THE EUROPEANISATION OF ENGLISH TORT LAW

Tort law is often regarded as the clearest example of traditional common law reasoning. Yet, in the past 40 years, the common law of England and Wales has been subject to European influences as a result of the introduction of the European Communities Act 1972 and, more recently, the implementation of the Human Rights Act 1998 in October 2000. EU Directives have led to changes to the law relating to product liability, health and safety in the workplace, and defamation, while *Francovich* liability introduces a new tort imposing State liability for breach of EU law. The 1998 Act has led to developments in privacy law and made the courts reconsider their approach to public authority liability and freedom of expression in defamation law.

This book explores how English tort law has changed as a result of Europeanisation – broadly defined as the influence of European Union and European human rights law. It also analyses how this influence has impacted on traditional common law reasoning. Has Europeanisation led to changes to the common law legal tradition or has the latter proved more resistant to change than might have been expected?

Volume 11 in the series Hart Studies in Private Law

The Europeanisation of English Tort Law

Paula Giliker

• HART •
PUBLISHING
OXFORD AND PORTLAND, OREGON
2014

Published in the United Kingdom by Hart Publishing Ltd
16C Worcester Place, Oxford, OX1 2JW
Telephone: +44 (0)1865 517530
Fax: +44 (0)1865 510710
E-mail: mail@hartpub.co.uk
Website: http://www.hartpub.co.uk

Published in North America (US and Canada) by
Hart Publishing
c/o International Specialized Book Services
920 NE 58th Avenue, Suite 300
Portland, OR 97213-3786
USA
Tel: +1 503 287 3093 or toll-free: (1) 800 944 6190
Fax: +1 503 280 8832
E-mail: orders@isbs.com
Website: http://www.isbs.com

Hart Publishing is an imprint of Bloomsbury Publishing plc

British Library Cataloguing in Publication Data
Data Available

ISBN: 978-1-84946-319-5

Typeset by Hope Services, Abingdon
Printed and bound in Great Britain by
CPI Group (UK) Ltd, Croydon CR0 4YY

Foreword

by The Rt Hon the Lord Mance, Justice of the Supreme Court of the United Kingdom

In appellate courts, European law has become an almost daily concern – whether one means the Brussels/Luxembourg or Strasbourg variety. Even in the Privy Council, the close linguistic association between the Westminster style constitutions of overseas jurisdictions and the European Convention on Human Rights makes it often relevant to analyse the Strasbourg case law. But the interface between domestic and European law is not always smooth. The changes effected and insights gained by European law and jurisprudence can be both stimulating and fruitful. But the time and effort necessary to obtain and digest them in submissions and judgments can also be frustrating. And there is a risk of alienation from other common law countries, who may see (or, to promote their own legal centres, even portray) British legal systems as undergoing a process of transmutation into an unfamiliar hybrid.

Professor Paula Giliker in this book addresses an important area of 'Europeanisation', that of English tort law. It is a novel subject and she is to be congratulated for the scholarly and at the same time readable way in which she does so. As a distinguished comparative lawyer, she chose tort law because it is largely judge made, commonly disregarded by students of European law (who tend to focus on public, rather than private law) but already quite significantly influenced by European law, of both the EU and Convention varieties. She sets out to analyse the areas of interface, to examine difficulties which common law courts and practitioners find and to study in particular the impact on traditional common law reasoning. But in her final pages she also acknowledges an underlying rationale in writing this book – by improving our knowledge base, to remove our fear of the unknown and engage on a more equal basis with these new forms of law – and she draws on her experience as an Erasmus tutor of long-standing to justify this.

To my mind these are extremely positive aims. There is absolutely no point in being a member of a community or council, unless one engages and seeks to make it work. This does not mean that, where there is room for disagreement or criticism, it should be stifled. On the contrary, but it should be uttered in an open spirit of debate or, in the favourite European buzz-word, dialogue. Provided the dialogue is truly mutual – and there is work to be done here – with each side listening to the others' concerns and an element of give and take, the result can only be beneficial. The significance of this – and indeed its potential relevance on issues of interpretation of EU law – was identified recently by the German

Constitutional Court in its judgment of 24 April 2013 on the *Counter-Terrorism Database Act*, 1 BvR 1215/07, para 91. The Supreme Court took the point up in its judgment in *HS2 Action Alliance Ltd v Secretary of State for Transport* [2014] UKSC 3, paras 111 and 202.

The structure which Professor Giliker adopts starts with areas where EU law has breached the levies surrounding English tort law – product liability, employers' liability, motor insurance and (in the limited area of innocent dissemination) electronic commerce. She moves, secondly, to the ever important area of state liability for breach of EU law – under principles established in the cases of C-6/90 *Francovich v Italian Republic* and C-46/93 and C-48/93 *Brasserie du Pêcheur v Germany* and (in a modified form in relation to state liability for failure correctly to apply EU law) in C-224/01 *Köbler v Austria*. She notes the difficulty that English courts have had in categorising these cases, seeking to bring them within the concept of statutory tort, whereas they should, in her view, be recognised as sui generis. She also notes the caution which they have exhibited towards *Köbler*-type liability – perhaps not surprising in a legal system which first encounters a prospect of a decision of its highest courts being challengeable in the County Court as 'manifestly' contrary to EU law. Thirdly, she examines the impact of the European Convention on Human Rights on defamation law. The Strasbourg case-law on the inter-relationship between the article 8 right to privacy and the article 10 right of freedom of expression has here been very influential on the private domestic legal position as between individuals and 'public watchdogs' like the press. She goes on to address the private law implications of the state's duty under article 2 to protect the right to life, and the proactive case law of the Strasbourg case law, which has extended this duty to bring about a body of European tort law overlapping with (and in relation to the scope and extent of liability differing from) domestic case law in circumstances involving the loss of or a threat to life. She discusses the recent cases such as *Rabone v Pennine Care* [2012] UKSC 2 and *Smith v Ministry of Defence* [2013] UKSC 41 in which the Supreme Court has sought to identify the boundaries of article 2 liability. Finally, she addresses the area of privacy (or perhaps one should call it 'confidence') where the Strasbourg court's jurisprudence has had its most major and obvious impact on the development of horizontal private rights.

In all these areas, Professor Giliker's critique of the authorities and principles is penetrating, interesting and balanced. She recognises the tensions which can arise in integrating or reconciling different habits of thought and expression, sometimes suggesting that the English courts may have been too cautious, on other occasions wondering whether they have not been too ready to abandon common law limitations, but she should certainly succeed in her aim of increasing understanding and promoting cooperation. I am very pleased to be able to recommend this innovative and well-written book to readers, both academic and practitioners alike.

London, February 2014

Preface

In 2010, I was asked to give a paper at the University of Sydney on the relationship between English and Australian tort law and whether European influences had led to changes to the framework of English tort law. This was a question, despite being an experienced tort lawyer and working in the field of comparative and European private law, I had not previously considered in any depth. I subsequently found out that this was a topic which had received very little attention from the private law community. Bearing in mind that European Union law had been part of the English legal system since 1973 and that the Human Rights Act 1998 had brought rights under the European Convention on Human Rights 'home' in October 2000, this seemed extraordinary. This book is therefore an attempt to fill this gap and uncover the extent to which European influences (taken broadly to include EU law but also the law of the European Convention on Human Rights) have changed the nature of English tort law.

The aim of the book is thus twofold: to identify sources of law in the domestic tort law system which are of European origin, but also to consider more broadly the consequences of introducing these new sources of law into the English common law legal tradition. European sources of law are primarily influenced by the civil law tradition and, as will be shown in this study, this requires lawyers to take account of different styles of reasoning, practice and methodology. The reception of these European sources is thus distinct from that of introducing rules from other common law jurisdictions. The language may be English, but it is a European form of English, requiring common lawyers to understand concepts such as 'proportionality', 'margin of appreciation' and 'sufficiently serious breach'. 'Europeanisation' therefore requires English tort lawyers not simply to identify new sources of law, but to adopt new forms of reasoning and language. A true understanding of this area of law requires effort and a willingness to adapt. The focus of this book will be to examine the extent to which the English tort law community has achieved this goal.

The aim, ultimately, is to encourage English tort lawyers to look again at their own legal system, recognise the impact of the European Communities Act 1972 and Human Rights Act 1998 and reconsider their currently conservative approach to such new sources. 'Europeanisation' is not simply a matter for public lawyers. Private lawyers are involved and the time has come to recognise the impact of such developments, both in terms of substantive law and in terms of legal reasoning itself.

This book was written during a period of research leave granted by the University of Bristol and I am very grateful for the university's support and, in particular, the award of a University Research Fellowship for 2012–13. This book would not, however, have been written without the support of colleagues and friends. Particular thanks go to Keith Stanton, Danny Nicol, Keith Syrett and Aaron Khan for commenting on specific chapters and their expertise and time is much appreciated. I am also grateful to Andrew Charlesworth, Tonia Novitz, Nina Boeger, Phil Syrpis, Dorota Leczykiewicz, James Lee and the SLS torts group for their helpful comments. I would also like to thank John Bell for introducing me to the importance of understanding judicial reasoning and the value of a comparative perspective. Thanks must also go to Hart Publishing and the assistance of Rachel Turner and, of course, Richard Hart. Finally, for putting up with numerous questions on human rights and public law (even at weekends), my thanks go to my family whose patience and support cannot be underestimated.

Bristol, January 2014.

Contents

Foreword v
Preface vii
Table of Cases xi
Table of Legislation xxvii
Table of Conventions xxxvi

1. Introduction 1
   I. The 'Europeanisation' of English Tort Law: What do we mean by 'Europeanisation'? 2
   II. Why Tort Law? 4
   Conclusion 14

2. Understanding 'Europeanisation': Transplanting European Union and Human Rights Law into Domestic Law 16
   Introduction 16
   I. Europeanisation and the National Court: Dealing With New Sources of Law 17
   II. Europeanisation and Legal Transplants: Integrating European Law into the English Legal System 27
   III. The Task Ahead 40

3. Breaking Down the Frontiers: EU Law in the English Law of Torts 42
   Introduction 42
   I. English Tort Law and the Product Liability Directive 46
   II. Employers' Liability and the European Framework Directive 63
   III. Road Accidents and Insurance: EU Directives relating to Compulsory Third Party Insurance Cover for Motor Vehicle Accidents 74
   IV. Defamation and the Internet: The Electronic Commerce Directive 2000/31/EC 77
   Conclusion 84

4. The European Tort: State Liability for Breach of European Union Law 89
   Introduction 89
   I. The Development of State Liability for Breach of EU Law 90
   II. English Tort Law and the Eurotort: Balancing European Policy and National Autonomy 93
   Conclusion 121

5. Tort Law and Human Rights: A European Culture of Rights? 123
Introduction 123
I. Defamation 126
II. Public Authority Liability in Tort 140
Conclusion 163

6. A Right to Personal Privacy in the English Law of Torts? 169
Introduction 169
I. From Breach of Confidence to a 'Tort' of Misuse of Private Information 171
II. A 'Euro' Tort of Misuse of Private Information? 185
Conclusion 192

7. Europeanisation and English Tort Law: The Way Forward 196
I. Finding Solutions 197
II. Conclusions 209

Index 213

Table of Cases

Australia

Giller v Procopets [2008] VSCA 236 192
Harris v Digital Pulse Pty Ltd (2003) 56 NSWLR 298 192
Sutherland Shire Council v Heyman (1985) 157 CLR 424 152

Canada

The Queen v Saskatchewan Wheat Pool [1983] 1 SCR 205; (1983) 143 DLR (3d) 9 67

Court of Justice of the European Union (formerly Court of Justice of the European Communities)

Alphabetical

Almeida v Companhia de Seguros Fidelidade–Mundial SA (Case C–300/10) [2013] 1 CMLR 39 ....74, 76
Amministrazione delle Finanze dello Stato v SpA San Giorgio (Case 199/82) [1983] ECR 3595 10
Banks v British Coal Corporation (Case C–128/92) [1994] ECR I–1209 119
Brasserie du Pêcheur v Germany; *R v Secretary of State for Transport, ex p Factortame (No 4)* (*Factortame III*) (Cases C–46/93 and C–48/93) [1996] ECR I–1029; [1996] QB 404 ....12, 19–20, 92, 94–95, 99–100, 102–107, 110, 112, 117, 122, 209
Brinkmann Tabakfabriken v Skatteministeriat (Case C–319/96) [1998] ECR I–5255 ....102–103, 107
Carvalho Ferreira Santos v Companhia Europeia de Seguros SA (Case C–484/09) [2011] RTR 32 ....74, 76
Centre hospitalier universitaire de Besançon v Thomas Dutrueux and Caisse primaire d'assurance maladie du Jura (Case C–495/10) [2012] 2 CMLR 1 49
Churchill Insurance Co Ltd v Wilkinson (Case C–442/10) [2012] RTR 10 74
CIA Security International SA v Signalson SA (Case C–194/94) [1996] ECR I–2201 10
Cofidis v Jean Louis Fredout (Case C–473/00) [2002] ECR I–10875 94

Commission of the European Communities v United Kingdom (Case C–127/05) [2007] ECR I–4619; [2007] All ER (EC) 986 .... 66, 71–72
Commission v France (Case C–52/00) [2002] ECR I–3827 48
Commission v Greece (Case C–154/00) [2002] ECR I–3879 48
Commission v Italy (Case C–379/10) 24 November 2011 (nyr) 117
Costa v ENEL (Case 6/64) [1964] ECR 585 21
Courage Ltd v Crehan (Case C–453/99) [2001] ECR I–6297; [2002] QB 507 .... 114, 119–120
DanskeSlagterier v Germany (Case C–445/06) [2009] ECR I–2119 104
Defrenne v SABENA (Case 43/75) [1976] ECR 455; [1976] 2 CMLR 98 120
Denkavit Internationaal BV v Bundesamt für Finanzen (Case C–283/94) [1996] ECR I–5063 99
Dillenkofer v Germany (Case C–178/94) [1996] ECR I–4845 .... 95, 97, 99, 102, 104, 113
EC Commission v France (Case C–177/04) [2006] ECR I–2461 48
EC Commission v Germany (Beer Purity) (Case 178/84) [1987] ECR1227; [1988] 1 CMLR 780 105
European Commission v United Kingdom (Case C–300/ 95) [1997] ECR I–2649; [1997] 3 CMLR 923 .... 52, 55, 58, 86
Evans v Secretary of State for the Environment, Transport and the Regions (Case C–63/01) [2003] ECR I–14447; [2005] All ER (EC) 763 102
Factortame litigation 10, 206
Farrell v Whitty (Case C–356/05) [2007] ECR I–3067 75–76
Francovich v Italian Republic (Case C–6/90) [1991] ECR I–5357; [1993] 2 CMLR 66 .... 11–12, 43, 71, 88–95, 97, 99, 104–106, 108–116, 118–122, 196, 203, 205
Fuß v Stadt Halle (No 2) (Case C–243/09) [2011] IRLR 176 102
González Sánchez v Medicina Asturiana SA (Case C–183/00) [2002] ECR I–3901 48
Haim v Kassenzahnaerztliche Vereinigung Nordrhein (Haim No 2) (Case C–424/97) [2000] ECR I–5123; [2002] 1 CMLR 11 .... 99, 112
Katja Candolin v Vahinkovakuutusosakeyhtio Pohjola and Jarno Ruokoranta (Case C–537/03) [2005] ECR I–5745 75–76
Köbler v Austria (Case C–224/01) [2003] ECR I–239; [2004] QB 848 .... 12, 108, 116–119, 204
Kraaljeveld (Case C–72/95) [1996] ECR I–5403 98
L'Oreal SA v eBay International AG (Case C–324/09) [2011] ECR I–6011 80
Laboratoires Pharmaceutiques Bergaderm SA v Commission of the European Communities (Case C–352/98P) [2000] ECR I–5291 .... 20, 92
Lavrador v Companhia de Seguros Fidelidade–Mundial SA (Case C–409/09) [2012] RTR 4 .... 74, 76
Leitner v TUI Deutschland GmbH & Co (Case C–168/00) [2002] ECR I–2631 98
Manfredi v Lloyd Adriatico Assicurazioni SpA (Joined Cases C–295/04 and C–298/04) [2006] ECR I–6619 120

Marleasing SA v La Comercial Internacional de Alimentacion SA (Case C–106/89) [1990] ECR I–4135 ....11, 21, 26, 52, 55, 77, 87
Marshall v SW Hampshire Health Authority (Teaching) (Case 152/84) [1986] ECR 723, [1986] 1 CMLR 688....................10, 120
Mendes Ferreira and Delgado Correia Ferreira (Case C–348/98) [2000] ECR I–6711 74
Metallgessellschaft Ltd and Hoechst v Commissioners of Inland Revenue (Cases C–397/98 and C–410/98) [2001] ECR I–1727 ....104, 106
Muñoz v Frumar Ltd (Case C–253/00) [2002] ECR I–7289 98
Norbrook Laboratories Ltd v Ministry of Agriculture, Fisheries and Food (Case C–127/95) [1998] ECR I–1531 ....95, 103
O'Byrne v Aventis Pasteur SA (Case C–358/08) [2009] ECR I–11305; [2010] 1 WLR 1375....................57
O'Byrne v Sanofi Pasteur MSD Ltd (Casc C–127/04) [2006] ECR I–1313; [2006] 1 WLR 1606....................56
Palmisani v INPS (Case C–261/95) [1997] ECR I–4025 94
Parliament v Council (family reunification) (Case C–540/03) [2006] ECR I–5769 14
Paul v Germany (Case C–222/02) [2004] ECR I–9425 98
Peterbroeck v Belgian State (Case C–312/93) [1995] ECR I–4599 90
Pfeiffer v Deutsches Rotes Kreuz, Kreisverband Waldshut eV (Cases C–397 to C–403/01) [2004] ECR I–8835....................11, 21
R v HM Treasury, ex p British Telecommunications plc (Case C–392/93) [1996] ECR I–1631; [1996] QB 615....................99, 102
R v Licensing Authority of the Department of Health, ex p Synthon (Case C–452/06) [2008] ECR I–7681....................99
R v Ministry of Agriculture, Fisheries and Food, ex p Hedley Lomas (Ireland) Ltd (Case C–5/94) [1996] ECR I–2553; [1997] QB 139 ....99, 102, 113
R v Secretary of State for Transport, ex p Factortame Ltd (No 2) (Case C–213/89) [1990] ECR I–2433 (*Factortame I*)....................10, 101, 112, 122
R v Secretary of State for Transport, ex p Factortame Ltd (No 3) (Case C–221/89) [1991] ECR I– 3905; [1992] QB 680 (*Factortame II*)....................101
Rechberger v Austria (Case C–140/97) [1999] ECR I–3499 ....97, 103–104
Rewe v Landwirtschaftskammer für das Saarland (Case 33/76) [1976] ECR 1989 90
Rewe–Handelsgesellschaft Nord v Hauptzollamt Kiel (Case 158/80) [1981] ECR 1805.................... 90–91
Rheinmuehlen v Einfuhr–und Vorratsstelle Getreide (Case 166/73) [1974] ECR 33....................108
Simmenthal (Case 106/77) [1978] ECR 629; [1978] 3 CMLR 263....................110
Skov Æg v Bilka Lavprisvarehus A/S (Case C–402/03) [2006] ECR I–199 48
Société Moteurs Leroy Somer v Société Dalkia France (Case C–258/08) [2009] ECR I–4733 48

Srl CILFIT and Lanificio di Gavardo SpA v Ministry of Health (Case 283/81) [1982] ECR 3415 .... 19–20, 38, 95, 117, 122
Traghetti del Mediterraneo SpA (In Liquidation) v Italy (Case C–173/03) [2006] ECR I–5177; [2006] 3 CMLR 19 117
Unibet Ltd v Justitiekanslern (Case C–432/05) [2007] ECR I–2271 90–91
Unilever Italia v Central Food (Case C–443/98) [2000] ECR I–7535 10
Van Duyn v Home Office (Case 41/74) [1974] ECR 1337; [1975] 1 CMLR 1 .... 10, 91
Van Gend en Loos v Nederlandse Administratie der Belastungen (Case 26/62) [1963] ECR 1; [1963] CMLR 105 .... 10, 19, 21, 90–91
Van Schijndel & Van Veen v Stichting Pensioenfonds voor Fysiotherapeuten (Cases C–430/93 to C–431/93) [1995] ECR I–4705 90
Veedfald v Arhus Amtskommune (Case C–203/99) [2001] ECR 1–3569; [2003] 1 CMLR 1217 56–57
Von Colson v Land Nordrhein–Westfalen (Case 14/83) [1984] ECR 1891 .... 10–11, 21, 52, 56, 90

Numerical

26/62 *Van Gend en Loos v Nederlandse Administratie der Belastungen* [1963] ECR 1, [1963] CMLR 105 .... 10, 19, 21, 90–91
6/64 *Costa v ENEL* [1964] ECR 585 21
166/73 *Rheinmuehlen v Einfuhr–und Vorratsstelle Getreide* [1974] ECR 33 108
41/74 *Van Duyn v Home Office* [1974] ECR 1337; [1975] 1 CMLR 1 .... 10, 91
43/75 *Defrenne v SABENA* [1976] ECR 455; [1976] 2 CMLR 98 120
33/76 *Rewe v Landwirtschaftskammer für das Saarland* [1976] ECR 1989 90
106/77 *Simmenthal* [1978] ECR 629; [1978] 3 CMLR 263 110
158/80 *Rewe–Handelsgesellschaft Nord v Hauptzollamt Kiel* [1981] ECR 1805 90–91
283/81 *Srl CILFIT and Lanificio di Gavardo SpA v Ministry of Health* [1982] ECR 3415 .... 19–20, 38, 95, 117, 122
199/82 *Amministrazione delle Finanze dello Stato v SpA San Giorgio* [1983] ECR 3595 10
14/83 *Von Colson v Land Nordrhein–Westfalen* [1984] ECR 1891 .... 10–11, 21, 52, 56, 90
152/84 *Marshall v SW Hampshire Health Authority (Teaching)* [1986] ECR 723; [1986] 1 CMLR 688 .... 10, 120
178/84 *EC Commission v Germany (Beer Purity)* [1987] ECR1227; [1988] 1 CMLR 780 105
C–106/89 *Marleasing SA v La Comercial Internacional de Alimentacion SA* [1990] ECR I–4135 .... 11, 21, 26, 52, 55, 77, 87
C–213/89 *R v Secretary of State for Transport, ex p Factortame Ltd (No 2)* [1990] ECR I–2433 (*Factortame I*) 10, 101, 112, 122

C–221/89 *R v Secretary of State for Transport, ex p Factortame Ltd (No 3)* [1991] ECR I–3905; [1992] QB 680 (*Factortame II*)..101
C–6/90 *Francovich v Italian Republic* [1991] ECR I–5357; [1993] 2 CMLR 66 .... 11–12, 43, 71, 88–95, 97, 99, 104–106, 108–116, 118–122, 196, 203, 205
C–128/92 *Banks v British Coal Corporation* [1994] ECR I–1209.........................119
C–46/93 and C–48/93 *Brasserie du Pêcheur v Germany*; *R v Secretary of State for Transport, ex p Factortame (No 4)* (*Factortame III*) [1996] ECR I–1029; [1996] QB 404... 12, 19–20, 92, 94–95, 99–100, 102–107, 110, 112, 117, 122, 209
C–312/93 *Peterbroeck v Belgian State* [1995] ECR I–4599....................................90
C–392/93 *R v HM Treasury, ex p British Telecommunications plc* [1996] ECR I–1631; [1996] QB 615...99, 102
C–430/93 to C–431/93 *Van Schjndel & Van Veen v Stichting Pensioenfonds voor Fysiotherapeuten* [1995] ECR I–4705...90
C–5/94 *R v Ministry of Agriculture, Fisheries and Food, ex p Hedley Lomas (Ireland) Ltd* [1996] ECR I–2553; [1997] QB 139.............................99, 102, 113
C–178/94 *Dillenkofer v Germany* [1996] ECR I–4845........ 95, 97, 99, 102, 104, 113
C–194/94 *CIA Security International SA v Signalson SA* [1996] ECR I–2201.......10
C–283/94 *Denkavit Internationaal BV v Bundesamt für Finanzen* [1996] ECR I–5063 99
C–72/95 *Kraaljeveld* [1996] ECR I–5403 98
C–127/95 *Norbrook Laboratories Ltd v Ministry of Agriculture, Fisheries and Food* [1998] ECR I–1531 ....95, 103
C–261/95 *Palmisani v INPS* [1997] ECR I–4025...94
C–300/ 95 *European Commission v United Kingdom* [1997] ECR I–2649; [1997] 3 CMLR 923 ....52, 55, 58, 86
C–319/96 *Brinkmann Tabakfabriken v Skatteministeriat* [1998] ECR I–5255...102–103, 107
C–140/97 *Rechberger v Austria* [1999] ECR I–3499 ....97, 103–104
C–424/97 *Haim v Kassenzahnaerztliche Vereinigung Nordrhein (Haim No 2)* [2000] ECR I–5123; [2002] 1 CMLR 11 ....99, 112
C–348/98 *Mendes Ferreira and Delgado Correia Ferreira* [2000] ECR I–6711......74
C–352/98P *Laboratoires Pharmaceutiques Bergaderm SA v Commission of the European Communities* [2000] ECR I–5291 ....20, 92
C–397/98 and C–410/98 *Metallgesellschaft Ltd and Hoechst v Commissioners of Inland Revenue* [2001] ECR I–1727 ....104, 106
C–443/98 *Unilever Italia v Central Food* [2000] ECR I–7535 10
C–203/99 *Veedfald v Arhus Amtskommune* [2001] ECR 1–3569; [2003] 1 CMLR 1217 56–57
C–453/99 *Courage Ltd v Crehan* [2001] ECR I–6297; [2002] QB 507..114, 119–120
C–52/00 *Commission v France* [2002] ECR I–3827...48
C–154/00 *Commission v Greece* [2002] ECR I–3879 48

C–168/00 *Leitner v TUI Deutschland GmbH & Co* [2002] ECR I–2631 98
C–183/00 *González Sánchez v Medicina Asturiana SA* [2002] ECR I–3901 48
C–253/00 *Muñoz v Frumar Ltd* [2002] ECR I–7289 98
C–473/00 *Cofidis v Jean Louis Fredout* [2002] ECR I–10875 94
C–63/01 *Evans v Secretary of State for the Environment, Transport and the Regions* [2003] ECR I–14447; [2005] All ER (EC) 763 102
C–224/01 *Köbler v Austria* [2003] ECR I–239; [2004] QB 848.....12, 108, 116–119, 204
C–397 to C–403/01 *Pfeiffer v Deutsches Rotes Kreuz, Kreisverband Waldshut eV* [2004] ECR I–8835 ....11, 21
C–222/02 *Paul v Germany* [2004] ECR I–9425 98
C–173/03 *Traghetti del Mediterraneo SpA (In Liquidation) v Italy* [2006] ECR I–5177; [2006] 3 CMLR 19...117
C–402/03 *Skov Æg v Bilka Lavprisvarehus A/S* [2006] ECR I–199 48
C–537/03 *Katja Candolin v Vahinkovakuutusosakeyhtio Pohjola and Jarno Ruokoranta* [2005] ECR I–5745 75–76
C–540/03 *Parliament v Council (family reunification)* [2006] ECR I–5769 14
C–127/04 *O'Byrne v Sanofi Pasteur MSD Ltd* [2006] ECR I–1313; [2006] 1 WLR 1606..56
C–177/04 *EC Commission v France* [2006] ECR I–2461 48
C–295/04 and C–298/04 *Manfredi v Lloyd Adriatico Assicurazioni SpA* [2006] ECR I–6619 120
C–127/05 *Commission of the European Communities v United Kingdom* [2007] ECR I–4619; [2007] All ER (EC) 986...66, 71–72
C–356/05 *Farrell v Whitty* [2007] ECR I–3067.. 75–76
C–432/05 *Unibet Ltd v Justitiekanslern* [2007] ECR I–2271 90–91
C–445/06 *DanskeSlagterier v Germany* [2009] ECR I–2119 104
C–452/06 *R v Licensing Authority of the Department of Health, ex p Synthon* [2008] ECR I–7681 99
C–258/08 *Société Moteurs Leroy Somer v Société Dalkia France* [2009] ECR I–4733 48
C–358/08 *O'Byrne v Aventis Pasteur SA* [2009] ECR I–11305; [2010] 1 WLR 1375..57
C–243/09 *Fuß v Stadt Halle (No 2)* [2011] IRLR 176...102
C–324/09 *L'Oreal SA v eBay International AG* [2011] ECR I–6011 80
C–409/09 *Lavrador v Companhia de Seguros Fidelidade–Mundial SA* [2012] RTR 4...74, 76
C–484/09 *Carvalho Ferreira Santos v Companhia Europeia de Seguros SA* [2011] RTR 32...74, 76
C–300/10 *Almeida v Companhia de Seguros Fidelidade–Mundial SA* [2013] 1 CMLR 39 ....74, 76
C–379/10 *Commission v Italy* 24 November 2011 (nyr) 117
C–442/10 *Churchill Insurance Co Ltd v Wilkinson* [2012] RTR 10 74
C–495/10 *Centre hospitalier universitaire de Besançon v Thomas Dutrueux and Caisse primaire d'assurance maladie du Jura* [2012] 2 CMLR 1 49

Factortame litigation 10, 206

European Commission on Human Rights

Earl Spencer v United Kingdom (1998) 25 EHRR CD 105 .... 173, 176
Khatun v United Kingdom (38387/97) (1998) 26 EHRR CD212 157
S v France (1990) 65 DR 250 161

European Court of Human Rights

Austin v United Kingdom (39692/09) (2012) 55 EHRR 14 156
Axel Springer AG v Germany (39954/08) (2012) 55 EHRR 6 184–185
BB v United Kingdom (2004) 39 EHRR 635 191
Chapman v United Kingdom (27238/95) [2001] ECHR 43 23
Chauvy & others v France (64915/01) (2005) 41 EHRR 29 128
Cooper v United Kingdom (2004) 39 EHRR 8 38
Cumpana v Romania (33348/96) (2005) 41 EHRR 200 128
Europapress Holding v Croatia (25333/06) (2011) 53 EHRR 27 135
Fressoz and Roire v France (2001) 31 EHRR 2 179
Guerra v Italy (14967/89) (1998) 26 EHRR 357 157
Handyside v United Kingdom (5493/72) (1976) 1 EHRR 737 24
Hatton v United Kingdom (36022/97) (2003) 37 EHRR 28 159–160
HL v United Kingdom (45508/99) (2005) 40 EHRR 32 155
Jain v United Kingdom (39598/09) [2010] ECHR 411 150
Jersild v Denmark (1994) 19 EHRR 1 179
Keenan v United Kingdom (27229/95) (2001) 33 EHRR 913 142
Lingens v Austria (1986) 8 EHRR 407 128
López –Ostra v Spain (16798/90) (1995) 20 EHRR 277 157
M v Newham LBC 145
MAK v Dewsbury Healthcare NHS TrustMAK v United Kingdom (45901/05) (2010) 51 EHRR 14 145–146
Malone v UK (8691/79) (1985) 7 EHRR 14 173
McVicar v United Kingdom (46311/99) (2002) 35 EHRR 22 135
MGN Ltd v United Kingdom (39401/04) (2011) 53 EHRR 5 .... 132, 177
Mosley v United Kingdom (48009/08) (2011) 53 EHRR 30 187
Osman v United Kingdom (23452/94) (1998) 29 EHRR 245 .... 13, 38, 140–145, 148–149, 152, 163–165, 167–168, 207
Peck v United Kingdom (44647/98) (2003) 36 EHRR 41 .... 173, 176–177, 180
Pfeifer v Austria (12556/03) (2007) 48 EHRR 175 128
PG and JH v United Kingdom (44787/98) [2001] ECHR 550 177
Reynolds v UK (2694/08) (2012) 55 EHRR 35 .... 151, 163, 167
Sciacca v Italy (50774/99) (2006) 43 EHRR 20 181
Stafford v United Kingdom (2002) 35 EHRR 1121 38

Steel v United Kingdom (68416/01) (2005) 41 EHRR 22......................131–132, 139
Steel and Morris v United Kingdom (68416/01) (2005) 41 EHRR 403 136–137
Tammer v Estonia (2001) 37 EHRR 857...179
Times Newspapers (Nos 1 and 2) v United Kingdom (3002/03 and 23676/03)
[2009] EMLR 14...138
Tolstoy Miloslavsky v United Kingdom (A/323) (1995) 20 EHRR 442 ....127, 131
TP v United Kingdom (2002) 34 EHRR 2... 144–145
Tyrer v United Kingdom (5856/72) (1979–1980) 2 EHRR 1 24
Van Colle v United Kingdom (7678/09) (2013) 56 EHRR 23 148
Von Hannover v Germany (No 1) (59320/00) (2005)
40 EHRR 1...177, 179–186, 190–192, 195
Von Hannover v Germany (No 2) (40660/08) (2012) 55 EHRR 15............. 184–185
Wainwright v United Kingdom (12350/04) (2007) 44 EHRR 40..........................170
Wall Street Journal Europe SPRL v United Kingdom (Admissibility) (28577/05)
(2009) 48 EHRR SE19 135
Yasa v Turkey (22495/93) (1999) 28 EHRR 408...151
Z v Finland (1997) 25 EHRR 371 179
Z v United Kingdom (2001) 34 EHRR 97 ....38, 142
Z v United Kingdom (29392/95) (2002) 34 EHRR 3............................144–145, 207

European General Court (formerly Court of First Instance of the European Communities)

Case T–230/94 *Farrugia v Commission* [1996] ECR II–195................................106

Germany

BGH 9 May 1995 NJW 1995, 2162...87
BGH 24 October 1996 BGHZ 134, 30; NJW 1997, 123; [1997] CMLR 971 105

Netherlands

Schulten v Sanquin Bloedvoorziening, District Court of Amsterdam, 3 February
1999 NJ 1999, 621 55

New Zealand

Hosking v Runting [2004] NZCA 34; [2005] 1 NZLR 1 ....186, 192

United Kingdom

A v B plc [2002] EWCA Civ 337; [2003] QB 195 .... 176, 181, 191
A v National Blood Authority [2001] 3 All ER 289 .... 6, 51–53, 55, 61–62, 87
Abouzaid v Mothercare (UK) Ltd [2000] Lloyd's Rep Med 280 50–51
Abouzaid v Mothercare (UK) Ltd, The Times, 20 February 2001 ... 51, 53, 55, 61–62
Al–Fagih v HH Saudi Research and Marketing (UK) [2001] EWCA Civ 1634; [2002] EMLR 13 130
Allied Maples Group v Simmons & Simmons [1995] 1 WLR 1602 106
Alstom Transport v Eurostar International Ltd [2012] EWHC 28 (Ch) 26
Anns v Merton LBC [1978] AC 728 5
Anufrijeva v Southwark London Borough Council [2003] EWCA Civ 1406; [2004] QB 1124 191
Application des Gaz SA v Falks Veritas Ltd [1974] 1 Ch 381 109
Archer v Brown [1985] QB 401 107
Argyll v Argyll [1967] Ch 302 175
Arscott v Coal Authority [2004] EWCA Civ 892; [2005] Env LR 6 161
Arthur JS Hall & Co v Simons [2002] 1 AC 615 143
Assange v The Swedish Prosecution Authority [2012] UKSC 22; [2012] 2 AC 471 21
Associated Newspapers Ltd v HRH Prince of Wales [2006] EWCA Civ 1776 178
Aston Cantlow v Wallbank [2003] UKHL 37; [2004] 1 AC 546 .... 124, 163
Atkinson v Newcastle Waterworks Co (1877) 2 Ex D 441 111
Attorney General v Blake [2000] UKHL 45; [2001] 1 AC 268 188
Attorney–General v Guardian Newspapers Ltd (No 2) [1990] 1 AC 109 ...... 126, 175
Attorney–General v Guardian Newspapers Ltd (No 2) [2007] UKHL 21 .... 175, 178, 191
Austin v Commissioner of Police of the Metropolis [2005] EWHC 480 (QB); [2005] HRLR 20 154
Austin v Commissioner of Police of the Metropolis [2007] EWCA Civ 989; [2008] QB 660 .... 154–155, 167
Austin v Commissioner of Police of the Metropolis [2009] UKHL 5; [2009] 1 AC 564 .... 153–155, 167
Baker v Quantum Clothing Group Ltd [2011] UKSC 17; [2011] 1 WLR 1003 73
Ball v Street [2005] EWCA Civ 76 68
Barnett v Chelsea & Kensington Hospital Management Committee [1969] 1 QB 428 .... 58, 105
Barrett v Enfield LBC [2001] 2 AC 550 143–145
Barretts & Baird (Wholesale) v IPCS [1987] IRLR 3 90
Baturina v Times Newspapers Ltd [2011] EWCA Civ 308; [2011] 1 WLR 1526 133
Bellinger v Bellinger (Lord Chancellor Intervening) [2003] UKHL 21; [2003] 2 AC 467 25

Berezovsky v Forbes Inc (No 2) [2001] EWCA Civ 1251; [2001] EMLR 45..........135
Bernstein v Skyviews Ltd [1978] 1 QB 479..........172
Bolam v Friern Hospital Management Committee [1957] 1 WLR 583..........6
Bonnard v Perryman [1891] 2 Ch 269..........139, 166
Bonnick v Morris [2003] 1 AC 300..........129
Bourgoin SA v Ministry of Agriculture, Fisheries and Food [1986] QB 716..........1, 109
Branson v Bower (No 2) [2002] QB 737..........128
British Chiropractic Association v Singh [2010] EWCA Civ 350; [2011] 1 WLR 133..........138
Brooks v Comr of Police of the Metropolis [2005] UKHL 24; [2005] 1 WLR 1495..........148–149
Browne v Associated Newspapers Ltd [2007] EWCA Civ 295; [2008] QB 103..........178, 182, 186
Buck v Nottinghamshire Healthcare NHS Trust [2006] EWCA Civ 1576..........73
Bulmer v Bollinger [1974] Ch 401..........20, 37
Bunt v Tilley [2006] EWHC 407 (QB); [2007] 1 WLR 1243..........79–81
Butler (or Black) v Fife Coal Co Ltd [1912] AC 149..........111
Bux v Slough Metals Ltd [1973] 1 WLR 1358..........73
Byrne v Motor Insurers' Bureau [2008] EWCA Civ 574; [2009] QB 66..........101
Campbell v Mirror Group Newspapers Ltd [2004] UKHL 22; [2004] 2 AC 457..........42, 169, 176–183, 185–189
Campbell v Mirror Group Newspapers Ltd (Costs) [2005] UKHL 61; [2005] 1 WLR 3394..........132
Caparo v Dickman [1990] 2 AC 605..........141, 143, 152
Cassell v Broome [1972] AC 1027..........139, 187
Caswell v Powell Duffryn Colliery Co [1940] AC 152..........72
Charman v Orion Publishing Group Ltd [2007] EWCA Civ 972; [2008] 1 All ER 750..........130
Churchill Insurance Co Ltd v Fitzgerald [2012] EWCA Civ 1166; [2012] 3 CMLR 49..........26, 74, 77
Clift v Slough BC [2010] EWCA Civ 1484; [2011] 1 WLR 1774..........153, 162–163
Coco v AN Clark (Engineers) Ltd [1969] RPC 41..........175
Connolly v DPP [2007] EWHC 237 (Admin); [2008] 1 WLR 276..........25
Cooper v Attorney General [2010] EWCA Civ 464; [2011] 2 WLR 448..........12, 118
Cornelius v De Taranto [2000] EWHC 561 (QB); [2001] EMLR 12..........177
Couch v Steel (1854) 3 E & B 402; 118 ER 1193..........110
Cream Holdings Ltd v Banerjee [2004] UKHL 44; [2005] 1 AC 253..........139, 186
Crehan v Inntrepreneur Pub Company [2004] EWCA Civ 637; [2004] 2 CLC 803..........114, 120
Cullen v Chief Constable of the Royal Ulster Constabulary [2003] 1 WLR 1763 (HL(NI))..........112
Culnane v Morris [2005] EWHC 2438 (QB); [2006] 1 WLR 2880..........133
Customs and Excise v Samex ApS [1983] 3 CMLR 194..........20

D v East Berkshire Community NHS Trust (also known as *JD*) [2003] EWCA Civ 1151; [2004] QB 558 ....145–146, 149–150, 153, 164
D v East Berkshire Community Health NHS Trust and others [2005] UKHL 23; [2005] 2 AC 373 ....123, 146, 164
Davie v New Merton Board Mills [1959] AC 604 63
Dennis v Ministry of Defence [2003] EWHC 793 (QB); [2003] Env LR 34........158, 161
Derbyshire CC v Times Newspapers Ltd [1993] AC 534........126
Devenish Nutrition Ltd v Sanofi–Aventis SA [2007] EWHC 2394 (Ch); [2008] 2 WLR 637; [2008] EWCA Civ 1086; [2009] Ch 390........107, 188
Director General of Fair Trading v First National Bank Plc [2001] UKHL 52; [2002] 1 AC 481 ....28, 52
Dobson v Thames Water Utilities Ltd [2009] EWCA Civ 28; [2009] 3 All ER 319........159–160
Dobson v Thames Water Utilities Ltd [2011] EWHC 3253 (TCC); 140 Con LR 135........160–161
Donoghue v Stevenson [1932] AC 562 ....4–5, 11, 45, 47, 60, 206
Douglas and Others v Hello! Ltd (No 1) [2001] QB 967 ....175–176, 186, 190, 195
Douglas v Hello! Ltd (No 3) [2005] EWCA Civ 595; [2006] QB 125........177, 181, 185–188
Douglas v Hello! [2007] UKHL 21; [2008] 1 AC 1........175, 178–179
Duke of Brunswick v Harmer (1849) 14 QB 185........137
E v Chief Constable of the Royal Ulster Constabulary [2008] UKHL 66; [2009] 1 AC 536 142
Elguzouli–Daf v Commissioner of Police of the Metropolis [1995] QB 335........150
Entick v Carrington (1765) 2 Wils KB 275; 95 ER 807........171
Ferdinand v MGN Ltd [2011] EWHC 2454 (QB)........180, 185
Flood v Times Newspapers [2010] EWCA Civ 804; [2011] 1 WLR 153........129, 131
Flood v Times Newspapers [2012] UKSC 11; [2012] 2 AC 273 129–131
Forsyth–Grant v Allen [2008] EWCA Civ 505; [2008] Env LR 41........188
Foster v Biosil (2001) 59 BMLR 178 (CC (Central London)) 50
Froom v Butcher [1976] 1 QB 286 75–76
Fytche v Wincanton Logistics plc [2003] EWCA Civ 874; [2003] ICR 1582...67, 111
Fytche v Wincanton Logistics plc [2004] UKHL 31; [2004] 4 All ER 221; [2004] ICR 975........63–64, 67–70, 114
Galloway v Telegraph Group Ltd [2006] EWCA Civ 17; [2006] EMLR 11 130–131
Garden Cottage Foods Ltd v Milk Marketing Board [1982] QB 1114 (CA)........109
Garden Cottage Foods Ltd v Milk Marketing Board [1984] AC 130........109, 112
Ghaidan v Godin–Mendoza [2004] UKHL 30; [2004] 2 AC 557 25–26
Godfrey v Demon Internet Ltd [2001] QB 201 80
Godfrey v Demon Internet Ltd [2012] All ER (EC) 501 80
Goldsmith v Bhoyrul [1998] QB 459........126
Gorringe v Calderdale MBC [2004] UKHL 15; [2004] 1 WLR 1057........164
Gorris v Scott (1874) LR 9 Exch 125........114

Grant v Australian Knitting Mills [1936] AC 85 60
Greene v Associated Newspapers Ltd [2004] EWCA Civ 1462; [2005] QB 972 ....128, 139
Gregg v Scott [2005] UKHL 2; [2005] 2 AC 176 105
Groves v Lord Wimborne [1898] 2 QB 402 63–64
Guardian News and Media Ltd, Re [2010] UKSC 1; [2010] 2 AC 697 128
Gur v Avrupa Newspaper Ltd [2008] EWCA Civ 594; [2009] EMLR 4.... 131–132
Hellewell v Chief Constable of Derbyshire [1995] 1 WLR 804....175
Henderson v Merrett Syndicates Ltd [1995] 2 AC 145....153
Hide v Steeplechase Co (Cheltenham) Ltd [2013] EWCA Civ 545; [2013] PIQR P22....66
Hill v Chief Constable of West Yorkshire [1988] QB 60 148–149
Hill v Chief Constable of West Yorkshire [1989] AC 53....142, 164
Howlett v Holding [2006] EWHC 41 (QB) 125
HRH Prince of Wales v Associated Newspapers Ltd [2006] EWCA Civ 1776....182
Hulton & Co v Jones [1910] AC 20 132–133
Hunter v Canary Wharf Ltd [1997] AC 655....157, 159–160, 172
Ide v ATB Sales Ltd [2008] EWCA Civ 424 60
Jain v Trent SHA [2009] UKHL 4; [2009] 1 AC 853....146, 149–150, 164, 209
Jameel (Yousef) v Dow Jones & Co Inc [2005] EWCA Civ 75; [2005] QB 946....133–134, 136
Jameel (Mohammed) v Wall Street Journal Europe Sprl [2005] EWCA Civ 74; [2005] QB 904....135
Jameel v Wall Street Journal Europe SPRL (No 3) [2006] UKHL 44; [2007] 1 AC 359 ....127–131, 136
John v Mirror Group Newspapers Ltd [1997] QB 586....131–132, 187
Joseph v Spiller [2010] UKSC 53; [2011] 1 AC 852....128
K v News Group Newspapers Ltd [2011] EWCA Civ 439; [2011] 1 WLR 1827 ...183
Kaschke v Gray [2010] EWHC 690 (QB); [2011] 1 WLR 452....79
Kay v Lambeth LBC [2006] UKHL 10; [2006] 2 AC 465....183, 192
Kaye v Robertson [1991] FSR 62 ....172–173, 189
Kent v Griffiths [2001] QB 36 143
Khorasandjian v Bush [1993] QB 727 172
Kiam v MGN Ltd [2002] EWCA Civ 43; [2003] QB 281....131
King v Sussex Ambulance NHS Trust [2002] EWCA Civ 953; [2002] ICR 1413....66
Kirklees Metropolitan Borough Council v Wickes Building Supplies [1993] AC 227 109
Kuddus v Chief Constable of Leicestershire Constabulary [2002] 2 AC 122 107
L (A Child) v Reading Borough Council [2001] EWCA Civ 346; [2001] 1 WLR 1575....144
Lawrence v Pembrokeshire CC [2007] EWCA Civ 446; [2007] 1 WLR 2991 146
Litster v Forth Dry Dock & Engineering Co Ltd [1989] ICR 341 49
Litster v Forth Dry Dock & Engineering Co Ltd [1990] 1 AC 546....21
Lochgelley Iron & Coal Co v M'Mullan [1934] AC 1....72

Lough v First Secretary of State [2004] EWCA Civ 905; [2004] 1 WLR 2557 160–161
Loutchansky v Times Newspapers Ltd (Nos 2–5) [2001] EWCA Civ 1805; [2002] QB 783 .... 6, 127, 137
M (a minor) v Newham LBC 141
Maccaba v Lichtenstein [2004] EWHC 1580 (QB) 134
Marcic v Thames Water Utilities Ltd [2002] EWCA Civ 64; [2002] QB 929 158
Marcic v Thames Water Utilities Ltd [2003] UKHL 66; [2004] 2 AC 42 .... 153, 157–158, 160–161, 165
McGrath v Dawkins [2012] EWHC B3 (QB) 81
McKenna v British Aluminium Ltd [2002] Env LR 30 .... 157, 159
McKennitt v Ash [2006] EWCA Civ 1714; [2008] QB 73 .... 178, 181–183, 185, 187, 189–192
Metropolitan International Schools Ltd v Designtechnica Corpn [2009] EWHC 1765 (QB); [2011] 1 WLR 1743 80
Mitchell v Glasgow City Council [2009] UKHL 11; [2009] 1 AC 874 149
Moorcock, The (1889) 14 PD 64 97
Mosley v News Group Newspapers Ltd [2008] EWHC 1777 (QB); [2008] EMLR 20 .... 182, 187, 189, 191–192
Murphy v Brentwood DC [1991] 1 AC 398 5
Murray v Big Pictures (UK) Ltd [2008] EWCA Civ 446; [2009] Ch 481 6
Murray v Express Newspapers plc [2008] EWCA Civ 446; [2009] Ch 481 .... 182–183, 192
Neil Martin Ltd v The Commissioners of Her Majesty's Revenue and Customs [2006] EWHC 2425 (Ch); [2007] STC 823 111
Ntuli v Donald [2010] EWCA Civ 1276; [2011] EMLR 10 182
O'Byrne v Aventis Pasteur MSD Ltd [2007] EWCA Civ 966; [2010] UKSC 23; [2010] 1 WLR 1412 57
O'Rourke v Camden LBC [1998] AC 188 112
O'Shea v MGN Ltd [2001] EMLR 40 .... 129, 132–134, 140
OB v Aventis Pasteur [2008] UKHL 34; [2008] 3 CMLR 10 57
OBG Ltd v Allan. See *Douglas v Hello!* [2007] UKHL 21; [2008] 1 AC 1
Office of Fair Trading v Abbey National plc [2009] UKSC 6; [2010] 1 AC 696 108
Officer L, Re [2007] 1 WLR 2135 149
Osman v Ferguson [1993] 4 All ER 344 (CA) 13, 142
Palmer v Palmer [2006] EWHC 1284 (QBD (Admin)) 53
Patel v Patel [1988] 2 FLR 179 115
Pemberton v Southwark LBC [2000] 1 WLR 1672 158
Pepper v Hart [1993] AC 593 34
Phelps v Hillingdon LBC [2001] 2 AC 619 144–145
Phonographic Performance Ltd v Department of Trade and Industry [2004] EWHC 1795 (Ch); [2004] 1 WLR 2893 110
Pickstone v Freemans plc [1988] ICR 697 49
Poole v HM Treasury [2007] EWCA Civ 1021; [2007] All ER 379 .... 96–97, 108

Prince Albert v Strange (1849) 2 De G & Sm 652; 1 Mac & G 25 175
Prince Radu of Hohenzollern v Houston [2008] EWCA Civ 921; [2009] EMLR 13 130
Qualcast (Wolverhampton) Ltd v Haynes [1959] AC 743 72
R v Bournewood Community and Mental Health NHS Trust, ex p L [1999] 1 AC 458 ....155, 167
R v Briggs–Price (Robert William) [2009] UKHL 19; [2009] 1 AC 1026 25
R v Department of Social Security, ex p Scullion [1999] 3 CMLR 798 (QBD) 101, 106
R v Horncastle [2009] UKSC 14; [2010] 2 AC 373 22
R v Home Secretary, ex p Simms [2000] 2 AC 115 25
R v Lambert (Steven) [2001] UKHL 37, [2002] 2 AC 545 26
R v Secretary of State for the Home Department, ex p Brind [1991] 1 AC 696 126
R v Secretary of State for the Home Department, ex p Gallagher [1996] 2 CMLR 951 (CA) 105–107
R v Secretary of State for Transport, ex p Factortame Ltd (No 2) [1991] 1 AC 603 37
R v Secretary of State for Transport, ex p Factortame Ltd (No 5) [1997] Eu LR 475 (Divisional Court); [1997] EWHC Admin 756; [1998] CMLR 1353; [2000] 1 AC 524 ....12, 100–102, 107, 110
R v Secretary of State for Transport, ex p Factortame Ltd (No 7) [2000] EWHC (Tech) 179; [2001] 1 WLR 942 ....94, 102, 107, 109–111, 114
R v Spear [2002] UKHL 31; [2003] 1 AC 734 22
R (Al–Skeini) v Secretary of State for Defence [2007] UKHL 26; [2008] 1 AC 153 23
R (Alconbury Developments Ltd and Others) v Secretary of State for the Environment, Transport and the Regions [2001] UKHL 23; [2003] 2 AC 295 ....22, 207
R (Anderson) v Secretary of State for the Home Department [2002] UKHL 46; [2003] 1 AC 837 25
R (Faulkner) v Secretary of State for Justice [2009] EWHC 1507 (Admin) 147
R (Greenfield) v Secretary of State for the Home Department [2005] UKHL 14; [2005] 1 WLR 673 ....147, 159
R (Laporte) v Chief Constable of Gloucestershire Constabulary [2006] UKHL 55; [2007] 2 AC 105 155
R (Negassi) v Secretary of State for the Home Department [2013] EWCA Civ 151; [2013] 2 CMLR 45 ....100, 106
R (Pennington) v Parole Board [2010] EWHC 78 (Admin) 147
R (Sturnham) v Parole Board [2013] UKSC 23; [2013] 2 WLR 1157 ....25, 147, 156
R (Ullah) v Special Adjudicator [2004] UKHL 26; [2004] 2 AC 323 ....23, 151, 180–181, 207
R (Wilkinson) v Inland Revenue Commissioners [2005] UKHL 30; [2005] 1 WLR 1718 25

Rabone v Pennine Care NHS Trust [2012] UKSC 2; [2012] 2 AC 72 .... 24, 141, 146, 150–152, 164, 191
Rantzen v Mirror Group Newspapers (1986) Ltd [1994] QB 670 .... 126–127, 131
Reynolds v Times Newspapers Ltd [2001] 2 AC 127 .... 127–131, 133, 139–140
Richardson v LRC Products 50–51
RK v Oldham NHS Trust 145
Robb v Salamis (M & I) Ltd [2006] UKHL 56; [2007] ICR 175 68–69
Roberts v Gable [2007] EWCA Civ 721; [2008] QB 502 130–131
Robinson v Balmain New Ferry [1910] AC 295 154
Rocknroll v News Group Newspapers Ltd [2013] EWHC 24 (Ch) 183
Rookes v Barnard [1964] AC 1129 .... 106–107, 187
S (a child), Re [2004] UKHL 47; [2005] 1 AC 593 .... 139, 178
Sam B v McDonald's Restaurants Ltd [2002] EWHC 490 (QBD) 52–53
Savage v South Essex Partnership NHS Foundation Trust [2008] UKHL 74; [2009] 1 AC 681 149
Secretary of State for Employment v Mann [1997] ICR 209 94
Secretary of State for Work and Pensions v M [2006] UKHL 11; [2006] 2 AC 91 23
Sempra Metals Ltd v Inland Revenue Comrs [2007] UKHL 34; [2008] 1 AC 561 110
Sheldrake v DPP [2004] UKHL 43; [2005] 1 AC 264 .... 25, 167
Sim v Stretch [1936] 2 All ER 1237 133
Smith v Chief Constable of Sussex Police [2008] EWCA Civ 39; [2008] HRLR 23 .... 153, 162
Smith v Chief Constable of Sussex Police [2008] UKHL 50; [2009] 1 AC 225 .... 147–149, 162–163, 203
Smith v Ministry of Defence [2013] UKSC 41; [2013] 3 WLR 69 .... 151–153, 165
Smith v Northamptonshire CC [2009] UKHL 27; [2009] ICR 734 68–69
South Hetton Coal Co Ltd v North Eastern News Association Ltd [1894] 1 QB 133 136
Spencer v Secretary of State for Work and Pensions [2008] EWCA Civ 750; [2009] QB 358 94
Spencer–Franks v Kellogg Brown & Root Ltd & Ors (Scotland) [2008] UKHL 46; [2008] ICR 863 68
Stanton v Collinson [2010] EWCA Civ 81 75
Stephens v Avery [1988] Ch 449 174
Stoke–on–Trent City Council v W & J Wass Ltd (No 1) [1988] 1 WLR 1406 188
Stokes v Guest Keen & Nettlefold (Bolts and Nuts) Ltd [1968] 1 WLR 1776 73
Stovin v Wise [1996] AC 923 141
Stubbings v Webb [1993] AC 498 165
Sugar v Associated Newspapers Ltd (unreported) 6 February 2001 128
Tamiz v Google Inc [2012] EMLR 24; [2012] EWHC 449 (QB); [2013] EWCA Civ 68 80–81
Tesco Stores Ltd v Pollard [2006] EWCA Civ 393; (2006) 150 SJLB 537 .... 53, 61–62

Thames Trains Ltd v Health and Safety Executive [2003] EWCA Civ 720 113
Thompson v James [2013] EWHC 515 (QB)..162
Thornton v Telegraph Media Group Ltd [2010] EWHC 1414 (QB); [2011] 1 WLR 1985...133
Three Rivers District Council [1996] 3 All ER 558 96
Three Rivers District Council [2000] 2 WLR 15 96
Three Rivers District Council v Bank of England (No 3) [2000] UKHL 33; [2003] 2 AC 1 ....92, 95–98, 108, 111, 113
Three Rivers District Council v Bank of England [2004] 3 All ER 168; [2004] EWCA Civ 218; [2004] QB 916; [2004] 2 WLR 1065 108
Tolley v Fry [1931] AC 333...172
Van Colle v Chief Constable of Hertfordshire [2008] UKHL 50; [2009] 1 AC 225 ....146–149, 164, 166, 203
Vodafone 2 v Revenue and Customs Commissioners [2009] EWCA Civ 446; [2010] Ch 77 26
W v Essex County Council [2001] 2 AC 592...144
W v Westminster City Council [2005] EWHC 102 (QB); [2005] 4 All ER 96..162
Wainwright v Home Office [2003] UKHL 53; [2004] 2 AC 406 ....115, 168–171, 173, 177, 193–194
Walsh v Shanahan [2013] EWCA Civ 411..188
Warren v Random House Group Ltd [2008] EWCA Civ 834; [2009] QB 600......134
Waterson v Lloyd [2013] EWCA Civ 136; [2013] EMLR 17 129
Watkins v Secretary of State for the Home Department [2004] EWCA Civ 966; [2005] QB 883..153
Watkins v Secretary of State for the Home Department [2006] UKHL 17; [2006] 2 AC 395 ....150, 166
Williams v Settle [1960] 1 WLR 1072 172
Wilsons & Clyde Coal Co Ltd v English [1938] AC 57...................................... 63–64
Worsley v Tambrands Ltd [2000] PIQR P95..50
X v Bedfordshire CC [1995] 2 AC 633........................ 13, 66, 112–113, 141, 143, 145
X v Schering Health Care Ltd [2002] EWHC 1420; (2003) 70 BMLR 88 60
Yuen Kun–Yeu v Attorney General of Hong Kong [1988] 1 AC 175........................98

United States of America

Greenman v Yuba Power Products Inc 377 P 2d 897 (Cal 1963) 46
Scholten v Sanguin Foundation (NJ 1999)..87

Table of Legislation

European Union

Charter of Fundamental Rights of the European Union 14
Art 47 11
EEC Treaty. *See* Treaty of Rome in 1957
Lisbon Treaty 11, 14
Treaty establishing the European Communities (TEC)
Art 30 105
Art 81 (now Art 101 TFEU) 107
Treaty on European Union (TEU) 10
Art 4(3) 11, 42, 91
Art 6(1)–(3) 14
Art 19 11
Art 19(1) 89
Treaty on the Functioning of the European Union (TFEU) 10, 36, 119
Art 36 (ex Art 30 TEC) 105
Art 45 116
Art 49 110
Art 101 .... 44, 109, 112, 114, 119–120
Art 101(1) 119
Art 102 .... 44, 109, 112
Art 153 (ex Art 137 TEC) 64
Art 255 36
Art 258 (ex Art 226 TEC) 38, 54, 86, 89
Art 260 (ex Art 228 TEC) 38, 54, 86, 89
Art 267 .... 21, 38, 54, 56, 58, 86–87, 89, 96, 108, 114–115, 122, 151, 206–207
Art 267(3) 89, 94, 108, 117
Art 268 92
Art 288 (ex Art 249 TEC) 42, 91, 120
Art 288(3) 42
Art 340(2) (ex Art 288(2) TEC) 19–20, 38, 92
Treaty of Rome 1957 (EEC Treaty) 9–10, 20, 44, 107, 112
Art 7 100
Art 52 (now Art 49 TFEU) 100–101
Art 59 100
Art 86 109
Art 177 100
Art 221 100

Directives

Dir 72/166/EEC of 24 April 1972 on the approximation of the laws of Member States relating to insurance against civil liability in respect of the use of motor vehicles, and to the enforcement of the obligation to insure against such liability 1972 OJ, English Special Edition (II), p 360 (First Motor Insurance Directive)....................45, 74
Art 3(1)....................75
Dir 73/239/EEC of 24 July 1973 First Council Directive on the coordination of laws, regulations and administrative provisions relating to the taking–up and pursuit of the business of direct insurance other than life assurance [1973] OJ L228/3....................96
Dir 77/780/EEC First Council Banking Co–ordination Directive [1977] OJ L322/30....................95–96, 98
Dir 79/7/EEC on equal treatment of men and women in matters of social security....................101
Dir 80/987/EEC of 20 October 1980 on the approximation of the laws of the Member States relating to the protection of employees in the event of the insolvency of their employer [1980] OJ L283/23....................91
Dir 84/5/EEC of 30 December 1983on the approximation of the laws of the Member States relating to insurance against civil liability in respect of the use of motor vehicles [1984] OJ L8/17 (Second Motor Vehicle Insurance Directive)....................45, 102
Art 2(1)....................75
Dir 85/337/EEC on the assessment of the effect of certain public and private projects on the environment [1985] OJ L175/ 40....................118
Dir 85/374/EEC of 25 July 1985 on the approximation of the laws, regulations and administrative provisions of the Member States concerning liability for defective products [1985] OJ L210/29 (Product Liability Directive)....................11, 16, 44–63, 84–87, 201, 205, 209
Preamble....................46
Recitals 1–2....................46
Recital 6....................51
Recitals....................51–53
Art 1....................57
Art 3....................57
Art 6....................50
Art 7(e)....................49, 54–55
Art 8(2)....................49
Art 9....................58
Arts 10–11....................56
Art 13....................48, 59
Art 15(1)(a)....................49

Art 15(1)(b) 49, 54
Art 15(3) 58
Art 16 49
Art 16(2) 58
Art 19 ....47, 54
Art 20 86
Art 21 ....58, 86
Dir 86/188/EEC of 12 May 1986 on the protection of workers from the risks related to exposure to noise at work [1986] OJ L137/28 73
Dir 89/299/EEC of 17 April 1989 on banking law 98
Dir 89/391/EEC of 12 June 1989 on the introduction of measures to encourage improvements in the safety and health of workers at work [1989] OJ L183/1 (Health and Safety of Workers at Work Directive/Framework Directive) 45, 64, 66, 69, 71–72, 85
Art 5(4) 66
Art 16 (1) 66
Dir 89/646/EEC of 15 December 1989 on banking law 98
Dir 89/655 on the minimum health and safety requirements for the use of work equipment by workers at work (EU Workplace Directive) 68–69
Dir 89/656/EEC on the minimum health and safety requirements for the use by workers of personal protective equipment at the workplace (Personal Protective Equipment Directive) 67
Dir 90/232/EEC of 14 May 1990 on the approximation of the laws of the Member States relating to insurance against civil liability in respect of the use of motor vehicles [1990] OJ L129/33 (Third Motor Insurance Directive) 45, 74
Art 1 75
Dir 90/269/EEC of 29 May 1990 on the minimum health and safety requirements for the manual handling of loads where there is a risk particularly of back injury to workers (Manual Handling Directive) 66
Dir 90/314/EEC of 13 June 1990 on package travel, package holidays and package tours [1990] OJ L158/59 (Package Travel Directive) 97–98, 103
Art 7 ....97, 103
Dir 93/13/EEC of 5 April 1993 on unfair terms in consumer contracts [1993] OJ L95/21 (Unfair Terms in Consumer Contracts Directive) 28, 52, 85
Art 3 28
Dir 94/19/EC of 30 May 1994 on deposit–guarantee schemes [1994] OJ L135/5 98
Dir 95/63/EC 68
Dir 98/34/EC
Art 1(2) 77
Dir 1999/34/EC [1999] OJ L/1 ....49, 58
Dir 99/44/EC of 25 May 1999 on certain aspects of the sale of consumer goods and associated guarantees [1999] OJ L171/12 (Consumer Sales Directive) 59

Dir 2000/26/EC of 16 May 2000 (Fourth Motor Insurance Directive) ... 74
Dir 2000/31/EC of 8 June 2000 on certain legal aspects of information society services, in particular electronic commerce, in the Internal Market [2000] OJ L178/1 (Electronic Commerce Directive) ... 16, 45, 77–78, 81, 83–85, 137
Recital 41 ... 78
Art 2(a) ... 77
Arts 12–13 ... 78
Art 14 ... 78, 80
Art 15 ... 78
Dir 2004/35/EC of 21 April 2004 on environmental liability with regard to the prevention and remedying of environmental damage (Environmental Liability Directive) [2004] OJ L143/156 ... 43
Dir 2004/39/EC Markets in Financial Instruments Directive (MiFID) [2004] OJ L145 ... 43
Dir 2005/14/EC of 11 May 2005 (Fifth Motor Insurance Directive) ... 74
Dir 2005/29/EC [2005] OJ L149/22 (Unfair Commercial Practices Directive) ... 43
Dir 2007/30/EC of 27 June 2007 [2007] OJ L165 ... 64
Dir 2009/103/EC of 16 September 2009 relating to insurance against civil liability in respect of the use of motor vehicles, and the enforcement of the obligation to insure against such liability [2009] OJ L263/11 ... 74
Dir 2011/83/EU of 25 October 2011 on consumer rights [2011] OJ L304/65 ... 86
EU Motor Insurance Directives ... 74, 77, 87
Financial Services Directives ... 43

Regulations

Reg (EC) No 1/2003 of 16 December 2002 on the implementation of the rules on competition laid down in Arts 81 and 82 of the Treaty [2003] OJ L1 ... 44
Reg (EC) No 1882/2003 [2003] OJ L284 ... 64
Reg (EC) No 1137/2008 [2008] OJ L311 ... 64

France

Act No 389–98 of 19 May 1998 ... 47
Act No 2006–406 of 5 April 2006 ... 47
French Civil Code ... 9
Art 9 ... 194
Art 1382 ... 5
Arts 1386–1 to 1386–18 ... 47
Act No 70–643 of 17 July 1970 ... 194

Germany

Basic Law (*Grundgesetz*)
Art 1(1) 194
Art 2(1) 194
German Civil Code 14
para 823(1) 194

Portugal

Portuguese Civil Code 76
Arts 505–506 76
Art 570 76

United Kingdom

Competition Act 1998 44
Consumer Protection Act 1987 .... 11, 48–53, 55, 60–63, 85–86
Pt 1 .... 11, 16, 47, 49, 54, 59, 61–63, 205
s 1(1) 47, 49, 52, 55
s 1(2) 47
s 2(1) 47
s 2(2)(a)–(c) 47
s 2(3) 47
s 3 51–52
s 3(1) 11, 50
s 3(2) 50–51
s 3(2)(a) 50
s 3(2)(a)(i)–(iv) 50
s 3(2)(b)–(c) 50
s 4(1)(e) 51, 54–55
s 5(3)–(4) 47
s 41 111
Copyright, Designs and Patents Act 1988 172
s 85 172
Courts and Legal Services Act 1990
s 8 126
Data Protection Act 1998 172
Defamation Act 1952
s 2 134–135
s 5 135

s 10 ... 133
Defamation Act 1996 ... 80–81, 84, 124, 134
s 1 ... 77, 80–81, 86
s 1(1) ... 79–80
s 1(1)(a) ... 79
s 1(1)(b)–(c) ... 79–80
s 1(2)–(3) ... 79
s 1(3)(c) ... 79
s 1(3)(e) ... 79
s 1(5) ... 79
Defamation Act 2013 ... 124, 135
s 1 ... 133
s 1(1)–(2) ... 137
s 2(4) ... 135
s 4 ... 127, 130
s 4(3) ... 131
s 5 ... 82
s 5(1)–(2) ... 82
s 5(3) ... 82–83
s 5(3)(a) ... 82–83
s 5(3)(b) ... 82
s 5(3)(c) ... 83
s 5(4)–(5) ... 83
s 5(5)(a)–(d) ... 83
s 5(8)–(12) ... 83
s 6 ... 138
s 8 ... 138
s 11 ... 132
Employer's Liability (Defective Equipment) Act 1969 ... 63
Enterprise and Regulatory Reform Act 2013 ... 70
s 69 ... 70
s 69(3) ... 70
s 69(10) ... 70
Environmental Protection Act 1990
s 80 ... 160
s 82 ... 160
European Communities Act 1972 ... 1, 9, 17, 27, 34, 107, 110, 125, 197, 204, 208
s 2(1) ... 9, 109, 111
s 2(2) ... 9, 11, 69
s 3 ... 17–18
Sch 2 ... 9
Factories Act 1961 ... 65–66
Factory and Workshop Act 1878
s 5(4) ... 64

Fatal Accidents Act 1976 .... 124, 152
s 1A 150, 152, 164
Financial Services and Markets Act (FSMA) 2000 43
s 150 43
Health and Safety at Work etc Act 1974 .... 65–66, 69, 85
s 2(1) 65–66
s 15 65
s 47(1)(a) 65
s 47(2) 65, 67, 70, 72
Human Rights Act 1998 .... 1–2, 12–14, 16–17, 22, 25–28, 34, 36, 116, 123, 125–126, 129–132, 134, 136, 138–140, 142, 145–150, 152–154, 156, 158–161, 163–166, 168–170, 174, 176–178, 181, 186, 189–190, 192–197, 203–209
s 2 .... 22, 27, 204
s 2(1) 16, 22–23, 145, 174, 179, 206
s 2(1)(a)–(d) 22
s 3 .... 25–26, 124, 133, 152, 157, 204
s 3(1) 26
s 3(2) 25
s 4 .... 25, 152
s 6 .... 12–13, 16, 124, 140, 146, 157, 162, 169–170, 176, 196
s 6(3) 124–125
s 7 .... 12, 16, 124, 140, 146, 151, 164, 169–170, 196
s 7(1) 151
s 7(5) 125, 146
s 8 .... 12, 124, 140, 146–147, 165, 196
s 8(2) 124
s 8(3) 124, 146, 160
s 8(4) 147
s 12(4) 139, 178
s 60 44
Sch 1 124
Interception of Communications Act 1985 173
Law Reform (Contributory Negligence) Act 1945
s 1 75
s 1(1) 64
Law Reform (Personal Injuries) Act 1948
s 1(1) 64
Legal Aid, Sentencing and Punishment of Offenders Act 2012
s 44 132
Limitation Act 1980
s 2 .... 94, 114
s 11A(3) 56–57
s 28 101

s 35 56
Merchant Shipping Act 1988 100
Mines and Quarries Act 1954 65
Occupiers' Liability Acts 68
Offices, Shops and Railway Premises Act 1963 65
Protection from Harassment Act 1997 ....115, 172
Rehabilitation of Offenders Act 1974
s 8 172
Road Traffic Act 1988
s 151(8) 77
Sale of Goods Act 1979 59
Statute of Westminster 1285 110
Water Industry Act 1991 158
s 94 160

Statutory Instruments

Civil Procedures Rules 133
r 3.4 143
Code of Practice on noise at work 73
Competition Act 1998 and Other Enactments (Amendment) Regulations 2004 SI 2004/1261 44
Consumer Protection from Unfair Trading Regulations SI 2008/1277 43
Defamation (Operators of Websites) Regulations 2013/3028 83
Electronic Commerce (EC Directive) Regulations 2002 SI 2002/2013 ....16, 45, 78, 80–81, 137
Reg 17 78
Reg 18 78–79
Reg 19 78–81
Reg 19(a) 79
Reg 19(a)(i)–(a)(ii) 79
Reg 19(b) 79
Health and Safety (Display Screen Equipment) Regulations 1992 SI 1992/2792 65
Management of Health and Safety at Work Regulations 1992 SI 1992/2051 (now SI 1999/3242) 65
Reg 22 65
Management of Health and Safety at Work and Fire Precautions (Workplace) (Amendment) Regulations SI 2003/2457 (later amended by SI 2006/438, Reg 2) 65, 71
Manual Handling Operations Regulations 1992 SI 1992/2793 65–67
Personal Protective Equipment at Work Regulations 1992 SI 1992/2966 65–67
Reg 7(1) 66

Provision and Use of Work Equipment Regulations 1992 SI 1992/2932
(now SI 1998/ 2306)....65, 68
Provision and Use of Work Equipment Regulations 1998 SI 1998/ 2306....68
Reg 2(1)....68
Reg 3(2) 147....68
Reg 4(4)....66, 68
Reg 5....68
Reg 20....68
Unfair Terms in Consumer Contracts Regulations 1994 SI 1994/3159....52, 85
Unfair Terms in Consumer Contracts Regulations 1999 SI 1999/2083....85
Reg 5....28
Workplace (Health, Safety and Welfare) Regulations 1992 SI 1992/3004....65

United States of America

Restatement (Second) of Torts
§ 402A....46
§ 402A(1)....46
§ 402A(1)(a)–(b)....46
§ 402A(2)....46
§ 402A(2)(a)–(b)....46
§§ 652A–652I....171
Restatement (Third) Torts: Product Liability....53
§ 2(b)....53

Table of Conventions

European Convention of Human Rights 1950 .... 2, 8, 12, 14, 16–17, 25, 28–29, 35–36, 41, 77, 81, 123, 125, 128, 131, 140, 142, 145, 158, 170, 190, 195–196, 207–208, 210
Art 2 .... 124, 141, 145, 148–151, 153, 164
Art 2(2) 141
Art 3 .... 124, 141–142, 145–146, 164
Art 4 124
Art 5 .... 124, 153–156, 164, 167
Art 5(1) 154–156
Art 5(1)(a)–(f) 154–155
Art 6 .... 124, 131–134, 142, 145, 150
Art 6(1) 142
Art 7 124
Art 8 .... 124, 128–129, 131, 139, 141, 145–146, 148, 153, 156–164, 166, 168–170, 173, 176–187, 190–195, 209
Art 8(1) 157–158, 160
Art 8(2) 157, 162, 177
Art 9 124
Art 10 .... 81, 124–129, 131–136, 138–139, 163, 166, 176–178, 181–186, 190–191, 193, 195
Art 10(2) 128–129, 135, 191
Art 11 124
Art 13 207
Art 26 22
Art 27(2) 22
Art 31 22
Art 34 .... 150–151, 163
Art 35 12
Art 41 147
Art 45(2) 22
Art 46 .... 12, 22
Art 52(3) 14
Protocol 1, Art 1 .... 124, 141, 150, 153, 156, 158, 161
Strasbourg Convention on Products Liability in regard to personal injury and death 46–47
United Nations Convention on the Rights of the Child
Art 16 157

1

Introduction

> [R]emedies and procedures are best left to the law which is familiar to the country in which the right must be enforced. The good sense of that recognition can no doubt be shown in any number of different ways, but here it is enough to state the obvious, namely that the European Community is an economic and not a political community. Political systems and traditions vary, in some cases significantly, from member state to member state . . . What then can be the interest of Community law in endangering the continuation of this system?
>
> (Lord Justice Nourse).[1]

> Whatever then emerges will be a synthesis, a merging of the different national rivers, not an inundation. Common lawyers have proved as least as good as other European lawyers elsewhere in interpreting and applying European principles where they have already developed . . . Endless reiteration of hostility to such moves is likely only to be counter-productive.
>
> (Lord Mance).[2]

We see above two judicial statements and two different attitudes displayed by the English judiciary to the potential impact of European law on traditional common law principles. Lord Justice Nourse seeks to preserve the identity and culture of the common law. His faith is therefore placed in the common law legal tradition and its principles developed over centuries of practice. Europe is therefore a matter of economics or trade with limited impact on national law. Lord Mance, speaking 20 years later, is the more positive, seeking to diminish the perception of Europe as a threat to the common law and to highlight the possible benefits from a more proactive involvement in the interpretation and application of European Union (EU) law. And yet the title of his article – 'Is Europe Aiming to Civilise the Common Law?' – identifies the key issue which this book seeks to address: to what extent are European influences changing the nature of the common law legal tradition? As we shall see, in the last 40 years, the combined impact of the European Communities Act 1972, the Human Rights Act 1998 and increased contact between European scholars, lawyers and judges has resulted in what Lord Cooke

[1] *Bourgoin SA v Ministry of Agriculture* [1986] QB 716, 789–90.

[2] J Mance, 'Is Europe Aiming to Civilise the Common Law?' (2007) 18 *European Business Law Review* 77, 99.

has described as the diminishing Englishness of the common law.[3] In identifying the road ahead for English tort law, this book will examine the extent to which an area of law, traditionally a bastion of English case law methodology and practice, is changing both in terms of substantive law and how the courts reason. While a number of books have already addressed the Europeanisation of contract law[4] or consumer law,[5] tort law has received less attention and yet the factors which have encouraged interest in contract law – intervention at EU level, harmonisation proposals, European interaction at scholarly, professional and judicial level – apply equally to tort law. Further, the European Convention of Human Rights, brought into English law via the HRA 1998, has had greater impact on tort law than the law of contract, providing, as it does, a remedy for breaches of Convention rights by public authorities. This chapter will explain why tort law has been chosen as a particularly revealing example of the impact of European influences on English private law and what insights this study can bring to English common lawyers who continue to regard Europeanisation as introducing alien and 'un-British' concepts into the English legal system. It will start, however, with a key initial question: what do we mean by 'Europeanisation'?

I. The 'Europeanisation' of English Tort Law: What do we mean by 'Europeanisation'?

Miller has noted that in common with the term 'globalisation',[6] the term 'Europeanisation' is used frequently, but often with little definitional care.[7] There is no single grand theory of Europeanisation.[8] She notes that the term indicates a process of transformation, but gives little guidance as to its content, mechanisms and the extent of its influence. Miller identifies three possible meanings: (i) the

[3] R Cooke, 'The Road Ahead for the Common Law' (2004) 53 *International & Comparative Law Quarterly* 273.

[4] See, eg, L Miller, *The Emergence of EU Contract Law: Exploring Europeanization* (Oxford, Oxford University Press, 2011), R Schulze and J Stuyck (eds), *Towards a European Contract Law* (Munich, Sellier, 2011), C Twigg-Flesner, *The Europeanisation of Contract Law*, 2nd edn (Abingdon, Routledge-Cavendish, 2013), K Boele-Woelki and W Grosheide (eds), *The Future of European Contract Law* (The Hague, Kluwer, 2007), J Smits (ed), *The Need for a European Contract Law* (Groningen, Europa Law Publishing, 2005).

[5] eg, S Leible, *European Consumer Law* (Oxford, Hart Publishing, forthcoming), I Benohr, *EU Consumer Law and Human Rights* (Oxford, Oxford University Press, 2013), H Schulte-Nölke and L Tichy (eds), *Perspectives for European Consumer Law: Towards a Directive on Consumer Rights and Beyond* (Munich, Sellier, 2010), S Weatherill, *EU Consumer Law and Policy* (Cheltenham, Edward Elgar, 2005).

[6] W Twining, *Globalisation and Legal Theory* (Cambridge, Cambridge University Press, 2000); W Twining, 'Globalisation and Comparative Law' in E Örücü and D Nelken (eds), *Comparative Law: A Handbook* (Oxford, Hart Publishing, 2007) 69–75.

[7] Miller, *The Emergence of EU Contract Law* (n 4) 3.

[8] JP Olsen, 'The Many Faces of Europeanisation' (2002) 40 *Journal of Common Market Studies* 921, 944, who argues that Europeanisation may be less useful as an explanatory concept than as an attention-directing device and a starting point for further exploration.

development of transnational law at European level, (ii) the entrance of European-derived rules at national level and (iii) the process of harmonisation itself. In contrast, Michaels and Jansen have favoured a broader threefold division, which covers not only the instrumental (EU law), but also the academic (transnational legal science) and the regulatory (competition between legal rules governed by the inner rationality of the market).[9] Other authors have preferred a narrower focus, for example on the harmonisation of European private law,[10] on the impact of EU legislation on domestic private law,[11] or in terms of European integration including its indirect and sometimes unintended consequences with regard to national, EU or international law.[12]

In this book, 'Europeanisation' is taken in a broader sense. It will examine the impact of European Union law on domestic English law, but will also consider the relevance of the case law of the European Court of Human Rights and the degree to which cross-fertilisation with tort law generally has taken place. There is surprisingly little literature on this topic taken as a whole. The perspective is that of an English tort lawyer, who, by virtue of her training as a comparative and European private lawyer, is seeking to identify European influences which may affect the traditional common law approach to English tort law. 'Europeanisation' is not, however, simply a question of substantive law. It must also be taken as a cultural phenomenon, changing our outlook on law and its development. The book will thus consider to what extent English lawyers may now be said to possess a 'European' legal perspective. It will also examine cross-jurisdictional European dialogue. Professional bodies such as the International Association of Judges,[13] the Council of Bars and Law Societies of Europe (CCBE)[14] and the Council of the Notariats of the European Union (CNUE)[15] bring practitioners from European Member States together. Institutions have been established for the dissemination and development of European law such as the Academy of European Law (ERA), which provides a centre for the continuing education of lawyers in order to improve the application

[9] R Michaels and N Jansen, 'Private Law Beyond the State? Europeanization, Globalisation, Privatization' (2006) 54 *American Journal of Comparative Law* 843, 861–64.

[10] O Lando, 'Optional or Mandatory Europeanization of Contract Law' (2000) 8 *European Review of Private Law* 59: 'The term to "Europeanise" the law . . . means to unify or harmonise European law i.e. the law of the countries which are, or will, become members of the European Union.' Lando also distinguishes between optional Europeanisation (left to national courts to determine whether to bring laws of Europe closer together) and the more controversial mandatory Europeanisation by which unification is imposed by the legislators in the European Union or Member States.

[11] Twigg-Flesner, *The Europeanisation of Contract Law* (n 4). See also J Engstrom, *Europeanisation of Remedies and Procedures Through Judge-Made Law* (Oxford, Hart Publishing, forthcoming).

[12] FG Snyder (ed), *The Europeanisation of Law: The Legal Effects of European Integration* (Oxford, Hart Publishing, 2000).

[13] www.iaj-Uim.org/, including the regional group of the European Association of Judges (43 countries).

[14] The CCBE is the representative organisation of around 1 million European lawyers through its member bars and law societies from 31 full member countries, and 11 further associate and observer countries.

[15] The CNUE is the official body representing the notarial profession in dealings with the European institutions. Speaking for the profession, it negotiates and makes decisions for the European Union's notariats.

of European law,[16] and, more recently, the European Law Institute, founded in June 2011 as an entirely independent organisation to initiate, conduct and facilitate research, to make recommendations, and to provide practical guidance in the field of European legal development.[17] Academic projects such as the Trento Common Core project[18] and the work of the European Centre of Tort and Insurance Law[19] bring together academics and legal professionals from across Europe by hosting annual conferences and engaging in ongoing research on European private law. Information exchange, facilitated by electronic resources and greater internet access and promoted by, for example, the European Commission has led to greater awareness of European principles and case law. Tort law is not immune from these influences. The two main reasons for focusing on tort law in this study will be set out below.

II. Why Tort Law?

A. A Key Exemplar of Common Law Values

Tort law is generally regarded as a clear example of common law methodology. It is largely case-based and as an area of law where the legal rules have been developed by judges with limited statutory intervention, it provides a good illustration of how English judges reason.[20] It also highlights the ongoing importance to common lawyers of legal procedure (the system of nominate torts representing the legacy of the writ system) and its focus on remedies rather than principle.[21] MacCormick, for example, used the leading tort case of *Donoghue v Stevenson*[22] as a running example in his work *Legal Reasoning and Legal Theory*.[23] In stating the

[16] See www.era.int.

[17] www.europeanlawinstitute.eu/home/. See R Zimmermann, 'Challenges for the European Law Institute' (2012) 16 *Edinburgh Law Review* 5.

[18] www.common-core.org/ (which has a distinct tort section) and whose stated aim is to seek 'to unearth the common core of the bulk of European private law, i.e., of what is already common, if anything, among the different legal systems of European Union member states.'

[19] www.ectil.org/.

[20] See J Bell, *Policy Arguments in Judicial Decisions* (Oxford, Clarendon Press, 1983) 41.

[21] Rudden, for example, has noted the extraordinary level of intellectual energy which common lawyers devote to identifying whether the conduct in question amounts to a nominate tort in contrast to their civil law counterparts: B Rudden, 'Torticles' (1991–92) 6/7 *Tulane Civil Law Forum* 105, 109.

[22] *Donoghue v Stevenson* [1932] AC 562, described by Lord Rodger as 'probably the most famous case in the whole Commonwealth world of the common law': A Rodger, 'Mrs Donoghue and Alfenus Varus' (1988) 41 *Current Legal Problems* 1, 2. An international conference was held in May 2012 to mark the 80th anniversary of this case, demonstrating the continued reverence with which the common law community holds this particular case: 'The Paisley Snail: *Donoghue v Stevenson*, International Conference on the Law of Negligence', held naturally in Paisley where the facts of the case took place.

[23] N MacCormick, *Legal Reasoning and Legal Theory* (Oxford, Clarendon Press, 1978). See also N MacCormick, '*Donoghue v Stevenson* and Legal Reasoning' in PT Burns (ed), *Donoghue v Stevenson and the Modern Law of Negligence* (Vancouver, Continuing Legal Education of British Columbia, 1991) 191–213.

'neighbour principle', Lord Atkin established the test for the duty of care in negligence.[24] While such a general statement of principle may be compared with the general clauses found in civil law codes,[25] the reality, as known to all common lawyers, is different. Case law development post *Donoghue v Stevenson* did not proceed on the basis of broad principle,[26] but developed categories of liability, echoing Lord Macmillan's comment in *Donoghue* that 'the categories of negligence are never closed'.[27] The gradual development of the tort of negligence into the twenty-first century illustrates both how the common law courts reason and the importance placed on the doctrine of precedent, giving legal certainty and predictability to the law.[28]

For English lawyers, therefore, tort law epitomises the 'Englishness' of the common law and this is emphasised by the fact that its definition is classically linked to its place in society itself: it is the law of *civil* wrongs, that is, conduct deemed wrongful in our society. Lord Denning, for example, emphasised that the province of tort law is to allocate responsibility in our society for injurious conduct.[29] *Street on Torts* also finds it helpful to focus on tort law as a means of remedying breach of a relevant norm of conduct which infringes the claimant's interest.[30] McBride and Bagshaw express similar views, albeit more pragmatically: 'the function of tort law is to determine what legal rights we have against other people, free of charge and without our having to make special arrangements for them, and what remedies will be available when those rights are violated'.[31] Whichever definition one prefers,[32] all commentators highlight the connection between tort law and domestic values, giving rise to right of reparation to specific individuals. Tort law is thus about citizens within our society and the duties (and rights) they owe to each other. It establishes when (legally) we must take care, when we are permitted to defend ourselves, to what extent we can act freely on our own land even if it

[24] *Donoghue* (n 22) 580: 'Who then in law is my neighbour? The answer seems to be – persons who are so closely and directly affected by my act that I ought reasonably to have them in contemplation as being so affected when I am directing my mind to the acts or omissions which are called in question.'

[25] See, eg, the French Civil Code, art 1382: 'Any act whatever of man, which causes damage to another, obliges the one by whose fault it occurred, to compensate it': translation: www.legifrance.gouv.fr.

[26] See R Heuston, '*Donoghue v Stevenson* in Retrospect' (1957) 20 *Modern Law Review* 1; D Ibbetson, *A Historical Introduction to the Law of Obligations* (Oxford, Oxford University Press, 1999) 190–91. Note the rejection of the 'Anns' test in *Anns v Merton LBC* [1978] AC 728 by the House of Lords in *Murphy v Brentwood DC* [1991] 1 AC 398.

[27] *Donoghue* (n 22) 619.

[28] K Stanton, 'Professional Negligence: Duty of Care Methodology in the Twenty-first Century' (2006) 22 *Journal of Professional Negligence* 134; J Morgan, 'The Rise and Fall of the General Duty of Care' (2006) 22 *Journal of Professional Negligence* 206.

[29] Review of Winfield (3rd edn) (1947) 63 *Law Quarterly Review* 517. Winfield had famously defined tort law as a 'breach of a duty primarily fixed by law', but this is accepted to be too vague: PH Winfield, *The Province of the Law of Tort* (Cambridge, Cambridge University Press, 1931) 32.

[30] J Murphy and C Witting (eds), *Street on Torts*, 13th edn (Oxford, Oxford University Press, 2012) 4.

[31] NJ McBride and R Bagshaw, *Tort Law*, 4th edn (Harlow, Pearson, 2012) 1.

[32] K Oliphant (ed), *The Law of Tort*, Butterworths Common Law Series, 2nd edn (London, Butterworths, 2007) para 1.2 comments that 'Attempts at more precise definition may give something of the flavour of tort law, or some aspect of it, but they are inevitably over- or under-inclusive, or otherwise inaccurate in one respect or another'.

may be to the detriment of other citizens. It determines when and to what extent a NHS doctor owes a duty to take reasonable care for my welfare,[33] a newspaper can accuse me of criminal activities,[34] a freelance photographer can take pictures of my children[35] and when the blood transfusion service will be held responsible for supplying me with infected blood in circumstances where the virus in question was incapable of detection.[36] The decision of what exactly constitutes a civil wrong remains primarily a matter for the courts, drawn from centuries of judicial decision-making, although increasingly legislation is having some impact.[37]

English tort law also reflects the divide between the common law countries of Europe (England and Wales; Ireland) and the majority of states whose legal system are based on civil law or mixed common and civil law legal traditions.[38] Although it inevitably shares certain values, solutions[39] and practices with other continental systems, it also bears the imprint of its own historical development and legal culture, which may be identified as the values, practices and concepts which are integrated into the operation of legal institutions and the interpretation of legal texts.[40] Most notably, English law stood outside the wave of codification in the eighteenth and nineteenth century, which marked the displacement of the *ius commune* based on canon law and the law of Rome[41] in favour of the unification of national law through codification and the growth of the modern nation-state in Continental Europe.[42]

This has led to a common/civil law divide which goes beyond the mere difference in terminology of tort law or delict. Zimmermann comments that 'It is just about out of the question that the House of Lords would refer to the textbooks of Medicus or Flume; likewise the German Federal Supreme Court does not normally consult Treitel on Contract or Fleming on Torts'.[43] Nevertheless scholars such as Zimmermann have sought to highlight that this division is far from

[33] *Bolam v Friern Hospital Management Committee* [1957] 1 WLR 583.

[34] *Loutchansky v Times Newspapers Ltd and others (Nos. 2–5)* [2001] EWCA Civ 1805; [2002] QB 783.

[35] *Murray v Big Pictures (UK) Ltd* [2008] EWCA Civ 446; [2009] Ch 481.

[36] *A and others v National Blood Authority and another* [2001] 3 All ER 289.

[37] P Cane and J Conaghan (eds), *The New Oxford Companion to Law* (Oxford, Oxford University Press, 2008) 1171.

[38] Some authors would go further and suggest that common and civil law paths are irreconcilable: P Legrand, 'European Legal Systems are not Converging' (1996) 45 *International & Comparative Law Quarterly* 52. As will be seen in ch 2, the author does not go this far, but notes that there are differences which go beyond black-letter law and affect the culture within which law operates.

[39] R Zweigert and H Kötz, *An Introduction to Comparative Law*, 3rd edn (Oxford, Oxford University Press, 1998) 34, BS Markesinis, 'The Not So Dissimilar Tort and Delict' (1977) 93 *Law Quarterly Review* 78.

[40] See J Bell, 'English Law and French Law: Not So Different? (1995) 48(2) *Current Legal Problems* 63.

[41] See R Zimmermann, *The Law of Obligations: Roman Foundations of the Civilian Tradition* (Oxford, Oxford University Press, 1996).

[42] See P Stein, 'The ius commune and Its Demise' (2004) 25 *Journal of Legal History* 161.

[43] R Zimmermann, 'Civil Code and Civil Law: The "Europeanization" of Private Law within the European Community and the Re-emergence of a European Legal Science' (1994–95) 1 *Columbia Journal of European Law* 63, 66.

watertight,[44] and the influence of civil law was particularly evident in the English ecclesiastical courts and the Court of Admiralty.[45] Indeed, it would be unlikely that a country where Roman law had been taught in its universities from the Middle Ages[46] and whose commercial law, notably in relation to maritime law, inevitably came into contact with civil law scholastic thinking and procedures[47] would bear no imprint of Roman law influences. Ibbetson identifies at the beginning of the eighteenth century the 'stirrings of theorization' in tort law, and the influence of natural lawyers such as Grotius and Pufendorf whose work brought continental ideas into English law,[48] although such principles were largely developed indigenously from the 18th-century natural law base.[49] He observes, however, that although English law undoubtedly received 'injections' of Roman law, these were immediately assimilated into the specifically English legal framework and cut off from their Roman roots.[50] English tort law has thus remained distinctive in many ways from its civil law counterparts. Baker notes that the common law withstood two waves of Romanist influence which swept across the Continent in the wake of the rediscovery of Justinian's *Digest* and Renaissance humanism which drove out older methods of proof and encouraged the application of rational legal principles based on civil law.[51] Tort law remains the law of the courts, with limited intervention by legislature, uncodified and – as a law of social wrongs – reflective of changes in society, be they political or socio-economic. It also bears the imprint of the distinct procedures of the English courts, notably the writ system, its legal profession and the centralised court system of England and Wales.

It is inevitable, therefore, that new European sources, be they EU law or European human rights law, will challenge the common law/civil law divide. More fundamentally, if tort law is about society, are we moving towards a European society in which the civil wrongs in question are those contrary to the societal values of Europe, not

[44] Zimmermann, argues that, in reality, English law was never entirely isolated from Continental legal culture: see R Zimmermann, 'Der europäische Charakter des englischen Rechts' [1993] *Zeitschrift für Europäisches Privatrecht* 4.

[45] JH Baker, *An Introduction to English Legal History*, 4th edn (London, Butterworths, 2002) 123–24, 126–34.

[46] P Stein, *The Teaching of Roman Law in England around 1200* (London, Selden Society, 1990), Supplementary Volume 8, Introduction. Zimmermann has noted that up until the nineteenth century, the two universities of England and Wales (Oxford and Cambridge) followed the Continental model of study and leading Roman law works, such as German jurist Heineccius' *Elementa iuris civilis*, were used as textbooks in universities ranging from Cracow to Oxford: R Zimmermann, 'Roman Law and the Harmonization of Private Law in Europe' in AS Hartkamp et al (eds), *Towards a European Civil Code*, 4th edn (The Hague, Kluwer Law International, 2011) 33, 45.

[47] As noted by the great commercial judge, Lord Mansfield: see T Lowry, 'Lord Mansfield and the Law Merchant: Law and Economics in the Eighteenth Century' (1973) 7 *Journal of Economic Issues* 605, CP Rodgers, 'Continental Literature and the Development of the Common Law by the King's Bench, c. 1750–1800' in V Piergiovanni (ed), *The Courts and the Development of Commercial Law* (Berlin, Duncker & Humblot, 1987).

[48] And whose work had been translated into English by the mid eighteenth century, Zimmermann, *The Law of Obligations* (n 41) 46–47.

[49] Ibbetson, *A Historical Introduction to the Law of Obligations* (n 26) 153–54.

[50] DJ Ibbetson, 'A Reply to Professor Zimmermann' in TG Watkin, *The Europeanisation of Law* (London, UKNCCL, 1998) 229.

[51] Baker, *An Introduction to English Legal History* (n 45) 28.

simply England and Wales? Europeanisation is therefore not simply a question of introducing new legal rules, but bringing in new forms of policy and remedial frameworks, threatening the autonomy of the common law to develop its own law of tort and for English lawyers to make policy judgements at a localised level. The challenge for the common law legal community is self-evident.[52]

B. Lack of Awareness of European Influences on English Tort Law

i. Isn't It Public, Not Private, Law?

There is, however, a second reason for focusing on tort law. Until recently, tort law has been seen as immune to or, at best, relatively unaffected by Europeanisation. European Union law and the European Convention on Human Rights have been seen as matters for public and human rights lawyers. The Law Society and the General Council of the Bar's list of 'The Foundations of Legal Knowledge', required for completion of the academic stage of training in an undergraduate law degree, provides for the following key elements and general principles of legal study:

i. Public Law, including Constitutional Law, Administrative Law and Human Rights;
ii. Law of the European Union;
iii. Criminal Law;
iv. Obligations including Contract, Restitution and Tort;
v. Property Law; and
vi. Equity and the Law of Trusts.[53]

Human rights, it will be noted, are expressly considered as an element of public law, while EU law remains distinct from other elements of private law. Indeed, a glance at the syllabi of UK universities will generally serve to emphasise this subject division. Tort law, often taught as a first-year subject, preceding study of EU law and distinct from the public law coverage of human rights law, is seen as part of the private law brand and often, as stated above, used as a means for demonstrating the methodology of common law reasoning. One of the aims of this book is to dispel the myth that Europeanisation is solely of interest to public lawyers. It also impacts on private law and private lawyers continue to ignore changes to their legal system at their peril. Admittedly, it may take private lawyers out of their comfort zone to consider new sources of law and unfamiliar concepts 'foreign' to the traditional

[52] For a perspective of the challenges of Europeanisation to civil law systems, see JM Smits, 'The Europeanisation of National Legal Systems: Some Consequences for Legal Thinking in Civil Law Countries' in M Van Hoecke (ed), *Epistemology and Methodology of Comparative Law* (Oxford, Hart Publishing, 2004) 229.

[53] This applies to all law degrees commenced after 1 September 2001 and was prepared jointly by the Law Society and the Bar Standards Board, setting out the conditions a law degree course must meet in order to be termed a 'qualifying law degree': see www.sra.org.uk/students/academic-stage.page.

common law system. However, subsequent chapters will highlight that a failure to recognise Europeanisation may lead to incorrect application of the law and the danger of a conflict between the UK courts and the Court of Justice of the European Union (CJEU) or European Court of Human Rights (ECtHR). Further, lawyers commencing a law degree after September 2001 have no excuse for ignorance, having studied EU law as part of their qualifying degree programme.

ii. *What Has EU Law to Do with English Private Law?*

On 1 January 1973 the United Kingdom became a Member State of the then European Communities. The European Communities Act 1972 marked the necessary step[54] to make European law applicable within the national legal system. Section 2(1) of the 1972 Act provides:

> All such rights, powers, liabilities, obligations and restrictions from time to time created or arising by or under the Treaties, and all such remedies and procedures from time to time provided for by or under the Treaties, as in accordance with the Treaties are without further enactment to be given legal effect or used in the United Kingdom shall be recognised and available in law, and be enforced, allowed and followed accordingly; and the expression 'enforceable EU right' and similar expressions shall be read as referring to one to which this subsection applies.

On this basis, provisions of EU law that are directly applicable or have direct effect are automatically enforceable in the United Kingdom without the need for any further enactment. Section 2(2) applies to measures that are neither directly applicable nor have direct effect and which may be introduced into national law by means of delegated legislation.[55] EU law is thus capable of giving rise to rights and liabilities which must be recognised by the English courts. Nevertheless, as the statement from Lord Justice Nourse indicates, in 1973 most UK lawyers thought about the European Union primarily in economic terms. Indeed, it may be questioned whether a common market promoting trade between Member States would have been expected to impact on domestic principles of private law. As Caruso explains, the six European nations that signed the Treaty of Rome in 1957 each had a functioning civil code dealing with private law[56] and, therefore,

[54] In relation to international treaties, the UK is a dualist system.

[55] European Communities Act 1972, s 2(2):

> Subject to Schedule 2 to this Act, at any time after its passing Her Majesty may by Order in Council, and any designated Minister or department may by order, rules, regulations or scheme, make provision – (a) for the purpose of implementing any EU obligation of the United Kingdom, or enabling any such obligation to be implemented, or of enabling any rights enjoyed or to be enjoyed by the United Kingdom under or by virtue of the Treaties to be exercised; or (b) for the purpose of dealing with matters arising out of or related to any such obligation or rights or the coming into force, or the operation from time to time, of subsection (1) above; and in the exercise of any statutory power or duty, including any power to give directions or to legislate by means of orders, rules, regulations or other subordinate instrument, the person entrusted with the power or duty may have regard to the objects of the EU and to any such obligation or rights as aforesaid.

[56] West Germany, France, Italy, Belgium, the Netherlands and Luxembourg; the French Civil Code dating back to 1804.

the Treaty of Rome was exclusively public in inspiration and scope. However, as the EU expanded and became more politically active, this 'reassuring breakwater' could not hold for long.[57] The initial policy goal of removing barriers to trade came to be interpreted broadly to encompass measures dealing with issues such as health, environmental protection and the protection of consumer rights. This has led inevitably to an increase in litigation in private law. While in 1995, the number of cases before the ECJ on substantive private law legislation and civil procedure numbered no more than six,[58] by 2007, this had risen to 29.[59]

At present, the Treaty on European Union (TEU) and the Treaty on the Functioning of the European Union (TFEU) create a wide framework of powers, duties and individual rights.[60] The national court is expected to provide a remedial framework to ensure that the rights granted to individuals are respected and thus give citizens effective protection. Perhaps most well known is the development of the doctrine of direct effect by which the national courts are expected to provide a remedial response to the breach of EU legal provisions which are sufficiently clear, precise and unconditional to be considered justiciable.[61] While national courts are, with some exceptions,[62] given considerable remedial autonomy, the remedy awarded must comply with the principles of effectiveness[63] and equivalence (or non-discrimination).[64] Further, the doctrine of indirect effect states that national courts now have duties to interpret existing legislation in line

[57] D Caruso, 'The Missing View of the Cathedral: The Private Law Paradigm of European Legal Integration' (1997) 3 *European Law Journal* 3, 8–9. This does not signify, however, that the domestic courts were ready to accept such an extension: for a discussion of the response of the English, French and German Supreme Courts, see J Bell, *Judiciaries within Europe* (Cambridge, Cambridge University Press, 2006) 378–80.

[58] Not counting cases in which private law was a side issue.

[59] E Hondius, 'The Impact of Community Law on Domestic Private Law' (2010) 18 *European Review of Private Law* 425.

[60] Consolidated versions of the Treaty on European Union and the Treaty on the Functioning of the European Union, OJ C83 of 30 March 2010.

[61] Case 26/62 *Van Gend en Loos v Nederlandse Administratie der Belastungen* [1963] ECR 1, [1963] CMLR 105 and Case 41/74 *Van Duyn v Home Office* [1974] ECR 1337. Generally, P Craig and G de Búrca, *EU Law: Text, Cases and Materials*, 5th edn (Oxford, Oxford University Press, 2011) ch 7. Note that the rule remains that the direct effect of a directive may only be pleaded against the State and not against an individual (vertical not horizontal effect): Case 152/84 *Marshall v Southampton and South-West Hampshire Area Health Authority (Teaching)* [1986] ECR 723. This rule is mitigated to a certain extent by the doctrine of incidental horizontal effects, permitting the use of unimplemented directives in certain cases between private parties: Craig and de Búrca, *EU Law*, 207 (who also describe it as complex and confusing); Case C-194/94 *CIA Security International SA v Signalson SA* [1996] ECR I-2201; Case C 443/98 *Unilever Italia v Central Food* [2000] ECR I-7535.

[62] eg, the right of restitution under the San Giorgio principle for illegally levied taxes (Case 199/82 *Amministrazione delle Finanze dello Stato v SpA San Giorgio* [1983] ECR 3595). Note also the willingness to set aside national restrictions on remedies, as seen in *Factortame* below.

[63] The principle of effectiveness requires that it should not be practically impossible to exercise EU rights in the national law: see Case C-213/89 *R v Secretary of State for Transport, ex parte Factortame Ltd* [1990] ECR I-2433 (full effectiveness of EU law impaired if rule of national law prevented court from granting interim relief against the Crown, thereby setting aside a rule of national law).

[64] The principle of equivalence means that the remedies and procedures for dealing with such claims in domestic law must give rise to remedies which are no less favourable than those available in domestic law: see Case 14/83 *Von Colson v Land Nordrhein-Westfalen* [1984] ECR 1891.

with EU law.[65] English courts are thus expected to respond positively to EU law and give priority to establishing the meaning of the relevant legal provision when determining how it should apply at national level.[66] Article 19 TEU[67] re-iterates that 'Member States shall provide remedies sufficient to ensure effective legal protection in the fields covered by Union law'.[68]

EU law is thus a significant source of English law. Commentators now acknowledge that 'A major proportion of the law in the United Kingdom is in fact made by or through the EU'.[69] English judges are also more willing to utilise 'European' concepts such as legitimate expectation and proportionality in shaping rules of domestic law.[70] It would be surprising, therefore, if tort law remained unaffected. As will be discussed in chapter 3, EU law has affected areas of tort law as diverse as product liability, health and safety law, road accidents and defamation. The impact of EU law may be seen most clearly by returning to tort law's most iconic case: *Donoghue v Stevenson*.[71] As tort lawyers know, the fault-based liability established by this case now exists side-by-side with the strict liability provisions found in Part 1 of the Consumer Protection Act 1987.[72] Yet, this notable piece of consumer legislation derives not from a Law Commission report or government White Paper, but from European Union Directive 85/374/EEC, commonly known as the Product Liability Directive.[73] The 1987 Act thus creates a new head of liability in English tort law whose origin is European. As such, it provides an excellent example of the influence of European law striking at the heart of English tort law.

Further, the European Court of Justice in *Francovich*[74] created a new head of tort liability that would be applied by the domestic courts of Member States: State liability for breach of EU law. The key challenges of *Francovich* liability, as set out in chapter four, are as follows: it is a head of tortious liability in which the English

[65] Case 14/83 *Von Colson* (n 64); Case C-106/89 *Marleasing SA v La Comercial Internacional de Alimentacion SA* [1990] ECR I-4135; Cases C-397–403/01 *Pfeiffer v Deutsches Rotes Kreuz, Kreisverband Waldshut eV* [2004] ECR I-8835. This follows from art 4(3) TEU: 'The Member States shall take any appropriate measure, general or particular, to ensure fulfilment of the obligations arising out of the Treaties or resulting from the acts of the institutions of the Union.'

[66] C van Dam, *European Tort Law*, 2nd edn (Oxford, Oxford University Press, 2013) para 204–3.

[67] Introduced following the Lisbon Treaty.

[68] See also Charter of Fundamental Rights, art 47: '[e]veryone whose rights and freedoms guaranteed by the law of the union are violated has the right to an effective remedy before a tribunal in compliance with the conditions laid down in this Article'.

[69] R Ward and A Akhtar, *Walker & Walker's English Legal System*, 11th edn (Oxford, Oxford University Press, 2011) 110.

[70] M Hunt, 'The Human Rights Act and Legal Culture: The Judiciary and the Legal Profession' (1999) 26 *Journal of Law and Society* 86, 101.

[71] *Donoghue* (n 22). The House of Lords determined that the manufacturer would owe the ultimate consumer a duty to take reasonable care in the production of the item in question.

[72] Consumer Protection Act 1987, pt 1, s 3(1).

[73] Council Directive 85/374/EEC of 25 July 1985 on the approximation of the laws, regulations and administrative provisions of the Member States concerning liability for defective products: [1985] OJ L210, 29. Part I of the Consumer Protection Act 1987 marked the first occasion on which the UK government had implemented an EU Directive by means of an Act of Parliament rather than by means of delegated legislation, as permitted by s 2(2) of the European Communities Act 1972.

[74] *Francovich v Italian Republic* (C6/90) [1991] ECR I-5357; [1993] 2 CMLR 66.

courts are applying a test for liability established by the CJEU not the English courts[75] and potential defendants (the 'State') may include the UK government[76] or even the national court itself.[77] As will be discussed in chapter four, *Francovich* liability may be seen as a threat to the autonomy of the national courts on matters of tort law development and yet remains surprisingly under-analysed by tort lawyers (although not EU lawyers) despite its recent 20-year anniversary.

iii. Do Tort Lawyers Need to Know about Human Rights?

For many tort lawyers, Europeanisation will be equated with the introduction of the Human Rights Act 1998 (HRA 1998). Although the European Convention on Human Rights had been signed in Rome in 1950 and ratified by the UK in 1951, it had limited impact on the English legal system and indeed it was not until 1966 that the UK government permitted British citizens to petition the ECtHR in Strasbourg. As an international agreement, the Convention's impact was naturally limited. The ECtHR may find a Contracting State in breach of one or more of the Convention rights and guarantees, but its judgments are only binding on the countries concerned.[78] Further, litigants are required to exhaust all domestic remedies and bring the complaint within six months of the final decision of the domestic court.[79] Bringing a case to Strasbourg was therefore a time-consuming and expensive process. While commentators had noted that even prior to the 1998 Act the English courts had at times been influenced by the Convention, for example, in seeking to interpret statutes or the common law in a Convention-compliant way when the relevant law was ambiguous or the law undeveloped or uncertain,[80] it was the introduction of the 1998 Act by the then Labour government[81] which enabled individual litigants to enforce Convention rights in the domestic courts without having to travel to Strasbourg.[82] In permitting actions against public authorities,[83] where tort law traditionally adopted a restrictive

[75] See C-46/93 and C-48/93 *Brasserie du Pêcheur v Germany; R v Secretary of State for Transport, ex p Factortame (No.4)* (also known as '*Factortame III*') [1996] ECR I-1029; [1996] QB 404, paras 28 and 29.

[76] *R v Secretary of State for Transport, ex p Factortame (No 5)* [2000] 1 AC 524.

[77] *Köbler v Austria* (C224/01), [2003] ECR I-239; [2004] QB 848. For a recent application of *Köbler* liability in the UK courts, see *Cooper v Attorney General* [2010] EWCA Civ 464; [2011] 2 WLR 448.

[78] ECHR, art 46: Binding force and execution of judgments.

[79] ECHR, art 35: Admissibility criteria.

[80] A Lester, 'Human Rights and the British Constitution' in J Jowell and D Oliver, *The Changing Constitution*, 7th edn (Oxford, Oxford University Press, 2011) 76–77. Steele also notes that the influence of the Convention was apparent prior to 2000, for example in relation to the treatment of freedom of expression in the tort of defamation: J Steele, '(Dis)owning the Convention in the Law of Tort' in J Lee (ed), *From House of Lords to Supreme Court* (Oxford, Hart Publishing, 2011) 104.

[81] Labour Party, *Bringing Rights Home: Labour's Plans to Incorporate the European Convention on Human Rights into UK Law* (London, Labour Party, 1996).

[82] It is important to note that litigants may still complain to Strasbourg if, for example, they disagree with the ruling of the English courts that their rights have not been violated. See M Amos, 'The Impact of the HRA on the UK's Performance before the European Court of Human Rights' [2007] *Public Law* 655.

[83] HRA 1998, ss 6–8. Section 6 of the Act, which permits claims against local authorities which have acted in a way which was incompatible with a Convention right, thus provides an alternative to negligence claims.

approach towards liability[84] and potentially impacting on the judgments of ordinary courts (classified as public authorities under the Act) in private litigation,[85] the Act required tort lawyers at least to consider how it would relate to existing tort law principle.

However, it was the *Osman* effect, that is, a ruling of the ECtHR in 1998 that the application of the duty of care test in the tort of negligence had been contrary to Article 6 of the European Convention on Human Rights (ECHR), which awakened tort lawyers to the potential impact of the Act.[86] As will be detailed in chapter five, the fact that this ruling was delivered in 1998 – the same year as the Act – was particularly significant. The government had delayed implementation to permit the legal profession to come to terms with the new provisions and *Osman v United Kingdom* indicated that private lawyers would not be immune from this process. Wright in 2001 argued that tort lawyers needed to both consider the impact of the Act and develop tort law from a human rights perspective.[87] *Osman* had indicated the potential of the HRA 1998 to change fundamental principles of tort law. The response of the English courts to this case will be analysed in chapter five.

Yet, the most challenging area for tort lawyers has perhaps been the development of privacy law. This has led to a succession of cases seeking to protect private information ranging from the infidelity of various footballers to photographs of Princess Caroline of Monaco tripping over at her beach club. The abundant literature in this field tends to derive from public lawyers such as Phillipson, Fenwick and Masterman at the University of Durham, and yet, as is discussed in chapter six, one key question is whether the courts are developing a new tort of misuse of private information. The input of tort lawyers in this debate is of obvious value, but requires, naturally, an understanding of the human rights framework.

More broadly, to participate in these debates tort lawyers need to understand the new rights-based framework and to determine the relationship between damages claims for breach of Convention rights and traditional claims for compensation in tort. This may give rise to issues on the cusp of private and public law, but human rights can no longer be dismissed as solely the remit for public and international lawyers. Chapters five and six will examine the extent to which the English tort law community – judges, lawyers and academics – has embraced the possibilities for legal development presented by the 1998 Act.

[84] See *X v Bedfordshire CC* [1995] 2 AC 633.

[85] See, eg, G Phillipson, 'The Human Rights Act, "Horizontal Effect" and the Common Law: A Bang or a Whimper?' (1999) 62 *Modern Law Review* 824.

[86] *Osman v United Kingdom* (23452/94) (1998) 29 EHRR 245, criticising the Court of Appeal's ruling in *Osman v Ferguson* [1993] 4 All ER 344.

[87] J Wright, *Tort Law & Human Rights: The Impact of the ECHR on English Law* (Oxford, Hart Publishing, 2001). Mullender, in contrast, argued Wright's view of the limitations of common law culture is unduly negative: R Mullender, 'Tort, Human Rights and Common Law Culture' (2003) 23 *Oxford Journal of Legal Studies* 301.

iv. Does It Really Make Any Difference in Terms of Legal Reasoning?

The first part of this book will deal, however, with a different topic. The application of European sources in terms of substantive law will be examined in chapters three to six, but chapter two will set out the legal framework for interpretation of EU and European human rights law and consider the difficulties involved in 'transplanting' sources of law which primarily reflect the civil law tradition into English private law. While European Treaties and the European Convention on Human Rights may be considered more imprecise and less detailed than Continental Codes, for example the notoriously complex and abstract German Civil Code, these sources are far closer to the civil law tradition than that of the common law in terms of structure, judicial style and, particularly troubling for common lawyers, the absence of any strict doctrine of precedent.[88] As will be detailed in chapter two, this raises problems in terms of different methods of statutory interpretation, understanding judgments written in a different legal style and comprehending legal language, which may technically be in English, but utilises concepts unfamiliar to a common law audience. This is a challenge which, not only judges, but the whole legal community must address in order to understand the changes detailed in this book.

Conclusion

This book will argue that 'Europeanisation' is something which tort lawyers *need* to understand if they are to participate fully in the debate regarding European influences on English tort law. 'Europeanisation' requires not only an awareness of the HRA 1998, but also that European law generally (EU and ECHR) impacts on core elements of tort law. Further, following the Lisbon Treaty, the division between EU and ECHR law is less distinct; Article 6(1) of the Treaty on European Union providing that the EU recognises the rights, freedoms and principles set out in the Charter of Fundamental Rights of the European Union[89] and Article 6(3) that the fundamental rights of the ECHR, together with the constitutional traditions common to Member States, constitute general principles of EU law.[90] Article 6(2) also provides for the EU to accede to the ECHR in due course, although negotiations on this point continue.[91]

[88] Although the CJEU and ECtHR in practice will often follow leading judgments.

[89] The Charter itself provides that when its provisions overlap with the ECHR, the meaning and scope of such rights should be the same as that laid down by the Convention; the Charter extending beyond the civil and political rights of the ECHR to include social and economic rights: ECHR, art 52(3). See Case C-540/03 *Parliament v Council (family reunification)* [2006] ECR I-5769.

[90] This has led Hugh Collins to argue that national courts, when applying EU law, should interpret the relevant provision in a manner which is compatible with the Charter: 'On the (In)compatibility of Human Rights Discourse and Private Law' (2012) 7 *LSE Working Paper*, 8 (www.lse.ac.uk/collections/law/wps/WPS2012–07_Collins.pdf).

[91] See C Eckes, 'EU Accession to the ECHR: Between Autonomy and Adaption' (2013) 76 *Modern Law Review* 254; S Douglas-Scott, 'The European Union and Human Rights after the Treaty of Lisbon'

Inevitably, inherent in this discussion are different policy views on the merits or otherwise of Europeanisation. It may be seen as having a positive influence on legal development in terms of political and economic goals, protecting both consumers and individual rights. Alternatively, it may be viewed as diminishing national autonomy, disrupting traditional practices and limiting the role of both the domestic judiciary and legislator in the creation and development of legal norms. Dehousse has remarked on the tensions between institutions operating at different levels, for example the EU with its emphasis on market integration and ensuring a free market by the removal of factors distorting competition, and the domestic concerns of the national court.[92] Doctrinal discomfort, combined with pressure to engage in debates and apply legal rules on subjects once the prerogative of the national courts, has led, Caruso has noted, to resistance at national level: 'In the legal culture of Europe, private law is perceived as and may actually function as a bulwark against the flood of European regulation, a sort of antidote to the dilution of regional identities'.[93] In examining signs of Europeanisation, therefore, this book will simultaneously analyse the receptivity of English tort law to these new influences and the extent to which, explicitly or implicitly, signs of opposition continue to exist. In so doing, it will consider whether Europeanisation has led to a change in English legal culture and how English judges reason. Fundamentally, this book will question whether the English tort law community is ready to welcome Europeanisation, or whether the common law legal culture has proven more resistant to change than might have been expected.

(2011) 11 *Human Rights Law Review* 645; P Gragl, *The Accession of the European Union to the European Convention on Human Rights* (Oxford, Hart Publishing, 2013). If this occurs, CJEU decisions concerning Convention rights will be open to review in Strasbourg.

[92] R Dehousse, 'Comparing National and EC Law: The Problem of the Level of Analysis' (1994) 42 *American Journal of Comparative Law* 761. See also C Joerges, 'Interactive Adjudication in the Europeanisation Process? A Demanding Perspective and a Modest Example' (2000) 1 *European Review of Private Law* 1, who argues that the only way these tensions may be overcome is by an active European judiciary.

[93] Caruso, 'The Missing View' (n 57) 4.

2

Understanding 'Europeanisation': Transplanting European Union and Human Rights Law into Domestic Law

Introduction

This chapter has two aims. The first section will establish the extent to which Europeanisation has required the English courts to utilise new sources of law based primarily on the civil law legal tradition. These possess what Markesinis has termed a distinct 'style' to that of the common law.[1] Accession to the European Union in 1973 led to the introduction of European Union law into the English legal system, acting as a 'catalyst for change and for bringing international law directly into the legal system of the UK'.[2] More recently the Human Rights Act 1998 (HRA 1998) has obliged the English courts to 'take into account' the jurisprudence of the European Court of Human Rights[3] and allows claimants to bring an action against public authorities for breach of Convention rights.[4] English judges must now interpret Treaty provisions and the content of rights under the European Convention on Human Rights (ECHR) and consider the case law of the Court of Justice of the European Union (CJEU) and European Court of Human Rights (ECtHR) when delivering judgments in the domestic courts. This is particularly challenging in the private law context, where the law has traditionally been developed by the courts with minimal statutory intervention. The courts must now integrate new legislative provisions such as Part 1 of the Consumer Protection Act 1987[5] and the Electronic Commerce (EC Directive) Regulations 2002[6] into the existing common law framework.

[1] See BS Markesinis, 'A Matter of Style' (1994) 110 *Law Quarterly Review* 607; K Zweigert and H Kötz, *An Introduction to Comparative* Law, 3rd edn (Oxford, Oxford University Press, 1998) ch 5: 'The Style of Legal Families'.

[2] M Kirby, 'The Common Law and International Law : A Dynamic Contemporary Dialogue' (2010) 30 *Legal Studies* 30, 31.

[3] HRA 1998, s 2(1).

[4] HRA 1998, ss 6 and 7.

[5] Implementing the 1985 Council Directive 85/374/EEC of 25 July 1985 concerning liability for defective products.

[6] SI 2002/2013, implementing. Directive 2000/31/EC of the European Parliament and of the Council of 8 June 2000 on certain legal aspects of information society services, in particular electronic commerce, in the Internal Market (Directive on Electronic Commerce): [2000] OJ L178/1.

While chapters three to six of this book will examine the practical implementation of these developments in the English law of tort, this chapter will consider the difficulties that arise when new sources of law are introduced into a legal system. It will thus provide a foundation for the analysis in subsequent chapters. The division is, as stated above, one of the classic common/civil law divide.[7] The majority of EU States (and indeed all the founding six countries of the EEC) represent civil law jurisdictions and it is unsurprising that this has influenced the content of EU law.[8] While British lawyers had an important role in the drafting of the ECHR, again the substantive and procedural law of the Strasbourg court bears a far closer relationship to civil, rather than common, law. This presents English courts with a dual challenge: to apply correctly new sources of law and to integrate them into the existing common law system. The second half of this chapter will utilise the legal transplant debate[9] to highlight the advantages and disadvantages of introducing external sources of law into a particular legal system and the extent to which true integration is possible. As will be seen, Europeanisation is not simply a question of identifying new rules, but applying them correctly within an existing legal framework.

The common law courts thus find themselves with a dilemma: how (and to what extent) to respond to case law and different interpretative techniques originating in the courts of Luxembourg and Strasbourg? They must respond to the changes introduced by the European Communities Act 1972 and HRA 1998, but simultaneously maintain the integrity of the English legal system. They must deal with (and understand) case law and legislation drafted in an unfamiliar form and overcome their natural reluctance to deal with 'alien'[10] case law, legal terminology and legislative instruments. This chapter will set out the challenge for the English courts. Subsequent chapters will consider how well the courts have responded to this challenge.

I. Europeanisation and the National Court: Dealing With New Sources of Law

Section 3 of the European Communities Act 1972 provides that, in interpreting the meaning or effect of the European Treaties or the validity, meaning or effect of

[7] JH Merryman and R Pérez-Perdomo, *The Civil Law Tradition: An introduction to the Legal Systems of Europe and Latin America*, 3rd edn (Stanford, CA, Stanford University Press, 2007).

[8] See M de S-O l'E Lasser, *Judicial Deliberations: A Comparative Analysis of Judicial Transparency and Legitimacy* (Oxford, Oxford University Press, 2004).

[9] The term was coined in the 1970s by the Scottish-American legal scholar, Alan Watson, and indicates the moving of a legal rule or system of law from one country to another: A Watson, *Legal Transplants*, 1st edn (Edinburgh, Scottish Academic Press, 1974).

[10] Nolan, for example, has commented that 'the process of convergence [of tort and HRA claims] would serve to distort the law of negligence both by undermining established principles and by introducing alien concepts': D Nolan, 'Negligence and Human Rights Law: The Case for Separate Development' (2013) 76 *Modern Law Review* 286, 302.

any EU instrument, the courts shall decide in accordance with the principles laid down by and any relevant decision of the European Court of Justice (ECJ). Judicial notice will be taken of the Treaties themselves and any decision of the ECJ on the point in question. The impact of section 3 of the Act is therefore twofold: courts must decide cases in accordance with the principles laid down by the CJEU, and take judicial notice of its decisions. This requires the English courts to utilise a new source of law which bears little resemblance to traditional English case law.[11] A collegiate court states the court's decision, with no dissenting or concurring opinions.[12] There is also no formal doctrine of stare decisis (although in practice the Court does follow its previous decisions in almost all cases);[13] a doctrine regarded by common lawyers as a vital source of certainty and predictability within the legal system.[14] Lord Goff extra-judicially noted the challenges this creates to the common lawyer schooled in moving gradually from case to case, reasoning by analogy: 'Continental lawyers love to proclaim some great principle, and then knock it into shape afterwards. Instead, the boring British want to find out first whether and, if so, how these great ideas are going to work in practice. This is not at all popular with the propagators of the great ideas'.[15] His Lordship openly confessed to a preference to the approach with which he was accustomed, which enabled him to have 'an instinctive feel' for the result of any case. It is likely that many English judges share this view.

Judges must also cope with a new style of legislative drafting which, in comparison with common law statutes, is imprecise.[16] Arnull has remarked that such ambiguity, notably in Treaty provisions, makes it wholly implausible for the Court of Justice to purport to be the mouthpiece of the written law.[17] The Court of Justice is, therefore, in a sense forced on many occasions to adopt a style of interpretation which focuses not on the exact wording of the instrument, but, more broadly, on

[11] See A Arnull, *The European Union and its Court of Justice*, 2nd edn (Oxford, Oxford University Press, 2006) chs 16 and 17.

[12] See M Kirby, 'Judicial Dissent: Common Law and Civil Law Traditions' (2007) 123 *Law Quarterly Review* 379. Koopmans has noted the clear resemblance to French law, including the fact that the single impersonal judgment will be preceded by an individual advisory opinion by the advocate general in often a highly personal style: T Koopmans, 'The Birth of European Law at the Cross-Roads of Legal Traditions' (1991) 39 *American Journal of Comparative Law* 493, 500.

[13] JJ Barcelo, 'Precedent in European Community Law' in N MacCormick and RS Summers (eds), *Interpreting Precedent: A Comparative Study* (Aldershot, Dartmouth Publishing, 1997). It now seems clear that both the CJEU and ECtHR have informal doctrines of precedent which give greater authority to certain judgments, notably those of constitutional importance.

[14] R Cross and JW Harris, *Precedent in English Law*, 4th edn (Oxford, Clarendon Press, 1991).

[15] R Goff, 'The Future of the Common Law' (1997) 46 *International & Comparative Law Quarterly* 745, 753.

[16] See N MacCormick and RS Summers (eds), *Interpreting Statutes: A Comparative Study* (Aldershot, Dartmouth Publishing Co Ltd, 1991) ; G Beck, *The Legal Reasoning of the Court of Justice of Justice of the EU* (Oxford, Hart Publishing, 2013). Vogenauer notes that the typical style of drafting in the common law tradition is casuistic and specific; drafters seeking to cover all eventualities. In contrast, the Continental style, influencing EU law, is far less detailed and often framed in general and abstract language with no attempt made to cover every conceivable case: S Vogenauer, 'The Drafting of the CESL: An Assessment and Suggestions for Approval' (European Union, 2012) para 3.1.

[17] Arnull, *The European Union and its Court of Justice* (n 11) 637.

its objective. On this basis, a purposive or teleological approach is commonly adopted, although it has been noted that the teleological approach is only one of a range of methods employed by the courts to resolve questions of interpretation.[18] In *Van Gend en Loos*, for example, the Court of Justice, in determining whether a Treaty provision had direct effect, found it necessary to consider the spirit, general scheme and the wording of the provisions in question.[19] The Court has stated that 'every provision of [EU] law must be placed in its context and interpreted in the light of the provisions of [EU] law as a whole, regard being had to the objectives thereof and to its state of evolution at the date on which the provision in question is to be applied.'[20] This latter statement also hints at the significance of judicial policy. Hartley notes that one of the distinctive characteristics of the decisions of the Court of Justice is the extent to which policy – primarily strengthening the Union, increasing the scope and effectiveness of Union law and enlarging the powers of the Union institutions – impact on its decision making.[21] In the tort law context, Article 340(2) TFEU presents a good example of this process in action. This provision, which deals with the institutional liability of the European Union, provides that 'In the case of non-contractual liability, the Union shall, in accordance with the general principles common to the laws of the Member States, make good any damage caused by its institutions or by its servants in the performance of their duties.'[22] Koopmans has commented that this vague wording was in all likelihood included out of embarrassment in the absence of any better solution,[23] but nevertheless reference to 'common general principles' has been used to facilitate the growth and expansion of EU law, notably by the ECJ in *Brasserie du Pêcheur v Germany; R v Secretary of State for Transport, ex p Factortame (No 4)*.[24] As discussed in chapter four below, the Court relied on 'the general principle familiar to the legal systems of the Member States that an unlawful act or omission gives rise to an obligation to make good the damage caused'[25] to develop the principle of State liability for breach of EU law. Subsequently, this line of case law has been used, in

[18] Ibid, 607; A Albors Llorens, 'The European Court of Justice: More than a Teleological Court' (1999) 2 *Cambridge Yearbook of European Legal Studies* 373.

[19] Case 26/62 *Van Gend en Loos v Nederlandse Administratie der Belastungen* [1963] ECR 1; [1963] CMLR 105.

[20] Case 283/81 *Srl CILFIT and Lanificio di Gavardo SpA v Ministry of Health* [1982] ECR 3415, para 20.

[21] TC Hartley, *The Foundations of European Union Law*, 7th edn (Oxford, Oxford University Press, 2010) 72.

[22] Ex Art 288(2) TEC. See, eg, L Antoniolli, 'Community Liability' in H Koziol and R Schulze, *Tort Law of the European Community* (Wien, Springer, 2008); P Craig and G de Búrca, *EU Law: Text, Cases and Materials*, 5th edn (Oxford, Oxford University Press, 2011) ch 16.

[23] T Koopmans, 'Comparative Law and the Courts' (1996) 45 *International & Comparative Law Quarterly* 545, 546. Koopmans is a former CJEU judge. Van Gerven has suggested that it would include principles accepted by the prevailing opinion in a sufficiently large number of Member States, but this seems equally vague: W van Gerven, 'Harmonization of Private Law: Do We Need It?' (2004) 41 *Common Market Law Review* 505, 516.

[24] *Brasserie du Pêcheur v Germany; R v Secretary of State for Transport, ex p Factortame (No 4)* C-46/93 and C-48/93 [1996] ECR I- 1029; [1996] QB 404.

[25] Ibid, para 29.

the absence of particular justification, to assist in the interpretation of Art 340(2) TFEU itself.[26]

The multilingual nature of EU law, drafted in several languages, should also be noted.[27] There are currently 24 official languages in the EU. The ECJ in *Cilfit* acknowledged that as all different language versions are equally authentic, interpretation of a provision of EU law may involve a comparison of different language versions, whilst bearing in mind that EU law will use terminology specific to EU law and distinct from that used in the national legal system.[28]

This has presented considerable challenges to the common law courts. Treaty provisions bear a greater resemblance to Continental codes than English legislation. Case law equally does not resemble the dialogue traditionally found in common law judgments between bench and advocates, but the collective wisdom of the civil law court.[29] It is unsurprising, therefore, that English judges first reacted to EU law with misgivings.[30] Lord Denning spoke for many common lawyers when, seeking to interpret the Treaty of Rome, he famously stated:

> How different is this Treaty. It lays down general principles. It expresses its aims and purposes. All in sentences of moderate length and commendable style. But it lacks precision. It uses words and phrases without defining what they mean. An English lawyer would look for an interpretation clause, but he would look in vain. There is none. All the way through the Treaty there are gaps and lacunae. These have to be filled in by the Judges, or by Regulations or Directives. It is the European way.[31]

Lord Bingham has also described the process as involving 'not [that] familiar to common lawyers of laboriously extracting the meaning from words used but the more creative process of supplying flesh to a spare and loosely constructed skeleton.'[32] Mak, in an interesting survey on the use of foreign law by the UK Supreme Court and the Supreme Court of the Netherlands, reports comments that UK judges find the judgments of the CJEU difficult to read, describing them as 'Delphic', and openly criticise their 'flabby reasoning' which they attribute to the need to find a compromise with the other judges deciding the case.[33]

[26] C-352/98 P *Laboratoires Pharmaceutiques Bergaderm SA v Commission of the European Communities* [2000] ECR I-5291, para 41. See *Brasserie du Pêcheur* (n 24) para 42.

[27] See, generally, G Dannemann, S Ferreri and M Graziadei, 'Language and Terminology' in C Twigg-Flesner, *The Cambridge Companion to European Union Private Law* (Cambridge, Cambridge University Press, 2010); E Paunio and S Lindroos-Hovinheimo, 'Taking Language Seriously: An Analysis of Linguistic Reasoning and its Implications in EU Law' (2010) 16 *European Law Journal* 395.

[28] *Cilfit* (n 20) paras 18–19.

[29] B Rudden, 'Courts and Codes in England, France and Soviet Russia' (1973–74) 48 *Tulane Law Review* 1010.

[30] Dagtoglou notes the comment of a Court of Appeal judge a few weeks after British entry into the EEC who remarked that what Community law needed was a strong injection of common law common sense: 'The English Judges and European Community Law' (1978) 37 *Cambridge Law Journal* 76, 97.

[31] *Bulmer v Bollinger* [1974] Ch 401, 425.

[32] Bingham J in *Customs and Excise v Samex ApS* [1983] 3 CMLR 194, 211.

[33] E Mak, 'Why Do Dutch and UK Judges Cite Foreign Law?' (2011) 70 *Cambridge Law Journal* 420, 433–35. In contrast, she finds that British judges have a certain ideological affinity with the Strasbourg court, notwithstanding reservations expressed concerning the quality of its judgments (p 432).

Both the open-textured nature of many EU legislative provisions and the Court of Justice's form of reasoning present challenges to national courts seeking to interpret EU law within the national court system.[34] A true understanding of the jurisprudence of the CJEU cannot be achieved without an appreciation that the Court will examine the whole context in which a particular provision is situated and give the interpretation most likely to further what the Court considers to be the aim of the provision in question.[35] The supremacy of EU law means that domestic courts are required to give legal effect to its provisions and, where necessary, bring domestic law into line with EU law.[36] Individual citizens may also under the doctrine of direct effect be able to bring claims in the national courts for breach of their rights under EU law.[37] The doctrine of indirect effect takes this process a step further. Under the *Marleasing* principle,[38] in applying national law, the domestic court should interpret domestic legislation as far as possible in the light of the wording and purpose of the relevant directive to achieve the result pursued by the latter. In so doing, the court should consider its national law as a whole in order to assess to what extent any particular national law may be applied so as not to produce a result contrary to that sought by the directive.[39] Article 267 TFEU also provides a preliminary reference procedure for questions of interpretation the national courts are unable to resolve, but is dependent on the willingness of the English courts to make such references and the clarity of the guidance received from the CJEU.[40]

Despite initial doubts, Whittaker has noted that English courts now firmly and completely accept the principle of the supremacy of EU law and the necessity of following European principles and interpretative practices.[41] The challenge is thus

[34] The 'European way', as Arnull has recognised, will usually involve the use of the teleological and contextual method of interpretation: Arnull, *The European Union* (n 11) 612.

[35] P Craig and G de Búrca, *EU Law: Text, Cases and Materials*, 5th edn (Oxford, Oxford University Press, 2011) 64, who also note that the Court, in adopting a purposive approach, does not seek the precise purpose of the authors of the text and is thus not adopting a narrowly historical approach.

[36] Case 6/64 *Costa v ENEL* [1964] ECR 585.

[37] Case 26/62 *Van Gend en Loos* (n 19).

[38] Case C-106/89 *Marleasing SA v La Comercial Internacional de Alimentacion SA* [1990] ECR I-4135. See Case 14/83 *Von Colson v Land Nordrhein-Westfalen* [1984] ECR 1891 and Cases C-397–403/01 *Pfeiffer v Deutsches Rotes Kreuz, Kreisverband Waldshut eV* [2004] ECR I-8835.

[39] *Marleasing* (n 38) para 115.

[40] For the difficulties raised by insufficiently precise guidance, see JE Levitsky, 'The Europeanization of the British Legal Style' (1994) 42 *American Journal of Comparative Law* 347, 363–68. Nicol notes that the nature of the procedure obliges the Luxembourg court to frame its judgments in the form of abstract principles for the national court to apply: D Nicol, 'Lessons from Luxembourg: Federalisation and the Court of Human Rights' [2001] *European Law Review* 3, 6.

[41] S Whittaker, 'Precedent in English Law: A View from the Citadel' (2006) 14 *European Review of Private Law* 705, 739–40. See also N Grief, 'The Pervasive Influence of European Community Law in the United Kingdom' in TG Watkin, *The Europeanisation of Law* (London, UKNCCL, 1998) who argues that the House of Lords judgment in *Litster v Forth Dry Dock and Engineering Co Ltd* [1990] 1 AC 546 demonstrates how far UK judges have travelled since the early years of membership of the EU. Most recently, see Lord Mance in *Assange v The Swedish Prosecution Authority* [2012] UKSC 22, [2012] 2 AC 471, para 203.

no longer one of acceptance – that debate has passed[42] – but one of engaging in the process correctly.

A similar position arises under the Human Rights Act 1998. In interpreting the meaning of Convention rights, section 2 of the Act requires the court to 'take into account' any relevant judgment of the ECtHR; the question of relevance being a matter for the opinion of the court or tribunal.[43] This is a lesser obligation, reflecting the different position of the ECtHR and CJEU with respect to national law. Strasbourg case law will be 'persuasive' only, but nevertheless introduces a new source of law into the English system which is different in style.[44] The Strasbourg court decides cases by majority vote and therefore gives a single judgment, although, in contrast to the Luxembourg court, it does permit individual concurring or dissenting opinions.[45] In the absence of any indication in section 2(1) of the degree to which judgments and decisions of the ECtHR should be taken into account (or the weight given to them), there is an ongoing debate as to the extent to which domestic courts may go beyond existing Strasbourg case law in applying Convention rights.[46] Case law indicates that while the Supreme Court reserves the right to refuse to follow Strasbourg jurisprudence,[47] the courts, in the absence of special circumstances, should follow any clear and constant jurisprudence of the ECtHR, fearing that if they do not do so there is at least a possibility of a successful appeal to the Strasbourg court, which is likely to follow its own constant jurisprudence.[48] In the view of Lord Bingham, national courts should not, therefore, without strong reason dilute or

[42] Ward noted even in 1995 a tendency to regard EU law as a 'necessary evil': I Ward, 'The Limits of Comparativism: Lessons from UK–EC Integration' (1994) 2 *Maastricht Journal of European & Comparative Law* 23, 26.

[43] HRA 1998, s 2:

> Interpretation of Convention rights: '(1) A court or tribunal determining a question which has arisen in connection with a Convention right must take into account any – (a) judgment, decision, declaration or advisory opinion of the European Court of Human Rights,(b) opinion of the Commission given in a report adopted under Art 31 of the Convention,(c) decision of the Commission in connection with Art 26 or 27(2) of the Convention, or(d) decision of the Committee of Ministers taken under Art 46 of the Convention, whenever made or given, so far as, in the opinion of the court or tribunal, it is relevant to the proceedings in which that question has arisen.

[44] A Mowbray, *Cases, Materials and Commentary on the European Convention on Human Rights*, 3rd edn (Oxford, Oxford University Press, 2012) 52–57 notes that the structure of the judgment will consist of a statement of the facts as established by the Court, following by an application of the law of the Convention to these facts and, where breach is found and just satisfaction requested, a determination on this point.

[45] ECHR, art 45(2). This, it has been argued, enhances its persuasive power towards government officials: L Helfer and AM Slaughter, 'Toward a Theory of Effective Supranational Adjudication' (1997) 107 *Yale Law Journal* 273, 328.

[46] See, eg, J Wright, 'Interpreting Section 2 of the Human Rights Act 1998: Towards an Indigenous Jurisprudence of Human Rights' [2009] *Public Law* 595; R Masterman, 'Taking the Strasbourg Jurisprudence into Account: Developing a "municipal law of human rights" under the Human Rights Act' (2005) 54 *International & Comparative Law Quarterly* 907.

[47] *R v Spear* [2002] UKHL 31; [2003] 1 AC 734, *R v Horncastle* [2009] UKSC 14; [2010] 2 AC 373.

[48] *R (Alconbury Developments Ltd and Others) v Secretary of State for the Environment, Transport and the Regions* [2001] UKHL 23; [2003] 2 AC 295, para 26 per Lord Slynn.

weaken the effect of ECtHR case law.[49] This reflects the fact that the Convention is an international instrument, the correct interpretation of which can only be authoritatively expounded by the Strasbourg court: '[t]he duty of national courts is to keep pace with the Strasbourg jurisprudence as it evolves over time: no more, but certainly no less.'[50] This final phrase 'no more but no less' does suggest a conservative approach to human rights by which the national courts 'mirror' the interpretation of Convention rights given by the ECtHR. Lord Irvine has recently expressed concern that this may lead English courts to believe that they are bound by the Strasbourg court when in fact they must decide the case for themselves.[51] Sir Philip Sales in response notes, however, that the 'mirror' principle provides what the common law needs: guidance on how to apply the section 2(1) interpretative duty.[52] Attention must, however, be paid to the changing nature of rights and the fact that some case law may become less relevant with time.[53]

In reality, the fact remains that not all Strasbourg case law is clear and consistent. In common with EU law, there is no formal doctrine of stare decisis, although the court will in practice be guided by previous case law,[54] and the courts have a tendency to give rulings which turn on the specific facts of the case and from which it is difficult to extract clear rules. As Gearty has noted:

> This is not precedent as the common lawyer understands the term. The judgments of the Court never engage with past case law in the way familiar to a student of the common law. There are no attempts to steer a path through earlier cases, identifying strengths and weaknesses and setting out clear, principled guidance for the future . . . Another disconcerting recent tendency has been the Court's habit of setting out tests that need to be applied without making explicit their nature, their roots in the Convention or their origin in the case law. This has given to some recent decisions the feel of a private conversation among *cognoscenti*, where all are presumed to know why certain formulae or phrases are being deployed. [55]

[49] *R (on the application of Ullah) v Special Adjudicator* [2004] UKHL 26; [2004] 2 AC 323, para 20, stating the so-called 'mirror principle'.

[50] Ibid, para 20. Compare Lord Brown's more restrictive reformulation in *R (on the application of Al-Skeini) v Secretary of State for Defence* [2007] UKHL 26; [2008] 1 AC 153, para 106; 'no less, but certainly no more'. For recent criticism, see R Clayton 'Smoke and Mirrors: The Human Rights Act and the Impact of Strasbourg Case Law' [2012] *Public Law* 639, who argues that the rule is not consistently applied by the domestic courts and that it would be preferable if domestic courts regarded the ECtHR case law as a floor, not a ceiling.

[51] Lord Irvine of Lairg, 'A British Interpretation of Convention Rights' [2012] *Public Law* 237. See also Lady Hale, '*Argentoratum locutum*: Is Strasbourg or the Supreme Court Supreme?' (2012) 12 *Human Rights Law Review* 65 and more recently Lord Judge 'Constitutional Change: Unfinished Business' lecture 4 December 2013 (UCL, London).

[52] P Sales, 'Strasbourg Jurisprudence and the Human Rights Act: A Response to Lord Irvine' [2012] *Public Law* 253. Sir Philip Sales is a High Court Judge.

[53] *Secretary of State for Work and Pensions v M* [2006] UKHL 11; [2006] 2 AC 91, para 131: 'In an evolving area, a domestic court may perhaps also have to consider whether relatively elderly jurisprudence reflects the result that the court would still reach' per Lord Mance.

[54] See *Chapman v United Kingdom* (27238/95) [2001] ECHR 43, para 70: 'The Court considers that, while it is not formally bound to follow any of its previous judgments, it is in the interests of legal certainty, foreseeability and equality before the law that it should not depart, without good reason, from precedents laid down in previous cases.'

[55] CA Gearty, 'Unravelling *Osman*' (2001) 64 *Modern Law Review* 159, 188.

Further, some matters will be held to fall within the margin of appreciation of the national authorities, and left to be determined by the domestic court.[56] This may be seen as an attempt by the ECtHR to uphold its aim of subsidiarity and to allow Member States leeway on issues where there is no consensus. Former vice-president of the Court, Christos Rozakis has commented that

> [T]he margin of appreciation has many times acted as a vehicle of judicial restraint, limiting the spectrum of the ECtHR's interference in certain matters to an 'external' review of the compatibility of domestic acts with the Convention . . . The rule is that a State party to the Convention has a wider margin of appreciation to construe its obligations under it whenever there is no established European consensus delimiting a right protected.[57]

The doctrine has nevertheless proved contentious – for those concerned at Strasbourg intervention into national affairs the margin is insufficiently wide,[58] while other commentators have expressed concern that, without clear guiding principles, a domestic court may seek to avoid proportionality decisions in difficult cases.[59] More significantly, the very form of Convention rights are general, often qualified, lacking in detail and leaving much for the national court to interpret. It is accepted that the rudimentary nature of its provisions and the social and economic changes which have occurred since 1950 require 'interpretative latitude', adapting the Convention to modern needs: it is, to use a commonly used phrase, a 'living instrument'.[60] This is not, however, indicative of certainty. In the recent case of *Rabone and another v Pennine Care NHS Trust*,[61] for example, Baroness Hale remarked on the difficulties of interpreting ECtHR case law in view of its tendency to state the applicable principle in very broad terms without defining precisely in what circumstances it would apply. 'Such broad statements of principle', she commented, 'are hard to interpret and even harder to apply'.[62]

[56] *Handyside v United Kingdom* (5493/72) (1976) 1 EHRR 737; M Amos, 'The Dialogue between United Kingdom Courts and the European Court of Human Rights' (2012) 61 *International & Comparative Law Quarterly* 557; Baroness Hale, 'Common law and Convention law: The limits to interpretation' [2011] European Human Rights Law Review 534; MR Hutchinson, 'The Margin of Appreciation Doctrine in the European Court of Human Rights' (1999) 48 *International & Comparative Law Quarterly* 638.

[57] CL Rozakis, 'The European Judge as Comparatist' (2005) 80 *Tulane Law Review* 257, 272–73.

[58] Lord Hoffmann, 'The Universality of human rights' (2009) 125 *Law Quarterly Review* 416, 424: 'the Court has not taken the doctrine of the margin of appreciation nearly far enough. It has been unable to resist the temptation to aggrandise its jurisdiction and to impose uniform rules on Member States. It considers itself the equivalent of the Supreme Court of the United States, laying down a federal law of Europe.'

[59] Lord Lester, 'Universality versus Subsidiarity: A Reply' [1998] *European Human Rights Law Review* 73; R Clayton and H Tomlinson, *The Law of Human Rights*, 2nd edn (Oxford, Oxford University Press, 2009) 319–20.

[60] Clayton and Tomlinson, *Law of Human Rights* (n 59) 260–61. The concept was first used in *Tyrer v United Kingdom* (5856/72)) (1979–1980) 2 EHRR 1 at 31.

[61] *Rabone and another v Pennine Care NHS Trust* [2012] UKSC 2; [2012] 2 AC 72.

[62] Ibid, para 97. See also Lord Mance (para 123): 'it is perhaps worth remembering expressly that individual section decisions of the [European Court of Human Rights] are not, and may not respond well to the same close linguistic analysis that a common lawyer would give to, binding precedents.'

Lord Reed experienced similar difficulties in a later case when seeking guidance as to the assessment of damages, noting that the Strasbourg court rarely articulates clear principles either in explaining when damages should be awarded and how they should be assessed.[63] The Court rarely provides the precise legal tests which common lawyers expect.[64] Whittaker argues that, on balance, UK judges do engage closely with the case law of the ECtHR, but do so in a distinctive way, understanding its international and minimal character and ultimately that they are not bound by it.[65] Örücü is more positive, noting that, in seeking to answer the question of compatibility with the ECHR under the HRA 1998, UK judges are rapidly becoming conversant with human rights issues and the utility of using Convention cases to assist interpretation of the relevant law.[66]

In relation to interpretation of UK legislation, section 3 of the HRA 1998 places an obligation on the English courts, so far as it is possible to do so, to interpret primary and subordinate legislation in a way which is compatible with the Convention rights covered by the Act. Again, the obligation is not absolute ('so far as it is possible') and section 3 represents a compromise by which the judiciary is unable to affect the validity, continuing operation or enforcement of any incompatible primary or subordinate legislation,[67] but may under section 4 make a declaration of incompatibility, thereby respecting the principle of Parliamentary Sovereignty. As stated in the Government's White Paper, 'The courts will be required to interpret legislation so as to uphold the Convention rights unless the legislation itself is so clearly incompatible with the Convention that it is impossible to do so.'[68] The abundant case law on this provision indicates that the courts are willing to strain if necessary legislative language to adopt a Convention-compliant construction,[69] but that they cannot ignore a clear decision of Parliament to legislate in a non-compliant way.[70] Lord Bingham in *Sheldrake v DPP*[71] acknowledged that while the interpretive obligation under section 3 is a very strong and far reaching one, there is a limit beyond which a Convention-compliant interpretation is not possible and may

[63] *R (on the application of Sturnham) v Parole Board* [2013] UKSC 23; [2013] 2 WLR 1157, paras 34–39, contrasting this approach with the detailed, fact-specific approach of the common law court.

[64] Lord Reed also remarked somewhat caustically on the 'blizzard' of Strasbourg authorities presented by counsel and the need for litigants to identify cases capable of providing a statement of principle rather than a one-off decision on its own facts: 'Otherwise, to adapt Mark Twain's remark about life, the citation of authorities is liable to amount to little more than one damn thing after another' *R (on the application of Sturnham)* (n 63) para 103. See also Lord Carnwath (ibid, para 114).

[65] Whitaker, 'Precedent in English Law' (n 41) 744.

[66] E Örücü, 'Comparative Law in Practice: The Courts and the Legislator' in E Örücü and D Nelken (eds), *Comparative Law: A Handbook* (Oxford, Hart Publishing, 2007) 429.

[67] HRA 1998, s 3(2).

[68] 'Rights Brought Home: the Human Rights Bill' (London, HMSO, 1997) Cm.3782.

[69] See, notably, *R v Home Secretary, ex parte Simms* [2000] 2 AC 115, *Ghaidan v Godin-Mendoza* [2004] UKHL 30; [2004] 2 AC 557, *Sheldrake v DPP* [2004] UKHL 43; [2005] 1 AC 264, *R (Wilkinson) v Inland Revenue Commissioners* [2005] UKHL 30; [2005] 1 WLR 1718, *Connolly v DPP* [2007] EWHC 237 (Admin); [2008] 1 WLR 276, *R v Briggs-Price (Robert William)* [2009] UKHL 19; [2009] 1 AC 1026.

[70] See *R (Anderson) v Secretary of State for the Home Department* [2002] UKHL 46; [2003] 1 AC 837 and *Bellinger v Bellinger (Lord Chancellor Intervening)* [2003] UKHL 21; [2003] 2 AC 467.

[71] *Sheldrake v DPP* [2004] UKHL 43 (n 69) para 28.

require the court to depart from the legislative intention of Parliament. As might be imagined, there is considerable academic debate as to the degree to which the judiciary are able to use section 3 to re-interpret statutory provisions.[72]

Analogies may be found between the *Marleasing* principle and section 3.[73] The courts have found that the interpretative obligation under EU law is similar to that under section 3 HRA, and, although the context is different, the same general approach should apply.[74] This may require the court to go well beyond conventional domestic law modes of interpretation.[75] Lord Steyn in *Ghaidan v Godin-Mendoza* found that the *Marleasing* principle – that national courts should, as far as possible, interpret national legislation in the light of the wording and purpose of directives – provided a significant signpost to the meaning of section 3(1) in the 1998 Act.[76] Both interpretative duties, therefore, expect the national court to look for a contextual and purposive interpretation and present a challenge for traditional methods of construing legislation.[77]

Europeanisation thus brings with it new sources of law which the national courts must utilise and understand. This gives rise to inevitable challenges both in terms of interpretation and application. The next four chapters will examine how the English courts have applied EU and European human rights law in the context of English tort law. However, one further preliminary issue remains to be discussed: what potential difficulties arise when new non-native sources of law are introduced into a pre-existing legal system?

[72] See, eg, Lord Lester, 'The Art of the Possible: Interpreting Statutes under the Human Rights Act' [1998] *European Human Rights Law Review* 665, R Clayton, 'The Limits of What's "Possible": Statutory Construction under the Human Rights Act' (2002) *European Human Rights Law Review* 559 and A Kavanagh, 'The Elusive Divide between Interpretation and Legislation under the Human Rights Act 1998' (2004) 24 *Oxford Journal of Legal Studies* 259.

[73] See recently P Sales, 'Judges and Legislature: Values into Law' (2012) 71 *Cambridge Law Journal* 287, 293–94.

[74] *Alstom Transport v Eurostar International Ltd* [2012] EWHC 28 (Ch), para 37; Lord Steyn in *R v Lambert (Steven)* [2001] UKHL 37, [2002] 2 AC 545, para 44: 'The difficulties involved in applying section 3 can be exaggerated. The exercise is analogous to interpreting legislation in line with European Community Directives so far as it is possible to do so provided it does not distort clear statutory language.'

[75] Sales, 'Judges and Legislature' (n 73) at 294, relying upon *Ghaidan v Godin-Mendoza* [2004] UKHL 30, [2004] 2 AC 557.

[76] *Ghaidan* (n 75) para 45, adding 'It was envisaged that the duty of the court would be to strive to find (if possible) a meaning which would best accord with Convention rights. This is the remedial scheme which Parliament adopted': para 46.

[77] See also Aikens LJ in *Churchill Insurance Co Ltd v Fitzgerald* [2012] EWCA Civ 1166; [2012] 3 CMLR 49, para 50, who identified various parameters for the interpretation of domestic statutes which satisfied the national court's obligations under EU law and the HRA 1998. See also Sir Andrew Morritt in *Vodafone 2 v Revenue and Customs Commissioners* [2009] EWCA Civ 446; [2010] Ch 77, paras 37–38.

II. Europeanisation and Legal Transplants: Integrating European Law into the English Legal System

This section will examine an issue which is, regrettably, little debated: the extent to which EU and European human rights law are capable of being integrated into the national legal system. As a result of the European Communities Act 1972 and Human Rights Act 1998, new sources of law have been introduced (or, to use a commonly used metaphor, 'transplanted') into the existing common law system.[78] As Graziadei explains, the 'transplant' metaphor is used to describe the gradual diffusion of law and legal change through the introduction of 'foreign' ideas.[79] By virtue of the choices of the legislator in the 1972 and 1998 Acts, the English courts have been forced to adopt an 'inter-systemic approach' in which English courts interact with the courts of Luxembourg and Strasbourg. Amos has noted the particular difficulties which arise when there is continued 'donor' involvement in the development of national law, which renders domestic assimilation more difficult and requires domestic law-makers to possess an excellent command of both EU and Strasbourg jurisprudence.[80] Van Hoecke and Warrington observe that this requires judges in all recipient systems to confront new forms of reasoning and conceptual frameworks which have, to a certain extent, to be integrated into their own system and own legal language.[81] They comment, in particular, on the potentially disruptive effect of EU Directives, which introduce new values and principles and disturb the coherence of existing national law. EU law enjoys supremacy over national law and will therefore become an integral part of the national legal system, regardless of the views of national judges. Schmid has commented that the private law in Europe may be said to serve 'two masters', the competences of which are not clearly delimited, which leads to legal fragmentation and the overlapping of different layers of law.[82] Such a multi-level regime renders the task of the judges all the more difficult. As will be seen in chapters three and four, EU law has affected only specific areas of tort law, permitting the law otherwise to develop organically. The question, therefore, is how to integrate these new sources – designated superior sources of law – into the traditional legal system. Teubner, commenting on the implementation of

[78] Xanthaki notes the particular problems such transplants cause for legislative drafters: H Zanthaki, 'Legal Transplants in Legislation: Defusing the Trap' (2008) 57 *International & Comparative Law Quarterly* 659.

[79] M Graziadei, 'Comparative Law as the Study of Transplants and Receptions' in M Reimann and R Zimmermann, *The Oxford Handbook of Comparative Law* (Oxford, Oxford University Press, 2008).

[80] M Amos, 'Transplanting Human Rights Norms: The Case of the United Kingdom's Human Rights Act' (2013) 35 *Human Rights Quarterly* 386, 401–2. She argues that s 2 HRA has, in fact, prevented the English courts better reflecting UK norms.

[81] M Van Hoecke and M Warrington, 'Legal Cultures, Legal Paradigms and Legal Doctrine: Towards a New Model for Comparative Law' (1998) 47 *International & Comparative Law Quarterly* 495, 533.

[82] CU Schmid, 'The Emergence of a Transnational Legal Science in European Private Law' (1999) 19 *Oxford Journal of Legal Studies* 673.

the Unfair Terms in Consumer Contracts Directive[83] into English law has noted that new rules introduced by EU Directives may act (and be viewed) as 'legal irritants'.[84] The rules, he argued, are likely to be re-contextualised to suit the recipient legal system, noting, in particular, the potential difficulties caused by rules which challenge deeply imbedded values within a legal system, in this instance the introduction of a test of 'good faith'.[85] In Teubner's view the natural reaction of the common law system is to reinterpret the rule in question; in this context, the civilian concept of 'good faith' would be treated simply as a principle which outlaws certain excesses of economic action as opposed to its more communitarian interpretation in civil law.[86] Collins has also noted that difficulties will arise when 'the English confident appeal to reason and common sense is rejected in favour of a more metaphysical civilian formula'[87] particularly where new legal rules are deemed to threaten the cultural identity and values of the legal community.[88] Human rights law may also raise transplant difficulties. Amos argues that in introducing the HRA 1998, the UK government overestimated the esteem in which the ECHR was held with the result that ECHR rights are still not regarded as sufficiently 'British' and calls are increasing for the HRA 1998 to be replaced with a British, rather than European, Bill of Rights.[89]

Inevitably, this leads to problems. The judiciary, having no choice, may nevertheless resist change and seek to adopt the most restrictive interpretation of such sources to minimise the disruption to national law. Further, it may seek to 'anglicise' the incoming law, opting for the familiar rather than seeking to respond to difference. For one schooled in the tradition of the common law, such forced transplants require, as Kahn-Freund recognised in 1974, the legal system and its judiciary to adjust to foreign patterns,[90] which will require not simply a knowledge of the law, but also a willingness to change and recognition of its social and political context. Further, supra-national law does require some form of consistency in its application across different legal systems and it can therefore never be completely 'domesticated'. This will only occur if the judiciary in each relevant state seeks to engage in a cross-jurisdictional dialogue.

The question posed here is quite simple: is it even possible for English judges to interpret and apply correctly 'foreign' law deriving from the European legal

[83] Council Directive 93/13/EEC of 5 April 1993 on unfair terms in consumer contracts OJ L095, 21 April 1993.

[84] G Teubner, 'Legal Irritants: Good Faith in British Law and How Unifying Law Ends up in New Divergencies' (1998) 61 *Modern Law Review* 11.

[85] Now Regulation 5, The Unfair Terms in Consumer Contracts Regulations 1999 SI 1999/ 2083, implementing Art 3 of the Directive.

[86] Consider, for example, *Director of Fair Trading v First National Bank* [2001] UKHL 52.

[87] H Collins, 'Good Faith in European Contract Law' (1994) 14 *Oxford Journal of Legal Studies* 229, 246.

[88] H Collins, 'European Private Law and the Cultural Identity of States' (1995) 3 *European Review of Private Law* 353.

[89] Amos, 'Transplanting Human Rights Norms' (n 80) 406–7. See, eg, the report of the UK Commission on a Bill of Rights, *A UK Bill of Rights?: The Choice Before Us*, published in December 2012.

[90] O Kahn-Freund, 'On Uses and Misuses of Comparative Law' (1974) 37 *Modern Law Review* 1, 3–4.

tradition with a stronger resemblance to civil rather than common law or will their own legal training and common law focus render a true appreciation of the operation of EU and ECHR law impossible?[91] Such an issue is fundamental to the successful application of EU and ECHR law within the English tort law system and will be addressed below.

A. The Impossibility of Legal Transplants?

The challenge for the English courts is to integrate European legal sources into the common law system. It has been questioned, however, to what extent this is possible. Montesquieu famously stated in 1748 that it would only be by chance ('*un grand hazard*') if laws from one system successfully transferred to another legal system. Laws, in his view, were localised and a product of their home environment: 'They should be relative to the physical qualities of the country . . . to the degree of liberty which the constitution can admit, to the religion of the inhabitants, to their inclinations, to their wealth, to their numbers, to their commerce, to their mores, to their manners'.[92] On this basis, geographical, economic, social, cultural and political factors all render successful legal transplants improbable. Legrand has further argued that legal rules travel encumbered by their own historical, epistemological and cultural baggage.[93] On this basis, he suggests, it is impossible for a legal system with a distinct legal culture to understand fully legal rules deriving from a different system, highlighting in particular the civil and common law divide.[94] Legrand argues that the very different *mentalités* (that is, ways of thinking about law) of the common and civil law give rise to an unbridgeable cultural divide, rendering full harmonisation impossible to achieve:[95]

> The civil law and common law must, therefore, be seen as two discrete epistemological formations with the latter having elected . . . not to formulate itself as rules (although the possibility to do so was technically open to it) and not to fashion itself as a system,

[91] Such a question naturally also affects civil law systems faced with supranational law which exposes its own legal culture to a dual system of national and supranational elements: see, eg, A Janssen and R Schulze, 'Legal Cultures and Legal Transplants in Germany' (2011) 19 *European Review of Private Law* 225 and JM Smits, 'The Europeanisation of National Legal Systems: Some Consequences for Legal Thinking in Civil Law Countries' in M van Hoecke (ed), *Epistemology and Methodology of Comparative Law* (Oxford, Hart Publishing, 2004).

[92] Charles Secondat de Montesquieu, *De l'esprit des Lois, Book 1, Ch 3* (reprinted by Ulan Press, Red Lion PA, 2012). See R Launay, 'Montesquieu: The Spectre of Despotism and the Origins of Comparative Law' in A Riles (ed), *Rethinking the Masters of Comparative Law* (Oxford, Hart Publishing, 2001).

[93] P Legrand, 'The Impossibility of Legal Transplants' (1997) 4 *Maastricht Journal of European & Comparative Law* 111, 114.

[94] See also C Harlow, 'Voices of Difference in a Plural Community' (2002) 50 *American Journal of Comparative Law* 339, 348: 'conceptual differences between legal systems go much deeper than procedure, presentation of argument or methods of construction. They spring from different cultural traditions, reflecting "different justifications for the imposition of legal obligations and the creation of rights", which derive from "the moral and political foundations" of different societies'.

[95] P Legrand, 'European Legal Systems Are Not Converging' (1996) 45 *International & Comparative Law Quarterly* 52. See also 'The Impossibility of Legal Transplants' (n 93).

> that is, to take the road not travelled. These epistemologies are conditioned by, and constantly reinforce in their turn, deeply-embedded world-views within the societies.[96]

In his view, therefore, EU law represents a distinct legal culture which is far from value-free, but is socially derived from the negotiation process which leads to EU legislation. It has a socio-cultural dimension inherent in its rules which national states will struggle to understand and apply.[97] In relation to human rights, presumably Legrand would share the view of Lord Hoffmann that human rights may be universal in abstraction, but should be national in application and that the concept of having an international court of human rights to deal with the concrete application of those rights in different countries is fundamentally flawed.[98] Such views are consistent of the early views of Montesquieu and von Savigny who spoke of the '*Volksgeist*': the organic connection between the law and the particular character (spirit/*Geist*) of the people.[99]

Such comments do identify a genuine source of concern – can common law judges really understand law based on the civil law system? – but many would disagree with Legrand's conclusion that such an understanding is impossible to achieve. Lando, the father of the harmonisation of European contract law,[100] has argued that the legal values held by European lawyers are very similar.[101] While there are undoubtedly differences between legal systems, this does not mean that it is impossible to find common values and similar economic and political concerns. Markesinis has also noted that transplanting 'foreign' law requires explanation and presentation in a shape and form which renders it accessible to a common law audience,[102] but opines nevertheless that there is 'no doubt that convergence is taking place . . . There is thus a convergence of solutions in the area of private law as the problems faced by courts and legislators acquire a common and international flavour'.[103] Smits has equally noted that with globalisation, the idea of distinct national cultures becomes outdated as most legal jurisdictions will come into contact with new influences.[104] This is, of course, particularly so in relation to

[96] P Legrand, 'Against a European Civil Code' (1997) 60 *Modern Law Review* 44, 48.

[97] Ibid, at 57.

[98] Lord Hoffmann, 'The Universality of Human Rights' (2009) 125 *Law Quarterly Review* 416, 423.

[99] FC von Savigny, *Vom Beruf unserer Zeit für Gesetzgebung und Rechtswissenschaft* (Heidelberg, Bey Mohr und Zimmer, 1814). The concept of the *Volksgeist* was actually developed by German philosopher Johann Gottfried von Herder. See R Zimmermann, 'Savigny's Legacy: Legal History, Comparative Law, and the Emergence of a European Science' (1996) 112 *Law Quarterly Review* 576.

[100] Establishing the Commission on European Contract Law in the 1980s.

[101] O Lando, 'Optional or Mandatory Europeanisation of Contract Law' (2000) 8 *European Review of Private Law* 59.

[102] BS Markesinis, 'Judge, Jurist and the Study and Use of Foreign Law' (1993) 109 *Law Quarterly Review* 622.

[103] BS Markesinis, 'Learning from Europe and Learning in Europe' in BS Markesinis (ed), *The Gradual Convergence: Foreign Ideas, Foreign Influences, and English Law on the Eve of the 21st Century* (Oxford, Oxford University Press, 1994) 30.

[104] JM Smits, 'Law Making in the European Union: On Globalisation and Contract Law in Divergent Legal Cultures' (2007) 67 *Louisiana Law Review* 1181; 'Legal Culture as Mental Software, or: How to Overcome National Legal Culture?' in T Wilhelmsson, E Paunio and A Pohjolainen (eds), *Private Law and the Many Cultures of Europe* (The Hague, Kluwer, 2007). See also G Canivet, 'Influence croisée de la Common Law et du Droit Civil' (2003) 63 *Louisiana Law Review* 945, 946: 'La culture n'est pas un

supranational treaties and conventions which apply across a number of different states.

Watson has argued in contrast that legal transplants are not only possible, but inevitable. He has famously argued that 'successful borrowing could be made from a very different legal system, even from one at a much higher level of development and of a different political complexion'[105] and, from a historical perspective, he is correct. The influence of Roman law, for example, demonstrates the vitality of legal ideas which are capable of influencing Continental European countries despite differences in culture, language and time. Watson concedes, however, that transplanting the 'idea' does not mean that it will develop identically in every single State.[106] This is obviously problematic in relation to a supranational law, such as EU law, where it is sought to implement common standards in every Member State. Ewald also comments that Watson's arguments seem particularly directed to private law rules and fare less well in relation to public law rules which cannot be said to be insulated from political, economic and social forces.[107] While Watson may over-estimate, therefore, the ease with which national legal systems apply externally sourced rules, he does make the valid point that legal history evidences that transplants happen and it falls to the national legal system to deal with them.

On this basis, it is submitted that there is room for a middle-ground. A more moderate position is that English lawyers must simply make more effort to respond to the difficulties caused by legal transplants and ensure that our judges are adequately trained how to deal with these new sources of law. Legal culture[108] may be an obstacle to integration, but it is not static[109] and indeed difficult to define with any degree of precision.[110] It is nevertheless a useful concept in assisting us to

dogme intangible et figé, elle n'est pas un refus du renouvellement; elle est une réalité dynamique, interactive et vivante'.

[105] A Watson, 'Legal transplants and law reform' (1976) 92 *Law Quarterly Review* 79. See also A Watson, *Legal Transplants*, 1st edn (Edinburgh, Scottish Academic Press, 1974); 2nd edn (Athens, Ga, University of Georgia Press, 1993).

[106] A Watson, 'Legal Transplants and European Private Law' (2000) 4(4) *Electronic Journal of Comparative Law*: 'from early days I have argued that a rule once transplanted is different in its new home'.

[107] W Ewald, 'Comparative Jurisprudence (II): The Logic of Legal Transplants' (1995) 43 *American Journal of Comparative Law* 489, 503.

[108] Nelken has argued that legal culture, in its most general sense, provides a way of describing patterns of legally orientated social behaviour and attitudes, ranging from the operation of the legal profession to the very values and ideas underlying the legal system in question: D Nelken, 'Using the Concept of Legal Culture' (2004) *Australian Journal of Legal Philosophy* 1.

[109] Friedman has argued that legal culture constantly undergoes changes, reacting and adjusting itself to the surrounding society: LM Friedman, 'Some Comments on Cotterell and Legal Transplants' in D Nelken and J Feest (eds), *Adapting Legal Cultures* (Oxford, Hart Publishing, 2001) 93.

[110] See, eg, D Nelken, 'Defining and Using the Concept of Legal Culture' in Örücü and Nelken (eds) *Comparative Law* (n 66), who describes it as a term which may be used prescriptively as well as descriptively. See also D Nelken, 'Legal Culture', ch 39 in JM Smits (ed), *Elgar Encyclopedia of Comparative Law*, 2nd edn (Cheltenham, Edward Elgar Publishing, 2012) and R Cotterell, 'Comparative Law and Legal Culture' in Reimann and Zimmermann (eds) *Oxford Handbook* (n 79). Zimmermann has described it as a 'notoriously intractable concept': R Zimmermann, 'Challenges for the European Law Institute' (2012) 16 *Edinburgh Law Review* 5, 15.

understand the multi-textured nature of the reception of 'foreign' law into the domestic legal system, whether one prefers to call it 'culture', 'tradition',[111] 'style' or even '*mentalité*'. It is clear that historical, socio-economic, psychological and ideological factors influence the content and application of legal rules and render it more difficult for legal actors from a different jurisdiction to understand correctly how law functions. Common lawyers will thus have to do more than simply identifying new legal rules. As Markesinis has noted, understanding the law of Luxembourg and Strasbourg is not just a question of knowing the substance of the law, but also adjusting traditional processes of reasoning and style.[112]

B. The Possibility of Legal Transplants?

In an era of international travel and trade, when ordinary citizens regularly make contracts using the laws of different legal systems when purchasing items on the internet – the choice of law of the retail giant Amazon is, for example, Luxembourg – arguments based on the localised nature of law seem outdated. One might question to what extent globalisation has made such isolationism unrealistic. Many lawyers now do not think solely in terms of localised law, but globally.[113] Changes to the national legal system from external sources are thus inevitable due to contact through trade, politics, international treaties and conventions and the migration of populations and religions.

The successful application of European rules will therefore depend on the willingness of national judges to go beyond the formal application of rules of the 'foreign' law and to understand their social and political context.[114] Ewald argues that 'to understand a legal system is not just a matter of possessing *information* about a text or a body of rules, but is rather akin to possessing a certain kind of ability: to have mastered the enactment principles, and to be able, with a certain degree of skill, to marshall a legal argument, and to offer reasons for one's conclusions'.[115] It is necessary, therefore, to appreciate the significance of the differences in legal style, reasoning and statutory interpretation explained in the first section of this chapter. In identifying what Sacco has called the 'legal formants' in the

[111] Patrick Glenn argues the concept of 'legal tradition' is to be preferred in that it accommodates multiple sources of law and gradations in the force of their normativity: 'Comparative Legal Families and Comparative Legal Traditions' in Reimann and Zimmermann (eds) *Oxford Handbook* (n 79). See also H Patrick Glenn, 'Legal Cultures and Legal Traditions' in M van Hoecke (ed), *Epistemology and Methodology of Comparative Law* (Oxford, Hart Publishing, 2004).

[112] BS Markesinis, 'Judicial Style and Judicial Reasoning in England and Germany' (2000) 59 *Cambridge Law Journal* 294.

[113] Teubner has remarked that 'globalising processes have created one world-wide network of legal communications which downgrades the laws of the nation state to mere regional parts of this network which are in close communication with each other': G Teubner, 'Legal Irritants: Good Faith in British Law and How Unifying Law Ends Up in New Divergencies' (1998) 61 *Modern Law Review* 11, 16. See also W Twining, 'Globalisation and Comparative Law' in Örücü and Nelken (eds) (n 66).

[114] Kahn-Freund, 'On Uses and Misuses' (n 90).

[115] WB Ewald, 'Comparative Jurisprudence (I): What Was it Like to Try a Rat?' (1995) 143 *University of Pennsylvania Law Review* 1889, 2137 (emphasis in text).

living law, one must go beyond identifying operative rules stated by statute or case law and consider the role played by the practices that shape the law, but are not expressly acknowledged (which Sacco terms 'cryptotypes'), be they situated at the level of operative rules or at other levels, such as the ideology permeating a given legal system.[116] Understanding legal rules thus goes beyond positive law to recognition of the role which tacit assumptions play in the interpretation of the law. As Teubner has indicated, it is not enough merely to cite European authority. Without a change of approach, such 'continental noise' will only lead to new dissonances and different versions of the same law in different Member States.[117]

The key issue, therefore, is that understanding the law of the European Union and European Court of Human Rights requires work. Here, comparative law provides a particularly useful insight. It warns of the difficulty of approaching non-domestic rules objectively and the natural tendency after years of training within one particular legal system to assume its superiority to less familiar systems.[118] Such inherent bias, which derives from one's own cultural, social, economic, political and even personal background, inevitably impacts on legal reasoning with a tendency to regard the 'new' law as an intruder whose presence must be justified. Van Erp notes that these factors shape how judges think and reason and, more generally, mould how we perceive ourselves as lawyers.[119] Comparative law informs us that to understand external rules, it is necessary to appreciate their distinct context and the sources from which they derive. This, as Palmer notes, will not always be easy, but we must do our best.[120] Retaining a national bias may lead to resistance, an unwillingness to embrace change and a desire to isolate such rules and interpret them as narrowly as possible. This may be overt – the Eurosceptic, for example – but perhaps more dangerously, subconscious as the lawyer naturally adopts the traditional stance of his or her legal system without considering why such a response seems instinctively correct. Arvind suggests that a distinction may be made according to the strength of the new law which is introduced. Formal sources of law – such as law transposed under an EU Directive – cannot be ignored, but when it is deemed to clash with existing ideas of justice and fairness, the result may be a reception which, without technically violating the letter of the formal rule, seeks to mitigate or alter its effect.[121] In such circumstances, the tendency will be to adjust the way in which the new law is interpreted

[116] R Sacco, 'Legal Formants: A Dynamic Approach to Comparative Law (I) and (II)' (1991) 39 *American Journal of Comparative Law* 1, 349.

[117] Teubner, 'Legal Irritants' (n 84) 20.

[118] See, eg, G Frankenberg, 'Critical Comparisons: Re-thinking Comparative Law' (1985) 26 *Harvard International Law Journal* 411, who notes a crucial home bias that drives the comparativist's approach to 'foreign' law. See also P Zumbansen, 'Comparative Law's Coming of Age? Twenty Years after Critical Comparisons' (2005) 6 *German Law Journal* 1073.

[119] S van Erp, 'Comparative Private Law in Practice: The Process of Law Reform' in Örücü and Nelken (eds) *Comparative Law* (n 66) 407.

[120] V Palmer, 'From Lerotholi to Lando: Some Examples of Comparative Law Methodology'(2004) 4(2) *Global Jurist Frontiers* 1, 5–6.

[121] TT Arvind, 'The "Transplant Effect" in Harmonization' (2010) 59 *International & Comparative Law Quarterly* 65, 79.

or applied so as to suit domestic policy judgments. This is particularly easy where the legal rule in question provides for general concepts rather than precise technical rules and does not derive from a well-established legal-cultural background.[122] Inevitably, however, forcing European concepts into a common law box (or, if one prefers, cause of action) will lead to distortion, misunderstandings and a response which may be inconsistent with that of other Member States.[123] The conclusion must be, therefore, that legal transplants are possible, but not, without effort, inevitably successful.

C. The Reception of European Sources: So Different?

It is submitted that in relation to the transplantation of European law, be it EU law or European human rights case law, a distinctive picture arises. Whatever the views of individual politicians or judges, European law *is* part of the English legal system. EU Directives must be transposed into English law and the subsequent legislation interpreted by the English court. The HRA 1998 requires the English courts to take into account the case law of the ECtHR. To dismiss such law as 'alien' or 'foreign' neglects the fact that the English courts have no choice in the matter and must respond to these new sources of law, as must the legal community as a whole. The European Communities Act 1972 and the HRA 1998 require the English courts to adapt to new forms of reasoning and legislation and consider case law from outside the common law courts. Two key factors, however, indicate that the process of transplantation may not be as difficult as anticipated.

i. Legal Culture Is Not Static

Much has changed since 1972. Lawyers practise across different jurisdictions and UK legal education now includes a compulsory EU law unit with optional units in international, comparative and human rights law. Changes in rules of statutory construction,[124] the transformation from the House of Lords to the Supreme Court consistent with the separation of powers,[125] and the acceptance of concepts

[122] C van Dam, 'European Tort Law and the Many Cultures of Europe' in T Wilhelmsson (ed), *Private Law and the Cultures of Europe* (The Hague, Kluwer Law International, 2007) 72.

[123] Graziadei has warned that disguising foreign elements in familiar clothes may render them more familiar and hence more acceptable to the national legal community, but indicates a failure to understand change in its own terms: Graziadei, 'Comparative Law' (n 79) 462.

[124] Consider, for example, the rule in *Pepper v Hart* [1993] AC 593 that, contrary to their previous self-denying ordnance, the courts will permit themselves to look at the report of Parliamentary proceedings in *Hansard* for the purpose of resolving ambiguity in the construction of statute. Grief notes that although this relaxation of the previous rule was not expressly attributed to EU law, there can be little doubt that judicial experience of the EU law was a contributing factor: N Grief, 'The pervasive influence of European Community law in the United Kingdom' in TG Watkin, *The Europeanisation of law* (London, UKNCCL, 1998) 94.

[125] See J Lee (ed), *From House of Lords to Supreme Court: Judges, Jurists and the Process of Judging* (Oxford, Hart Publishing, 2011); L Blom-Cooper QC, B Dickson and G Drewry (eds), *The Judicial House of Lords: 1876–2009* (Oxford, Oxford University Press, 2009).

such as 'legitimate expectation' and 'proportionality' in public law[126] all demonstrate the influence of European sources on the development of the common law. Politically, economically and even socially, European States have much in common and this is underpinned by common membership of the European Union and adherence to common statements of values such as the ECHR. Bell argues that 'in an important sense, there is a common western European legal culture. We have common liberal democratic political values which are operated in capitalist, secular, pluralistic societies under the rule of law.'[127] Such commonalities will render any legal transplants all the easier. Significantly also the debate is in English. Judgments from Luxembourg and Strasbourg are published in English, together with an abundance of textbooks detailing the provisions of EU and European human rights law. The 'peril' of understanding a foreign language, highlighted by Stapleton who warns practitioner and judge to exercise extreme caution in using comparative materials from foreign language systems,[128] does not exist. This is not to ignore the fact that there is a 'European' legal language which has developing, using terms such as 'proportionality', 'margin of appreciation' and 'sufficient serious breach' which possess their own specific dictionary meaning,[129] but the fact that the debate takes place in English renders it far easier for the English court to participate.

The lawyers of today also differ from their counterparts of 1973 or 2000. Law students graduating in 2014 will have studied EU and European human rights law as part of the *English* law degree and will be familiar with the doctrines of 'direct effect' and rights-based discourse as their harassed public law tutors explain once again the distinction between EU and ECHR law. Their tutor in EU law may indeed have been schooled in another European jurisdiction or at least had the opportunity to study at the European University Institute in Florence,[130] and thereby able to give a particularly clear insight into the European legal tradition. Students and academics may have also taken advantage of the Erasmus programme which, since its

[126] See, eg, P Craig, *Administrative Law*, 7th edn (London, Sweet and Maxwell, 2012) chs 21 and 22.

[127] J Bell, 'English Law and French Law: Not So Different? (1995) 48(2) *Current Legal Problems* 63, 64. See also F Wieacker, 'Foundations of European Legal Culture' (1990) 38 *American Journal of Comparative Law* 1, 6: 'it is obvious that the legal systems of the common law represent the peculiarly European cultural context just as definitely as those of the continent, not only because of the similar ways of life but also because of the longstanding commonality of the crucial religious, ideological, philosophical and scientific foundations.'

[128] J Stapleton, 'Benefits of Comparative Tort Reasoning: Lost in Translation' (2007) 1(3) *Journal of Tort Law* 1, 33: 'the perils involved when tort practitioners and judges in English speaking jurisdictions resort to foreign-language legal materials are even graver because most common law judges and practitioners are fully fluent only in English.' (Electronic copy available at: http://ssrn.com/abstract=1015370).

[129] C Robertson, 'EU Legal English: Common Law, Civil Law, or a New Genre?' (2012) 20 *European Review of Private Law* 1215, 1237, argues that EU legal texts, increasingly drafted in English, may also cause interpretative difficulties to civil law courts in view of the distinctive linguistic style found in such texts, which are generally a product of interstate negotiation between common and civil law Member States.

[130] See www.eui.eu/Home.aspx. The EUI's mission, laid down in the 1970s, is to 'foster the advancement of learning in fields which are of particular interest for the development of Europe'. A convention was signed in 1972 cementing the commitment of Member States to create the EUI as a pillar for research and development.

introduction in 1987, has allowed over two and a half million students to engage in a period of study at another European university.[131] While the current generation of judges will not have benefited from such training, they will nevertheless have been exposed to cases involving the HRA 1998 and EU law and therefore, perforce, required to respond to the new forms of law and the interpretative duties outlined in first half of this chapter. It does no justice to English judges (and the legal profession as a whole) to assume that they are not capable of responding to the challenges which are raised. Some judges have a particularly pro-European background. Lord Slynn, for example, worked as Advocate General and Judge at the ECJ between 1981 and 1992 before becoming a House of Lords judge. Lord Bingham was one of the first major figures as Lord Chief Justice to support the incorporation of the ECHR into English law and as a barrister acted for the European Commission and advised on issues of EU law, rendering him extremely well-placed as a judge to take an informed view on both human rights and EU law.[132] Lord Mance (currently in the Supreme Court) represented the UK on the Council of Europe's Consultative Council of European Judges from 2000 to 2011, being elected its first chair from 2000 to 2003, and currently chairs the Executive Council of the International Law Association and the Lord Chancellor's Advisory Committee on Private International Law. He is further a member of the Judicial Integrity Group and of the seven person panel set up under the Treaty on the Functioning of the European Union (Art 255) to give an opinion on candidates' suitability to perform the duties of Judge and Advocate-General of the European Court of Justice and General Court. The positive influence of these judges will be noted in the course of this book.

The English legal tradition has therefore changed over time. This is inevitable. In the case of the introduction of the Human Rights Act 1998, a definite step was taken to make the judiciary more 'rights aware'. The introduction of the Act in 2000 was preceded by a vigorous training process for UK judges to ensure that they fully appreciated the nature of Convention rights and how to apply such rights in a common law context. Bell notes the systematic training undertaken which involved the provision of seminars and manuals ('benchbooks') to support the judiciary.[133] Indeed, it is reported that the government spent £4.5 million training judges, magistrates and tribunal chairpersons for the implementation of the HRA 1998.[134] This may be contrasted with the position in 1973 when

[131] www.britishcouncil.org/erasmus-about-erasmus.htm.

[132] See F Jacobs, 'European Law and the English Judge' in M Andenas and D Fairgrieve (eds), *Tom Bingham and the Transformation of the Law: A Liber Amicorum* (Oxford, Oxford University Press, 2011) 420 and 427.

[133] J Bell, *Judiciaries within Europe* (Cambridge, Cambridge University Press, 2006) 319. See also the comments of Lord Woolf who noted that 'Preparation for legislation on this scale was unprecedented in the United Kingdom . . . [and was] worthwhile since it meant not only judges, but officials, Ministers and advocates were immersed in a human rights culture. Change of culture is the most important aspect of the introduction of the Human Rights Act': 'Opening of the judicial year European Court of Human Rights: Strasbourg', available at www.judiciary.gov.uk/media/speeches/2003/opening-judicial-year-european-courts-human-rights-strasbourg.

[134] The Lord Chancellor wrote to judges stating that 'With proper training and planning, I am confident that all courts and tribunals will be able to give full effect to the rights recognised by the

the potential impact of EU law on the English legal system was clearly underestimated.[135] Acceptance of the role of EU law in the domestic legal system was, in fact, slow and met with initial judicial resistance.[136] Nevertheless, post-*Factortame*,[137] the English courts have recognised the supremacy of EU law and that it should be part of every lawyer's core training.

ii. Judicial Dialogue

It is important also to note the relationship between the English and European courts. In terms of EU and European human rights law, the Luxembourg and Strasbourg courts give guidance and seek to ensure the consistent application of the law, subject to the doctrines of subsidiarity and the margin of appreciation. English courts are bound by the rulings of the CJEU. The ECtHR is capable of giving binding judgments against individual States and, as seen above, under the 'mirror principle', the English courts are proving to be receptive to guidance given by this court and have embraced the need to bring English legal reasoning in line with the rights-based focus of that Court, although senior judges such as Sir John Laws and Lord Judge have recently been critical of any perceived subservience to Strasbourg. A central court, which seeks to guide and advise national courts, is clearly an extremely useful means of improving the ability of the national courts to apply correctly European law. Corradetti comments that human rights transplantability will only be successful if a mechanism for top-down guidance is present to prevent idiosyncratic interpretations of rights varying from one country to another.[138]

The dialogue between the Strasbourg and national court has been particularly evident.[139] Örücü notes that the ECtHR makes reference to national laws and that the Convention itself derives from principles already recognised under the domestic laws of democratic countries.[140] As will be discussed in chapter five, the

Convention and to make their distinctive contribution to fostering a culture of awareness of, and respect for, human rights throughout the whole of society': C Elliott and F Quinn, *English Legal System*, 12th edn (Harlow, Pearson Education, 2011) 293.

[135] D Nicol, *EC Membership and the Judicialization of British Politics* (Oxford, Oxford University Press, 2001), who questions the extent to which British MPs understood that membership of the then EEC entailed a shift in power from legislature to courts.

[136] Lord Denning famously stated in *Bulmer Ltd v Bollinger SA* [1974] Ch. 401, 418 that 'The treaty [of Rome] does not touch any of the matters which concern solely the mainland of England and the people in it.' Lord Bingham in a 1992 article was scathing of such attitudes, declaring it a 'national disgrace that there should continue to be widespread ignorance of Community law two decades after Britain joined the European Community': TH Bingham, '"There Is a World Elsewhere": The Changing Perspectives of English Law' (1992) 41 *International & Comparative Law Quarterly* 513, 519.

[137] *R v Secretary of State for Transport Ex p. Factortame Ltd (No 2)* [1991] 1 AC 603.

[138] C Corradetti, 'Can Human Rights Be Exported: On the Very Idea of Human Rights Transplantability' in AB Engelbrekt and J Nergelius (eds), *New Directions in Comparative Law* (Cheltenham, Edward Elgar Publishing, 2009), acknowledging, however, that such rights will inevitably be affected by the local culture itself (pp 51–52).

[139] See N Krisch, 'The Open Architecture of European Human Rights Law' (2008) 71 *Modern Law Review* 183; M Amos, 'The Dialogue between United Kingdom Courts and the European Court of Human Rights' (2012) 61 *International & Comparative Law Quarterly* 557.

[140] Örücü, 'Comparative Law in Practice' (n 66) 427.

negative response of the English legal community to the Strasbourg court's decision in *Osman v United Kingdom*[141] was taken on board by the Court in its later decision of *Z v United Kingdom.*[142] Other examples exist outside tort law where the Strasbourg court has shown itself to be receptive to the views of the English court[143] – it is clearly a two-way dialogue.[144]

A dialogue between the national court and CJEU is also fostered by the Article 267 TFEU preliminary reference procedure, which permits national courts to refer questions of interpretation to the CJEU when the answer is not clear.[145] This provides national courts with the opportunity to consult the CJEU on difficult points of interpretation and this procedure has been used by the UK courts on a number of occasions. While the *acte clair* doctrine permits the national court to decline to refer a question on the basis that the point is clear,[146] the standard is, in theory at least, relatively high: the correct application of European law must be so obvious as to leave no scope for any reasonable doubt as to the manner in which the question raised is to be resolved. Such a procedure meets two main goals: ensuring the consistent application of EU rules across Member States, but also involves the domestic court in the process of legal development, engaging in a dialogue with national courts to identify and subsequently apply correctly EU law. Koopmans has also noted that from the very beginning of its case law, the CJEU has sought to develop EU law while respecting the general principles of law which are common to the legal traditions of member states.[147]

Further, many UK judges are involved with organisations which seek to foster cross-jurisdictional understanding of the law. The British Institute of International and Comparative Law (BIICL), for example, was created in 1958 by the merger of the Society of Comparative Legislation (founded in 1895) and the Grotius Society (founded in 1915 and named after the sixteenth-century Dutch jurist regarded as one of the founders of international law). Former Presidents include Lords Bingham and Goff and its Board of Trustees includes judges, barristers and senior academics.[148] The Institute seeks to continue its mission first begun in 1895: to advance the understanding of international and comparative law, promote the rule

[141] *Osman v United Kingdom* (1998) 29 EHRR 245.

[142] *Z v United Kingdom* (2001) 34 EHRR 97.

[143] See, eg, *Cooper v United Kingdom* (2004) 39 EHRR 8 and *Stafford v United Kingdom* (2002) 35 EHRR 1121.

[144] See Jacobs, 'European Law and the English Judge' (n 132) 424.

[145] For recent guidance for national courts, see 2012/C 338/01 Recommendations to national courts and tribunals in relation to the initiation of preliminary ruling proceedings. The European Commission may equally assess whether the States have breached EU law under Art 258 TFEU (ex Art 226 TEC) and fine for serious and persistent breaches (Art 260 TFEU (ex Art 228 TEC)).

[146] Case 283/81 *Srl CILFIT* (n 20) para16. The court may also decline to refer where the answer to the question cannot affect the outcome of the case.

[147] T Koopmans, 'Comparative Law and the Courts' (1996) 45 *International & Comparative Law Quarterly* 545, 546. Art 340(2) TFEU provides a good example, providing that 'In the case of non-contractual liability, the Union shall, in accordance with the general principles common to the laws of the Member States, make good any damage caused by its institutions or by its servants in the performance of their duties'.

[148] www.biicl.org/governance/.

of law in international affairs; and promote their application through research, publications and events. Other UK organisations include the Franco-British Lawyers Society, whose current President is High Court judge, Mr Justice Tugendhat,[149] and the British–German Jurists Association, whose presidents since its inception in 1970 have been influential judges, namely Lord Diplock, Sir Edward Eveleigh, Sir Michael Kerr and Lord Hoffmann.[150]

At the European level, the European Court of Human Rights holds annual seminars entitled 'Dialogue between Judges' to foster greater understanding between national and Strasbourg judges.[151] Further, the Consultative Council of European Judges (CCJE)[152] is an advisory body of the Council of Europe on issues related to the independence, impartiality and competence of judges and is the first body within an international organisation to be composed exclusively of judges. In terms of the EU, lawyers are represented by the Council of Bars and Law Societies of Europe (CCBE), which is an international non-profit-making association founded in 1960.[153] It acts as the liaison between the EU and Europe's national bars and law societies on all matters of mutual interest relating to the exercise of the profession of lawyer. Dialogue between judges is also fostered by organisations such as the Association of European Administrative Judges (AEAJ),[154] European Judges and Prosecutors Association (EJPA),[155] the International Association of Judges (in particular the European section),[156] and European Network of Councils for the Judiciary (ENCJ).[157] Equally, the Network of the Presidents of the Supreme Judicial Courts of the EU was founded in 2004 to provide a forum through which European institutions would be given an opportunity to request the opinions of Supreme Courts and to bring them closer by encouraging discussion and the exchange of ideas. Finally, the founding of the European Law Institute (ELI) in 2011 marks an important step in encouraging lawyers to think of themselves as truly 'European', playing a role in the development of a supranational law. Zimmermann has argued that the ELI will perform an important role in monitoring, evaluating and stimulating the development of European law on a more permanent and systematic basis than in the past with the added benefit of institutional independence.[158]

[149] https://fbls.eu/.

[150] www.bgja.org.uk/.

[151] http://hub.coe.int/; the 2012 seminar entitled 'How can we ensure greater involvement of national courts in the Convention system?'

[152] www.coe.int/t/dghl/cooperation/ccje/default_en.asp.

[153] The CCBE is the representative organisation of around 1 million European lawyers through its member bars and law societies from 31 full member countries, and 11 further associate and observer countries.

[154] www.aeaj.org/ (founded in 2000).

[155] www.amue-ejpa.org/ (founded in 2004).

[156] www.iaj-uim.org/ (founded in 1953). The regional group of the European Association of Judges covers 43 countries.

[157] www.encj.eu (founded in 2004) whose aim is to improve cooperation between, and good mutual understanding amongst, the Councils for the Judiciary and the members of the Judiciary of the European Union (or candidate) Member States.

[158] Zimmermann, 'Challenges for the European Law Institute' (n 110) 12.

Such 'two way' traffic between national and European courts will inevitably make European legal rules seem less 'foreign'. It is clear that in contrast to legal transplants generally, a 'special' relationship exists between the courts of England and Wales and those of Luxembourg and Strasbourg in which dialogue is being fostered to ensure the necessary exchange of views and to promote a mutual understanding of these sources of European law. Örücü goes further and argues that judges play an important role in acting as the 'tuners' of the law, bridging societal divides by adapting the law.[159] She argues that we should not think in terms of transplanting foreign ideas into a new hostile environment, but think instead of the law as evolving in a period of transposition.[160] This insight is particularly useful in highlighting the key role of the courts in ensuring that this process of 'transposition, tuning and fitting' takes place. While the legislator chooses to 'transplant' law into the common law system, it is for the judiciary and, to a certain extent the legal community as a whole, to respond to these new sources and seek to apply them correctly within the existing domestic legal system. 'Tuning', as Örücü notes, is necessary at all levels, including legal education. The key message here is positive. Rather than viewing Europeanisation as likely to 'irritate' or disrupt the law, the common law legal system can respond and grow in response to European sources. As she notes:

> Internalisation of norms and standards by the people in a recipient system is crucial if there are to be fruitful developments. This is aided by the tuners. Harmony as a possibility of conversation can be achieved through appreciating diversity as well as by eliminating diversity.[161]

III. The Task Ahead

To suggest, therefore, that English lawyers, be they student, practitioner or judge, do not have the *mentalité* to understand European legal sources is, in my view, to underestimate the ability of the common law to evolve. Judges have been exchanging ideas in transnational networks and are more actively engaged than ever before with their other European counterparts.[162] Most importantly, EU and European human rights law are now part of the English legal system and therefore

[159] Örücü, 'Comparative Law in Practice' (n 66) 429.

[160] See E Örücü, 'Law as Transposition' (2002) 51 *International & Comparative Law Quarterly* 205. See also *The Enigma of Comparative Law: Variations on a Theme for the Twenty-First Century* (Leiden, Martinus Nijhoff, 2004).

[161] Ibid, 221.

[162] See S Muller and S Richards (eds), *Highest Courts and Globalisation* (The Hague, Asser Press, 2010); M Siems and M Gelter, 'Networks, Dialogue or One-Way Traffic? An Empirical Analysis of Cross-Citations Between Ten European High Courts' (2012) 8 *Utrecht Law Review* 88 who note that frequent cross-citations provide evidence of diffusion of ideas amongst legal systems; M Claes and M de Visser, 'Are You Networked Yet? On Dialogues within European Judicial Networks' (2012) 8 *Utrecht Law Review* 100.

all members of the English legal community will find themselves faced at some point with European sources of law.[163] Equally, with time, the students of today will be the judges of tomorrow, educated from the very beginning of their studies in the language of EU law and human rights. In the words of Lord Bingham, 'the 1990s will be remembered as the time when England – and I emphasise England – ceased to be a legal island, bounded to the north by the Tweed, and joined, or more accurately rejoined, the mainstream of European legal tradition, at least as an associate member'.[164]

The stage is thus set to examine the 'Europeanisation' of English tort law. This has attracted little attention in the private law community and yet provides a fascinating case study, giving us a clear insight into how judges reason and adapt to new sources of law. Many of the examples discussed in chapters three to six of this book have been wrongly overlooked or their full impact not appreciated. This chapter has identified three key challenges for the English courts in this field. First, the courts must adapt to new methods of statutory interpretation and understand and apply EU and European human rights case law. Secondly, the courts must determine how changes introduced by EU and ECHR law operate within the existing framework of English tort law and the extent to which Europeanisation will lead to a cross-fertilisation of ideas. Finally, the courts must resolve how they will deal with the inevitable diminution in autonomy when an area of law previously dominated by judge-made law is subjected to external European influences. The chapters which follow will examine the response the English judiciary – as 'tuners' of the law – to these challenges and whether it has reacted positively or sought to remodel 'foreign' rules into a more familiar common law pattern.

Europeanisation therefore represents more than the introduction of new rules of law, but a challenge to the existing legal structure and modes of reasoning. The ability or otherwise of the English courts to translate successfully these new rules of law into English tort law will be examined in the next four chapters.

[163] 'Europeanisation i.e. the increasing scope and influence of EU law and the ECHR in national legal systems, has led to the development of a "dialogue" between the national highest courts and the Luxembourg and Strasbourg courts': E Mak, 'Why Do Dutch and UK Judges Cite Foreign Law?' (2011) 70 *Cambridge Law Review* 420, 447.

[164] Bingham, '"There Is a World Elsewhere"' (n 136) 514.

3

Breaking Down the Frontiers: EU Law in the English Law of Torts

Introduction

This chapter will examine the influence of EU law on ordinary principles of English tort law following the entry of the UK into the European Economic Community (now European Union) in 1973. In common with other legal systems, English tort law has evolved to respond to changes in society, both at a socio-economic and political level, protecting a variety of interests including personal injury, property damage, financial loss and harm to reputation by means of a system of nominate torts. [1] Yet Article 288 of the Treaty on the Functioning of the European Union (TFEU)[2] makes it clear that European Union institutions, in the exercise of the Union's competences, possess law-making powers. They may adopt regulations, directives, decisions, recommendations and opinions that will impact on English law. From the perspective of tort law, directives are the most important source of law. This is significant in terms of the role of the national courts. While regulations are of general application and binding in their entirety on a par with national laws as soon as they are passed, directives generally require implementing legislation by the Member States and it is for the national authorities, then, to decide on the choice of form and method of transposition, subject to the supervision of the Commission.[3] In terms of EU policy, directives provide a less politically contentious means of bringing national laws into line on matters which affect the operation of the single market, giving Member States time to consider how best to integrate these new legal provisions into existing national law. As Craig and de Búrca have noted, the ability to act through directives gives the EU valuable flexibility,

[1] This list is not necessarily static and ch 6 will examine arguments that tort law should extend to the protection of privacy rights: see *Campbell v Mirror Group Newspapers Ltd* [2004] UKHL 22; [2004] 2 AC 457, paras 13–14 per Lord Nicholls of Birkenhead.

[2] ex Article 249 TEC.

[3] 'A directive shall be binding, as to the result to be achieved, upon each Member State to which it is addressed, but shall leave to the national authorities the choice of form and methods': Art 288(3) TFEU. See also Article 4(3) TEU: 'The Member States shall take any appropriate measure, general or particular, to ensure fulfilment of the obligations arising out of the Treaties or resulting from the acts of the institutions of the Union.'

particularly when the aim is to harmonise laws within the very different legal systems of the EU or introduce complex legislative change.[4]

This chapter will examine a number of directives which have been transposed into English law and which deal with matters traditionally dealt with at national level by the law of tort. It will not address liability of the State for breach of EU law (the so-called *Francovich* liability).[5] This is a new form of liability, which has been developed by the Court of Justice of the European Union (CJEU), and will be considered separately in chapter four. A distinction must also be drawn between directives which affect fundamental tort law principle, whose main focus is that of compensating for wrongs, and areas in which the directive is part of a broader regulatory framework which involves both public and private law. While the latter may also give rise to claims for breach of statutory duty, such a claim is merely part of this broad framework and it would be misleading to consider it in isolation. Examples may be found in the field of financial services, environmental law and competition law. Section 150 of the Financial Services and Markets Act (FSMA) 2000, for example, does provide for an action for damages for contravention by an authorised person of rules,[6] and this will include provisions under Financial Services Directives,[7] but it is clear that such provisions are part of a larger regulatory scheme and must be interpreted in this context. Equally, while EU law has introduced an environmental liability regime, the focus of the Environmental Liability Directive 2004/35/EC[8] is not compensation, but the regulation of environmental damage, and a key restrictive feature of the Directive is that it excludes damage to property, personal injury and pure economic loss.[9]

[4] P Craig and G de Búrca, *EU Law: Text, Cases and Materials*, 5th edn (Oxford, Oxford University Press, 2011) 105–6.

[5] So named after the leading case of C-6/90 *Francovich v Italian Republic* [1991] ECR I-5357; [1993] 2 CMLR 66.

[6] Although the term 'rule' is not defined under s 150, it is generally assumed that, subject to the reservations set out in the section itself, it will encompass any rule set out in the FSMA or any rule created by the FSA or other competent authority further to a power granted by the FSMA itself: A Hudson, *The Law of Finance*, 1st edn (London, Sweet and Maxwell, 2009) 26.55

[7] eg, the Markets in Financial Instruments Directive (MiFID) 2004/39/EC ([2004] OJ L145), whose provisions are incorporated into English law by means of rules contained in the Financial Services Authority Handbook: see K Stanton, 'The Neighbour Principle in the 21st Century: Yesterday's Revolution' (2012) 20 *Tort Law Review* 61, 74.

[8] Directive 2004/35/EC of the European Parliament and of the Council of 21 April 2004 on environmental liability with regard to the prevention and remedying of environmental damage (Environmental Liability Directive) [2004] OJ L143/156, 30 April 2004.

[9] S Wolf and N Stanley, *Wolf and Stanley on Environmental Law*, 5th edn (Abingdon, Routledge, 2011) 11.19. See also L Kramer, *EU Environmental Law*, 7th edn (London, Sweet & Maxwell, 2011); JH Jans and HHB Vedder, *European Environmental Law: After Lisbon*, 4th rev edn (Groningen, Europa Law Publishing, 2011); M Lee, *EU Environmental Law: Challenges, Change and Decision-Making* (Oxford, Hart Publishing, 2005). On this basis, this chapter will equally not consider the Unfair Commercial Practices Directive 2005/29/EC [2005] OJ L149/22, introduced into UK law by means of the Consumer Protection from Unfair Trading Regulations SI 2008/1277, on the basis that, at present, the Regulations do not give consumers the right to start civil actions to obtain compensation or other remedies and therefore involve public enforcement rather than private redress. For criticism, see the Law Commission 2012 Report No 332, *Consumer Redress for Misleading and Aggressive Practices*.

The case is even clearer in the area of competition law where the Competition Act 1998 replaced the pre-existing statutory framework for regulating competition law within the UK with a new regime modelled on the competition law provisions of the Treaty of Rome, now Articles 101 and 102 TFEU. Section 60 of the 1998 Act goes so far as to provide that the courts should so far as is possible (having regard to any relevant differences between the provisions concerned) determine questions relating to competition within the UK in a manner which is consistent with EU law. The aim, it has been remarked, is to ensure that EU and UK competition law develop in tandem and thereby ease the regulatory burden on businesses by applying in a UK context a series of rules with which they are familiar at EU level.[10] In fact, all Member States have implemented national competition rules which are broadly similar to the competition law provisions in Articles 101 and 102 TFEU; Council Regulation (EC) No 1/2003 establishing a pan-European framework for co-operation between the Commission and the judiciaries of the Member States.[11] In its recent consultation on options for encouraging private actions in competition law, the UK Department for Business, Innovation and Skills (BIS) was at pains to stress that any measures to improve private enforcement would have to complement public enforcement, enhancing overall the benefits of the competition regime to the UK economy.[12] As Stanton has argued, this may lead to divergence from traditional tort law policy, for example, it is clear that the primary function of competition law is deterrence which is not the focus of English tort law generally.[13] These specific regulatory areas therefore have little to add to a study of general tort law and will not be examined in this chapter.[14]

The focus of this chapter is therefore on the influence of EU Directives on core tort law principle and the extent to which evidence of 'Europeanisation' may be identified. It will focus on four important areas of tort law: liability for defective products, workplace accidents, road accidents, and the development of defamation claims against Internet service providers (ISPs). Council Directive 85/374/

[10] S Goodman, 'The Competition Act, Section 60: The Governing Principles Clause' (1999) 20 *European Competition Law Review* 73.

[11] Council Regulation (EC) No 1/2003 establishing a pan-European framework for co-operation between the Commission and the judiciaries of the Member States of 16 December 2002 on the implementation of the rules on competition laid down in Articles 81 and 82 of the Treaty [2003] OJ L1, implemented by the Competition Act 1998 and Other Enactments (Amendment) Regulations 2004 SI 2004/1261 in the United Kingdom. This is part of a policy of 'decentralised enforcement' by the European Commission, which seeks to empower national courts to enforce competition law while maintaining a certain degree of uniformity amongst Member States.

[12] BIS, *Private Actions in Competition Law: A Consultation on Options for Reform* (April 2012).

[13] Stanton, 'The Neighbour Principle' (n 7) 75. See also BIS, *Private Actions* (n 12) para 3.8.

[14] See K Stanton, 'Legislating for Economic Loss' in TT Arvind and J Steele, *Tort Law and the Legislature: Common Law, Statute and the Dynamics of Legal Change* (Oxford, Hart Publishing, 2012) 278: 'These torts exist as part of a wider regulatory scheme, and it would be very misleading to view them in isolation'. One might raise a similar point in relation to discrimination law which may give rise to a claim for breach of statutory duty, but is best treated as a distinct area of law which its own policy rationales: see E Ellis and P Watson, *EU Anti-Discrimination Law*, 2nd edn (Oxford, Oxford University Press, 2012); S Fredman, *Discrimination Law*, 2nd edn (Oxford, Clarendon Press, 2011).

EEC, commonly known as the Product Liability Directive,[15] is perhaps the most well-known of these examples. By imposing strict liability on manufacturers for defective products, it strikes at the heart of *Donoghue v Stevenson* fault-based liability.[16] Nevertheless, directives, such as Council Directive 89/391/EEC on Health and Safety of Workers at Work,[17] the Electronic Commerce Directive 2000/31/EC,[18] and other Council Directives, whose aim is to ensure that compulsory motor vehicle insurance allows all passengers who are victims of road accidents to be compensated for the injury or loss they have suffered,[19] are also relevant. These Directives do not create new areas of tort law, but do have the potential to affect the operation of core tort law principles, for example, by determining safety standards in relation to workplace accidents, providing defences for online intermediaries sued for defamation, and affecting the ability of insurers to rely on doctrines such as causation and contributory negligence to limit or exclude liability arising from road accidents. Transposition into national legislation has rendered the European character of these changes less obvious and one of the aims of this chapter is to highlight why the often overlooked European background to these measures is of importance in terms of interpretation and analysis. Faced with provisions which seek to bring English law closer to standards applicable across the Member States of the European Union, the English courts (and legislator) must determine to what extent English tort law policy must give way to European policy initiatives. Are we moving to what some commentators have called the gradual harmonisation of European private law by directives?[20]

[15] Council Directive 85/374/EEC of 25 July 1985 on the approximation of the laws, regulations and administrative provisions of the Member States concerning liability for defective products (Product Liability Directive) [1985] OJ L210/29.

[16] *Donoghue v Stevenson* [1932] AC 562.

[17] Council Directive 89/391/EEC of 12 June 1989 on the introduction of measures to encourage improvements in the safety and health of workers at work (Health and Safety of Workers at Work) [1989] OJ L183/1.

[18] Directive 2000/31/EC of the European Parliament and of the Council of 8 June 2000 on certain legal aspects of information society services, in particular electronic commerce, in the Internal Market (Directive on Electronic Commerce) [2000] OJ L178/1, implemented by the Electronic Commerce (EC Directive) Regulations 2002 SI 2002/2013.

[19] See, for example, Council Directive 72/166/EEC of 24 April 1972 on the approximation of the laws of Member States relating to insurance against civil liability in respect of the use of motor vehicles, and to the enforcement of the obligation to insure against such liability (OJ, English Special Edition 1972 (II), p. 360); Second Council Directive 84/5/EEC of 30 December 1983 on the approximation of the laws of the Member States relating to insurance against civil liability in respect of the use of motor vehicles [1984] OJ L8/17; Third Council Directive 90/232/EEC of 14 May 1990 on the approximation of the laws of the Member States relating to insurance against civil liability in respect of the use of motor vehicles [1990] OJ L129/33.

[20] See P-C Müller-Graff, 'EU Directives as a Means of Private Law Unification' in A Hartkamp et al, *Towards a European Civil Code*, 4th rev edn (The Hague, Kluwer, 2010); H Rösler, 'Europeanisation of Private Law through Directives: Determining Factors and Modalities of Implementation' (2010) 11 *European Journal of Law Reform* 305.

I. English Tort Law and the Product Liability Directive

Council Directive 85/374/EEC of 25 July 1985 concerning liability for defective products (the Product Liability Directive) introduced a common regime of strict liability for defective products into European Member States. Its preamble states that

> approximation of the laws of the Member States concerning the liability of the producer for damage caused by the defectiveness of his products is necessary because the existing divergences may distort competition and affect the movement of goods within the common market and entail a differing degree of protection of the consumer against damage caused by a defective product to his health or property . . . [L]iability without fault on the part of the producer is the sole means of adequately solving the problem, peculiar to our age of increasing technicality, of a fair apportionment of the risks inherent in modern technological production.[21]

The move towards a strict liability regime for faulty products in tort reflected developments in the United States,[22] where the 1965 US Second Restatement of Torts, section 402A provided that a seller would be strictly liable for defective products causing physical harm to the ultimate user or consumer, or to his property.[23] Further, the thalidomide tragedy, where a drug prescribed for pregnant women was later found to cause birth defects,[24] highlighted both the difficulties for litigants in obtaining compensation for defective products under a fault-based regime as well as the international impact of a globally distributed harmful product.[25] The English and Scottish Law Commissions and the Pearson Commission in the late 1970s had both recommended the adoption of a strict liability regime for personal injuries[26] caused by defective products.[27] Equally, the Council of Europe had endorsed strict liability in its Convention on Product Liability of

[21] Product Liability Directive, recitals 1 and 2.

[22] A key case being *Greenman v Yuba Power Products Inc* 377 P 2d 897 (Cal 1963) where the Supreme Court of California found a manufacturer strictly liable in tort for defective articles causing injury to a human being.

[23] US Second Restatement of Torts 1965, s 402 A. (Special Liability of Seller of Product for Physical Harm to User or Consumer): (1) One who sells any product in a defective condition unreasonably dangerous to the user or consumer or to his property is subject to liability for physical harm thereby caused to the ultimate user or consumer, or to his property, if (a) the seller is engaged in the business of selling such a product, and (b) it is expected to and does reach the user or consumer without substantial change in the condition in which it is sold. (2) The rule stated in subsection (1) applies although (a) the seller has exercised all possible care in the preparation and sale of his product, and (b) the user or consumer has not bought the product from or entered into any contractual relation with the seller. See GL Priest, 'Strict Products Liability: The Original Intent' (1988–89) 10 *Cardozo Law Review* 2301.

[24] See H Teff and CR Munro, *Thalidomide: The Legal Aftermath* (Westmead, Farnborough, Saxon House, 1976).

[25] See J Stapleton, *Product Liability* (London, Butterworths, 1994) 42–46; S Whittaker, *Liability for Products: English Law, French Law and European Harmonization* (Oxford, Oxford University Press, 2005) 432.

[26] The Law Commissions expressed doubts that strict liability was needed for property damage (para 121). This point was not dealt with by the Pearson Commission as it fell outside its terms of reference.

[27] English and Scottish Law Commission, *Liability for Defective Products* (Law Com No 82, Cmnd 6831, 1977); *Royal Commission on Civil Liability and Compensation for Personal Injury (Pearson Commission)* (Cmnd 7054, vol 1, ch 22, 1978).

1977.[28] The European Commission first drafted a proposal for reform in 1976,[29] which led to a fierce European debate which finally culminated in the 1985 Directive. Commentators noted, however, that the final version did not simply follow the then US model which was seen by many as a warning against an explosion of litigation and damages.[30]

Member States were given three years from the date of notification to comply with the Directive.[31] The United Kingdom, on 1 March 1988,[32] brought into force Part 1 of the Consumer Protection Act 1987, section 1(1) of which states that:

> This Part shall have effect for the purposes of making such provision as is necessary in order to comply with the product liability Directive and shall be construed accordingly.

Part I of the 1987 Act thus provides the clearest example of European Union law changing core tort law principle. The most famous case in English tort law is undoubtedly that of *Donoghue v Stevenson*[33]: the snail in the ginger beer bottle. Mrs Donoghue claimed that a bottle of ginger beer, purchased for her by her friend, had contained the decomposed remains of a snail; in other words she had suffered personal injury resulting from a defective bottle of ginger beer. In finding that the manufacturer owed a duty of care to the ultimate consumer of his product, the court determined that liability would arise on the basis of fault. Section 2(1) of the Act, in contrast, renders the manufacturer of a product (and others dealing with it) strictly liable where the personal injury or property damage (as defined by the Act)[34] has been caused wholly or partly by a defect in a product. The Act extends liability beyond manufacturers (or rather 'producers' as defined by sections 1(2) and 2(2)(a)) to include own-branders[35] and parties importing goods into the European Union.[36]

[28] Strasbourg Convention on Products Liability in regard to personal injury and death. See JG Fleming, 'Draft Convention on Products Liability (Council of Europe)' (1975) 23 *American Journal of Comparative Law* 729.

[29] Proposal for a Directive: [1976] OJ C241/9. This led to a revised proposal in 1979 ([1979] OJ C271/3) and the final directive was only reached after considerable debate and lobbying by industry, trade, insurance and consumer groups. The final result therefore differs considerably from the Commission's initial proposal.

[30] N Reich, 'Product Safety and Product Liability: An Analysis of the EEC Council Directive of 25 July 1985 on the Approximation of the Laws, Regulations, and Administrative Provisions of the Member States concerning Liability for Defective Products' (1986) 9 *Journal of Consumer Policy* 133, 136.

[31] Product Liability Directive, art 19.

[32] In so doing, it was more timely that many of its European counterparts, notably France which only implemented the Directive on May 23, 1998 (see Act No 389-98 of May 19, 1998). The final version only entered force in April 2006 – Act No 2006-406 of 5 April 2006 – and now constitutes Arts 1386-1 to 1386-18 of the French Civil Code. For a more detailed discussion of French product liability, see S Whittaker, *Liability for Products: English Law, French Law and European Harmonization* (Oxford, Oxford University Press, 2005).

[33] *Donoghue v Stevenson* [1932] AC 562.

[34] See Consumer Protection Act (1987), hereafter CPA 1987, ss. 5(3) and 5(4).

[35] CPA 1987, s 2(2)(b).

[36] ibid, s 2(2)(c). Liability under the Act is nevertheless not as wide as the common law, which extends to repairers, fitters, erectors and assemblers. Further, supplier liability is confined to an informational duty to enable the consumer to trace the producer through the chain of supply, as stated at s 2(3), and thus the primary source of supplier liability will continue to be the law of contract.

In seeking to remove divergences distorting competition between Member States and to provide a common level of protection for consumers injured by defective products, the Directive subjects English tort law to a new regime, imposed and supervised by the European Union itself.

A. Product Liability under the Consumer Protection Act 1987: Bringing EU Standards into English Tort Law

The aim of the Directive is to harmonise product liability across the European Union. Somewhat to the surprise of many, the CJEU in 2002 clarified that the Product Liability Directive is a maximum, rather than minimum, harmonisation directive, that is, imposes a common standard which Member States may not exceed.[37] States, such as France,[38] which had sought to improve on the protection provided, were found to have failed properly to transpose the Directive; the CJEU holding that

> the purpose of the Directive in establishing a harmonised system of civil liability on the part of producers in respect of damage caused by defective products is to ensure undistorted competition between traders, to facilitate the free movement of goods and to avoid differences in levels of consumer protection.[39]

Such a ruling does, however, seem at odds with Article 13 of the Directive which provides that the Directive would not affect 'any rights which an injured person may have according to the rules of the law of contractual or non-contractual [i.e. tortious] liability or a special liability system existing at the moment when this Directive is notified'. Subsequent case law has clarified that it is a question of the scope of the Directive. Law outside the Directive, for example for breach of a contractual warranty, will not be affected. Controversially, provisions which provide for compensation for matters not covered by the Directive, for example damage to commercial property, may also be subject to a separate regime at national law.[40]

[37] Case C-52/00 *Commission v France* [2002] ECR I-3827; Case C-154/00 *Commission v Greece* [2002] ECR I-3879; Case C-183/00 *González Sánchez v Medicina Asturiana SA* [2002] ECR I-3901. Note also subsequent litigation: Case C-177/04 *EC Commission v France* (C177/04) [2006] ECR I-2461 (failure to take the necessary measures to comply fully with the judgment in Case C-52/00 *Commission* v *France*) and Case C-402/03 *Skov Æg v Bilka Lavprisvarehus A/S* [2006] ECR I-199 (liability of supplier).

[38] France was found to have failed properly to transpose the Directive by (a) providing that suppliers would be liable to the same extent as producers, (b) making some of the defences of a producer contingent upon appropriate steps having been taken to prevent the harmful consequences of the defect and (c) compensating damage even under the €500 threshold.

[39] Case C-52/00 *Commission v France* (n 37) para 17. Whittaker has convincingly argued that such goals are impossible to attain in view of diversity in the implementation of the Directives and the broader context, notably social security and first party insurance, in which the law operates: see Whittaker, *Liability for Products* (n 32). Note, also, his earlier work: 'The EEC Directive on Product Liability' (1985) 5 *Yearbook of European Law* 233.

[40] See Case C-258/08 *Société Moteurs Leroy Somer v Société Dalkia France* [2009] ECR I-4733. See J-S Borghetti, 'Le dommage réparable en matière de responsabilité du fait des produits défectueux' (2008) *Recueil Dalloz* 2318; J Rochfeld, 'Les ambiguïtés des directives d'harmonisation totale. Nouvelle

Maximum harmonisation is thus limited to the scope of the Directive. The force of the Directive is further weakened by political compromises which have led to certain provisions being optional, for example the development risks defence at Article 7(e),[41] which inevitably leads to divergence amongst Member States.

As will be seen from the survey of English case law below, while maximum harmonisation has not been a problem in England and Wales – the Conservative government of the time seeking to restrict liability as much as possible to minimise the cost of liability for industry[42] – the courts have struggled to interpret Part 1 of the 1987 Act according to the section 1(1) obligation to construe the law in compliance with the Directive. In particular, the legacy of fault-based liability has proven particularly difficult to shake.

i. From Negligence to Strict Liability: Interpreting the Concept of 'Defect' Purposively

As discussed in chapter two, in transposing EU law into national legislation, the courts are expected to adopt a purposive approach to interpretation, that is, one which will construe the resultant legislation as far as possible in the light of the objectives and purposes of the directive rather than focusing on the literal meaning of the words used. This presents particular challenges to the English courts in terms of unfamiliar interpretative techniques, but also in resisting the temptation to adhere to traditional forms of reasoning. The treatment of the concept of 'defect' – a central concept in the Directive and Act – represents a good example of the tendency of the English courts to resort to type: to adopt traditional common law reasoning instead of the purposive rules of construction of the European court. This is particularly problematic in relation to a strict liability rule. English courts are more familiar with fault-based liability, influenced by cost/benefit analysis whereby the benefits of a product are balanced against the magnitude of the danger inherent in the product and the cost of preventing that danger. Such an approach favours manufacturers and is thus inconsistent with the aims of the Directive to give a common level of consumer protection. As will be seen, despite the good intentions of the courts,[43] the ambiguous nature of the key concept of 'defect' in the Product Liability

répartition des compétences communautaires et interne' (2009) *Recueil Dalloz* 2047 and Case C-495/10 *Centre hospitalier universitaire de Besançon v Thomas Dutrueux and Caisse primaire d'assurance maladie du Jura* 27 October 2011 [2012] 2 CMLR 1. See, generally, R Sefton-Green, 'Multiculturalism, Europhilia and Harmonisation: Harmony or Disharmony' (2010) 6 *Utrecht Law Review* 50.

[41] Product Liability Directive, Art 15(1)(b). Art 15(1)(a) rendered the inclusion of primary agricultural products and game optional, but this was since overtaken by Directive 1999/34/EC/OJ 1999 L/1 which included such products within the Directive in the wake of the BSE crisis. Further options exist whether to place a cap on the producer's total liability for damage resulting from a death or personal injury (Art 16) and whether to allow a defence of contributory negligence (Art 8(2)).

[42] Whittaker, *Liability for Products* (n 32) 665.

[43] *Pickstone v Freemans plc* [1988] ICR 697; *Litster v Forth Dry Dock & Engineering Co Ltd* [1989] ICR 341.

Directive has led commentators to question just how 'strict' liability under the UK Act actually is.[44]

According to section 3(1) of the Act, a defect is said to exist in a product 'if the safety of the product is not such as persons generally are entitled to expect'.[45] Section 3(2) gives further guidance, providing that in assessing whether a defect exists, the court should take into account all the circumstances, including:

(a) (i) the manner in which and purposes for which the product has been marketed; (ii) the get-up (or packaging) of the product; (iii) the use of any mark (for example the 'kite mark') in relation to the product; (iv) any instructions for, or warnings with respect to doing or refraining from doing anything with or in relation to the product;
(b) what might reasonably be expected to be done with or in relation to the product; and
(c) the time when the product was supplied by its producer to another. It is irrelevant that products supplied after that time are generally safer than the product supplied to the claimant.[46]

This definition lacks the precision usually found in a UK statute and has been rightly criticised as both circular and vague. Who are 'persons generally': consumers? manufacturers? random members of the public? More importantly, how does one assess what they may legitimately expect? There is no definition of what one is 'entitled' to expect in terms of safety. This raises immediate problems in relation to products such as knives which, by their very nature, may cause harm due to their sharpness, but are nevertheless useful when used properly. Further if one chooses a cheap product, is it legitimate to expect the same level of safety as a top of the range model double in price? In a number of early cases, such as *Richardson v LRC Products*,[47] the English courts appeared reluctant to stray too far from the negligence standard. In this case, Mrs Richardson had become pregnant when a condom used by her husband failed. In the absence of any convincing explanation for its failure, the judge examined the care taken by the manufacturer in producing the goods and noted that its standards exceeded the relevant British Standard. On this basis, the action was unsuccessful. While the decision may be justified on the basis that the public do not expect condoms to be 100 per cent effective, it is

[44] One notable critic has been Professor Jane Stapleton: see, eg, 'Products Liability Reform: Real or Illusory?' (1986) 6 *Oxford Journal of Legal Studies* 392 and *Product Liability* (n 25). See also C Newdick, 'The Future of Negligence in Product Liability' (1987) 103 *Law Quarterly Review* 288.

[45] CPA 1987, s 3(1), implementing Art 6 of the Directive. S 3(1) further defines 'safety' to include safety with respect to products comprised in that product and safety in the context of risks of damage to property, as well as in the context of risks of death and personal injury.

[46] Expanding on the wording of Art 6 of the Directive.

[47] *Abouzaid v Mothercare (UK) Ltd* [2000] Lloyd's Rep Med 280 (Ian Kennedy J). See also *Worsley v Tambrands Ltd* [2000] PIQR P95 (toxic shock syndrome resulting from use of tampon) and the highly questionable decision of *Foster v Biosil* (2001) 59 BMLR 178 (CC (Central London)) (ruptured breast implant). Freeman comments that in these three cases, the claimants fared no better under the Act than they would under the common law action in negligence: R Freeman, 'Strict Product Liability Laws' [2001] *Journal of Personal Injury Law* 26. 'Early' is a relative term in that the Act has produced very little case law. The reasons for this will be discussed below.

difficult to reconcile the judge's reasoning with a regime of strict liability, particularly as the judge made no effort to consider the Directive, focusing solely on the wording of section 3 and general case law.

Subsequent case law has, nevertheless, focused more on the wording of the Directive and its recitals. In *Abouzaid v Mothercare (UK) Ltd*,[48] Pill LJ relied on recital 6 to the Directive to determine that the standard for section 3 is 'the safety which the public at large is entitled to expect' and drew a distinction between liability in negligence (which would not have arisen on the facts) and liability under the Act. The leading case remains that of *A v National Blood Authority*.[49] This was a group action brought by 114 claimants who had been infected with the virus Hepatitis C through blood transfusions which had used blood or blood products obtained from infected donors. Although the risk of the virus had been known since at least the 1970s, it was, at the time of infection, impossible to detect. Screening for the virus was available only from September 1991. On that basis, the defendants argued that the most that the public could have legitimately expected up to that date was that all reasonable precautions would be carried out, not that the blood would be 100 per cent clean. In the view of the judge, this was a blatant attempt to re-introduce fault-based ideas. This was contrary to the purpose of the Directive. Section 3 would be confined to *relevant* circumstances,[50] and the steps taken by the manufacturer to avoid the risk would not be relevant in a no-fault regime. On this basis, 'avoidability' of the harmful characteristic would be ignored,[51] as would the impracticality, cost or difficulty of taking precautionary measures and the benefit to society and utility of the project.[52] Burton J thus expressly rejected a cost/benefit analysis. The public at large were entitled to expect that the blood transfusion would be free from infection. Burton J further cast doubt on earlier decisions such as *Richardson*.[53]

What is interesting about the judgment of Burton J is his use of EU law and reference to case law from outside the common law world including case law from Germany, France and the Netherlands. More questionable is his choice to refer to the wording of the Directive, rather than the UK Act, in applying the tests under section 3 and section 4(1)(e) of the Act. As stated in chapter two, the

[48] *The Times*, 20 February 2001 (buckle on elastic strap fixing cover to pushchair amounted to defect in design). This was the first full judgment of the Court of Appeal on the Act. His Lordship also made reference to *A v National Blood Authority* [2001] 3 All ER 289, 334 which provided that 'the court will act as . . . the appointed representative of the public at large'.

[49] *A v National Blood Authority* [2001] 3 All ER 289. Comment: C Hodges, 'Compensating Patients' (2001) 117 *Law Quarterly Review* 528; G Howells and M Mildred, 'Infected Blood: Defect and Discoverability: A First Exposition of the EC Product Liability Directive' (2002) 65 *Modern Law Review* 95.

[50] This is not obvious from the wording of s 3(2), which states that 'all the circumstances shall be taken into account': see Hodges, 'Compensating Patients' (n 49) 530.

[51] 'Indeed . . . had it been intended that it would be included as a derogation from, or at any rate a palliation of [the purpose of the Directive] then it would certainly have been mentioned': *A v National Blood Authority* (n 49) 336.

[52] Except in the context of whether, with full information and proper knowledge, the public had and should have accepted the risk.

[53] See Burton J in *A v National Blood Authority* (n 49) 319.

doctrine of indirect effect requires the national courts to interpret existing legislation in line with EU law.[54] This is also expressly stated at section 1(1) of the 1987 Act.[55] It does not, however, require Member States to use the Directive as the source of law. As Lord Steyn has commented, the role of the domestic court is to apply the concepts of the Directive within national law, while appreciating their autonomous meanings so as to ensure uniform application of the Directive across Member States so far as possible.[56] This means, therefore, that the domestic court should focus on the relevant *national* legal provisions, but interpret them as far as possible in light of the wording and the purpose of the relevant provisions of EU law.[57] In Arnull's view, Burton J went further and, in so doing, threatened to undermine the distinction between the vertical and horizontal direct effect of directives. He concluded, however, that the sheer size of the case and the impact of the ECJ ruling in *European Commission v United Kingdom*[58] on the interpretation of the Act (discussed below) rendered *A* a special case and that such an approach would be unlikely to be widely used.

Subsequent case law has supported Arnull's analysis. In *Sam B v McDonald's Restaurants Limited*,[59] the claimants consisted of a number of children, all of whom had visited a branch of McDonalds with an adult. Each had been scalded by a spilt hot drink from a lidded cup whose lid had become detached. The resulting burns were in many cases full thickness and the scarring and tenderness permanent. The judge, Field J, found that the defendants had not been negligent and that any claim would rest on section 3 of the Act. His Honour found that:

> Persons generally expect tea or coffee purchased to be consumed on the premises to be hot . . . They expect precautions to be taken to guard against this risk but not to the point that they are denied the basic utility of being able to buy hot drinks to be consumed on the premises from a cup with the lid off. Given that the staff were trained to cap the drinks securely and given the capabilities of the cups and lids used, I am satisfied that the safety of the hot drinks served by McDonald's was such as persons generally are entitled to expect.[60]

In applying the test of Burton J, with reference both to the Directive and its recitals,[61] it is interesting to note that the court addresses the question of 'safety' by taking account of the benefits to the public of being able to purchase hot drinks and the precautions taken by the defendants to serve the drinks safely in addition

[54] Case 14/83 *Von Colson v Land Nordrhein-Westfalen* [1984] ECR 1891; Case C-106/89 *Marleasing SA v La Comercial Internacional de Alimentacion SA* [1990] ECR I-4135.

[55] CPA 1987, s 1(1): 'This Part shall have effect for the purposes of making such provision as is necessary in order to comply with the product liability Directive and shall be construed accordingly.'

[56] *Director General of Fair Trading v First National Bank Plc* [2001] UKHL 52; [2002] 1 AC 481, para. 32. The case concerned Council Directive 93/13/EEC [1993] OJ L95/29) as implemented in the Unfair Terms in Consumer Contracts Regulations 1994 (SI 1994/3159), but his Lordship makes a generally valid point.

[57] A Arnull, 'Product Liability and the Effect of Directives' (2001) 26 *European Law Review* 213, 213–14.

[58] *European Commission v United Kingdom* Case C-300/ 95 [1997] ECR I-2649; [1997] 3 CMLR 923.

[59] *Sam B v McDonald's Restaurants Limited* [2002] EWHC 490 (QBD).

[60] Ibid, para 80,

[61] Ibid, paras 71–73.

to the more legitimate question of the capabilities of the cups and lids used. In the later case of *Tesco Stores Ltd v Pollard*,[62] the Court of Appeal favoured a similar approach, finding a cap to a bottle of dishwasher powder not to be defective when the producer had used a child-resistant closure (CRC) cap which was more difficult to open than if it had used an ordinary screwtop, but was less safe than that specified in the British Standard certificate.[63] In the view of Laws LJ, the public were only entitled to expect that the bottle would be more difficult to open than if it had an ordinary screwtop.[64] The Court of Appeal made no effort to consider the Directive or its recitals, but focused on the wording of the English statute. Commentators have noted that the Court of Appeal's robust approach to interpretation may have set back the trend towards a more purposive construction of the Act.[65]

Despite *A* and its strong advocacy of an approach which focused on the Product Liability Directive and its recitals, the English courts do seem to be reverting to type and applying traditional tort principles of construction. In particular, one may note that in relation to the defective design cases of *Sam B* and *Pollard*, the shadow of the traditional cost/benefit fault-based test is difficult to escape. Even in *Abouzaid*, one might question whether the court's concern that more could have been done to render the product safe[66] is wholly consistent with the view of Burton J that avoidability of the accident was not a relevant concern. Such case law suggests that English tort law appears, in relation to defective design cases at least, to be adopting a position arguably closer to that of the US Third Restatement of Torts: Product Liability,[67] which has reverted to fault-based liability in relation to design and marketing defects, than the more purposive approach required by EU law.

ii. Guidance from the CJEU: The Development Risks Defence, the Definition of Damage and the 10 Year Long-Stop

An important element in the transposition of directives into national law is that of EU supervision, notably the ability of the national court to make references to the

[62] *Tesco Stores Ltd v Pollard* [2006] EWCA Civ 393; (2006) 150 SJLB 537 (were child-resistant closure caps defective?)

[63] For criticism, see M Mildred [2006] *Journal of Personal Injury Law* C130, who argues that there may be good commonsense grounds for tying the public expectation test to that of the British Standard. Contrast *Palmer v Palmer* [2006] EWHC 1284 (QBD (Admin)): 'Klunk Klip' device, which introduced slack into seat-belts to make them more comfortable, was defective.

[64] *Pollard* [2006] EWCA Civ 393, para.18.

[65] M Mildred, 'Pitfalls in Product Liability' [2007] *Journal of Personal Injury Law* 141.

[66] eg, a non-elasticated method of attachment or instructions to fasten the straps from behind the seat unit, together with a warning: Pill LJ (n 48) para 27.

[67] See Third Restatement Torts: Product Liability § 2(b) where a product is defined as 'defective in design when the foreseeable risks of harm posed by the product could have been reduced or avoided by the adoption of a reasonable alternative design.' Equally, a product is 'defective because of inadequate instructions or warnings when the foreseeable risk of harm posed by the product could have been reduced or avoided by the provisions of reasonable instructions or warnings'. Strict liability is retained only for manufacturing defects.

CJEU on points of interpretation under Article 267 TFEU and the ability of the Commission itself, as guardian of the Treaties, to bring an action before the CJEU if it believes that a State is in breach of its obligation to transpose the directive correctly.[68] This serves, of course, to distinguish such legislation from purely domestic legal provisions.

This process has indeed been utilised in relation to the UK transposition of the Product Liability Directive. The resultant litigation is helpful in identifying the relationship between national and EU courts in this field. In April 1989, the European Commission initiated infringement proceedings against the UK which alleged that Part 1 of the 1987 Act did not properly transpose the Directive into English law, as required by Article 19 of the Directive. The case concerned the controversial development risks defence, inserted after considerable lobbying by industrialists. Article 7(e) provides for an optional defence[69] where 'the state of scientific and technical knowledge at the time when [the producer] put the product into circulation was not such as to enable the existence of the defect to be discovered.'

Section 4(1)(e) of the UK statute introduced, however, a differently worded provision:

> the state of scientific and technical knowledge at the relevant time was not such that a producer of products of the same description as the product in question *might be expected* to have discovered the defect if it had existed in his products while they were under his control. (emphasis added)

Comparing the two provisions, while the Directive suggests that the producer must establish, objectively, that the knowledge available at the time of circulation would not have alerted the defendant to the particular risk, section 4(1)(e) appears more generous. Its wording indicates that the producer need only show that a 'reasonable producer', that is, another producer in the same market, would not have known of the risks in question. Such a test is reminiscent of the negligence test for breach of duty with a reversed burden of proof; an argument which leading academics did not fail to raise.[70]

[68] Art 258 TFEU enables the Commission to initiate legal proceedings against a Member State that has adopted or maintained in force rules or administrative practices which contravene EU law. Art 260 TFEU provides that 'If the European Court of Justice finds that a Member State has failed to fulfil an obligation under the treaty, the State shall be required to take the necessary measures to comply with the judgement of the Court of Justice'.

[69] This defence is optional to Member States (see Art 15(1)(b)), although it has generally been implemented within the European Union except in Finland and Luxembourg. Spain excludes the defence for food and medicinal products and France excludes the defence for products derived from the human body. Germany has permitted liability for development risks in the area of pharmaceutical products since 1978.

[70] This matter provoked a considerable academic debate: see, for example, J Stapleton, *Product Liability* (n 25) and C Newdick, 'The Development Risk Defence of the Consumer Protection Act 1987' (1988) 47 *Cambridge Law Journal* 455. Mildred suggests that the real issue is that the wording of Art 7(e) is not clear as a result of a compromise form of wording agreed during negotiations which glossed over national differences: M Mildred, 'The Development Risks Defence' in D Fairgrieve (ed), *Product Liability in Comparative Perspective* (Cambridge, Cambridge University Press, 2005) 169.

In Case C-300/95 *European Commission v United Kingdom*,[71] the ECJ, perhaps surprisingly, rejected the Commission's claim. It held that Article 7(e) imposed an objective test on the producer as to the state of scientific and technical knowledge at the time the product was put in circulation. This would include the most advanced level of knowledge in the relevant field, provided that such knowledge was accessible at the relevant time. In the view of the court, there was no clear indication that section 4(1)(e) was inconsistent with a proper interpretation of the Directive. Whilst the section *could* be interpreted in a broader sense, the court held that its wording did not suggest that the availability of the defence depended on the subjective knowledge of the producer. There was, in any event, no English decision which indicated that the English courts would interpret the section in a way which would conflict with their duty, stated in section 1(1) of the Act, to construe the Act in accordance with the Directive. Advocate General Tesauro suggested that, in this light, the Commission's application had been 'overhasty, to say the least'. One might consider that, due to the absence of case law, English law had a fortunate escape.[72]

As Craig and de Búrca acknowledge, the ECJ in this decision was essentially relying on the doctrine of indirect effect and that national courts would construe their domestic legislation as far as possible in the light of the wording and purpose of the Product Liability Directive to achieve the result pursued by the latter.[73] Burton J in *A & Others v National Blood Authority*[74] indeed sought to follow this decision and focused on the wording of Article 7(e) of the Directive and the judgment of the ECJ in ruling that it would be inconsistent with the purpose of the Directive if a producer, knowing of a risk of infection to blood by means of accessible information, could continue to supply the product without liability simply because he or she could not identify in which of the products the defect would occur.[75] The Court of Appeal in *Abouzaid v Mothercare (UK) Ltd*[76] equally rejected a defence that as no record of any comparable incident had been recorded by the Department of Trade and Industry accident database, the state of scientific and technical knowledge did not indicate a problem at the relevant time. The defence existed to deal with technical advances, and a simple practical test would have

[71] Case C-300/95 *European Commission v United Kingdom* [1997] ECR I-2649; [1997] 3 CMLR 923. Comment: C Hodges, 'Development Risks: Unanswered Questions' (1998) 61 *Modern Law Review* 560.

[72] Howells, however, argues that this argument demonstrates a lack of understanding how UK case law works. In view of the costs of litigation, it was very unlikely that there would have been enough litigation to allow the principles to be tested regularly: G Howells, 'Product Liability and the European Tort Landscape' in R Schulze (ed), *Compensation of Private Losses: The Evolution of Torts in European Business Law* (Munich, Sellier, 2011) 72.

[73] Craig and de Búrca, *EU Law* (n 4) 426. See Case C-106/89 *Marleasing SA v La Comercial Internacional de Alimentacion SA* [1990] ECR I-4135.

[74] *A & Others v National Blood Authority* [2001] 3 All ER 289. Contrast, however, the different application of the defence in the Dutch case of *Schulten v Sanquin Bloedvoorziening*, District Court of Amsterdam, 3 February 1999 NJ 1999, 621.

[75] *A & Others v National Blood Authority* (n 74) 340.

[76] *The Times*, 20 February 2001.

revealed how an accident could arise with a buckle on an elastic strap. Further, Pill LJ doubted whether an accident database fell within the category of 'scientific and technical knowledge'.[77] Such case law does suggest a positive response by the English courts to the interpretative challenges posed by the Directive. It also highlights the role played by the Commission and CJEU in ensuring the correct application of the Directive in national law.

It must be noted, however, that for obvious political reasons, the Commission has only rarely brought actions against Member States for their faulty transposition of directives, preferring less confrontational methods. Equally, the intervention of the CJEU has been less helpful on other occasions in guiding national courts. In, for example, the Danish kidney case of *Veedfald*,[78] the ECJ avoided ruling on the question whether flushing a kidney with a defective fluid which rendered it unusable for transplant was personal injury or property damage under the Directive. It found that the term 'damage' was not defined in the Directive and so it was left to national legislatures to determine the precise content of the relevant heads of damage, provided that its rules did not impair the effectiveness of the Directive and were interpreted in the light of its wording and purpose.[79]

The *O'Byrne* litigation also serves to demonstrate the difficulties of relying on CJEU guidance under the Article 267 TFEU reference procedure. The case involved an application to substitute as defendant the parent company and manufacturer of the vaccine instead of its English subsidiary against whom the action had been originally brought. This involved a clash of national legislation with that introduced by the Directive. Section 35 of the UK Limitation Act 1980 grants a discretion to the court to substitute a new party. However, section 11A(3) of the same Act – implementing Article 11 of the Product Liability Directive – provides that an action shall not be brought after the expiration of the period of 10 years from the time the product was put into circulation. This raised the question whether it was still permissible to substitute a new party to the action under section 35 after the 10 year long-stop had expired.

The English High Court, at the request of both parties, made a preliminary reference to the European Court of Justice. In *O'Byrne v Sanofi Pasteur MSD Ltd*,[80] the ECJ held that the question of the substitution of parties after the 10 year long-stop was a matter for the national court to decide:

> [I]t is as a rule for national law to determine the conditions in accordance with which one party may be substituted for another in the context of such an action. A national

[77] Ibid, para 29.

[78] Case C-203/99 *Veedfald v Arhus Amtskommune* [2001] ECR 1–3569; [2003] 1 CMLR 1217. See G Howells (2002) 10 *European Review of Private Law* 847; P Rott, 'What is the Role of the ECJ in EC Private Law?' (2005) 1 *Hanse Law Review* 6.

[79] *Veedfald* (n 78) para 27, citing Case 14/83 *Von Colson and Kamann* [1984] ECR 891, para 26. Similarly, matters of procedure are left to the national courts subject to these principles, although the Directive does make specific provision for limitation (Arts 10 and 11).

[80] *O'Byrne v Sanofi Pasteur MSD Ltd* Case C-127/04 [2006] ECR I-1313; [2006] 1 WLR 1606.

> court . . . must, however, ensure that due regard is had to the personal scope of Directive 85/374, as established by articles 1 and 3 thereof.[81]

With this rather oblique statement, the matter was then referred back to the English courts.

Perhaps unsurprisingly, a second reference to the European Court of Justice was made in 2008.[82] The ECJ was asked, bluntly, whether the Directive, which sought to harmonise limitation periods for defective products, nevertheless permitted national legislation which allowed the substitution of one defendant for another after the expiry of the 10 year long-stop period. The Grand Chamber in 2009[83] held that where national legislation allowed for substitution of parties, it should *not* be applied in a way which permitted the producer to be sued after the expiry of the long-stop period even though the action had been begun within time, albeit against the wrong defendant. It did accept, however, that where the proceedings had been issued within time against a wholly owned subsidiary of the producer, the Product Liability Directive did not prevent the national court from substituting the producer for that subsidiary if the court had found that the putting into circulation of the product in question was, in fact, carried out by that producer.

Applying this ruling, the UK Supreme Court in *O'Byrne v Aventis Pasteur MSD Ltd*[84] held in 2010 that a new party could not be substituted in this case, despite the fact that the manufacturer wholly owned its English subsidiary. The ECJ's core ruling had been that a national rule allowing substitution should not be invoked against a producer after expiry of the 10-year period. The exception for wholly owned subsidiaries was interpreted narrowly to indicate a situation where, as a matter of fact, a distribution subsidiary was so closely involved with the parent producer that they could, in effect, also be regarded as a producer. This was not the case here. O'Byrne, therefore, finally lost his battle for compensation some 18 years after the initial injury had taken place.

What the *O'Byrne* and *Veedfald* sagas demonstrate is that even when a direct question is asked of the CJEU, one will not always obtain clear guidance; the European Court merely deferring to the national court subject to the principles of effectiveness and equivalence. Further, obtaining guidance may be a lengthy process and may raise new questions such as the meaning of 'the most advanced level of knowledge' or 'accessible knowledge' in relation to the development risks defence. In its 1997 decision, the Court acknowledged that these terms may lead to difficulties in interpretation which the national courts would have to resolve,

[81] Ibid, para 39. The ECJ did resolve, however, that a product was put into circulation for the purposes of s 11A(3) when it leaves the production process operated by the producer and enters a marketing process in the form in which it is offered to the public in order to be used or consumed: ibid, para 27.

[82] *OB v Aventis Pasteur* [2008] UKHL 34; [2008] 3 CMLR 10.

[83] Case C-358/08 *O'Byrne v Aventis Pasteur SA* [2009] ECR I-11305; [2010] 1 WLR 1375. Comment G Howells (2010) 3 ERCL 284.

[84] *O'Byrne v Aventis Pasteur MSD Ltd* [2010] UKSC 23; [2010] 1 WLR 1412, reversing Court of Appeal in [2007] EWCA Civ 966.

but that any such difficulties could be resolved by use of the Article 267 TFEU procedure, that is, by means of a (time-consuming) reference to the ECJ![85] To this may be added issues such as causation and non-material damage which are not dealt with by the Directive and thereby left to the national court to determine.[86] A national court is likely to adhere to its traditional tort principles – in English law, the 'but for' test for causation[87] and restrictive rules applying to pure economic loss claims.[88] The result is a maximum harmonisation directive subject to divergent national rules on causation and non-material damage. Howells has described the Directive as 'non-exhaustive full harmonisation' whereby EU rules cannot be deviated from but other regimes remain in place.[89] The result is, however, an ongoing risk of divergence between Member States on key issues to which the Commission remains worryingly complacent.[90]

B. How has the 1985 Product Liability Directive Changed Core Tort Law Principle?

The current regime thus leaves an active role for the national courts to supplement the core harmonisation regime established by the Directive. This arises due to deference by the CJEU to the national courts, but also from the unwillingness of the Commission, in its five yearly reviews of the Directive,[91] to engage in reform, bar the limited addition of primary agricultural products under the 1999 Directive.[92]

85 Case C-300/95 *European Commission v United Kingdom* (n 71) para 29.

86 While Art 9 expressly states that recovery of non-material damage eg damages for pain and suffering is a matter for national law, other issues such as causation are simply not mentioned.

87 *Barnett v Chelsea & Kensington Hospital Management Committee* [1969] 1 QB 428. For differences between EU legal systems, see B Wininger et al, *Essential Cases on Natural Causation,* Digest of European Tort Law (Wien, Springer, 2010); L Khoury, *Uncertain Causation in Medical Liability* (Oxford, Hart Publishing, 2006).

88 See, eg, WVH Rogers, *Damages for Non-Pecuniary Loss in a Comparative Perspective,* Tort and Insurance Law (Vienna, Springer, 2001).

89 G Howells, 'Product Liability: A History of Harmonization' in AS Hartkamp et al, *Towards a European Civil Code,* 4th edn (The Hague, Kluwer, 2011) 894.

90 D Fairgrieve and G Howells, 'Rethinking Product Liability: A Missing Element in the European Commission's Third Review of the European Product Liability Directive' (2007) 70 *Modern Law Review* 962.

91 The Commission has to report regularly to the Community institutions on the state of the application of the Directive. Art 21 of the Directive stipulates that it must report every 5 years on the general application of the Directive. Arts 15(3) and 16(2) stipulate that it must report every 10 years after notification of the Directive on development risks and financial limits. The Commission has subsequently published four reports (COM (1995) 617 final, COM (2000) 893 final, COM (2006) 496 final, COM (2011) 547 final) plus a number of studies, such as the Lovells Report (published in 2003) and the Fondazione Rosselli Report (published in 2004), and a Green Paper on Product Liability adopted in July 1999, COM (1999) 396 final. The fourth report covers the period 2006–10 and analyses the application of the Directive in the 27 Member States: see http://ec.europa.eu/enterprise/policies/single-market-goods/documents/internal-market-for-products/liability/index_en.htm.

92 Directive 1999/34/EC of the European Parliament and of the Council of 10 May 1999. Note that efforts to establish a parallel regime governing liability for services were unsuccessful: Proposal for a Council Directive on the Liability of Suppliers of Services, COM (1990) 482 final [1991] OJ C12/8. The Commission officially withdrew the draft on 24 June 1994 COM (1994) 260 final.

The most recent 2011 report acknowledged continued lobbying to reform the burden of proof and the defence of development risks, and to review the question of the 500 euro threshold for material damage, but concluded that it would be premature to propose a review of the Directive at this stage.[93] In a global study, Reimann noted that despite its theoretical importance, the Directive has had very little impact on the law in action; the majority of claims continuing to be brought under the traditional tort of negligence or for breach of a contractual warranty.[94] There remains across the EU very limited case law under the Directive.[95]

In the light of these findings, this section will examine the real impact of the Directive on English tort law and the extent to which the much-heralded strict liability provisions of Part 1, Consumer Protection Act 1987 have actually changed fundamental principles of English tort law.

i. Why So Few Cases?

The fourth report of the European Commission on the Directive noted that there had been an increase since 1986 in the number of product liability cases brought under national laws, but that data indicated that the costs of the action discouraged this type of proceedings in some Member States, for example in the United Kingdom.[96] The limited case law in the UK is, however, due to a combination of factors.[97] Article 13 of the Directive expressly permits the retention of alternative bases for liability in contract law and it seems clear that for many claimants it is far easier to use the consumer-friendly provisions of the Sale of Goods Act 1979 than attempt to bring a claim against a usually more distant producer.[98] For small items consumers may further prefer to use non-legal mechanisms, such as complaining to the store's customer complaints department. The Lovells 2003 report on the Directive noted that, in reality, the Directive is part of a broader system involving a wide variety of factors (such as safety and consumer protection laws, judicial practices and procedures, cultural and social factors), all of which affect the practical functioning of product liability systems.[99]

[93] Fourth report on the application of Council Directive 85/374/EEC of 25 July 1985 on the approximation of the laws, regulations and administrative provisions of the Member States concerning liability for defective products amended by Directive 1999/34/EC of the European Parliament and of the Council of 10 May 1999 (Fourth Report on Product Liability Directive) COM (2011) 547 final, giving as reasons that the information available is not sufficiently fact-based and that any amendment to one or more provisions might have a detrimental effect on the current balance between a balance between consumer protection and the producers' interests under the Directive.

[94] M Reimann, 'Product Liability in a Global Context: The Hollow Victory of the European Model' (2003) 7 *European Review of Private Law* 128, 146.

[95] For an overview of the case law across the EU, see P Shears, 'The EU Product Liability Directive: Twenty Years On' [2007] *Journal of Business Law* 884.

[96] Fourth report on Product Liability Directive COM(2011) 547 final, 4.

[97] See J Stapleton, 'Products Liability in the United Kingdom: The Myths of Reform' (1999) 34 *Texas International Law Journal* 45, 63–65.

[98] The 1979 Act further contains the improved consumer remedies for faulty products introduced by the Consumer Sales Directive (Directive 99/44/EC of the European Parliament and of the Council of 25 May 1999 on certain aspects of the sale of consumer goods and associated guarantees [1999] OJ L171/12, 7 July 1999.

[99] *Product Liability in the European Union* (2003) 63 (European Commission Study MARKT/2001/11/D).

Much will also depend on the nature of the problem. In not addressing the issue of causation, the Directive leaves litigants with a hurdle to overcome which, notably with respect to design defects, may be difficult to surmount.[100] In the third-generation oral contraceptive pill litigation, for example, Mackay J in *X v Schering Health Care Ltd*[101] concluded, in a judgment of 200 pages after a trial lasting three months and hearing the conflicting evidence of 10 experts, that there was insufficient evidential basis to establish that an increased risk of cardiovascular injury was caused by the product. On this basis, he did not proceed to examine the law under the Act. Such cases can only render litigants more nervous of bringing such claims in future. Further, the Directive itself has limitations such as the 10-year long-stop which, for litigants where the disease has developed over time, may prove a real obstacle to establishing liability. Equally damages are confined to death, personal injury and non-commercial property greater than £275 in value. While undoubtedly many cases will be settled before reaching court and, therefore, there is a danger of reading too much into the limited number of reported cases, it cannot be denied that difficulties in establishing a claim under the Act and the availability of more user-friendly alternatives have diminished the utility of the Act as a means of consumer protection.

ii. Limited Practical Impact

A further concern arises when one examines to what extent the Consumer Protection Act 1987 has provided greater consumer protection than the original fault-based liability it sought to replace. In some respects the benefits are obvious – it is a strict liability statute and covers defendants such as importers and own-branders for the first time – but it might be questioned whether, in general, it produces significantly different results from the previous regime. If, for example, one considers manufacturing defects (non-standard products), even under the *Donoghue v Stevenson* principle, claimants in many cases find fault relatively easy to establish where there has been variance from the norm of production. The courts, in fact, readily infer fault.[102] Winfield and Jolowicz remark that in many cases this comes very close to the imposition of strict liability.[103] It is thus in the

[100] See *Ide v ATB Sales Ltd* [2008] EWCA Civ 424 where two alternative explanations for the cause of Mr Ide's accident were put before the court. The court indicated, however, that in Consumer Protection Act cases in contrast to negligence, it was unnecessary to determine the precise mechanism by which the product was defective: the question was whether the claimant could prove on the balance of probabilities that the defect caused the damage sustained.

[101] *X v Schering Health Care Ltd* [2002] EWHC 1420, (2003) 70 BMLR 88. See M Mildred [2002] *Journal of Personal Injury Law* 428.

[102] Consider, eg, *Grant v Australian Knitting Mills* [1936] AC 85: 'The appellant is not required to lay his finger on the exact person in all the chain who was responsible, or to specify what he did wrong. Negligence is found as a matter of inference from the existence of the defects taken in connection with all the known circumstances' per Lord Wright at 101.

[103] WVH Rogers, *Winfield and Jolowicz on Tort*, 18th edn (London, Sweet and Maxwell, 2010) 10–16 (hereafter *Winfield and Jolowicz*). MA Jones (ed), *Clerk and Lindsell on Torts*, 20th edn (London, Sweet and Maxwell, 2010) (hereafter *Clerk and Lindsell*) agrees at 11.28 that absent fairly clear evidence that the defect was unforeseeable or not reasonably avoidable, the defendant will rarely escape liability in practice for manufacturing defects.

context of design faults that the greatest advantage for litigants might be anticipated. If, however, *Tesco v Pollard* is representative of a move towards an approach which takes account of the comparative costs and benefits of a particular design, one might wonder to what extent the Directive has led to a fundamental change to the law applicable prior to the 1987 Act. Nolan has gone so far as to suggest that 'In manufacturing defect cases, the common law approximates to strict liability in any case, and in design and marketing defect cases, liability under the CPA 1987 will generally require evidence of fault'.[104] Winfield and Jolowicz note that while the test in negligence (was it reasonable to market this design?) will differ from that under the Act (what level of safety can the public legitimately accept?), both involve questions of cost and benefit, leading to a substantial overlap between the two approaches.[105] While in the light of *A* and *Abouzaid* there is clearly a distinction between negligence and liability under the Act, one might wonder whether this will always lead to different results.

iii. Tort Textbooks and Teaching

A further factor in assessing the impact of the Act on traditional tort law principle is to consider the extent to which such liability is treated by practitioners and academics as a core part of English tort law. While leading tort textbooks and practitioners' texts cover Part 1 of the Consumer Protection Act 1987 as part of their discussion of liability for defective products,[106] it remains the case that few universities cover product liability as part of their tort law unit and certainly little emphasis is placed on the objectives and purposes of the 1985 Product Liability Directive. This is underlined by the fact that two of the leading statute books for Contract, Tort and Restitution contain no reference to the Directive, presumably baffling students attempting to understand the judgment of Burton J in *A* (above).[107] In a crowded syllabus, clearly product liability is not a priority. As a topic which brings together liability in contract and tort, national and EU law, one might argue that it is perhaps better taught as consumer law, particularly as an understanding of the role of Directive in national legal systems requires an understanding of EU law.[108] Whittaker notes that this is consistent with the government's decision to make implementation of the Directive part of a larger reform of consumer law under the Consumer Protection Act 1987 including ambitious regulatory measures and criminal sanctions, and that the debate at the

[104] D Nolan, 'Product Liability' in K Oliphant (ed), *The Law of Tort*, Butterworths Common Law, 2nd edn (London, LexisNexis, 2007) 19.38.

[105] *Winfield and Jolowicz* (n 103) 10–21.

[106] See, eg, *Winfield and Jolowicz* (n 103) Ch 10; S Deakin, A Johnston and B Markesinis, *Markesinis and Deakin's Tort Law*, 7th edn (Oxford, Oxford University Press, 2012) ch 20; *Clerk and Lindsell* (n 103) ch 11.

[107] See F Rose, *Blackstone's Statutes on Contract, Tort & Restitution 2013–2014*, 24th edn (Oxford, Oxford University Press, 2013); J Devenney and H Johnson, *Contract, Tort and Restitution Statutes 2012–2013*, 4thedn (Aldershot, Routledge, 2012). Both do, however, contain extracts from the 1987 Act.

[108] See, eg, S Weatherill, 'Consumer Policy' in P Craig and G de Búrca (eds), *The Evolution of EU Law*, 2nd edn (Oxford, Oxford University Press, 2011) ch 27.

time was focused on the need to reform product liability rather than EU economic policy.[109] Certainly the best coverage of the law is found in specialist texts.[110] There are further strong arguments that one should not teach product liability without at least reference to the consumer's most frequent recourse when faced with a defective product: a claim against the retailer for breach of contract or to trading standards for breach of regulations imposed by criminal law. The net result is that the average LLB student is unlikely to appreciate the significance of having a maximum harmonisation Directive transposed into English tort law and the tensions between national and European courts which follow. Cases such as *Pollard* (above), which make no reference to EU law, mark a worrying tendency to treat the statute as simply another national legislative provision and thereby diminish the European nature of this legislative provision.

These three factors have combined to diminish the impact of the Directive on English tort law. In treating Part 1 of the 1987 Act as part of an English consumer law regime, there is a danger of paying little attention to the European origins of this area of law. The Act is far more likely to be treated as a rare example of strict liability in an area of law dominated by the tort of negligence.[111] This is a pity in that while it took almost 12 years from the introduction of the 1987 Act for a claimant to bring a successful claim, the two important cases of *Abouzaid* and *A* mark attempts by the English courts to respond to the distinctive nature of such claims with reference to EU law and case law from the CJEU and Member States.[112] The pro-European approach of Burton J, however, seems to have made little lasting impact on national law, bar recognition that the development risks defence is to be applied restrictively which, of course, comes from the ECJ case itself. Equally one might question the extent to which European supervisory mechanisms have assisted in placing a European stamp on law deriving from the Directive in that the examples shown above demonstrate a limited desire to intervene both at CJEU level and by the Commission itself. Bearing in mind the distinctive nature of common law tort rules on causation, remoteness, assessment of damages and civil procedure and the general dominance of fault-based reasoning in the English courts, clearly the natural instinct of the English courts is to adhere to traditional practices unless, as we see in *A*, a positive effort is made. A limited 'maximum' harmonisation Directive which leaves key national tort principles in place whilst providing limited guidance for those rules within its scope is unlikely to achieve uniform application across Member States without considerable intervention by

[109] Whittaker, *Liability for Products* (n 32) 465–66.

[110] eg, leading practitioner works: CJ Miller and RS Goldberg, *Product Liability*, 2nd edn (Oxford, Oxford University Press, 2004) and G Howells, *The Law of Product Liability*, 2nd edn (London, Butterworths, 2007).

[111] eg, M Lunney and K Oliphant, *Tort Law: Text and Materials*, 5th edn (Oxford, Oxford University Press, 2013) place product liability in a chapter on 'Special Liability Regimes' for example.

[112] See E Deards and C Twigg-Flesner, 'The Consumer Protection Act 1987: Proof At Last That It Is Protecting Consumers?' (2001) 10 *Nottingham Law Journal* 1.

the CJEU. As we know, this has not occurred.[113] Equally citation of EU case law, relevant case law from other Member States or even the Directive itself will only occur if there is a positive change in practice by the courts and the legal profession in general.[114]

One can only conclude that rather than striking at the heart of core tort law principle, the impact of Part 1 of the 1987 Act has been to provide an additional remedy for defective products, merely supplementing the existing armoury of contract and tort law actions. If, as is commonly accepted, the law under the Act provides limited improvement to the position of the consumer from the pre-existing common law, one might have sympathy with the view of Stapleton, who remarks: 'One might be forgiven for asking . . . why (apart from Euro-window-dressing) was such energy wasted on such a "reform" as the Directive?'[115]

II. Employers' Liability and the European Framework Directive

Workplace safety has long been a concern of the law of tort. While in modern times, the question of employers' liability raises more general regulatory concerns, tort law does play a part in compensating employees, notably by means of the torts of negligence and breach of statutory duty. *Wilsons & Clyde Coal Co Ltd v English*[116] famously stated the personal non-delegable duty of the employer in the tort of negligence towards his employees.[117] Further, the tort of breach of statutory duty may place the employer under a stricter duty to protect the employee than that applied in negligence, subject, of course, to the wording of the statutory provision in question. While it is commonly accepted that the tort of breach of statutory duty now plays a limited role in English tort law, a more generous approach has traditionally been taken towards legislation relating to health and safety in the workplace.[118] Baroness Hale noted in *Fytche v Wincanton Logistics plc*[119] that:

[113] On this basis, Fairgrieve, Howells and Pilgenstorfer have recently argued that in the absence of any signs of imminent Commission intervention, soft law guidance may provide helpful assistance to resolve uncertainty as to the meaning of some key provisions: see D Fairgrieve, G Howells and M Pilgerstorfer, 'The Product Liability Directive: Time to get Soft?' (2013) 4 *Journal of European Tort Law* 1.

[114] As regards the collection of information, the *Product Liability Forum of the British Institute of International and Comparative Law* has a database on liability for defective products: www.biicl.org/plf.

[115] Stapleton, 'Products Liability in the United Kingdom' (n 97) 65.

[116] *Wilsons & Clyde Coal Co Ltd v English* [1938] AC 57.

[117] Supplemented by the Employer's Liability (Defective Equipment) Act 1969, which reverses the House of Lords decision in *Davie v New Merton Board Mills* [1959] AC 604.

[118] See K Stanton, 'New Forms of the Tort of Breach of Statutory Duty' (2004) 120 *Law Quarterly Review* 324, 326; G Williams, 'The Effect of Penal Legislation in the Law of Tort' (1960) 23 *Modern Law Review* 233, 258; *Groves v Lord Wimborne* [1898] 2 QB 402.

[119] *Fytche v Wincanton Logistics plc* [2004] UKHL 31; [2004] ICR 975.

> [I]t has been accepted that legislation protecting safety in the workplace gives rise to an action for breach of statutory duty and the same was generally true for provisions protecting health. Indeed, because of certain well-known defects in the law of negligence until the decision in *Wilsons & Clyde Coal Co Ltd v English* [1938] AC 57,[120] the action for breach of statutory duty was often the only one available to an injured worker. It is not surprising that a more relaxed and purposive construction was given to provisions designed for the worker's protection even if they also created criminal offences, usually minor and rarely prosecuted.[121]

Since the landmark decision of *Groves v Lord Wimborne*,[122] therefore, the tort of breach of statutory duty has proven to be particularly adept at finding a remedy for damages where the employer has breached industrial safety legislation; in *Groves*, an employee being injured by unfenced machinery in breach of the duty to maintain fencing for dangerous machinery imposed on the employer by section 5(4) of the Factory and Workshop Act 1878.

However, workplace safety has also been a major concern for the European Union. Under Article 153 TFEU,[123] the EU will 'support and complement' the activities of Member States in improving health and safety in the workplace. To this end, the European Parliament and Council are empowered to adopt measures designed to encourage cooperation between Member States through initiatives aimed at improving knowledge, developing exchanges of information and best practices, promoting innovative approaches and evaluating experiences, and, more significantly, may adopt, by means of directives, minimum requirements for gradual implementation, having regard to the conditions and technical rules obtaining in each Member State. These are thus *minimum* standards and there is nothing to prevent Member States providing employees with better protection. While between 1970 and 1985, only six directives had been adopted by the European Council, in 1987 a third action programme on safety, health and hygiene at work was adopted,[124] which led to the 1989 Directive.[125]

The so-called 1989 Framework Directive[126] is one of the cornerstones of the EU's policy for health and safety in the workplace. It seeks to improve the protec-

[120] Namely the 'unholy trinity' of defences: the doctrine of common employment (finally abolished by the Law Reform (Personal Injuries) Act 1948, s1(1)) and the pro-employer application of the defences of contributory negligence and *volenti non fit injuria*. The doctrine of contributory negligence, in particular, as understood in the 19th century, afforded an employer a complete defence against any claim brought by an employee until it was reformed by s 1(1) of the Law Reform (Contributory Negligence) Act 1945. As long as an employer could show that the employee was also negligent to some degree and contributed to the harm caused, the employer would be completely exonerated.

[121] *Fytche* (n 119) para. 61.

[122] *Groves v Lord Wimborne* [1898] 2 QB 402.

[123] Ex Art 137 TEC.

[124] Third Community Action Programme on safety, hygiene and health at work of 23 October 1987 [1988] OJ C28/3.

[125] D Kloss, *Occupational Health Law*, 5th edn (Oxford, Wiley-Blackwell, 2010) 10.

[126] Council Directive 89/391/EEC of 12 June 1989 on the introduction of measures to encourage improvements in the safety and health of workers at work, OJ 183, 29 June 1989 (Framework Directive), subsequently amended by Regulation (EC) No 1882/2003 OJ L284, 31 October 2003; Directive 2007/30/EC OJ L165, 27 June 2007 and Regulation (EC) No 1137/2008 OJ L311, 21 November 2008.

tion of workers with regard to accidents at work and occupational diseases by ensuring that preventive measures are taken with the provision of information, consultation, balanced participation and training for both the workers and their representatives. It covers all workers in the EU, whether in the public or private sector and forms the basis for 'daughter directives'. These provide more detailed provisions on particular aspects of workplace safety, such as the safety of machinery and work equipment, use of visual display units and the handling of heavy loads. Such measures were transposed into English law by regulations made under section 15 of the Health and Safety at Work etc. Act 1974 (hereafter the 1974 Act).

While the 1974 Act represents the means by which the UK has responded to this series of Directives, a number of factors should be noted. First, the view was taken that the Directives did not necessitate great changes to UK law in that it already provided significant provision for workplace safety. The necessary amendments would, in the view of the Health and Safety Commission (HSC; now merged with the Health and Safety Executive (HSE)) largely make explicit what was previously implicit.[127] Secondly, section 2(1) of the 1974 Act provides that it shall be the duty of every employer to ensure, so far as is reasonably practicable, the health, safety and welfare at work of all his employees, but this is qualified by section 47(1)(a) which states that this will not confer a right of action in civil proceedings – liability is penal. Until recent reforms (detailed below), section 47(2) of the 1974 Act did, nevertheless, provide that breach of a duty imposed by health and safety *regulations* should, so far as it causes damage, be civilly actionable except in so far as the regulations provide otherwise. On this basis, breach of such regulations would allow employees to sue for breach of statutory duty, provided, of course, such an action was not excluded by the regulation itself.

Subsequent case law has thus focused on claims for breach of statutory duty under the numerous regulations which have implemented EU Health and Safety Directives. In addition to the 'six pack' regulations of 1992,[128] subsequent regulations have served to replace much of the old law contained in statutes such as the Factories Act 1961, Mines and Quarries Act 1954 and the Offices, Shops and Railway Premises Act 1963. This has not been without some difficulties in transposition. The Management of Health and Safety at Work Regulations 1992 were amended, following representations by the European Commission, to permit a civil action.[129] Regulation 22, nevertheless, still excludes claims by non-employees.[130] In contrast,

[127] A Emir, *Selwyn's Law of Employment*, 17th edn (Oxford, Oxford University Press, 2012) 11.76.

[128] Management of Health and Safety at Work Regulations 1992 SI 1992/2051 (now SI 1999/3242); Personal Protective Equipment at Work Regulations 1992 SI 1992/2966; Provision and Use of Work Equipment Regulations 1992 SI 1992/2932 (now SI 1998/ 2306); Workplace (Health, Safety and Welfare) Regulations 1992 SI 1992/3004; Manual Handling Operations Regulations 1992 SI 1992/2793; Health and Safety (Display Screen Equipment) Regulations 1992 SI 1992/2792.

[129] Management of Health and Safety at Work and Fire Precautions (Workplace) (Amendment) Regulations SI 2003/2457.

[130] McBride and Bagshaw remark that the negative wording of Reg 22 (there shall not be a right of action in any civil proceedings insofar as that duty applies for the protection of a third party) is no doubt attributable to the fact that the government was forced into changing the law: N McBride and R Bagshaw, *Tort Law*, 4th edn (Harlow, Pearson Education, 2012) para 22.3.

in *King v Sussex Ambulance NHS Trust*,[131] Hale LJ was able to interpret the relevant provisions of the Manual Handling Directive[132] and the 1992 Manual Handling Operations Regulations 1992[133] to avoid any inconsistency, despite their different wording.[134] The Commission also took the United Kingdom to the European Court of Justice, challenging section 2(1) of the 1974 Act which qualifies the employer's duty to ensure the health, safety and welfare at work of all his employees by the term 'so far as reasonably practicable'.[135] While this is a phrase long used by the English legislator, notably in the Factories Act 1961, the addition of this term had been expressly rejected at the drafting stage of the 1989 Directive, although some qualification had been accepted.[136] The ECJ found that the Commission could not show that the UK had failed in its obligations to transpose Council Directive 89/391 and that there had been no intention that the provisions in question would subject the employer to strict liability. Welcoming the ECJ's decision, Bill Callaghan, HSC Chair, stated, 'We continue to believe that the right way forward is a proportionate and risk-based approach protecting employees and others effectively, whilst allowing commonsense to be applied when deciding on what protective measures to adopt.'[137]

Nevertheless, it remains the case that EU Directives have reshaped the regulation of workplace safety. However, the method of transposition – fitting them into the existing framework of national law largely deriving from the 1974 Act – has served to render their European origins less obvious. From the perspective of the Europeanisation of tort law, the impact of these Directives is interesting in two ways. First, it is an area of law which has given renewed life to the tort of breach of statutory duty, which, as previously stated, applies restrictively in other areas of law.[138] Secondly, while the torts of breach of statutory duty and negligence

[131] *King v Sussex Ambulance NHS Trust* [2002] EWCA Civ 953; [2002] ICR 1413, para 17.

[132] Council Directive 90/269/EEC of 29 May 1990 on the minimum health and safety requirements for the manual handling of loads where there is a risk particularly of back injury to workers (fourth individual Directive within the meaning of Article 16 (1) of Directive 89/391/EEC) [1990] OJ L156/ 9 (Manual Handling Directive).

[133] SI 1992/2793.

[134] The Court of Appeal similarly in *Hide v Steeplechase Co (Cheltenham) Ltd* [2013] EWCA Civ 545; [2013] PIQR P22 was able to interpret Reg 4(4) of the Provision and Use of Work Equipment Regulations 1998 consistently with Art 5(4) of the 1989 Framework Directive by placing the burden of proof on the defendant to prove that any relevant accident was due either to unforeseeable occurrences beyond the defendant's control or to exceptional events the consequences of which could not be avoided despite the exercise of all due care. The Court expressly criticised the trial judge for interpreting the relevant law in a 'classic common law manner': para 12.

[135] *Commission of the European Communities v United Kingdom* (C-127/05) [2007] ECR I-4619; [2007] All ER (EC) 986.

[136] Council Directive 89/391/EEC, Art 5(4) provides that:

> This Directive shall not restrict the option of Member States to provide for the exclusion or the limitation of employers' responsibility where occurrences are due to unusual and unforeseeable circumstances, beyond the employers' control, or to exceptional events, the consequences of which could not have been avoided despite the exercise of all due care.

[137] Callaghan, (2007) 14(12) *Health and Safety at Work* 668.

[138] See *X and others (minors) v Bedfordshire County Council* [1995] 2 AC 633, discussed in ch. 4.

are distinct,[139] such regulatory standards are capable of assisting courts in determining the appropriate standard of care in negligence and therefore have a secondary effect in the development of negligence liability in the workplace.

A. Breach of Statutory Duty

The tort of breach of statutory duty requires that the claimant must show that the legislation in question is intended to be actionable at private law, the harm suffered must be within the ambit of the statute, the duty must have been breached, and the breach must have caused the loss suffered, subject to any defences.[140] Until recently, section 47(2) of the 1974 Act indicated that, unless stated otherwise, the health and safety regulations were intended to be civilly actionable. Although recent reforms (see below) have reversed this presumption, the cases examined in this section give an insight into the manner in which the English courts have applied law transposed from EU Directives. In *Fytche v Wincanton Logistics plc*,[141] for example, the claim for breach of statutory duty turned on a difficult point on the true construction of the Personal Protective Equipment at Work Regulations 1992.[142] The majority of the House of Lords found that the injury suffered by Mr Fytche was not of the kind for which the protective equipment had been supplied. Fytche was the driver of a milk tanker and had been provided with steel toe capped boots by his employer to reduce the risk of impact injuries. The boots were not supposed to be waterproof and one of the boots had a tiny hole in it which, when delivering milk in snow, led to Fytche suffering mild frostbite to this toe due to water penetration. Regulation 7(1) requires that every employer shall ensure that personal protective equipment provided is maintained in good repair. The majority refused to adopt a literal interpretation, which would have imposed an absolute duty on the employer, and held that the provision had to be construed in relation to the purpose for which the equipment had been provided, here to protect against the risk of impact injury, not injuries caused by bad weather. It is interesting that, unlike the Court of Appeal,[143] their Lordships made express reference to Directive 89/656/EEC on Personal Protective Equipment, noting differences in drafting between the Directive and the 1992 Regulations, and considering the wider scheme of the EU legislation. Lord Walker commented that 'If the scheme and context of the Regulations strongly suggests that a restricted meaning is appropriate, it should not be rejected merely because health

[139] Contrast Canada: *The Queen v Saskatchewan Wheat Pool* [1983] 1 SCR 205; (1983) 143 DLR (3d) 9 breaches of statute are merely to be used as evidence for breach of an established tort such as negligence.

[140] *Clerk and Lindsell* (n 103) para 9-04.

[141] *Fytche v Wincanton Logistics plc* [2004] UKHL 31; [2004] ICR 975.

[142] SI 1992/2966. With the exception of sea transport, the Regulations give effect as respects Great Britain to Council Directive 89/656/EEC on the minimum health and safety requirements for the use by workers of personal protective equipment at the workplace.

[143] *Fytche v Wincanton Logistics plc* [2003] EWCA Civ 874; [2003] ICR 1582.

and safety are in issue'.[144] Such a view may be contrasted with the minority view of Baroness Hale that '[t]here are good policy reasons for imposing strict liability on employers for many of the injuries which their employees suffer at work'.[145]

The question of statutory intention, an inherent difficulty in the tort of breach of statutory duty, is thus rendered more difficult when, as in *Fytche*, the court is faced with two pieces of legislation whose wording is not necessarily consistent and where domestic legislation may exceed than the minimum standards of the Directive. In *Smith v Northamptonshire CC*,[146] the House of Lords again struggled to interpret regulations – this time, the Provision and Use of Work Equipment Regulations (PUWER) 1998, Regulations 2(1) and 3(2)[147] – in determining whether a driver and carer, collecting a wheelchair user who accessed her home by means of a wooden ramp, could claim that she had been injured by work equipment 'provided for use or used by an employee . . . at work' when the ramp crumbled and caused her to sustain injury. The ramp had not been installed by her employer[148] and she was not on work property at the time of the incident. Again the House of Lords was divided; the majority refusing to adopt a literal interpretation of the regulation which would lead to extensive liability, preferring again to construe the Regulations on the basis of the relevant Directive 89/655. Lord Mance held that:

> Courts should be careful not to impose on employers responsibilities which go far beyond those at which Directive 89/655 and the 1998 Regulations can in my opinion have been intended to impose. The judge's (over) generous interpretation of the concept of control would, if accepted, add both unjustified stringency and undesirable uncertainty into this area.[149]

In his Lordship's view, the Regulations did not provide all-embracing protection and existed alongside other forms of liability, such as that found under the Occupiers' Liability Acts and ordinary common law duties of care.

In contrast, *Robb v Salamis (M & I) Ltd*,[150] the House of Lords adopted a more generous approach to liability for breach of Regulations 4(4) and 20 of the 1998 PUWER Regulations. In construing those regulations, Lord Hope found it helpful

[144] *Fytche* (n 141) para 52, but cf. *Ball v Street* [2005] EWCA Civ 76; [2005] *Personal Injuries and Quantum Reports* P22 (in relation to PUWER Regulations 1998, reg 5).

[145] *Fytche* (n 141) para 70. Lord Hope also dissented.

[146] *Smith v Northamptonshire CC* [2009] UKHL 27; [2009] ICR 734.

[147] SI 1998/ 2306. The Regulations revoke and re-enact the Provision and Use of Work Equipment Regulations SI 1992/2932, which gave effect as respects Great Britain, except in relation to certain matters, to Council Directive 89/655/EEC on the minimum health and safety requirements for the use of work equipment by workers at work, including provisions required by Directive 95/63/EC.

[148] It had been installed by the NHS. Stockwell suggests that the claimant missed an opportunity in not joining the NHS as a defendant which might have led to a different result: M Stockwell [2009] *Journal of Personal Injury Law* C132.

[149] *Smith* (n 146) para 69.

[150] *Robb v Salamis (M & I) Ltd* [2006] UKHL 56; [2007] ICR 175. It is noticeable that the leading judgment in this case was delivered by Lord Hope, who was in the minority in both the cases above. This is suggestive of divergent approaches to interpretation in their Lordship's House. Note also the more generous interpretation of the 1998 Regulations in *Spencer-Franks v Kellogg Brown and Root Ltd & Ors (Scotland)* [2008] UKHL 46 [2008] ICR 863 on the meaning of work equipment.

to refer to both the EU Framework Directive 89/391/EEC and the EU Workplace Directive 89/655/EEC in determining that the aim of these regulations was to ensure that work equipment, which is made available to workers, may be used by them without impairment to their safety or health. This created an obligation to anticipate situations which may give rise to accidents, rather than simply waiting for them to happen.[151] On that basis, an employee, who fell from a removable ladder giving access to bunk-beds in the sleeping quarters provided by his employer, could successfully sue for breach of statutory duty in that it was foreseeable that a removable ladder might not be replaced properly, subject to a 50 per cent reduction for contributory negligence. Lord Clyde agreed:

> [T]he general purpose of the Directives has been to encourage improvements to the existing levels of protection for the health and safety of workers. While they seek to lay down minimum standards it might be expected that they may not necessarily be looking to preserve standards which have existed at common law in relation to the employer's liability in reparation to his employees and which may now be too low for current requirements for safety.[152]

A brief glance at these leading cases indicates tension in interpreting the regulations, and, in particular, difficulties in determining the extent to which employees should be protected against injuries in the workplace, bearing in mind the often loose wording of the regulations and limited definitional assistance. There are also signs of tension as to the level at which policy should be determined: national or European Union? In *Smith*, Baroness Hale, dissenting, argued that it has long been established that as between the non-negligent employer who benefited from the employee's labour and the non-negligent employee who suffered illness or injury at work, the law might often (though not invariably) favour the employee. Her Ladyship questioned the extent to which European Directives, in setting a minimum standard which the UK could exceed, would be helpful as an aid to construing national legislation 'made, not under the *vires* of section 2(2) of the European Communities Act 1972, but under the *vires* of the Health and Safety at Work etc Act 1974.'[153] If minimum harmonisation does permit Member States to provide a higher level of protection at national level, it raises an interesting question as to what role the aims and objectives of the Directive should play in interpreting the resultant legal provision and, in particular, to what extent the minimum agreed standard may be relied upon to justify a refusal to extend liability. This is particularly relevant in an area of law where the courts are willing to depart from a literal interpretation of the provisions in question in favour of what they perceive to be the intent of Parliament, particularly when, as seen in *Fytche* and *Smith*, the Supreme Court is divided as to what this intent may be.

[151] *Robb* (n 150) para 24. See also Lord Rodger ibid at para 53.
[152] *Robb* (n 150) para 48.
[153] *Smith* (n 146) para 42.

Such case law provides a good illustration of the tensions which exist in integrating minimum harmonisation EU Directives into English law where a pre-existing legal framework exists for dealing with such claims. The minimum standards set by the Directives allows for superior national rules as Baroness Hale has suggested. In her view, the national level of employee protection is something to be applauded and protected from any threat that it might be watered down by EU law. In contrast, Lord Walker in *Fytche* uses EU policy as a reason for limiting employee protection under the legislation in question.

B. Reform to Claims for Breach of Statutory Duty under Section 47(2), Health and Safety at Work etc Act 1974

This debate must now be considered in the light of the reforms introduced by the coalition Government under the Enterprise and Regulatory Reform Act 2013. The Government had previously expressed its support for a recommendation that regulatory provisions which impose strict liability on employers should be reviewed by June 2013 and either qualified with 'reasonably practicable' where strict liability is not absolutely necessary or amended to prevent civil liability from attaching to a breach of these provisions.[154] Section 69 of the Enterprise and Regulatory Reform Act 2013, however, goes further and amends section 47(2) of the 1974 Act to state that 'Breach of a duty imposed by a statutory instrument containing (whether alone or with other provision) health and safety regulations shall not be actionable except to the extent that regulations under this section so provide.'[155] This reverses the previous presumption that a regulation *would* give rise to civil liability unless otherwise provided. In future, therefore, there will be no civil liability for breach of a duty imposed by health and safety legislation unless specific provision is made.[156]

This raises difficulties for claimants in that current regulations make no such express provision, perhaps understandably when, in the past, there was no need to do so. The government has expressed no intention to amend the regulations. Business minister Matthew Hancock MP explained government policy as follows:

> [I]t is unhelpful when health and safety becomes a byword for regulations that get in the way and stop businesses competing or, for instance, children from being taken on school trips once reasonable precautions have been put in place, and instead bring the whole system into disrepute. That is what the Government are trying to stop. The key

[154] Department of Work and Pensions, *A Progress Report on Implementation of Health and Safety Reforms* (June 2012). See also the report of Professor Ragnar Löfstedt reviewing UK health and safety law: *Reclaiming Health and Safety for All: An Independent Review of Health and Safety Legislation* (November 2011): www.dwp.gov.uk/docs/lofstedt-report.pdf

[155] Enterprise and Regulatory Reform Act 2013, s 69(3). It adds that 'Breach of a duty imposed by an existing statutory provision shall not be actionable except to the extent that regulations under this section so provide (including by modifying any of the existing statutory provisions)'.

[156] This provision came into effect on 1 October 2013. It will only apply to breaches of duty after the commencement date: s 69(10).

> defence of negligence ensures that if people breach health and safety rules or have not acted reasonably, that will – of course – be taken into account under the system, and the new clause will not change criminal health and safety procedures. We must, however, ensure that unreasonable claims, and the existing perception of health and safety legislation, do not get in the way of Britain's ability to compete.[157]

On this basis, in future, civil claims for breach of health and safety duties will generally be brought on the basis of proof that the employer has been negligent. This weakens the position of employees who must now satisfy the requirements of the tort of negligence and raises the question whether this complies with the UK's obligations at EU level. What one sees here is *national* government policy, responding to what the government perceives to be over-burdensome civil liability and a fear of the 'compensation culture'. Enforcement of the regulations will in future be solely under the mandate of the Health and Safety Executive, although commentators have warned that its enforcement rates are currently low due to under-funding.[158] It is clear that the UK government favours an approach to workplace safety which is risk- and evidence-based.[159]

The government reforms have unsurprisingly caused an outcry from unions and personal injury lawyers. There has, however, been little reference to the EU dimension, although some commentators have suggested that the Government may face challenges under the principle of State liability for breach of EU law for failing to effectively implement EU Health and Safety Directives (the so-called *Francovich* liability examined in ch 4) and that public bodies may be challenged under the principle of direct effect.[160] This lack of attention might seem surprising in view of the changes made by the Labour government in 2003 to the Management of Health and Safety at Work Regulations in response to a demand by the European Commission that correct implementation of the health and safety framework Directive required the removal of the 'civil liability exclusion' introduced by the Conservative government to protect employers.[161] Nevertheless it may be argued that in view of the government concession at the time, this point was never tested. In the later decision of the ECJ in *Commission of the European Communities v United Kingdom (C-127/05)*,[162] Advocate General Mengozzi noted that the Framework Directive did not require Member States to adopt a specific form of liability and that Member States remain free to choose the form of that liability,[163] but that 'a proper assessment of the United Kingdom's position must,

[157] *Hansard* HC Deb 16 October 2012, col 194.

[158] Z Nanji, 'Health and Safety Update' (2013) 157(3) *Solicitors Journal* 23.

[159] This is the position of the HSE, which is currently working on the UK report on the practical implementation of EU law as part of the European Commission's review of EU health and safety law.

[160] See, eg, I Pennock, 'Shifting the Burden' (2012) 156(44) *Solicitors Journal* 10; K Patten, 'Step Back in Time' (2013) 163 *New Law Journal* 62; N Tomkins, 'The Enterprise and Regulatory Reform Bill' [2013] *Journal of Personal Injury Law* 1.

[161] Management of Health and Safety at Work and Fire Precautions (Workplace)(Amendment) Regulations SI 2003/2457 (later amended by SI 2006/438, reg 2).

[162] *Commission of the European Communities v United Kingdom* (C-127/05) [2007] ECR I-4619; [2007] All ER (EC) 986.

[163] Ibid, paras 124–125 of opinion.

in my view, include consideration of whether the civil liability to which employers are subject under the common law is at least as extensive as the form of civil liability which emerges from the provisions of the framework Directive'.[164] It should be noted that the Government stresses that breach will still lead to criminal liability and that there remains a duty of care on employers to provide a safe system of work for their employees. Further, the social security system continues to provide an underlying level of protection for injured employees.[165] The Government is clearly confident that in reversing the presumption in section 47(2) of the 1974 Act in favour of the employer, it is nevertheless still acting within the 'margin of manoeuvre'[166] available to the Member States in transposing the provisions in the EU Directives into national law. It remains to be seen if this confidence is well-placed.

The reform does indicate, however, a belief in a national, as opposed to European, framework for health and safety regulation. This, it may be argued, is not new. Our analysis indicates that even when there was a presumption of civil liability under section 47(2), apart from adding to the complexity of the law, EU intervention in this area of law did little to change national attitudes to health and safety protection. Indeed, one might argue that its main impact has been to revitalise the tort of breach of statutory duty; an impact now under threat. There is little sign at present of a dominant European, rather than UK, policy imperative in this area of law.

C. Negligence

The government reform outlined above seeks to emphasise the role of the tort of negligence, rather than breach of statutory duty, as the basis for employee claims. This raises a different dimension to the question of European influences on national law, namely that the introduction of EU Directives on health and safety law may impact on the standard of care required in negligence claims involving workers. Employers' liability in negligence has long provided an alternative claim for injured employees. While it is established law that an employer owes a personal and non-delegable duty of care to the employee, the employee must still prove that this duty has been breached.[167] It is now generally accepted that a breach of a statutory duty may provide evidence of negligence,[168] but that it must be considered in relation to the facts of the case, allowing for the fact that employees may be inadvertent or

[164] Ibid, at para 129 of opinion.

[165] See P Cane, *Atiyah's Accidents, Compensation and the Law*, 8th edn (Cambridge, Cambridge University Press, 2013) ch 13.

[166] *Commission v United Kingdom* (C-127/05) (n 162) para 49 of judgment.

[167] See *Clerk and Lindsell* (n 103) paras 13-03 ff.

[168] See Lord Keith in *Qualcast (Wolverhampton) Ltd v Haynes* [1959] AC 743, 756. Earlier suggestions that breach of statutory duty might be equated with negligence (see Lord Atkin in *Lochgelley Iron & Coal Co v M'Mullan* [1934] AC 1, 9; Lord Macmillan in *Caswell v Powell Duffryn Colliery Co* [1940] AC 152, 168) are now generally disregarded.

become heedless of risks over time. A failure to establish breach of statutory duty does not necessarily prevent a successful claim in negligence, or vice versa.[169] Lee has commented on the uncertainty which exists as to the extent to which regulatory norms may shape the standard of care in personal injury cases in negligence.[170] Nevertheless, statutory duties may provide guidance to the courts of the precautions a reasonable person would take in that situation, and provide a useful source of information as to appropriate standards.[171] They therefore help inform the content of the duty of care.[172] In *Baker v Quantum Clothing Group Ltd*,[173] for example, the Supreme Court found that a Code of Practice on noise at work was official and clear guidance, which could set the standard for the reasonable and prudent employer without specialist knowledge,[174] although it was emphasised that there is no set rule and that the employer's duty also requires him to keep up to date when faced with reforms indicating that more protection is required.[175] As Stephenson LJ remarked in *Bux v Slough Metals Ltd*,[176] 'The statutory obligation may exceed the duty at common law or it may fall short of it or it may equal it.' It does, however, provide a point of reference in determining whether the employer has satisfied his duty of care towards the employee.

On this basis, logically, the regulations transposing the EU Directives into English law will have some influence on claims for negligence in the workplace. As Stephenson LJ noted, this does not prevent the English courts requiring a *higher* standard of care, but it gives courts information of the regulatory framework in place for dealing with such accidents. Employers' liability for negligence in the workplace thus provides an interesting example of the indirect impact of EU legislation, affecting how domestic courts apply core principles of English tort law.

[169] *Clerk and Lindsell* (n 103) paras 9-56 and 13-29.

[170] M Lee, 'Safety, Regulation and Tort: Fault in Context' (2011) 74 *Modern Law Review* 555; M Lee, 'Tort Law and Personal Injury in the Regulatory State' [2011] *Journal of Personal Injury Law* 137

[171] See *Stokes v Guest Keen and Nettlefold (Bolts and Nuts) Ltd* [1968] 1 WLR 1776, 1783: 'the overall test is still the conduct of the reasonable and prudent employer, taking positive thought for the safety of his workers in the light of what he knows or ought to know . . . where there is developing knowledge, he must keep reasonably abreast of it and not be too slow to apply it.' Cane notes that 'The main area in which breach of regulatory standards is actionable in tort is occupational health and safety': P Cane, 'Tort Law as Regulation' (2002) 31 *Common Law World Review* 305, 320.

[172] *Buck v Nottinghamshire Healthcare NHS Trust* [2006] EWCA Civ 1576, para 40 per Waller LJ.

[173] *Baker v Quantum Clothing Group Ltd* [2011] UKSC 17; [2011] 1 WLR 1003.

[174] Lord Mance, delivering the lead judgment, stated: 'there is, in my opinion, no basis for the court to disturb the judge's conclusion . . . that the Code of Practice was an official and clear guidance which set an appropriate standard upon which a reasonable and prudent employer could legitimately rely in conducting his business until the late 1980s': para 36.

[175] Here an EU Directive 86/188 ([1986] OJ L137/28) which lowered the noise level for which action would be required.

[176] *Bux v Slough Metals Ltd* [1973] 1 WLR 1358, 1369–1370.

III. Road Accidents and Insurance: EU Directives Relating to Compulsory Third Party Insurance Cover for Motor Vehicle Accidents

This third example concerns the interplay of EU Motor Insurance Directives[177] with national rules relating to road traffic accidents.[178] The Directives, now consolidated in the interests of clarity into Directive 2009/103,[179] have the objectives of ensuring free movement of vehicles across Member States, guaranteeing that victims of vehicle accidents receive comparable treatment irrespective of where in the EU the accident takes place, and of protecting motor vehicle passengers, regarded as a particularly vulnerable category, by filling any gaps in the compulsory motor insurance cover of passengers in Member States.[180]

The Directives do not claim to harmonise the national liability rules of Member States. The aim is to ensure that victims injured in road accidents are covered by a common system of insurance. Member States are expressly held to remain free to determine the rules of civil liability applicable to road accidents,[181] although they are expected to exercise their powers in compliance with EU law. In *Churchill Insurance Co Ltd v Fitzgerald*,[182] the English Court of Appeal noted the tension between national tort rules governing the claim of the insured person, which may provide, for example, for the reduction of liability for contributory negligence and the exclusion of liability under the doctrine of *novus actus interveniens*, and national rules which define or limit the scope or extent of the obligation to provide insurance cover against civil liability for damage caused to third parties by motor vehicles. The latter is defined and guaranteed by European Union legislation and it is for the court to ensure that national law does not conflict with its objectives and provisions.[183] The former is, essentially, governed by national law, subject to the rule of not rendering the relevant EU Directives ineffective.[184]

[177] The Directives are, as follows: Council Directive 72/166/EEC of 24 April 1972; Second Council Directive 84/5/EEC of 30 December 1983; Third Council Directive 90/232/EEC of 14 May 1990; Fourth Directive 2000/26/EC of the European Parliament and of the Council of 16 May 2000; Fifth Directive 2005/14/EC of the European Parliament and of the Council of 11 May 2005.

[178] See H Heiss, 'Liability Insurance' in R Schulze (ed), *Compensation of Private Losses: The Evolution of Torts in European Business Law* (Munich, Sellier, 2011).

[179] Directive 2009/103/EC of the European Parliament and of the Council of 16 September 2009 relating to insurance against civil liability in respect of the use of motor vehicles, and the enforcement of the obligation to insure against such liability [2009] OJ L263/11, 7 October 2009.

[180] *Churchill Insurance Co Ltd v Wilkinson* (C-442/10) [2012] RTR 10, para 27.

[181] *Mendes Ferreira and Delgado Correia Ferreira* (C-348/98) [2000] ECR I-6711 paras 23 and 29.

[182] *Churchill Insurance Co Ltd v Fitzgerald* [2012] EWCA Civ 1166; [2012] 3 CMLR 49, para 44.

[183] Ibid, para 45.

[184] *Lavrador v Companhia de Seguros Fidelidade-Mundial SA* (C-409/09) [2012] RTR 4, ECJ (Third Chamber), para 25, *Carvalho Ferreira Santos v Companhia Europeia de Seguros SA* (C-484/09) [2011] RTR 32, ECJ (2nd Chamber) para 31 and *Almeida v Companhia de Seguros Fidelidade-Mundial SA* (C-300/10) [2013] 1 CMLR 39 para 28.

The potential for a clash of national and EU policy may be found in the decision of the Court of Justice in *Candolin v Pohjola.*[185] National law had provided that a passenger who knew or ought to have known that the driver had consumed alcohol above a stipulated limit, so that his ability to drive correctly was considerably impaired, would not be able to recover under the vehicle's insurance policy unless a special reason could be found. The ECJ held that:

> The Member States must exercise their powers in compliance with Community law and, in particular, with Article 3(1) of the First Directive, Article 2(1) of the Second Directive and Article 1 of the Third Directive, whose aim is to ensure that compulsory motor vehicle insurance allows all passengers who are victims of an accident caused by a motor vehicle to be compensated for the injury or loss they have suffered. The national provisions which govern compensation for road accidents cannot, therefore, deprive those provisions of their effectiveness. Such would be the case specifically where, solely on the basis of the passenger's contribution to the occurrence of his injuries, national rules, established on the basis of general and abstract criteria, either denied the passenger the right to be compensated by the compulsory motor vehicle insurance or limited such a right in a disproportionate manner. It is only in exceptional circumstances that the amount of the victim's compensation may be limited on the basis of an assessment of his particular case.[186]

On this basis, a national rule which allows the insurance company to refuse to pay or to limit the amount of compensation paid in a disproportionate manner is precluded.[187] Whilst dealing with a limited category of claims– victims in motor vehicle accidents where national law limits or excludes their ability to recover compensation from the insurer – one English commentary has questioned the extent to which this may potentially impact on the English court's discretion under section 1 of the Law Reform (Contributory Negligence) Act 1945 to reduce the claimant's damage to the extent which is 'just and equitable' in road traffic accident cases.[188] In *Froom v Butcher,*[189] Lord Denning, for example, set out guidance for the apportionment of damages for contributory negligence in road traffic accidents. Subsequent case law has acknowledged that there is a powerful public interest in having a well-understood formula, which will avoid enquiry into fine degrees of contributory negligence and ensure that the vast majority of tort cases can be settled.[190] Lunney and Oliphant comment that 'In an area of law where the relevant principles were considered relatively settled and uncontroversial, the ECJ's *Candolin* decision constitutes something of a bombshell',[191] suggesting that

[185] Case C-537/03 *Katja Candolin and Others v Vahinkovakuutusosakeyhtio Pohjola and Jarno Ruokoranta* [2005] ECR I-5745.

[186] Ibid, paras 27–30.

[187] *Candolin and Others*, para 35. Confirmed in *Farrell v Whitty* (C-356/05) [2007] ECR I-3067, para 35.

[188] M Lunney and K Oliphant, *Tort Law: Text and Materials*, 5th edn (Oxford, Oxford University Press, 2013) 304–5.

[189] *Froom v Butcher* [1976] 1 QB 286.

[190] *Stanton v Collinson* [2010] EWCA Civ 81, para 26 per Hughes LJ.

[191] Lunney and Oliphant, *Tort Law* (n 188) 304. Despite the cases discussed below, Lunney and Oliphant maintain that in the absence of a judicial decision, the compatibility of the *Froom v Butcher* guidelines with *Candolin* remains an open question: ibid.

reduction of the victim's damages under the *Froom v Butcher* guidelines may be seen as potentially in conflict with *Candolin*. Clearly such a practice is common in road traffic accident cases and, as stated above, practically very useful. Insurance expert, Robert Merkin, is, however, more sanguine: 'Happily, English law complies with these rules'.[192] The question is how narrowly *Candolin* should be interpreted: what is signified by a 'disproportionate' reduction of damages and what circumstances will be judged 'exceptional'?

More recent case law would appear to support Merkin's view. In *Lavrador v Companhia de Seguros Fidelidade-Mundial SA*,[193] the ECJ distinguished the situation in *Candolin*, where the right to compensation for victims of the accident had been affected by an absolute limit on the insured driver's cover against civil liability, from that in *Lavrador*. Here the Portuguese Civil Code provided that the strict liability provisions relating to traffic accidents did not apply where the victim was solely and exclusively responsible for the accident. This was acceptable, provided that the court undertook an individual assessment of the contribution of the particular victim to his or her own loss or injury:[194]

> Unlike the respective legal contexts which led to the judgments in *Candolin and Others* and in *Farrell*, that legislation does not have the effect, therefore, where the victim contributes to his own loss or injury, of *automatically* excluding or limiting disproportionately this right . . . Thus, it does not affect the obligation under European Union law to ensure that civil liability arising under national law is covered by insurance which complies with the provisions of the three abovementioned directives.[195]

On this basis, English law, in which the court applies the rules of causation and defences to the facts of each case and does not apply an absolute bar to recovery, would seem to satisfy the *Candolin* test. The percentage reduction set by Lord Denning MR in *Froom v Butcher* remains merely guidance; the ultimate test being the reduction that the court deems to be 'just and equitable' in the circumstances. It would seem, therefore, that *Candolin* is unlikely to have the dramatic effect on English tort law that some commentators feared. Nevertheless, it remains a good illustration of the tensions between domestic tort law and the policy goals of the

[192] R Merkin (2005) 17 *Insurance Law Monthly* 12.

[193] *Lavrador v Companhia de Seguros Fidelidade-Mundial SA* C-409/09 [2012] RTR 4, ECJ (Third Chamber). See also C-484/09 *Carvalho Ferreira Santos v Companhia Europeia de Seguros SA* [2011] RTR 32, ECJ (2nd Chamber).

[194] Arts 505 and 570 of the Portuguese Civil Code state that strict liability under the Code for road traffic accidents can be excluded if the accident is attributable to the victim or to a third party, or is the result of *force majeure*, or, where the injured person's fault has contributed to the occurrence or aggravation of the injury or loss, compensation may be reduced by the competent court subject to the seriousness of the fault of each party and the consequences thereof.

[195] *Lavrador* (n 193), para 34 (emphasis added). See also *Carvalho Ferreira Santos* (n 193), para 43, where, in contrast to the legal position in *Candolin*, Art 506, Portuguese Civil Code does not automatically exclude or limit disproportionately the right of the victim. Here a driver of a motor vehicle suffered personal injury in a collision with another motor vehicle and the Code provided that civil liability would be apportioned in accordance with the contribution of each of the vehicles to the occurrence of the damage. Note also the recent case of C-300/10 *Almeida v Companhia de Seguros Fidelidade-Mundial SA* [2013] 1 CMLR 39.

European legislator. The Court of Appeal in *Churchill v Fitzgerald*[196] did ultimately find itself obliged to re-interpret the UK legislative provision dealing with motor insurance indemnities in accordance with the EU Directives, taking note of the *Marleasing* duty to interpret national law in conformity with EU law, discussed in chapter two.[197] Again while dealing with a particular policy question, the domestic court needs to be aware of the potential impact of EU law on even well-established rules of English tort law and that, as seen above, this may involve applying concepts such as '[dis]proportionality', which are ill-defined and difficult to interpret.[198]

IV. Defamation and the Internet: The Electronic Commerce Directive 2000/31/EC[199]

The final example of the tension between EU and national tort law provisions arises in the controversial area of defamation law. Chapter five will discuss the debate concerning the relationship of this tort with law under the European Convention on Human Rights, but there is an EU dimension which receives less attention and limited mention in tort textbooks. The Directive on Electronic Commerce 2000/31/EC contains provisions which overlap with the national defence of innocent dissemination, set out in section 1, Defamation Act 1996, and makes provision for defences for 'information society service providers'[200] when 'illegal'[201] material is found on their sites. The question of the liability of intermediary service providers is one of the many challenges facing the traditional tort of defamation with the rise of information technology. Electronic media, such as

[196] *Churchill* (n 182).

[197] In order to allow the Road Traffic Act 1988, s 151(8) to be interpreted in accordance with EU motor insurance Directives, the notional addition of some wording was required; the court preferring the proposed wording of the insurers.

[198] For criticism of the ambiguity of proportionality in this context, see I Pennock, 'Court Places Limits on Insurers' Right to Recover Compensation from Drivers' (2012) 156(37) *Solicitors Journal* 12.

[199] Directive 2000/31/EC of the European Parliament and of the Council of 8 June 2000 on certain legal aspects of information society services, in particular electronic commerce, in the Internal Market (Electronic Commerce Directive): [2000] OJ L178/1. See AR Lodder, 'European Union E-Commerce Directive: Article by Article Comments', *Guide to European Union Law on E-Commerce*, vol 4, available at: http://papers.ssrn.com/sol3/papers.cfm?abstract_id=1009945.

[200] Electronic Commerce Directive, Art 2(a), defines 'information society services' as services within the meaning of Art 1(2) of Directive 98/34/EC, that is, services normally provided for remuneration, at a distance, by electronic means and at the individual request of a recipient of services. It is generally accepted that commercial Internet intermediaries, such as ISPs, bulletin board operators, and web hosting services will usually satisfy this definition: M Collins, *The Law of Defamation and the Internet*, 3rd edn (Oxford, Oxford University Press, 2010) para 16.32.

[201] This term highlights that the Directive goes beyond defamatory material to include child pornography and the infringement of intellectual property rights. It is interesting that the UK legislator preferred the term 'unlawful' to that of 'illegal' in transposing the Directive into UK law.

Usenet newsgroups and material posted on Facebook and Twitter,[202] 'publish' in a different way to traditional printed material and facilitate spontaneous exchanges of ideas between multiple recipients across the world. While promoting freedom of expression, there is a corresponding risk of abuse in terms of misuse of information and the publication of defamatory remarks which may harm a claimant's reputation. Online intermediaries, which facilitate communication in a variety of ways by acting as go-betweens between the creators and receivers of the information, present an obvious target to a claimant who believes herself to be defamed and cannot identify or locate the creator of the posting in question. They are usually solvent, visible in the market and may intervene directly by removing the material in question. Liability may, however, discourage such intermediaries from displaying controversial information (thereby restricting freedom of expression), threaten their financial stability, and put them in a difficult legal position whereby removal of the posting may place them in breach of their contractual arrangements with the posting's creator.[203]

On this basis, Articles 12–15 of the Directive seek to strike a balance between the different interests at stake,[204] and provide intermediary service providers with defences when 'illegal' material is found on their sites. This was implemented into the UK by the similarly worded Regulations 17–19, Electronic Commerce (EC Directive) Regulations 2002.[205]

These regulations adopt the framework of the Directive in dividing protection for intermediaries into three categories: mere conduits, caching and hosts. For the first, the key issue is that the intermediary is passive and did not initiate the information transmitted, select the receiver of the transmission, nor select or modify the information contained in the transmission. In contrast, caching involves storing information temporarily and automatically on the computer system in order to make onward transmission of this information more efficient. Here, liability will be avoided if the information is stored for the sole purpose of making more efficient onward transmission of the information to other recipients of the service upon their request, and the service provider does not modify the information, complies with conditions on access to the information, complies with any rules regarding the updating of the information,[206] does not interfere with the lawful use of technology[207] to obtain data on the use of the information, and acts expeditiously to remove or to disable access to the information he has stored upon obtaining actual knowledge of the fact that the information at the initial source of the transmission has been removed from the network, or access to it has been

[202] Consider the McAlpine scandal in the UK in November 2012: R Williams, 'The Largest Number of Defendants in British Legal History? Twitter Users Brace Themselves for Barrage of Lawsuits from Lord McAlpine' *Independent* (19 November 2012).

[203] P Todd, *E-Commerce Law* (London, Cavendish Publishing, 2005) para 12.2.

[204] Recital 41, Electronic Commerce Directive.

[205] Electronic Commerce (EC Directive) Regulations 2002 SI 2002/2013.

[206] As specified in a manner widely recognised and used by industry.

[207] As widely recognised and used by industry.

disabled, or that a court or an administrative authority has ordered such removal or disablement.[208] Caching, in practice, rarely gives rise to claims.[209]

In contrast, a 'host' will store Internet content, such as web pages and bulletin board postings, on its networks on a non-temporary basis.[210] Regulation 19 provides that:

> Where an information society service is provided which consists of the storage of information provided by a recipient of the service, the service provider (if he otherwise would) shall not be liable for damages or for any other pecuniary remedy or for any criminal sanction as a result of that storage where –
>
> (a) the service provider –
>
> (i) does not have actual knowledge of unlawful activity or information and, where a claim for damages is made, is not aware of facts or circumstances from which it would have been apparent to the service provider that the activity or information was unlawful; or
>
> (ii) upon obtaining such knowledge or awareness, acts expeditiously to remove or to disable access to the information, and
>
> (b) the recipient of the service was not acting under the authority or the control of the service provider.

The defence is limited, however, to the storage of information and will not apply if the involvement of the operator goes beyond mere storage.[211]

It is clear that these provisions supplement, and do not replace, existing UK provisions providing defences for ISPs. In particular, section 1(1) of the Defamation Act 1996 provides a defence where the defendant:

> (a) was not the author,[212] editor or publisher[213] of the statement complained of,
>
> (b) took reasonable care in relation to its publication, and
>
> (c) did not know, and had no reason to believe, that what he did caused or contributed to the publication of a defamatory statement.[214]

Section 1(3) lists individuals who do *not* qualify as 'authors', 'editors' or 'publishers' under section 1(1)(a). Section 1(3)(e)[215] expressly covers the 'operator or provider

[208] SI 2002/2013, Reg 18.

[209] See *Bunt v Tilley* [2006] EWHC 407 (QB); [2007] 1 WLR 1243 (claim under Reg.18, Electronic Commerce (EC Directive) Regulations 2002 failed).

[210] See Collins, *Law of Defamation and the Internet* (n 200) para 16.62. Examples include Usenet newsgroups (as in *Bunt v Tilley* (n 209), and online chat rooms (as in *Kaschke v Gray* [2010] EWHC 690 (QB)).

[211] See *Kaschke v Gray* [2010] EWHC 690 (QB); [2011] 1 WLR 452.

[212] Defamation Act 1996, s 1(2) defines 'author' as originator of the statement, but does not include a person who did not intend that his or her statement be published at all.

[213] Publisher, in this context, has a narrower meaning than normal and is confined to a commercial publisher, that is, a person whose business is issuing material to the public, or a section of the public, who issues material containing the statement in the course of that business: Defamation Act 1996, s 1(2).

[214] In assessing the above criteria, the court will have regard to the extent of the defendant's responsibilities for the content of, or decision to publish, the statement; the nature or circumstances of the publication; and the previous conduct or character of the author, editor or publisher: Defamation Act 1996, s 1(5). For example, if the defendant distributes work by an author renowned for controversy, the defendant will be expected to vet the work carefully for defamatory material.

[215] See also s 1(3)(c).

of access to a communications system by means of which the statement is transmitted, or made available, by a person over whom he had no effective control' – essentially an ISP. Further, there is authority that where the role of the ISP is merely passive, it should not be regarded as a publisher at common law and thus need not establish a defence to escape liability.[216] The leading case of *Godfrey v Demon Internet Ltd*[217] demonstrates that the requirements of section 1(1) are cumulative. Morland J held that a failure to remove a defamatory posting, when told of its nature by the claimant victim, would lead to the loss of the section 1 defence. Once the defendant was informed of the defamatory content and took the decision not to remove it from its news server, it was no longer able to satisfy the requirements of section 1(1)(b) that reasonable care had been taken, nor of section 1(1)(c) that it did not know, and it had no reason to believe, that what it did caused or contributed to the publication of a defamatory statement. The defence would only be available if, having taken all reasonable care, the defendant had no reason to suspect that his act had that effect.

Godfrey has led commentators to question whether the section 1 defence is actually more difficult to establish than that under Regulation 19. *Gatley on Libel and Slander* notes that the 1996 Act and the Regulations do not necessarily produce consistent results, so that the defendant may find that he has a defence under the Regulations but not the Act.[218] It may be questioned, for example, whether the tests of 'acting expeditiously' when it is known (or should have been known) that unlawful information has been published (Reg 19), and of taking reasonable care in relation to the publication of material which it knew (or should have known) would cause or contribute to the publication of a defamatory statement (s 1) produce the same results. The Law Commission in its 2002 report inclined to the view that, despite some ambiguity, Regulation 19 and section 1 would act in the same manner, leaving the ISP potentially liable where it has been notified of an allegedly defamatory posting.[219] The ECJ (Grand Chamber) in *L'Oreal SA v eBay International AG* (C-324/09)[220] further clarified that an operator would not be able to rely on the Regulation if the defendant had been aware of facts or circumstances on the basis of which a diligent economic operator should have identified

[216] *Bunt v Tilley* [2006] EWHC 407 (QB); [2007] 1 WLR 1243 (although only a striking out application); *Metropolitan International Schools Ltd v Designtechnica Corpn* [2009] EWHC 1765 (QB); [2011] 1 WLR 1743 (operator of online search engine not publisher of material appearing on search return), but contra Morland J (obiter) in *Godfrey v Demon Internet Ltd* [2001] QB 201, 212. The Court of Appeal in *Tamiz v Google Inc* [2013] EWCA Civ 68 controversially overruled the view of Eady J at first instance ([2012] EWHC 449 (QB)), finding that Google's role as a platform provider was not purely passive when it provided tools to enable the blogger to design the layout, made the service available on terms of its own choice and could readily remove or block access to any blog that did not comply with those terms. The provision of a platform for blogs was deemed to be equivalent to the provision of a notice board: para 33.

[217] *Godfrey v Demon Internet Ltd* [2001] QB 201.

[218] P Milmo and WVH Rogers (eds), *Gatley on Libel and Slander*, 11th edn (London, Sweet & Maxwell, 2008) 6.28 : 'or even vice versa'.

[219] Law Commission, *Defamation and the Internet: A Preliminary Investigation* Scoping Study No 2 (December 2002) para.2.23.

[220] *Godfrey v Demon Internet Ltd* [2012] All ER (EC) 501, paras 120–21: the case concerned the interpretation of Art 14 of the E Commerce Directive upon which Reg 19 itself is based.

the illegality in question. Nevertheless, some commentators[221] have suggested that Regulation 19, in examining whether the service provider has knowledge that the activity or information is *unlawful*, imposes a higher threshold than the test under the 1996 Act. In order to be able to characterise something as 'unlawful' a person would need to know something of the strengths or weaknesses of available defences.[222] On this basis, while a notice showing that a statement is defamatory may be sufficient to defeat the section 1 defence, it may not be sufficient to defeat the Regulation 19 defence unless it also makes out a prime facie case of unlawfulness. Further, even during the pre-complaint period, section 1 requires that the defendant can show that it both took reasonable care in relation to the publication and did not know and had no reason to believe that what it did caused or contributed to the publication of a defamatory statement. This strongly suggests that there will be circumstances where a defendant can rely on the Regulation 19 defence, but where the section 1 defence will be lost.

Examining this area of law, one sees again tensions between the national and EU provisions, exacerbated by a lack of clarity as to the operation of the Regulations.[223] In an excellent survey of the application of the Directive across Europe in 2011, van Eecke identified ongoing uncertainty as to the meaning of the provisions dealing with online service providers, diverging case law at Member State level and a lack of understanding in many Member States of the role of online intermediaries and the reasons why it might be desirable to give them some protection.[224] In providing a defence which co-exists uneasily with national law, it is left to the domestic courts to speculate on overall policy and the degree to which online intermediaries should be protected against liability. A worrying concern is that the price of such uncertainty is paid by the ISPs themselves, forced to settle or engage in expensive litigation to determine the limits of their liability to claimants. On this basis, it seems legitimate to question whether a loosely phrased Directive which is now over 10 years old in a rapidly developing area of technology is capable of assisting Member States in their treatment of online intermediaries and, perhaps more pointedly, of giving the more principled assistance found by reference to the rights of freedom of expression and respect for private life under the ECHR to which the English courts increasingly make reference.[225]

[221] See GJH Smith, *Internet Law and Regulation*, 4th edn (London, Sweet and Maxwell, 2007) para 4-041; Collins, *The Law of Defamation and the Internet* (n 200) 16.75; *Gatley on Libel and Slander* (n 218) para 6.31.

[222] See Eady J in *Bunt v Tilley* (n 216), para 72 and, more recently, *McGrath & Anor v Dawkins & Ors* [2012] EWHC B3 (QB), para 43.

[223] Winfield and Jolowicz describe the law as a 'complex web of municipal and European legislation': *Winfield and Jolowicz* (n 103) para 12-23.

[224] P van Eecke, 'Online Service Providers and Liability: A Plea for a Balanced Approach' (2011) 48 *Common Market Law Review* 1455.

[225] 'Where the law is uncertain, in the face of rapidly developing technology, it is important that judges should strive to achieve consistency in their decisions and that proper regard should be paid, in doing so, to the values enshrined in the European Convention on Human Rights and Fundamental Freedoms. In particular, one should guard against imposing legal liability in restraint of Art.10 where it is not necessary or proportionate so to do': *Tamiz v Google Inc* [2012] EWHC 449 (QB); [2012] EMLR 24, para 37 (Eady J).

It is in this light that reforms introduced by the UK government are of particular relevance. The UK government had noted widespread concern that internet intermediaries, by facilitating the posting of defamatory material, might find themselves liable as publishers for the material despite their ignorance of its defamatory content. In its draft Defamation Bill of 2011, the government initiated consultation on the question of responsibility for publication on the internet and sought views on whether the law should be changed to give greater protection to secondary publishers such as ISPs, and discussion forums, alternatively how the existing law should be updated and clarified.[226] The Report of the Joint Committee on the Draft Defamation Bill[227] recommended reducing the pressure on hosts and service providers to take down material whenever it is challenged as being defamatory, in line with the core principle of protecting freedom of speech. It therefore proposed a new notice and take-down procedure, designed to provide everyone with easy access to the rapid resolution of disputes about online material. In its response, the Government rejected the proposed system as having too many practical and technical difficulties.[228] Importantly, however, it accepted the need to strike a balance which provided an effective means for people to protect their reputation when defamed on the internet, while ensuring that internet intermediaries are not unjustifiably required to remove material or deterred from properly monitoring content because of the fear that this will leave them potentially liable.[229] Section 5 of the Defamation Act 2013 now creates a new defence for the operators of websites where a defamation action is brought against them in respect of a statement posted on the website:

> Section 5 Operators of websites[230]
>
> (1) This section applies where an action for defamation is brought against the operator of a website in respect of a statement posted on the website.
> (2) It is a defence for the operator to show that it was not the operator who posted the statement on the website.
> (3) The defence is defeated if the claimant shows that –
>
>   (a) it was not possible for the claimant to identify the person who posted the statement,
>   (b) the claimant gave the operator a notice of complaint in relation to the statement, and

[226] *Draft Defamation Bill Consultation*, Consultation Paper CP3/11: www.justice.gov.uk/consultations/draft-defamation-bill.htm.

[227] *The Joint Committee on the Draft Defamation Bill Report* Session 2010–12, HL 203, HC 930-I, para 100; available at: www.publications.parliament.uk/pa/jt201012/jtselect/jtdefam/203/20307.htm#a40.

[228] *The Government's Response to the Report of the Joint Committee on the Draft Defamation*, Cm 8295 (London, HMSO, 2012); available at www.justice.gov.uk/downloads/publications/policy/moj/government-response-draft-defamation-bill.pdf. Interestingly the report made no reference to the 2000 Directive.

[229] Ibid, paras 85–88.

[230] Query whether the term 'website' is wide enough to cover all the activities of ISPs.

(c) the operator failed to respond to the notice of complaint in accordance with any provision contained in regulations.[231]

(4) For the purposes of subsection (3)(a), it is possible for a claimant to 'identify' a person only if the claimant has sufficient information to bring proceedings against the person.

. . .

(11) The defence under this section is defeated if the claimant shows that the operator of the website has acted with malice in relation to the posting of the statement concerned.

The procedure to be followed is set out in regulations which indicate what steps an operator must take in response to a notice of complaint and within what period of time.[232] The presumed defence does, however, put the onus on the claimant to satisfy section 5(3). Further section 5(12) adds that the defence is not to be defeated by reason only of the fact that the operator of the website moderates the statements posted on it by others.

The Government envisages the online intermediary acting as a liaison point between the person complaining about a defamatory posting and the person who has posted the material, where the identity and contact details of the latter are not known to the complainant. Upon receipt of a notice of complaint, the intermediary would have to contact the author of the material (or if this did not prove possible, take the posting down). If, after an initial exchange of correspondence, the issue remained in dispute, the intermediary would be required to provide details of the author to the complainant, who would then have to initiate legal proceedings against him or her to secure removal of the material (if the matter could not be resolved by other means), and could not pursue an action against the intermediary.[233] It is hoped that this new approach would have the benefit of resolving many cases without the need for court proceedings.[234]

This provision highlights the development of a UK-based approach to liability, side-lining the 2000 Directive in defamation cases although commentators continue to express concern at the failure of the UK government to ensure consistency

[231] Defamation Act 2013, s 5(5) provides that

> Regulations may (a) make provision as to the action required to be taken by an operator of a website in response to a notice of complaint (which may in particular include action relating to the identity or contact details of the person who posted the statement and action relating to its removal); (b) make provision specifying a time limit for the taking of any such action; (c) make provision conferring on the court a discretion to treat action taken after the expiry of a time limit as having been taken before the expiry; (d) make any other provision for the purposes of this section.

[232] Defamation Act 2013, ss 5(8)–(10). See now the Defamation (Operators of Websites) Regulations 2013/3028.

[233] Para 85, the *Government's Response to the Report of the Joint Committee on the Draft Defamation Bill* (n 228).

[234] Ibid, para 86.

between the two pieces of legislation.[235] The assumption seems to be that both the Defamation Act 1996 and 2000 Directive have failed to give sufficient protection to online intermediaries and it is therefore left to the *national* legislator to provide a framework which finds a correct balance between freedom of expression and the protection of reputation. This may be seen as a victory for national, rather than European policy, which places freedom of expression above the internal market concerns of the EU.

Conclusion

This chapter has examined how the introduction of new rules resulting from the transposition of EU Directives into UK law has affected English tort law. The examples given relate to key areas of English tort law: the liability of manufacturers to the ultimate consumer, the care owed by an employer to his or her employees, the operation of the tort of negligence in motor vehicle accidents and the defences available to ISPs in the tort of defamation. These new provisions seek either to ensure a minimum standard of protection for claimants in all Members States or, in the case of the Product Liability Directive, a common regime for those injured by defective products. At face value, it would seem that these Directives pose a threat to the autonomy of the English courts to develop organically core tort law principle.

However, this study has highlighted a distinction between the *existence* of new European tort law principles and their *impact*. Reading a standard tort law textbook, one would have little awareness that European Directives are changing core tort law principle and indeed, this seems not to be the case. Minimum standards, which offer a level of protection which UK law already exceeds (as in the example of health and safety law) or with which it is consistent (in our motor insurance/defamation examples), have made little difference in practice to claimants. Even a maximum harmonisation directive such as the 1985 Product Liability Directive has, perhaps surprisingly, done little to change the position of litigants suffering loss due to a defective product. Studies have shown that litigation costs have encouraged the use of informal dispute resolution mechanisms and that, for reasons of convenience, contract law may provide a more immediate solution. Further, the limited scope of the Directive, which permits litigants to seek remedies elsewhere when necessary, has diminished its impact on domestic systems of compensation.

Two main reasons may be identified for the limited impact of EU law, which has been highlighted in this chapter. First, the nature and scope of the Directives

[235] See, eg, Ashley Hurst comments on the Inforrm's blog: http://inforrm.wordpress.com/2012/12/14/clause-5-still-needs-work-joint-committee-on-human-rights-delivers-its-verdict-on-the-defamation-bill-ashley-hurst/.

themselves have restricted their ability to reform and harmonise national law. Directives are usually the result of compromise. The 10-year debate over the Product Liability Directive is a good example of where consensus came at the price of optional provisions and a watering down of the original framework of liability.[236] The final text, as a result, is often ambiguous and imprecise. Further, Directives grant Member States discretion how to transpose the text into national law. Transposition will involve translating EU legal terminology into nationally understood norms, while trying to retain their autonomous European meaning. The UK government guidance on transposition sets the general principle that Directives should be copied out, except where doing so would adversely affect UK interests.[237] This may lead to consistency, but the disadvantages of this approach were noted in a recent Law Commission report, which found that the 1993 Unfair Terms Directive,[238] which had been copied out into English law in the Unfair Terms in Consumer Contracts Regulations 1994/1999,[239] contained language which was too obscure to be accessible. It recommended that the law should be rewritten in a clear way, using terminology familiar in the UK.[240] More familiar legal language possesses, however, its own difficulties in that the national court is likely to interpret the transposed law according to ordinary common law principles. Further, by placing the transposed law into general domestic legislation,[241] it becomes difficult to distinguish rules having an EU origin from those developed organically.

The danger of assimilation of EU law into the common law system is exacerbated by the piecemeal and targeted nature of the Directives. The impact of EU law has been described as 'pointillist', consisting of a series of isolated steps without amounting to a system.[242] Minimum harmonisation directives set simply a basic line below which Member States cannot go. This leaves considerable scope for Member States to legislate above this line with resultant diversity across Member States. The health and safety Framework Directive of 1989, for example, was not regarded as significant to UK lawyers, who were confident that their own system already provided a higher level of protection. It simply made the law rather more complicated than it had been previously. Equally the defence for ISPs in the 2000 E-Commerce Directive was dismissed by the Law Commission as consistent

[236] It is widely acknowledged that the European Commission made a number of compromises to obtain agreement on the Product Liability Directive including the introduction of the development risks defence much to its reluctance: Howells, 'Product Liability' (n 89) 894–95.

[237] UK Department for Business, Innovation and Skills, *Transposition Guidance: How to Implement European Directives Effectively* (April 2013) 10, available at: www.gov.uk/government/publications/implementing-eu-directives-into-uk-law.

[238] Unfair Terms Directive 93/13/EEC.

[239] SI 1994/3159 and SI 1999/ 2083.

[240] English and Scottish Law Commissions, *Unfair Terms in Consumer Contracts: A New Approach? Issues Paper* (Crown copyright 2012) 9.8.

[241] eg, the Consumer Protection Act 1987 or the Health and Safety at Work etc Act 1974.

[242] A Harmathy, 'The Impact of the Practice of the European Court of Justice on the Civil and Commercial Law of the Member States of the European Union' (2010) 18 *European Review of Private Law* 429, 431. See also T Wilhelmsson, 'Private Law in the EU: Harmonised or Fragmented Europeanisation' (2002) *European Review of Private Law* 81.

with the previously enacted (UK) Defamation Act 1996, section 1. Maximum harmonisation directives are a rarity in view of the difficulties of achieving consent,[243] but even the maximum harmonisation Product Liability Directive does not touch on key issues such as causation, remoteness, the assessment of damages and civil procedure which are left to the national courts subject to the principles of effectiveness and equivalence. The provisions of EU law therefore exist alongside national rules and are integrated into classic tort frameworks: strict liability, breach of statutory duty, negligence, and defamation. This leads to what Stapleton has described as a localised application of the law – key matters left to national interpretation with limited EU guidance.[244]

This leads us to the second reason for the lack of impact of EU law on English tort law, which lies with the European Commission and CJEU themselves. Institutional limitations and practice have led to both these institutions playing only a limited role in promoting the uniform application of the law. At first glance, the supervisory role of both bodies seems significant. The 1985 Directive, for example, places a direct obligation on Member States to communicate to the Commission the texts of the main provisions of national law which they subsequently adopt in the field governed by the Directive[245] and on the Commission to report on the application of the Directive every five years.[246] Articles 258 and 260 TFEU also provide a means by which Member States may be held to account for failing to transpose any directive correctly. Article 258 TFEU establishes a general enforcement procedure which grants the European Commission a broad power to bring enforcement proceedings against Member States and this is supported by the Article 260 TFEU penalty mechanism.[247] This was successfully used in *European Commission v United Kingdom*[248] to ensure a more restrictive interpretation of the development risks defence under the 1987 Act. However, although this chapter has identified a number of cases brought by the Commission against the United Kingdom (and other States), the UK government has generally come out of such litigation relatively unscathed. In reality, the commencement of enforcement procedures is rare and inevitably politically controversial. The Article 267 TFEU preliminary reference procedure may seem more politically neutral in that it involves the domestic court itself asking for answers to specific questions of interpretation, but the nature of the exercise does limit the Court's ability to

[243] The difficulties experienced in gaining consensus for the 2011 Consumer Rights Directives offer an excellent example of this: see Directive 2011/83/EU of the European Parliament and of Council of 25 October 2011 on consumer rights [2011] OJ L304/65, 22 November 2011; C Twigg-Flesner and D Metcalfe, 'The Proposed Consumer Rights Directive: Less Haste, More Thought?' (2009) 5 *European Review of Contract Law* 368.

[244] J Stapleton, 'Products Liability in the United Kingdom: The Myths of Reform' (1999) 34 *Texas International Law Journal* 45, 66.

[245] Art 20.

[246] Art 21.

[247] See, generally, Craig and de Búrca (n 4) ch 12; but for criticism of the Art 260 mechanism, see P Wenneras, 'Sanctions against Member States under Article 260 TFEU: Alive, But Not Kicking?' (2012) 49 *Common Market Law Review* 145.

[248] *European Commission v United Kingdom* Case C-300/95 [1997] ECR I-2649.

intervene. Article 267 does not empower the CJEU to apply the law to the facts of the case and it must confine itself to responding to the questions posed by the national court.[249] Much will depend on the particular wording and scope of the questions asked, although it must be said that the Court on occasion has gone beyond its role in giving interpretative guidance.[250] Wurmnest and Heinze have commented, however, on the undue caution and self-restraint of European judges and identify a worrying trend to avoid difficult issues by giving open or evasive answers.[251] They also note that the development of private law principles is not assisted by the fact that most judges in the CJEU have a public law background, leading them often to address private law from a constitutional perspective. The point here is that if the CJEU and the Commission are not prepared to interfere and defer instead to the national courts, domestic courts are likely to continue to utilise localised forms of legal reasoning in interpreting the law. Even Burton J in *A*, in dutifully citing CJEU case law and case law from the Netherlands and Germany, arguably found it difficult to avoid common law reasoning, choosing to distinguish the Dutch case law and re-interpret the result of the German case.[252] Undue deference to national sensibilities serves only to diminish the impact of the Directives in national legal systems and de-emphasise the European policy goals involved.

This leads to an inevitable conflict at EU and UK level as to policy control. Tort law does not exist in a vacuum and essential policy questions arise as to the scope of intervention, the extent of compensation permissible and the treatment of risk. In all four examples, we have seen tensions between UK and EU policy goals and, notably in the case of health and safety law and defamation, direct intervention by the UK government to reform the law to render it more consistent with its own policy imperatives. In the motor insurance example, the main concern of the commentators was that core tort law principles might be changed by the unexpected intervention of the Motor Insurance Directives. The Product Liability Directive, in contrast, arose during a time when there were parallel suggestions of reform in the UK on the basis of strict liability, but its ghettoisation into consumer law has served to minimise its impact on general tort law principle where it is treated as a specific example of strict liability. Further, in practice, the courts have been reluctant to relinquish their previous adherence to cost/benefit analysis.

[249] See 2012/C 338/01 Recommendations to national courts and tribunals in relation to the initiation of preliminary ruling proceedings, para 7: 'under the preliminary ruling procedure the Court's role is to give an interpretation of European Union law or to rule on its validity, not to apply that law to the factual situation underlying the main proceedings. That is the task of the national court or tribunal'.

[250] Craig and de Búrca, *EU Law* (n 4) 473–74 (*Marleasing* itself being a classic example of the ECJ blurring this divide by providing a detailed response which simply required the Spanish court to execute the Court's ruling).

[251] W Wurmnest and C Heinze, 'General Principles of Tort Law in the Jurisprudence of the European Court of Justice' in R Schulze (ed), *Compensation of Private Losses: The Evolution of Torts in European Business Law* (Munich, Sellier, 2011) 61–62.

[252] *Scholten v Sanguin Foundation* February 3, 1999 NJ 1999, 621 (not followed); BGH 9 May 1995 NJW 1995, 2162 (re-interpreted).

These two factors serve to minimise 'Europeanisation' in this context. EU Directives have, in reality, made limited changes to national tort law. The English courts (and legislator) have demonstrated a resistance to loss of policy control and a tendency to absorb these piecemeal and targeted measures into the national common law framework. To this must be added a failure by the CJEU to establish clear European principles of tort law to be interpreted by the national courts. While deference to the national courts may be seen as politically astute and indeed a good means of limiting the work of the CJEU, well-known for its delays and over-burdensome case load, it does permit national courts considerable leeway in their interpretation of EU law provisions. Harmonisation by directives thus seems a long way away. EU tort law remains in its infancy, at least in the context of EU Directives affecting traditional tort law principle.

The next chapter will examine a potentially more significant source of Europeanisation in tort law: the ruling by the European Court of Justice in *Francovich v Italian Republic*[253] that each Member State may be liable in tort for breaching EU law and that this new cause of action would be applied by the national courts. The response of the English courts to this new source of tortious liability will be considered in chapter four.

[253] C6/90 *Francovich v Italian Republic* [1991] ECR I-5357; [1993] 2 CMLR 66.

4

The European Tort: State Liability for Breach of European Union Law

Introduction

This chapter will address an area of tort law where the interface between the European Union and English law is directly in issue. In 1991, the European Court of Justice in *Francovich v Italian Republic*[1] established the principle of State liability for breach of EU law. The court held that 'the effectiveness of [EU] rules would be impaired and the protection of the rights which they grant would be weakened if individuals were unable to obtain compensation when their rights are infringed by a breach of [EU] law for which a Member State can be held responsible.'[2] The importance of *Francovich* lies in the fact that this new form of liability would be applied by the national courts of Member States. The result is a novel form of tort law, which imposes liability not on private individuals but the State itself (including its courts of last instance). By requiring Member States to provide a non-contractual (or, for an English lawyer, tortious) remedy in damages, the ECJ, in effect, introduced a new hybrid form of tort law into the English legal system. This has no organic origin in the common law, but derives directly from case law of the Court of Justice of the European Union (CJEU). The task, therefore, for the national court is to apply this new form of tortious liability, bearing in mind the conditions established by the European Court and subject to its supervision, notably by means of preliminary rulings under Article 267 TFEU,[3] thereby providing an effective remedy which is equivalent to comparable domestic remedies.[4]

Francovich liability marks a new stage in the relationship between the English courts and the Court of Justice. The English courts are operating in a clear EU

[1] C6/90 *Francovich v Italian Republic* [1991] ECR I-5357; [1993] 2 CMLR 66 (hereafter *Francovich*).

[2] Ibid, para 33.

[3] Particularly relevant here is the obligation of the national court of last instance to refer questions to the CJEU where a decision is necessary to enable it to give judgment: see Art 267(3) TFEU. The Commission may equally assess whether the States have breached EU law under Art 258 TFEU and fine for serious and persistent breaches (Art 260 TFEU).

[4] See now also Art 19(1) TEU: 'Member States shall provide remedies sufficient to ensure effective legal protection in the fields covered by Union law.'

context. They must respond to the jurisprudence of the CJEU, while integrating this new cause of action into the traditional framework of the common law. As stated in the leading textbook of Craig and De Búrca, 'national courts [are required] to strike an appropriate, proportionality-based, case-by-case balance between the requirement of effective judicial protection for EU law rights and the application of legitimate national procedural and remedial rules'.[5] Nevertheless, English law has struggled to apply the conditions for liability, with, it must be stated, limited guidance from the CJEU, and indeed the classification of this form of liability itself remains contentious. This chapter will examine the response of the English courts to *Francovich* liability, colloquially known as the Eurotort,[6] and the extent to which this external source of tort law has been successfully integrated into the common law system of liability.

I. The Development of State Liability for Breach of EU Law[7]

As highlighted by the ECJ in *Van Gend en Loos*,[8] EU law not only leads to the imposition of obligations on individuals, but is capable of conferring rights which may be asserted against Member States and EU institutions. Such rights, if breached, require a remedy and national courts are expected to respect this. Nevertheless, the starting point for the CJEU was national procedural autonomy: 'in the absence of [EU] rules on this subject, it is for the domestic legal system of each Member State to designate the courts having jurisdiction and to determine the procedural conditions governing actions at law intended to ensure the protection of the rights which citizens have from the direct effect of [EU] law.'[9] This is subject, however, to a caveat: national law must satisfy the principles of equivalence (the remedy cannot be less favourable than those relating to similar actions of a domestic nature)[10] and effectiveness (the right to effective judicial protection should not be undermined).[11]

[5] P Craig and G de Búrca, *EU Law: Text, Cases and Materials*, 5th edn (Oxford, Oxford University Press, 2011) 231. See also K Lenaerts, 'National Remedies for Private Parties in the Light of the EU law Principles of Equivalence and Effectiveness' (2011) 46 *Irish Jurist* 13 and Case C-430–431/93 *Van Schijndel & Van Veen v Stichting Pensioenfonds voor Fysiotherapeuten* [1995] ECR I-4705 and Case C-312/93 *Peterbroeck v Belgian State* [1995] ECR I-4599.

[6] This term was first used by Henry J in *Barretts & Baird (Wholesale) v IPCS* [1987] IRLR 3, 5.

[7] See, generally, Craig and de Búrca, *EU Law* (n 5) ch. 8, esp 241–55.

[8] Case 26/62 *Van Gend en Loos v Nederlandse administratie der belastungen* [1963] ECR 1: [1963] CMLR 105.

[9] Case 33/76 *Rewe v Landwirtschaftskammer für das Saarland* [1976] ECR 1989, para 5.

[10] Case 158/80 *Rewe v Hauptzollamt Kiel* [1981] ECR 1805, para.44.

[11] See Case 14/83 *Von Colson and Kamann v Land Nordrhein-Westfalen* [1984] ECR 1891 and Case C-432/05 *Unibet* [2007] ECR I-2271, paras 37–44.

Over time, however, tensions have grown in the relationship between national courts and the CJEU. The doctrines of direct effect, which creates individual rights where legislation is clear, precise and unconditional, which the national courts must protect,[12] and, to a lesser extent, indirect effect, have served to underline the active role expected of national courts in enforcing EU law.[13] The ECJ in *Unibet* acknowledged that while, in principle, it did not require new remedies in national law, it might be otherwise if national law did not make it possible to ensure, even indirectly, respect for EU rights.[14] On this basis, despite the initial view that EU law did not require States to create new remedies in the national courts to ensure the observance of EU law,[15] this must now be qualified. One notable qualification arises from the ground-breaking decision of *Francovich v Italian Republic*[16] itself.

A. *Francovich*: A New Head of Tortious Liability

Francovich involved a number of claims against the Italian Republic for compensation for losses which, it was alleged, were due to Italy's delay in implementing Directive 80/987/EEC.[17] It was argued that had the Directive been implemented, the employees' losses following the insolvency of their employer would have been eliminated (or at least reduced). In providing that the effectiveness of EU rules would be impaired if individual citizens were unable to obtain compensation when their rights under EU law had been breached, the ECJ drew on the principle of effectiveness,[18] combined with the obligation of Member States to implement Directives and to make good loss and damage, now found in Article 4(3) TEU.[19] On this basis, it was inherent in the system of the Treaty that a State must be liable for loss and damage caused to individuals as a result of breaches of EU law. This new form of liability would be enforceable before the national courts.

Francovich represents a significant step in the relationship between the CJEU and the national courts of the EU. First, it involves an extension of liability beyond the doctrine of direct effect. In *Francovich*, the ECJ found a right to reparation,

[12] See Case 26/62 *Van Gend en Loos* [1963] ECR 1, [1963] CMLR 105 (Treaty articles); Case 41/74 *Van Duyn v Home Office* [1974] ECR 1337, [1975] 1 CMLR 1 (Directives); Art 288 TFEU (Regulations and decisions) and, generally, PP Craig, 'Once upon a Time in the West: Direct Effect and the Federalization of EEC Law' (1992) 12 *Oxford Journal of Legal Studies* 453.

[13] See Craig and de Búrca (n 5) ch 7.

[14] Case C-432/05 *Unibet Ltd v Justitiekanslern* [2007] ECR I-2271, para 41.

[15] Case 158/80 *Rewe-Handelsgesellschaft Nord v Hauptzollamt Kiel* [1981] ECR 1805, para 44.

[16] *Francovich* (n 1).

[17] Council Directive 80/987/EEC of 20 October 1980 on the approximation of the laws of the Member States relating to the protection of employees in the event of the insolvency of their employer [1980] OJ L283/23.

[18] See *Francovich* (n 1) paras 33 and 39.

[19] See *Francovich*, (n 1) para 36. Art 4(3) TEU provides that 'The Member States shall take any appropriate measure, general or particular, to ensure fulfilment of the obligations arising out of the Treaties or resulting from the acts of the institutions of the Union. The Member States shall facilitate the achievement of the Union's tasks and refrain from any measure which could jeopardise the attainment of the Union's objectives.'

despite the fact that the Directive in question was insufficiently precise to be directly effective.[20] Such liability therefore exists independently of the doctrine of direct effect, although it has been described as 'the necessary corollary of the direct effect of the Community provision whose breach caused the damage sustained.'[21] As Lord Hope explained in *Three Rivers District Council v Bank of England*,[22] this signifies that individuals now have two distinct routes by which to claim damages from a national authority: first, the principle of direct effect where damages are sought for the non-implementation or mis-implementation of a Directive, and, secondly, the broader ground of State liability. Both share the common goal of ensuring that EU provisions prevail over national provisions to ensure the full effectiveness of EU law. Secondly, by creating a right to damages, whose application would be determined by the national courts, the CJEU demonstrated its willingness to develop 'European' private law rights applicable in Member States, regardless of national legal traditions. This is an extension of Article 340(2) TFEU, which recognises that the tort liability of EU institutions is based on general principles common to the laws of Member States.[23] It is not surprising, therefore, that in the later case of *Brasserie du Pêcheur v Germany; R v Secretary of State for Transport, ex p. Factortame (No 4)*,[24] the Court expressly relied on Article 340(2) in stating the general European principle of tortious liability for breach of EU law.[25]

It is in *Brasserie du Pêcheur* that the CJEU established the three conditions necessary for determining liability:

> Community law confers a right to reparation where three conditions are met: the rule of law infringed must be intended to confer rights on individuals; the breach must be sufficiently serious; and there must be a direct causal link between the breach of the obligation resting on the state and the damage sustained by the injured parties.[26]

[20] The relationship between direct effect and *Francovich* liability is contentious: see S Prechal, 'Member State Liability and Direct Effect: What's the Difference After All?' [2006] *European Business Law Review* 299.

[21] C-46/93 and C-48/93 *Brasserie du Pêcheur v Germany; R v Secretary of State for Transport, ex p Factortame (No 4)* [1996] ECR I- 1029, para 22.

[22] *Three Rivers District Council v Bank of England (No 3)* [2000] UKHL 33; [2003] 2 AC 1, 198–99

[23] This provides for claims in tort against the European Union itself when an individual has suffered loss resulting from the legislative, administrative or executive functions of a European Union institution. See, generally, A Biondi and M Farley, *The Right to Damages in European Law* (The Hague, Kluwer Law International, 2009) ch 3; L Antoniolli, 'Community Liability' in H Koziol and R Schulze, *Tort Law of the European Community* (Wien, Springer, 2008).

[24] C-46/93 and C-48/93 *Brasserie du Pêcheur v Germany; R v Secretary of State for Transport, ex p Factortame (No 4)* (also known as '*Factortame III*') [1996] ECR I- 1029; [1996] QB 404 (hereafter *Brasserie du Pêcheur*) paras 28 and 29.

[25] Note also C-352/98 P *Laboratoires Pharmaceutiques Bergaderm SA v Commission of the European Communities* [2000] ECR I-5291 in which the ECJ acknowledged that the same criteria would be applied in the contexts of both State liability and EU liability under Art 340(2). Claims for institutional liability cannot be brought in the national courts and jurisdiction rests solely with the two Courts of the EU: Art 268 TFEU. On this basis, the English courts have not been required to deal with such claims and reference will only be made to case law under Art 340(2) TFEU when relevant to *Francovich* liability

[26] *Brasserie du Pêcheur* (n 24) para 51. For comment, see A Downes, 'Trawling for a Remedy: State Liability under Community Law' (1997) 17 *Legal Studies* 286 and P Craig, 'Once More unto the Breach: The Community, the State and Damages Liability' (1997) 113 *Law Quarterly Review* 67.

These conditions serve both to establish a framework for liability, but also keep liability within bounds. The national court will determine the facts and whether the conditions for liability have been satisfied. Further, it will lay down the substantive and procedural conditions for liability provided that they are not less favourable to similar domestic claims and not so framed as to make it virtually impossible or excessively difficult to obtain reparation.[27]

However, as will be seen, in a number of leading cases, the CJEU has found itself able to give guidance as to the correct application of these conditions, thereby blurring the division of roles between the European and domestic courts. Indeed, the relationship between the autonomy of the national court and the ability of the CJEU to intervene is an ongoing source of contention. While it is clear that the CJEU is willing on occasion to defer to the national courts, it exercises what Tridimas has called 'selective deference'.[28] In other words, although Member States are ostensibly permitted to develop principles of State liability subject to the principles of effectiveness and equivalence, the CJEU has at times adopted a more interventionist position which serves to remind national courts of the balance of power.

II. English Tort Law and the Eurotort: Balancing European Policy and National Autonomy

For an English tort lawyer, the first reaction to *Francovich* liability is likely to be one of lack of familiarity. Leading textbooks deal with it briefly as a subsection of the chapter concerning breach of statutory duty: *Winfield and Jolowicz on Tort* granting it one paragraph,[29] *Markesinis and Deakin's Tort Law* four pages.[30] It is perhaps unsurprising that it is the text and materials co-written by the former Director of the Institute for European Tort Law, Ken Oliphant, which provides the lengthiest account, albeit six pages.[31] Leading practitioners' text, *Clerk and Lindsell on Torts*, confines itself to three paragraphs.[32] In contrast, EU textbooks spend considerable time on the conditions of liability set at EU level, but understandably pay scant attention to their application at national level.[33] This leaves

[27] See *Francovich* (n 1) para 43.

[28] T Tridimas, 'Liability for Breach of Community Law: Growing up and Mellowing Down?' (2001) 38 *Common Market Law Review* 301.

[29] WVH Rogers, *Winfield and Jolowicz on Tort*, 18th edn (London, Sweet and Maxwell, 2010) para 7-12.

[30] S Deakin, A Johnston and BS Markesinis, *Markesinis and Deakin's Tort Law*, 6th edn (Oxford, Clarendon Press, 2008) 435–38

[31] M Lunney and K Oliphant, *Tort Law: Text and Materials*, 5th edn (Oxford, Oxford University Press, 2013) 617–22.

[32] M Jones et al, *Clerk and Lindsell on Torts*, 20th edn (London, Sweet and Maxwell, 2010) paras 9-46 to 9-48 (hereafter *Clerk and Lindsell*).

[33] Craig and de Búrca (n 5) ch 8; D Chambers, G Davies and G Monti, *European Union Law: Cases and Materials*, 2nd edn (Cambridge, Cambridge University Press 2010) 301–14, although not always: see, for example, PP Craig 'The Domestic Liability of Public Authorities in Damages: Lessons from the European Community' and M Hoskins, 'Rebirth of the Innominate Tort?' chs 6 and 7 in J Beatson and T Tridimas, *New Directions in European Public Law* (Oxford, Hart Publishing, 1998).

the reader somewhat short-changed subject to a few specialist texts such as the excellent Stanton, Skidmore, Harris and Wright, *Statutory Torts*,[34] or specialist works such as Biondi and Farley, *The Right to Damages in European Law*.[35] Even the term, Eurotort, does little to explain its significance in the English law of torts. This section will seek to remedy this omission and examine the application of the Eurotort in the English courts and the extent to which the common law judiciary has adapted to its particular hybrid EU/national law characteristics. Twenty years after the key *Francovich* decision, what has been the impact of this case in terms of both successful actions and the legal reasoning of the courts?

A. Applying *Francovich* Liability in the English Courts

In determining when the *Francovich/ Brasserie du Pêcheur* conditions are met, the national courts are given considerable autonomy, subject, as previously stated, to the principles of equivalence and effectiveness. It is for the national court to find the facts, decide whether the European legislation is intended to confer rights on individuals, whether the breach of European law is sufficiently serious and determine whether there is a direct causal link between the breach and the damage suffered. There is no precondition that the claimant should have exhausted all domestic remedies before relying on this cause of action.[36] Procedural rules are also generally a matter for the national courts, subject to the twin principles of equivalence and effectiveness. On this basis, limitation periods[37] and the choice of the relevant court[38] will be a matter for national courts as will rules of evidence. Judge Toulmin QC, therefore, in *Factortame (No 7)*,[39] determined that for limitation purposes *Francovich* liability should be treated in the same manner as breach of statutory duty. The Court of Appeal in *Spencer v Secretary of State for Work and Pensions* confirmed that section 2 of the Limitation Act 1980 would apply to such claims.[40]

It must be borne in mind, however, that the CJEU has given guidance as to the content of these conditions and its case law is binding on the English courts. There is also an obligation under Article 267(3) TFEU for courts of final appeal to

[34] K Stanton, P Skidmore, M Harris and J Wright, *Statutory Torts* (London, Sweet and Maxwell, 2003) ch 6. See also K Stanton, 'New Forms of the Tort of Breach of Statutory Duty' (2004) 120 *Law Quarterly Review* 324.

[35] A Biondi and M Farley, *The Right to Damages in European Law* (The Hague, Kluwer Law International, 2009).

[36] *Spencer v Secretary of State for Work and Pensions* [2008] EWCA Civ 750; [2009] QB 358 (hereafter *Spencer*).

[37] C-261/95 *Palmisani v INPS* [1997] ECR I-4025. Contrast Case C-473/00 *Cofidis v Jean Louis Fredout* [2002] ECR I-10875, where the ECJ found that a two-year time limit was incompatible with EU law (para 35).

[38] *Secretary of State for Employment v Mann* [1997] ICR 209: *Francovich* claims must be brought before the ordinary courts and industrial tribunals do not have jurisdiction.

[39] *R v Secretary of State for Transport ex p Factortame Ltd (No 7)* [2000] EWHC (Tech) 179, para 176.

[40] *Spencer* (n 36): action accrues from the time that claimants suffered personal injuries – s2, Limitation Act 1980 applies.

refer questions of interpretation to the CJEU when the answer is not clear.[41] While the *acte clair* doctrine permits the national court to decline to refer a question on the basis that the point is clear,[42] the standard is relatively high. The correct application of European law must be so obvious as to leave no scope for any reasonable doubt as to the manner in which the question raised is to be resolved. This will be assessed in the light of the specific characteristics of EU law, the particular difficulties to which its interpretation gives rise and the risk of divergences in judicial decisions within the EU.[43]

The application of the three conditions for liability will be examined below.

i. Condition 1: The rule of law infringed must be intended to confer rights on individuals

This first condition requires the court to interpret the provision in question: was it intended to confer rights on individual citizens? The case law of the CJEU indicates that a purposive approach should be taken to matters of interpretation. The court should thus consider what the rule in question is seeking to achieve in its general context. In *Dillenkofer v Germany*,[44] the ECJ advised that a right to damages would exist where the *result* prescribed by the Directive entails the grant of rights to individuals whose content is identifiable on the basis of the provisions of the Directive. Equally in *Norbrook Laboratories*,[45] the Court focused on whether the scope of the right could be 'adequately identified'. *Brasserie du Pêcheur* confirms that when the EU rule has direct effect, it will generally be deemed to confer rights on individuals enforceable in the national courts.[46]

The leading English case is that of *Three Rivers District Council v Bank of England*.[47] In this case, the claimants were more than 6,000 depositors in the UK branches of the Bank of Credit and Commerce International SA (BCCI) who suffered substantial losses when the bank collapsed; the principal cause of which was fraud on a vast scale perpetrated at a senior level of the bank. In addition to an (unsuccessful) claim under the tort of misfeasance in public office, the claimants alleged breaches of EU law, and, in particular, breaches of the requirements of the 1977 Banking Directive. The Directive[48] had introduced a statutorily based

[41] 'Where any such question is raised in a case pending before a court or tribunal of a Member State against whose decisions there is no judicial remedy under national law, that court or tribunal shall bring the matter before the Court.'

[42] Case 283/81 *Srl CILFIT and Lanificio di Gavardo SpA v Ministry of Health* [1982] ECR I-3415, para16. The court may also decline to refer where the answer to the question cannot affect the outcome of the case.

[43] Ibid.

[44] C-178/94 [1996] ECR I-4845, para 22. See also C6/90 *Francovich and Bonifaci v Italian Republic* [1991] ECR I-5357, para 40.

[45] C-127/95 *Norbrook Laboratories Ltd v Ministry of Agriculture, Fisheries and Food* [1998] ECR I-1531, para. 108.

[46] *Brasserie du Pêcheur* (n 24) para 23.

[47] *Three Rivers District Council v Bank of England (No 3)* [2000] UKHL 33; [2003] AC 1.

[48] First Council Banking Co-ordination Directive of 12 December 1977, Dir 77/780/EEC [1977] OJ L322, p. 30.

licensing system for deposit-taking institutions and it was argued that the Bank of England owed duties to depositors in terms of the initial licensing of BCCI, its failure to supervise BCCI and its failure to revoke its licence.

The House of Lords found that the Directive was not intended to confer rights on individual depositors. At first instance, Clarke J had concluded that even though the underlying purpose of supervision of credit institutions was to benefit savers, it did not confer rights on them.[49] Lord Hope, in his leading opinion, agreed:

> It placed duties of co-operation on the competent authorities where a credit institution was operating in one or more member state other than that in which its head office was situated. But it stopped short of prescribing any duties of supervision to be performed by the competent authority within each member state. It is not possible to discover provisions which entail the granting of rights to individuals, as the granting of rights to individuals was not necessary to achieve the results which were intended to be achieved by the Directive.[50]

Having examined the recitals and wording of the Directive and case law of the CJEU, his Lordship concluded that the Directive was the first step in a process of harmonisation of provisions for the regulation of credit institutions carrying on business within the EU and confined itself to imposing a number of minimum conditions and prohibitions on Member States as to the authorisation and supervision of credit institutions having their head offices in another Member State or having their head offices outside the Community. Controversially, and despite the strong dissenting judgment of Lord Justice Auld in the Court of Appeal,[51] Lord Hope rejected the request for a preliminary reference under (now) Article 267 TFEU on the basis that the House of Lords was unanimous and had the benefit of full submissions on the point.

Buxton LJ, in the later case of *Poole v HM Treasury*,[52] applied the same reasoning towards Council Directive 73/239/EEC which seeks to harmonise the rules relating to the business of direct insurance.[53] In this case, a substantial number of insurers (or names) on the Lloyd's insurance market had complained of losses suffered in the course of underwriting which were allegedly due to the market being inadequately regulated by the failure of the British government to transpose the 1973 Directive into English domestic law. In dismissing their claim, the Court applied the 'demanding' test whether the grant of a right to individuals in the national legal order was *necessary* to achieve the objectives of the Directive.[54] On

[49] *Three Rivers District Council* [1996] 3 All ER 558, 602.

[50] *Three Rivers District Council* [2003] AC 1, 218.

[51] *Three Rivers District Council* [2000] 2 WLR 15, 102–3, arguing that the 1977 Directive imposed clearly defined obligations on Member States and on their regulatory bodies and in doing gave rise to corresponding EU law rights in depositors to enforce those obligations by an action for damages.

[52] *Poole v HM Treasury* [2007] EWCA Civ 1021; [2007] All ER 379, approving Langley J at first instance.

[53] First Council Directive 73/239/EEC of 24 July 1973 on the coordination of laws, regulations and administrative provisions relating to the taking-up and pursuit of the business of direct insurance other than life assurance [1973] OJ L228, p. 3.

[54] *Poole* (n 52) para 23.

this basis, the Directive was not intended to protect insurers. The Court, in particular, dismissed the argument that an insurer had a right to be regulated by the government as 'nonsense'. [55] In its view, there was no support for the claimants' argument in European jurisprudence and therefore a reference to the ECJ was not required, nor permissible.

Three Rivers has received considerable criticism for its failure to embrace the broader objectives of EU law. Stanton et al question whether the decision of Lord Hope to exclude consideration of extrinsic materials relating to other EU banking legislation was consistent with the approach of the European Court.[56] Fairgrieve and Andenas[57] also argue that the provisions of the Directive needed to be read on the basis of the background for, and context of, the EU regulation of banking supervision and express concern that Lord Hope was importing the need for the legislation to be precise and unconditional when this is a requirement of direct effect, not *Francovich* liability.[58] This is evident in his Lordship's requirement that the 'contents of these rights is clear'[59] and taken a step further by the Court of Appeal in *Poole* by imposing a test of 'necessity', more reminiscent of the English test for implied terms than the approach of the ECJ.[60] Further, contrary to the assumption of the court in this case, the CJEU has shown a more flexible approach to this test, albeit in cases not cited by the Court of Appeal. In *Dillenkofer*,[61] the ECJ adopted a generous approach to consumers attempting to claim under Directive 90/314 on Package Travel,[62] despite the potential breadth of this category on the basis that '[a]ny other interpretation would be illogical, since the purpose of the security which organizers must offer under Article 7 of the Directive is to enable consumers to obtain a refund of money paid over or to be repatriated.'[63]

Examining the context of *Three Rivers* and *Poole*, the English courts are clearly reluctant to impose liability on regulators towards individual investors. This is consistent with the traditional principles of tort law whereby liability under the tort of misfeasance in public office is subject to a requirement of bad faith and

[55] *Poole* (n 52) para 41.

[56] Stanton et al, *Statutory Torts* (n 34) para 6.055.

[57] D Fairgrieve and M Andenas, 'Misfeasance in Public Office, Governmental Liability and European Influences' (2002) 51 *International & Comparative Law Quarterly* 757.

[58] As demonstrated by *Francovich* itself (Directive insufficiently precise to be directly effective).

[59] *Three Rivers* (n 47) 200. Note also that his Lordship was prepared to draw negative conclusions from the absence of a definition of the individuals in whose favour rights might be said to have been intended to be created by the Directive. Such reasoning ignores the fact that Directives often neglect to provide definitions for key concepts; a factor recognised by the European Commission in Communications such as 'A more coherent European contract law: An action plan' COM (2003) 68 final and 'European Contract Law and the revision of the *acquis*: The way forward' COM (2004) 651 final. The reasoning of Lord Millett (giving the only other reasoned opinion on this point) may equally be criticised for not fully embracing EU reasoning (232).

[60] *The Moorcock* (1889) 14 PD 64.

[61] C-178/94 *Dillenkofer v Germany* [1996] ECR I-4845.

[62] Council Directive 90/314/EEC of 13 June 1990 on package travel, package holidays and package tours [1990] OJ L158, p 59.

[63] *Dillenkofer* (n 61) para 36. See also Case C-140/97 *Rechberger, Geindl and Others v Austria* [1999] ECR I-3499.

negligence liability is generally excluded due to fears of indeterminate liability.[64] Indeed, the CJEU is not immune from such concerns. In *Paul v Germany*[65] a claim by depositors that the German banking supervisory authority had failed to supervise the bank adequately in accordance with the relevant directive equally failed. The Court found that the 1994 Directive on deposit-guarantee schemes[66] and other directives on banking law[67] conferred no right on individual depositors. While the directives imposed on the national authorities a number of supervisory obligations vis-a-vis credit institutions, it did not necessarily follow from that, or from the fact that the objectives pursued by the directives included the protection of depositors, that they sought to confer rights on depositors in the event of losses suffered by the allegedly defective supervision by competent national authorities. The ECJ, in particular, noted the complexity of banking supervision, the plurality of interests involved and the need to ensure the stability of the financial system.[68] Such restraint contrasts, however, with its treatment of holiday-makers under the Package Travel Directive: Advocate General Tizzano commenting that 'The very fact that holidays have assumed a specific socio-economic role and have become so important for an individual's quality of life, means that their full and effective enjoyment represents in itself an asset worth protecting'.[69] Equally, the CJEU seems more willing to allow individual claims when the legislation in question affects environmental protection and policy.[70] The context would therefore appear significant. Biondi and Farley suggest that the CJEU is reluctant to expose supervisory authorities to too many challenges in the delicate area of financial regulation and run the risk of possibly excessive litigation.[71]

While *Paul v Germany* may, therefore, be regarded as supporting the *Three Rivers* conclusion, it does not necessarily support a general application of its restrictive reasoning. It remains a matter of concern that future English courts will interpret *Three Rivers* as the 'English' authority for condition 1 and thereby introduce a distinctly narrow common law approach to liability.

[64] *Yuen Kun-Yeu v Attorney General of Hong Kong* [1988] 1 AC 175.

[65] Case C-222/02 *Paul v Germany* [2004] ECR I-9425. For criticism, see M Tison, 'Do Not Attack the Watchdog! Banking Supervisors Liability after Peter Paul' (2005) 42 *Common Market Law Review* 639, who notes that the German Supreme Court (*Bundesgerichtshof*), contrary to the English House of Lords, did consider the issue worthy of a preliminary referral to the ECJ.

[66] Directive 94/19/EC of the European Parliament and of the Council of 30 May 1994 on deposit-guarantee schemes [1994] OJ L135, p 5.

[67] Council Directives 77/780/EEC of 12 December 1977, 89/299/EEC of 17 April 1989 and 89/646/EEC of 15 December 1989.

[68] *Paul* (n 65) para 44. It should be noted, however, that the depositors were able to obtain some compensation (€20,000) from the German *Landgericht* for the late implementation of the Directive 94/19 EC.

[69] Case C-168/00, *Leitner v TUI Deutschland GmbH & Co* [2002] ECR I-2631 (Directive interpreted so as to give right to damage for non-material loss).

[70] A Arora, 'The Statutory System of the Bank Supervision and the Failure of BCCI' [2006] *Journal of Business Law* 487, 496: see C-253/00 *Muñoz v Frumar Ltd* [2002] ECR I-7289 (quality standards applicable to table grapes) and Case C-72/95 *Kraaljeveld* [1996] ECR I-5403 (environmental impact assessments).

[71] A Biondi and M Farley, *The Right to Damages in European Law* (The Hague, Kluwer Law International, 2009) 37.

ii. Condition 2: The breach must be sufficiently serious

Guidance as to the application of the second condition may be found in *Brasserie du Pêcheur* itself. The Court of Justice noted that while it was for the national courts to find the facts and determine whether the breach in question was 'sufficiently serious',[72] a sufficiently serious breach would exist where the Member State had manifestly and gravely disregarded the limits on its discretion, rendering the breach inexcusable.[73] Obvious examples include where the breach has occurred in the face of a CJEU judgment, preliminary ruling or settled case law which indicate a clear infringement of EU law. In the absence of case law, *Brasserie du Pêcheur* listed a number of non-exclusive factors which should be taken into account in determining whether the breach was sufficiently serious, namely:

> [T]he clarity and precision of the rule breached, the measure of discretion left by the rule to the national or EU authorities, whether the infringement and the damage caused was intentional or involuntary, whether any error of law was excusable or inexcusable, the fact that the position taken by a EU institution may have contributed towards the omission, and the adoption or retention of national measures or practices contrary to Community law.[74]

CJEU case law has further indicated that the complexity of the situation to be regulated, lack of clarity in the application or interpretation of the texts and the existence of a margin of discretion are all highly relevant.[75] There is clear authority that where the Member State has little or no discretion, for example in failing in its obligation to implement an EU directive, mere infringement may qualify in itself as a sufficiently serious breach.[76] In *Synthon*,[77] the ECJ held that the refusal of the British government to recognise the marketing authorisation of a drug certified by the Dutch authorities was sufficiently serious as the provision allowed States no discretion to refuse mutual recognition. In reality, much will depend, therefore, on the facts of each case and, in particular, the extent to which the breach in question is settled and clear. In *ex parte British Telecommunications*,[78] for example, the condition was not satisfied where the UK's interpretation of the

[72] *Brasserie du Pêcheur* (n 24) para 58.

[73] Ibid, para 45.

[74] *Brasserie du Pêcheur* (n 24) para 56. See also Case C-424/97 *Haim v Kassenzahnaertzliche Vereinigung Nordrhein* [2000] ECR I-5123, para 43.

[75] Tridimas comments: 'Other things being equal, the margin of discretion enjoyed by the Member State is in an inverse relationship with the likelihood of establishing a serious breach' Tridimas, 'Liability for Breach of Community Law' (n 28) 311.

[76] See *Francovich* itself (n 1). See also C-178/94 *Dillenkofer v Federal Republic of Germany* [1996] ECR I-4845; [1997] QB 259 (a Member State's complete failure to transpose a Directive constituted a 'sufficiently serious breach') and C-5/94 *R v Ministry of Agriculture, Fisheries and Food ex p Hedley Lomas (Ireland) Ltd* [1996] ECR I-2553; [1997] QB 139 (sufficient breach where there was no or very little room for discretion in granting a licence).

[77] C-452/06 *R v Licensing Authority of the Department of Health, ex p Synthon* [2008] ECR I-7681.

[78] C-392/93 *R v HM Treasury ex p British Telecommunications plc* [1996] ECR I-1631; [1996] QB 615. See also C-283/94 *Denkavit Internationaal BV v Bundesamt für Finanzen* [1996] ECR I-5063 (where other member states, after discussion with the Council, had adopted the same interpretation of the Directive as Germany and as there was no relevant case law of the Court breach not sufficiently serious).

Directive had not been manifestly wrong and was excusable in the absence of ECJ guidance on its meaning. The Court of Appeal in *R (on the application of Negassi) v Secretary of State for the Home Department*[79] equally argued that a genuine misapprehension of the true legal position which was not deliberate, cynical or egregious and which was shared not only by the Secretary of State but also, as a matter of first impression, by a number of judges would not, in the absence of guidance from the CJEU, amount to a sufficiently serious breach. Some commentators have suggested that this standard is too high. Stanton et al argue that '[t]his in many cases demanding standard offers Member State courts an easy opportunity to absolve their national public administration from the financial burden of a successful damages claim.'[80] Chalmers, Monti and Davies agree: 'liability occurs only when Members States are breaching EU law in a manner that must be obvious to them and one which leaves little room for doubt . . . It is there to penalise the very wayward state rather than to be concerned with redress for litigants. For, if it were the latter, there would be little justification for such a restrictive test'.[81]

The leading English case is *R v Secretary of State for Transport, ex p Factortame (No 5)*.[82] The question before the court was whether the British government's breach of EU law (as determined by the ECJ in the conjoined *Brasserie du Pêcheur v Germany/R v Secretary of State for Transport, ex p Factortame (No 4)* decision) amounted to a sufficiently serious breach to justify an award of damages.[83] The case itself related to the common fisheries policy and the controversial response of the UK government to quota hopping by Spanish fishermen, who had registered their fishing vessels on the British register as a means of obtaining access to UK fishing grounds. The government decided to intervene to protect British quotas and enacted the Merchant Shipping Act 1988 which changed the rules on registration and required that registered vessels were British owned, ie the legal owners and not less than 75 per cent of the beneficial owners were British citizens resident and domiciled in the UK. Questions as to the legality of the legislation under EU law were referred to the ECJ under the then Article 177 of the Treaty in March 1989 by the Divisional Court.[84] The ECJ in 1991 rejected the

[79] *R (on the application of Negassi) v Secretary of State for the Home Department* [2013] EWCA Civ 151; [2013] 2 CMLR 45, para 20.

[80] *Statutory Torts* (n 34) para 6.042.

[81] D Chalmers, G Davies and G Monti, *European Union Law: Cases and Materials*, 2nd edn (Cambridge, Cambridge University Press, 2010) 307. Lock, in a survey of English and German law, also observed the tendency of the national courts to deny sufficiently serious breach save in the most obvious of circumstances, for example, where there had been a failure to transpose a Directive in time or where the CJEU had previously established a breach: T Lock, 'Is Private Enforcement of EU Law through State Liability a Myth? An Assessment 20 years after *Francovich*' (2012) 49 *Common Market Law Review* 1675, 1697. The decision of the Court of Appeal in *Negassi* (n 79 above) lends further support to his argument.

[82] *R v Secretary of State for Transport, ex p Factortame (No 5)* [2000] 1 AC 524.

[83] The UK government accepted that, on the basis of the ruling in *Factortame No 4*, the relevant rules of EU law were intended to confer rights on individuals.

[84] It was alleged that the nationality condition was in breach of Arts 7, 52, 59 and 221 of the Treaty of Rome. On 18 May 1989 the House of Lords referred the further question as to whether under EU law English courts were required to have the power to grant interim protection for rights claimed under

UK's attempt to justify the conditions on residence and domicile as incompatible with the Treaty.[85]

In *Factortame (No 5)*, the government argued that the breaches were not sufficiently serious to justify an award of compensation. It had sought to respond to a serious economic problem and it had obtained and relied upon independent legal advice that the measures were acceptable under EU law. The House of Lords disagreed, holding that while the government had acted in good faith to protect its own fishing communities, the inevitable result of its policy had been to take away or seriously affect the rights to fish of the Spanish fishermen. The nationality condition was obviously discriminatory and in breach of Treaty provisions dealing with freedom of establishment. Further, the European Commission had advised the government of this prior to Royal Assent. Whilst the views of the Commission were not conclusive, its considered view in a case of this kind where the EU has a substantial role was found by Lords Slynn and Hope to be of importance.[86] On this basis, the deliberate adoption of legislation which was clearly discriminatory on the ground of nationality and which inevitably violated the relevant Treaty article (since it prevented establishment in the United Kingdom) was a manifest breach of fundamental treaty obligations.[87]

This approach was followed by the Court of Appeal in *Byrne v Motor Insurers' Bureau*.[88] Here, the Court was prepared to find a sufficiently serious breach where the Motor Insurers' Bureau had applied a stricter time limit for claims against untraced drivers than generally applied under national legislation The claimant had been subject to a hit-and-run accident in 1993 when three years old. The driver had never been traced and the child's parents only appreciated the possibility of bringing a claim against the MIB in 2001, which was out of time under the three year time limit of the MIB Untraced Drivers Agreement. A claim by a minor in the ordinary law of tort would, under section 28 of the Limitation Act 1980, be

Community law, a question answered in the affirmative by the European Court on 19 June 1990 in its judgment in Case C-213/89 *R v Secretary of State for Transport, Ex p Factortame Ltd* [1990] ECR I-2433 ('Factortame I').

[85] Case C-221/89 *R v Secretary of State for Transport, Ex p Factortame Ltd. (No 3)* [1991] ECR I- 3905; [1992] QB 680 (also known as '*Factortame II*'): requirement of nationality, residence and domicile for legal and beneficial owners, charterers, and managers and operators of fishing vessels registered on a Member State's register were contrary to Community law and in particular to Art 52 of the Treaty (now Art 49 TFEU).

[86] Lord Slynn commented that a Member State may choose to ignore the advice given but if it does so, it incurs the risk that, if it proves to be wrong and the Commission to be right, the Member State will be found to have gone ahead deliberately, well aware of the Commission's views, and that a court would be more likely to find that the breach had been manifest and grave and thus sufficiently serious: (n 82) 545. In contrast Lords Hoffmann and Clyde regarded the Commission's advice simply as a relevant matter to take into account in deciding whether a breach was sufficiently serious.

[87] It was agreed that 'domicile' fell to be treated in the same way as nationality. It was further clear that discrimination on grounds such as residence could constitute indirect or covert discrimination on the grounds of nationality.

[88] *Byrne v Motor Insurers' Bureau* [2008] EWCA Civ 574; [2009] QB 66. See also Sullivan J in *R v Department of Social Security ex p Scullion* [1999] 3 CMLR 798 (QBD): UK interpretation on a derogation in Directive 79/7 on equal treatment of men and women in matters of social security so unsustainable that amounted to sufficiently serious breach.

possible up to the age of majority. The claimant questioned whether the MIB time limit complied with EU law, as set out in the Second Motor Vehicle Insurance Directive,[89] in that it was less favourable than that applied in domestic law. Carnwath LJ applied the considerations identified in *Brasserie du Pêcheur* above, together with the test as applied *Factortame (No 5)*. His Lordship concluded that, in the light of ECJ case law,[90] which, at the very least, had warned the Government of the need to review the legality of the MIB Scheme, and the serious consequences of failing to comply, there was a sufficiently serious breach in not providing equivalent treatment of claims.

These decisions are interesting in terms of the ongoing relationship between the national courts and the CJEU. The courts focus on the rules of EU law and Lord Hope in *Factortame (No 5)* openly acknowledged 'the novel task' facing the English courts in applying the sufficiently serious test.[91] Nevertheless, concern may be raised whether English lawyers have fully appreciated that the *Brasserie du Pêcheur* test is not one based on fault, but a manifest and grave disregard to the limits of the State's discretion. *Brasserie du Pêcheur* makes it perfectly clear that whether the infringement and the damage caused was intentional or involuntary is a relevant issue, but reparation of loss is not conditional on proof of fault.[92] While not directly at issue in the cases above, which involved serious breaches of fundamental rights, the courts did place some emphasis on the failure of the UK government to take notice of evidence from the Commission and ECJ that the legislation might violate EU law. The Law Commission went further in its 2008 Consultation Paper, *Administrative Redress: Public Bodies and the Citizen*, and equated the test of sufficiently serious breach with that of serious fault.[93] In a perfect example of common law reasoning,[94] the relevant case law was deemed to provide evidence of the importance of fault: CJEU jurisprudence providing 'useful guidance' as to the sort of considerations that may lead a court to conclude

[89] Council Directive 84/5/EEC on the approximation of the laws of the Member States relating to insurance against civil liability in respect of the use of motor vehicles [1984] OJ L8, p.17).

[90] Notably C-63/01 *Evans v Secretary of State for the Environment, Transport and the Regions* [2003] ECR I-14447; [2005] All ER (EC) 763 on the same Directive.

[91] *Factortame (No 5)* (n 82) 550. See also Toulmin QC in *Factortame (No 7)* [2001] 1 WLR 942, 958.

[92] *Brasserie du Pêcheur* (n 24) para 56. See also Case C-243/09 *Fuß v Stadt Halle (No.2)* [2011] IRLR 176, para 67, noted J Tomkin (2012) 49 *Common Market Law Review* 1423, and indeed *Factortame (No 5)* (n 82) itself where Lord Slynn commented that: 'It was also clear from the cases that it is not necessary to establish fault or negligence on the part of the member state going beyond what is relevant to show a sufficiently serious breach' (541).

[93] Law Commission, *Administrative Redress: Public Bodies and the Citizen*, Consultation Paper No 187 (2008) para 4.148. In the later report, the Commission noted criticism of its position by senior English academics: Law Commission, *Administrative Redress: Public Bodies and the Citizen* (Report No 322) (2010) 3.33–3.35. Reform in this area has since been abandoned.

[94] The Law Commission relied on the cases of C-178/94 *Dillenkofer v Germany* [1996] ECR I-4845, C-5/94 *R v Ministry of Agriculture, Fisheries and Food ex p Hedley Lomas (Ireland) Ltd* [1996] ECR I-2553; [1997] QB 139, C-392/93 *R v HM Treasury ex p British Telecommunications plc* [1996] ECR I-1631; [1996] QB 615 and C-319/96 *Brinkmann Tabakfabriken v Skatteministeriat* [1998] ECR I-5255 (para 32) to support its argument that the test for 'sufficiently serious' breach is in fact a test of *fault* on the part of the Member State in question.

that certain conduct may constitute serious administrative failure. Granger, in her comparative study,[95] noted that English courts often make a thorough assessment of the nature of the breach even where EU law only requires a mere illegality. She attributes this to the general lack of familiarity of English judges with the idea that a mere illegality can constitute a basis for liability per se and a reluctance to find public authorities liable in tort: 'English judges, when applying state liability, probably feel that they need to justify their decisions very thoroughly since they depart from the national modus operandi'.[96] It is clear that there is a need for the English courts to appreciate the distinct nature of this test and that it does not necessarily replicate existing models for liability.

iii. Condition 3: There must be a direct causal link between the breach of the obligation resting on the State and the damage sustained by the injured parties.

The third condition of *Brasserie du Pêcheur* is that a direct causal link is needed. This is stated to be matter for the national court,[97] subject to the principles of equivalence and effectiveness, but in this area the ECJ has felt able to decide the issue when the necessary information was before it. In *Rechberger and Geindl v Austria*,[98] the Austrian government had argued that its failure to implement on time the relevant provisions of the Package Travel Directive, which would have provided refunds for travellers affected by the bankruptcy of a travel agent, did not directly cause the losses in that the real cause was the imprudent conduct of the travel organiser.[99] It could not, therefore, be held responsible for wholly exceptional and unforeseeable events. The ECJ disagreed. The national court had found a direct causal link and the provisions of the Directive, which guaranteed the refund of money paid over and repatriation in the event of the travel organisers' bankruptcy, could not be precluded by imprudent conduct on the part of the travel organiser or by the occurrence of exceptional and unforeseeable events. This may be contrasted with the Court's approach in *Brinkmann Tabakfabriken GmbH v Skatteministeriet*[100] where causation was used to restrict State liability. In this case, the ECJ found that the applicants' loss was more attributable to the mistaken interpretation of the Directive by the Danish tax authorities,[101]

[95] M-P Granger, 'National Applications of *Francovich* and the Construction of a European Administrative *ius commune*' (2007) 32 *European Law Review* 157.

[96] Ibid, 170.

[97] See *Brasserie du Pêcheur* (n 24) paras 51 and 65. See also *Norbrook* (n 45) para 110.

[98] Case C-140/97 *Rechberger and Geindl v Austria* [1999] ECR I-3499 concerning Art 7 of Council Directive 90/314/EEC of 13 June 1990 on package travel, package holidays and package tours [1990] OJ L158, p. 59.

[99] The case concerned an 'offer of a lifetime' arranged by a travel organiser for subscribers to a daily newspaper: a four-seven day trip to one of four European destinations free (save for airport taxes and a single-room supplement). Unsurprisingly the offer proved very successful, far more so than anticipated by the organisers who fell into logistical and financial difficulties ending in bankruptcy proceedings.

[100] Case C-319/96 *Brinkmann Tabakfabriken GmbH v Skatteministeriet* [1998] ECR I-5255.

[101] The Danish authorities had not, however, committed a sufficiently serious breach: ibid, para 29.

which had given immediate effect to the provisions of the Directive, than the failure of the State to transpose the Directive in time. Causation was therefore not established.

Despite these examples, a clear EU concept of causation does not yet exist. It is therefore left to the national courts to determine how to apply the test of direct causation. It is clear, however, that the CJEU would not permit a national court to adopt rules of causation which rendered it excessively difficult to prove causation. Tridimas goes further and finds that causation, as with the other conditions of liability, must be determined in the first place by EU law.[102] Yet, the fact remains that the CJEU to date has not chosen to elaborate any systematic principles of causation, but has approached issues that have arisen on a case by case basis. *Rechberger* indicates, however, that liability will not be precluded by the imprudent conduct of a third party or by exceptional and unforeseeable events. In contrast, *Brasserie du Pêcheur* states that the court will exclude losses caused by the claimant's own failure to mitigate his loss, setting the test: has the claimant shown reasonable diligence in order to avoid the loss or damage or limit its extent and, in particular, availed himself in time of all the legal remedies available to him?[103] No more than reasonable efforts seem to be required. In *Dillenkofer*,[104] for example, a package traveller, who had paid the whole travel price up front was not regarded as failing to mitigate his losses simply because he had not taken advantage of the possibility of not paying more than 10 per cent of the total travel price before obtaining documents of value. It is thus deemed a general principle that the injured party must show reasonable diligence in limiting the extent of the loss or damage, or risk having to bear the loss or damage himself.[105]

At national level, a number of problems emerge. First, it is well known that the tests for causation in the private law of Member States differ. French law, for example, states simply, that damage must be certain and direct, thereby excluding *dommage indirect* (indirect harm). This appears therefore to be consistent with the *Francovich* test, but in reality, as Steiner notes, the courts have 'vacillated' between two main tests for causation: equivalence of conditions (often referred to as the '*sine qua non*' test whereby an act or event may only be regarded as a cause of the harm if it is at least a condition of that harm) and the test for adequate causality (commonly regarded as a more restrictive test).[106] French commentators have remarked that the courts use either test as deemed appropriate and that the division between the two is contested.[107] The meaning, therefore, of a test of 'direct causation' is less than self-evident.

[102] Tridimas, 'Liability for Breach of Community Law' (n 28) 310.

[103] *Brasserie du Pêcheur* (n 24) para 84. See C-397/98 and C410/98 *Metalgesellschaft Ltd and Hoechst v Commissioners of Inland Revenue* [2001] ECR I-1727 and Case C-445/06 *DanskeSlagterier v Germany* [2009] ECR I-2119, para 60.

[104] C-178/94 *Dillenkofer v Federal Republic of Germany* [1996] ECR I-4845, para 73.

[105] *Brasserie du Pêcheur* (n 24) para 85.

[106] E Steiner, *French Law: A Comparative Approach* (Oxford, Oxford University Press, 2010) 359–60.

[107] F Terré, P Simler and Y Lequette, *Droit civil: Les obligations*, 10th edn (Paris, Dalloz 2009) no 860 (Charactère du lien de causalité). See also C Lapoyade Deschamps, 'La réparation du préjudice économ-

In *Brasserie du Pêcheur* itself, the question of causation was left to be determined by the German courts. The German Supreme Court (Bundesgerichtshof) held that it was a matter for the national legal systems of the individual Member States to implement the 'direct causation' test into national law while safeguarding the full effectiveness of Community law. In German law, the relevant test would be one of necessary and sufficient causation.[108] The *Brasserie du Pêcheur* case had been brought by a French brewing company which had been forced to discontinue exports of beer to Germany because its beer did not comply with the purity requirement laid down in German law. The ECJ in an earlier ruling[109] had held that this restriction was incompatible with Article 36 TFEU[110] (free movement of goods). The ECJ in *Brasserie du Pêcheur* had distinguished between provisions which prohibited the marketing under the designation 'Bier' of beers imported from other Member States (the 'marketing' provision) and the prohibition against the importing of beers containing additives (the 'import' provision).[111] It found that the marketing provision could be regarded as a serious breach of EU law,[112] but that the import provision, due to absence of conclusive case law, could not. The Bundesgerichtshof, in determining causation, found that the claimants' losses could not be said to be directly caused by marketing provision. The German authorities had taken no proceedings in respect of this rule and so the claim failed. The losses suffered by *Brasserie du Pêcheur* were in fact caused by the import provision, but this failed on the basis that the breach was not sufficiently serious. National rules of causation may thus serve to limit the scope of the *Francovich* doctrine, provided, of course, that they do not render reparation impossible or excessively difficult to obtain. [113]

It is therefore not greatly surprising to find that the English courts have applied the traditional 'but for' test to *Francovich* cases, requiring proof of causation on the balance of probabilities.[114] Although this may extend to a test of material contribution, the courts have rejected claims for loss of chance.[115] In *R v Secretary of*

ique pur en droit français' in E Banakas (ed), *Civil Liability for Pure Economic Loss* (The Hague, Kluwer Law International, 1996) 95: 'la jurisprudence n'hésitera pas à recourir, le plus souvent sans exprimer, à la méthode pourtant sommaire de l'équivalence des conditions chaque fois qu'elle *veut* indemniser'.

[108] BGH 24 October 1996 BGHZ 134,30; NJW 1997, 123; [1997] CMLR 971, para 15.

[109] Case 178/84 *EC Commission v Germany (Beer Purity)* [1987] ECR1227; [1988] 1 CMLR 780.

[110] Then Art 30, TEC.

[111] *Brasserie du Pêcheur* (n 24) para 59.

[112] The incompatibility of such rules with Art 30 TEC was manifest in the light of decisions of the Court already in existence at the time.

[113] See E Deards, '*Brasserie du Pêcheur*: Snatching Defeat from the Jaws of Victory' (1997) 22 *European Law Review* 620, who also notes that Mr Francovich's claim also ultimately failed at national level on the basis that his losses were not attributable to Italy's failure to implement the Directive in question.

[114] See *Barnett v Chelsea Hospital* [1969] 1 QB 428. Rebhahn notes that the balance of probabilities test applied by the English courts differs remarkably from the test used by German or Austrian courts: R Rebhahn, 'Non-Contractual Liability in Damages of Member States for Breach of Community Law' in Koziol and Schulze (n 23) para 9/78. In German or Austrian law, causation and other items are, in theory, only proved if there is a very high probability of proof.

[115] See recently *Gregg v Scott* [2005] UKHL 2; [2005] 2 AC 176.

State for the Home Department ex p Gallagher,[116] the Court of Appeal applied the 'but for' test: on the balance of probabilities, could Gallagher show that his exclusion from the UK was due to the Secretary of State's breach of EU law? His argument, that he would have had a better chance of securing a favourable result if the correct procedure had been followed, was a claim for loss of a chance which did not satisfy the balance of probabilities test.

Such analysis indicates that deference to national autonomy by the CJEU has left untouched disparities in relation to the test for causation in tort among Member States. Durant, in her survey of EU case law on causation, adds that there is uncertainty also at EU level in that the European courts seem to consider the *conditio sine qua non* test as the main test, but that they also require a direct causal link, thereby linking the two tests.[117] The English court's clear rejection of a claim for loss of chance may be contrasted with the recognition of claims based on *perte d'une chance* (loss of a chance) by the French courts, provided the loss is direct and certain,[118] and indications at EU level that liability may arise where the applicant had a 'strong chance' of gaining the benefit in question rendering the loss sufficiently direct and certain.[119]

Some uncertainty also exists as to whether the defendant is liable for *all* directly caused losses, regardless of their type. In *Brasserie du Pêcheur*, the ECJ stated that the damages awarded must be 'commensurate with the loss or damage sustained so as to ensure the effective protection for their rights',[120] and made it clear that they would extend to pure economic loss, including loss of profit (*lucrum cessans*).[121] Otherwise, the matter is left to the domestic courts, subject to the twin principles of equivalence and effectiveness. Although there have been few cases on this topic in English law, there has been some discussion whether exemplary or aggravated damages would be available. In relation to exemplary damages, *Brasserie du Pêcheur* advises that they may be awarded if available for a similar action founded on domestic law.[122] Under the leading case of *Rookes v Barnard*,[123] *Francovich* claims are most likely to fit within category one of 'oppressive, arbi-

[116] *R v Secretary of State for the Home Department ex p Gallagher* [1996] 2 CMLR 951 (CA). The Court of Appeal also found the breach not to be 'sufficiently serious'. See also *R (on the application of Negassi) v Secretary of State for the Home Department* (n 79) (N's claim was speculative and failed to establish a direct causal link).

[117] IC Durant, 'Causation' in Koziol and Schulze (n 23) para 3/28.

[118] Terré, Simler and Lequette, *Droit civil* (n 107) No 701. The only authority in favour of litigants in English law is the Court of Appeal decision of *Allied Maples Group v Simmons & Simmons* [1995] 1 WLR 1602 (Could it be said that but for the solicitor's negligent advice, the claimants would have had a substantial chance of negotiating a more profitable deal with a third party?) Argument on this basis was, however, rejected by the Court of Appeal in *Negassi* (n 79) para 23.

[119] Case T 230/94 *Farrugia v Commission* [1996] ECR II-195 para 44.

[120] *Brasserie du Pêcheur* (n 24) para 82.

[121] ibid, para 87. Including interest on payments: see Cases C-397/98 and C-410/98 *Metallgessellschaft and others v Commissioners of Inland Revenue* [2001] ECR I-1727 and *R v Department of Social Security ex. p. Scullion* [1999] 3 CMLR 798 (QBD).

[122] *Brasserie du Pêcheur* (n 24), para 90.

[123] *Rookes v Barnard* [1964] AC 1129. See PR Ghandhi, 'Exemplary Damages in English Tort Law' (1990) 10 *Legal Studies* 182.

trary or unconstitutional actions by government servants'. Under the old 'cause of action' test, however, such claims were not permitted in that damages were only available if previously awarded for the tort in question prior to *Rookes* or where the statute in question made express provision. The Divisional Court in *Factortame (No 5)* held that, in view of the failure of the European Communities Act 1972 (unsurprisingly) to make express provision for exemplary damages, they would not be granted in English law.[124] Although the House of Lords in *Kuddus v Chief Constable of Leicestershire Constabulary*[125] overturned the cause of action test, thus permitting exemplary damages where appropriate, the question remained whether a court would award exemplary damages today. Lewison J in *Devenish Nutrition Ltd v Sanofi-Aventis SA*[126] held that, under the principle of equivalence, exemplary damages should be available in such circumstances, although on the facts of this case an award was precluded as the defendant had already been fined for breach of competition law and this would lead to double punishment.[127] In contrast, Judge Toulmin QC in *Factortame (No 7)* held that aggravated damages were not recoverable. Such damages were necessary when the claimant's feelings and self-esteem were an integral part of the damage for which compensation was awarded. They were therefore inappropriate in relation to a claim for purely economic loss.[128] Restitutionary damages also remain contentious. The Court of Appeal in *Devenish Nutrition Ltd v Sanofi-Aventis SA*[129] rejected a claim for restitutionary damages in relation to a claim in competition law under Article 81 of the EC Treaty (now Article 101, TFEU) on the basis that purely compensatory damages were sufficient for the purpose of safeguarding the rights of private persons under the provision in question.

Causation and damages remain, therefore, primarily matters for the national courts and the European Court has paid scant attention to the policy issues that dominate causation discourse in every Member State. It must also be acknowledged that, as seen in *Brasserie du Pêcheur*, *Brinkmann* and *Gallagher*, causation may play an active role in limiting liability. Stanton et al argue that given the complex nature of the economic environment, causation may be difficult to establish in all but a few extreme cases.[130] As Woods and Smith indicate,[131] identifying the

[124] *R v Secretary of State for Transport, Ex p. Factortame (No5)* [1997] EWHC Admin 756; [1998] CMLR 1353, para 176. This finding was not appealed.

[125] *Kuddus v Chief Constable of Leicestershire Constabulary* [2002] 2 AC 122.

[126] *Devenish Nutrition Ltd v Sanofi-Aventis SA* [2007] EWHC 2394 (Ch); [2008] 2 WLR 637. Ruling not appealed to CA: [2008] EWCA Civ 1086; [2009] Ch. 390.

[127] *Archer v Brown* [1985] QB 401.

[128] *Factortame (No 7)* [2001] 1 WLR 942, 980, although his Honour expressly left open the question whether amendments to the Treaty of Rome importing social provisions into the Treaty would affect his decision.

[129] *Devenish Nutrition Ltd v Sanofi-Aventis SA* [2008] EWCA Civ 1086; [2009] Ch 390.

[130] Stanton et al, *Statutory Torts* (n 34) para 6.059. See also G Anagnostaras, 'Not as Unproblematic as You Might Think: The Establishment of Causation in Governmental Liability Actions' (2002) 27 *European Law Review* 663.

[131] L Woods and F Smith, 'Causation in *Francovich*: The Neglected Problem' (1997) 46 *International &Comparative Law Quarterly* 925.

State as the direct cause of economic loss in a marketplace where a number of factors will determine success is not necessarily a straightforward matter, particularly if the parties are not in a direct relationship. While it may be possible to establish that the State's breach increased the possibility of loss (or diminished the chance of avoiding loss), such claims are not admissible in English law. Such analysis suggests that this third condition may prove a real obstacle to potential claimants.

iv. Concluding remarks

In applying the *Francovich* test, the English courts have clearly struggled to apply EU law within the common law system. In particular, there must be concerns that the approach of the English courts in *Three Rivers* and *Poole* reveals reluctance by the courts to embrace the full potential of *Francovich* reasoning and adopt purposive reasoning in interpreting EU legislation. This is coupled with an evident disinclination to utilise the Article 267 TFEU reference procedure.[132] The House of Lords in *Three Rivers* refused to refer the case to the ECJ, despite strong differences of opinion between the judges during litigation. Article 267(3) imposes an obligation on the final court of appeal to refer, when necessary, questions of interpretation to the CJEU. The preliminary reference procedure is seen as essential for the preservation of the European character of the law established by the Treaty and to avoid divergences at national level.[133] The English courts, however, have been more than ready to rely on the *acte clair* doctrine to avoid the need for reference. At the very least it might be supposed that the strong dissenting judgment of Auld LJ in the Court of Appeal in *Three Rivers* would raise 'reasonable doubts' as to the meaning of the provision in question.[134] Further, in the light of *Köbler v Austria*,[135] which establishes that State liability may arise where a court of final appeal has failed to refer a matter to the CJEU in circumstances where it amounts to a manifest infringement of the applicable law, the reluctance to refer may potentially lead to a breach of EU law in its own right.[136]

An unwillingness to embrace the broader reasoning of EU law has, it is submitted, led the courts to place insufficient emphasis on the true characteristics of this

[132] See A Arnull, 'The Law Lords and the European Union: Swimming with the Incoming Tide' (2010) *European Law Review* 57.

[133] Case 166/73 *Rheinmuehlen v Einfuhr-und Vorratsstelle Getreide* [1974] ECR 33. See also I Maher, 'National Courts as European Community Courts' (1994) 14 *Legal Studies* 226 and 2012/C 338/01 Recommendations to national courts and tribunals in relation to the initiation of preliminary ruling proceedings, para 1: 'The reference for a preliminary ruling is a fundamental mechanism of European Union law aimed at enabling the courts and tribunals of the Member States to ensure uniform interpretation and application of that law within the European Union.'

[134] See also *Office of Fair Trading v Abbey National plc* [2009] UKSC 6; [2010] 1 AC 696. Here no reference was made despite a 3:2 divide whether the point was *acte clair* and a different interpretation of the relevant provision at Court of Appeal level. This decision was justified on the basis that even if the Court of Appeal had been correct in its interpretation, it had misapplied the law to the facts – a matter for national, not EU, law. Davies has described this as 'an unsatisfactory fudge' (PS Davies, 'Bank Charges in the Supreme Court' (2010) 69 *Cambridge Law Journal* 21).

[135] C224/01 *Köbler v Austria* [2003] ECR I-239; [2004] QB 848. See, further, below.

[136] See M Dougan, *National Remedies before the Court of Justice* (Oxford, Hart Publishing, 2004) 250.

hybrid EU/common law tort. As seen, it has led the courts to adopt a narrow reading of conditions 1 and 3 and to a tendency to seek out fault-based or deliberate misconduct for condition 2. One contributing factor to this confusion is, as will be discussed below, the refusal of English law to recognise the distinctive character of *Francovich* liability. Rather than recognising it as a new tort of State liability for breach of EU law, the English courts have preferred to identify *Francovich* liability as part of the existing tort of breach of statutory duty. As will be seen, such a classification is unhelpful in terms of application, and, most worryingly, serves to de-emphasise the European character of this area of law and the extent to which it is different in nature, reasoning and authority from the traditional English tort.

B. The Taxonomy of Torts: Classifying the Eurotort

In *Factortame (No 7)*, Judge Toulmin QC determined that *Francovich* liability should be treated as a form of the tort of breach of statutory duty, albeit 'somewhat different' from the requirements of English domestic law.[137] This built upon earlier case law, such as *Garden Cottage Foods Ltd v Milk Marketing Board*,[138] where Lord Diplock had chosen to categorise liability for breach of Article 102 TFEU (abuse of a dominant position in competition law)[139] as breach of statutory duty, imposed not only for the purpose of promoting the general economic prosperity of the common market, but also for the benefit of private individuals to whom loss or damage is caused by a breach of that duty. In so doing, his Lordship had rejected Lord Denning's alternative suggestion in *Application des Gaz SA v Falks Veritas Ltd*[140] that liability arising by virtue of the doctrine of direct effect should give rise to new forms of tort law.

As Judge Toulmin QC explained in *Factortame Ltd (No 7)*,[141] the breach of statutory duty analysis derives from a combination of the impact of section 2(1) of the European Communities Act 1972 and the EU legislation in question. Section 2(1) provides that domestic law should give effect to all rights, powers, liabilities, obligations and restrictions arising out of the Treaties and that where there is an enforceable Community right, it should be enforceable as a matter of domestic law. On this basis, where rights are conferred on individual citizens by virtue of EU law, these rights are deemed to fall within section 2(1) of the Act and effect

[137] *Factortame Ltd (No 7)* [2000] EWHC (Tech) 179, para 176.

[138] *Garden Cottage Foods Ltd v Milk Marketing Board* [1984] AC 130, 141. See also Mann J in *Bourgoin SA and Others v Ministry of Agriculture, Fisheries and Food* [1986] QB 716, 733.

[139] At that time Art 86 of the EEC Treaty. While doubts were thrown on such analysis by the Court of Appeal in *Bourgoin SA v Ministry of Agriculture* [1986] QB 716, it is now commonly accepted that *Bourgoin* cannot survive the ruling in *Francovich*: see Lord Goff in *Kirkless Metropolitan Borough Council v Wickes Building Supplies* [1993] AC 227, 281.

[140] *Application des Gaz SA v Falks Veritas Ltd* [1974] 1 Ch 381 obiter, 395–96, suggesting that the now Arts 101 and 102 TFEU would give rise to new torts called 'undue restriction of competition within the common market' and 'abuse of dominant position within the common market'. See also Denning MR in *Garden Cottage Foods Ltd v Milk Marketing Board* [1982] QB 1114, 1119 (CA).

[141] *Factortame Ltd (No 7)* [2000] EWHC (Tech) 179; [2001] 1 WLR 942, para 166.

must be given to them without any further enactment.[142] The 1972 Act, therefore, acts as a conduit or bridge, translating the EU rights into English law.[143] This is indeed supported by EU case law, which states that

> every national court must, in a case within its jurisdiction, apply Community law in its entirety and protect rights which the latter confers on individuals and must accordingly set aside any provision of national law which may conflict with it, whether prior or subsequent to the Community rule.[144]

It should be noted, however, that the courts have not stated that this is an exact match. In advocating classification as breach of statutory duty for limitation purposes, Judge Toulmin QC in *Factortame (No 7)* nevertheless preferred to use the term 'Eurotort' to distinguish this form of liability from the 'somewhat different' requirements of domestic law.[145] Equally, Hobhouse J in *Factortame (No 5)* described *Francovich* liability as '*sui generis*, of the character of a breach of statutory duty'.[146] Leading practitioners' text Clerk and Lindsell is more equivocal, stating that 'it remains unclear whether the right to damages is properly to be categorised as an action for breach of statutory duty.'[147] This section will examine why the courts have favoured classification of *Francovich* liability as a claim for breach of statutory duty, the arguments for and against such analysis and what insight this gives us into the English courts' treatment of *Francovich* liability.

i. Classification as Breach of Statutory Duty

Reliance on the tort of breach of statutory tort has the advantage of the familiar. The early history of the action may be traced back to the thirteenth century,[148] with a wealth of case law arising from the nineteenth century onwards.[149] It is a nominate tort with established conditions for liability, namely that Parliament must have intended that the statute in question was actionable at private law, the harm suffered must be within the ambit of the statute, the statutory duty must have been breached and the breach must have caused the loss suffered (subject to

142 See also *Sempra Metals Ltd v Inland Revenue Comrs*, [2007] UKHL 34; [2008] 1 AC 561, para 69 per Lord Nicholls, dealing with freedom of establishment under Art 49 TFEU. See also *Phonographic Performance Ltd v Department of Trade and Industry* [2004] EWHC 1795 (Ch); [2004] 1 WLR 2893.

143 Judge Toulmin QC in *Factortame Ltd (No 7)* (n 141) para 177.

144 Case 106/77 *Simmenthal* [1978] ECR 629, [1978] 3 CMLR 263.

145 *Factortame Ltd (No 7)* (n 141) para 176: '[i]t may well be that the term "Eurotort" is apt to describe the particular characteristics in *Brasserie du Pêcheur* to differentiate it from the somewhat different requirements under English domestic law.'

146 *Factortame (No 5)* [1997] Eu LR 475, 531 (Divisional Court).

147 *Clerk and Lindsell* (n 32) para 9-48.

148 Foster notes that c 50 of the second Statute of Westminster in 1285 sets out an early basis for a civil action based on statutory breach: N Foster, 'The Merits of the Civil Action for Breach of Statutory Duty' (2011) 33 *Sydney Law Review* 67, 68. See, generally, KM Stanton, *Breach of Statutory Duty in Tort* (London, Sweet and Maxwell, 1986) and K Stanton et al, *Statutory Torts* (n 34).

149 One of the earliest modern cases being *Couch v Steel* (1854) 3 E & B 402; 118 ER 1193.

any applicable defences).[150] In determining the intention of Parliament, the courts will construe the wording of the statute and when no indication is given, consider the scope and purpose of the statute and in particular for whose benefit it is intended.[151] As stated in *Neil Martin Ltd v The Commissioners of Her Majesty's Revenue and Customs*, 'the relevant question is not whether it would have been appropriate or reasonable for Parliament to have provided a private law remedy but whether, as a matter of construction, it actually intended to do so.'[152] In the absence of express provision for private law rights,[153] it is commonly accepted that this tort plays a limited role in English law save in specific contexts such as health and safety in the workplace.[154] On this basis, the Eurotort may be seen as revitalising a somewhat neglected area of English tort law.

In the English system of nominate torts, breach of statutory duty also bears the closest resemblance to *Francovich* liability. As an action against the State, the public law tort of misfeasance in public office might seem to be a more obvious starting point, but its key elements – deliberate abuses of power by a public official acting in bad faith – are far more stringent than those required by *Francovich* liability.[155] The public officer must act in the knowledge of, or with reckless indifference to the probability of, injury being caused to the claimant or a class of persons of which the claimant is a member.[156] Judge Toulmin QC in *Factortame (No 7)*[157] confirmed that misfeasance in public office is not a suitable home for *Francovich* liability. Equally unsuitable is the tort of negligence. There is no provision for duty of care and the 'sufficiently serious' breach test is not one of reasonable care. Other intentional torts do not provide any overall framework, despite the occasional overlap.

In this light, it is understandable that the award of damages for breach of EU legislation might seem closest to a tort which awards damages for breach of statutory duties.[158] Section 2(1) of the European Communities Act 1972, combined with the EU provision in question, serves to provide a legislative base. Both forms

[150] *Clerk and Lindsell* (n 32) para 9.04. This framework was approved in *Fytche v Wincanton Logistics plc* [2003] EWCA Civ 874; [2003] ICR 1582, para 17 per Waller LJ. See also, generally, RA Buckley, 'Liability in Tort for Breach of Statutory Duty' (1984) 100 *Law Quarterly Review* 204.

[151] *Butler (or Black) v Fife Coal Co. Ltd.* [1912] AC 149, 165 per Lord Kinnear; *Atkinson v Newcastle Waterworks Co.* (1877) 2 Ex D 441.

[152] *Neil Martin Ltd v The Commissioners of Her Majesty's Revenue and Customs* [2006] EWHC 2425 (Ch); [2007] STC 823, para 71 per Andrew Simmonds QC.

[153] See, eg, Consumer Protection Act 1987, section 41.

[154] See ch 3 of this book. See also K Stanton, 'New Forms of the Tort of Breach of Statutory Duty' (2004) 120 *Law Quarterly Review* 324, 326; G Williams, 'The Effect of Penal Legislation in the Law of Tort' (1960) 23 *Modern Law Review* 233, 258; *Groves v Lord Wimborne* [1898] 2 QB 402.

[155] See the now leading case on this intentional tort: *Three Rivers* (n 47).

[156] Intention may be proved by evidence of improper or ulterior motives (targeted malice) or that the officer has knowingly acted beyond his powers in the knowledge that such actions would probably result in injury to the claimant (untargeted malice).

[157] *Factortame (No 7)* (n 141) para 126.

[158] J Convery, 'State Liability in the United Kingdom after *Brasserie du Pêcheur*' (1997) 34 *Common Market Law Review* 603; M Hoskins, 'Rebirth of the Innominate Tort?' in J Beatson and T Tridimas, *New Directions in European Public Law* (Oxford, Hart Publishing, 1998) 93–96.

of liability require the claimant to establish that the legislation in question gives the claimant enforceable rights and that breach of these rights has caused damage to the claimant. Further, an existing body of law indicates that the directly effective competition rules in the Treaty of Rome (now Articles 101 and 102, TFEU) should be classified as the tort of breach of statutory duty.[159]

Nevertheless, differences do exist between the Eurotort and the tort of breach of statutory duty. Two fundamental distinctions may be drawn. First, *Francovich* liability is an action brought against the State for breaching the rights of individual citizens; 'State', in this context, defined broadly to include public authorities.[160] It is therefore a form of liability which seeks to render public bodies accountable to individual citizens.[161] *Factortame (No 2)*[162] highlighted that, in ensuring the full effectiveness of EU law, the national court may be required to grant remedies, such as interim relief against the Crown, previously precluded at common law. In contrast, domestic tort law is reluctant to find public bodies liable. Cases such as *X v Bedfordshire CC*[163] and *O'Rourke v Camden LBC*[164] indicate the unwillingness of the English courts to find public authorities liable for breach of statutory duty. Lord Browne-Wilkinson in *X* commented that 'The cases where a private right of action for breach of statutory duty have been held to arise are all cases in which the statutory duty has been very limited and specific as opposed to general administrative functions imposed on public bodies and involving the exercise of administrative discretions.'[165] Further, the availability and effectiveness of an alternative public law remedy, such as judicial review, may be a strong indication that damages should not be awarded for that breach.[166] The courts are aware that to impose a duty on a local authority to compensate all members of the public who suffer by its actions may give rise to a potentially large compensatory burden on bodies which are already over-stretched and would risk undermining their discretion. As recognised by the Law Commission,[167] where the defendant is

[159] *Garden Cottage Foods Ltd* (n 138), albeit not without criticism: see JS Davidson, 'Actions for Damages in the English Courts for Breach of EEC Competition Law' (1985) 34 *International & Comparative Law Quarterly* 178.

[160] Case C-424/97 *Haim v Kassenzahnaerztliche Vereinigung Nordrhein (Haim No 2)* [2000] ECR I-5123; [2002] 1 CMLR 11. See also *Brasserie du Pêcheur* (n 24) para 32.

[161] Consider, however, the view of Carol Harlow who questions whether the best way to enforce EU law is through the medium of damages, using litigation to redistribute limited resources, or whether enforcement would be better achieved by having judicial review as the standard procedure, with annulment or declaratory orders as the standard remedy: '*Francovich* and the Problem of the Disobedient State' (1996) 2 European Law Journal 199, 204.

[162] Case C-213/89 *Secretary of State for Transport, ex p Factortame Limited (No 2)* [1990] ECR I-2433.

[163] *X v Bedfordshire CC* [1995] 2 AC 633.

[164] *O'Rourke v Camden LBC* [1998] AC 188 (housing for the homeless was provided in the general public interest and therefore the statute could not create a private right of action for damages). See R Carnwath [1998] *Public Law* 407

[165] *X* (n 163) 732.

[166] See *Cullen v Chief Constable of the Royal Ulster Constabulary* [2003] 1 WLR 1763 (HL(NI)): adequate public law remedies justified denying the claimant a private law claim.

[167] Law Commission, *Administrative Redress*, Consultation Paper (n 93) para 4.75.

a public body, courts have, with the exception of health and safety legislation,[168] been extremely reluctant to hold that a statutory provision was actually intended to confer a private law right to compensation. This is especially the case where the statutory duty breached forms part of an overall regulatory system or a scheme of social welfare for the benefit of the public at large.[169] This restrictive approach in domestic law towards the liability of public bodies under the tort of breach of statutory duty presents a clear contrast with the *Francovich* principle of state liability.[170]

Secondly, although the conditions of *Francovich* liability – conferral of rights; sufficiently serious breach; causation – resemble those of breach of statutory duty, differences exist. In determining whether the legislation intends to confer private law rights on individuals, the domestic tort focuses on the actual wording of the statutory provision in question. As stated in the leading case of *X v Bedfordshire CC*,[171] the court must examine whether, as a matter of construction, the statutory duty was imposed for the protection of a limited class of the public and Parliament intended to confer on members of that class a private right of action.[172] *Clerk and Lindsell* have noted that this can be a somewhat haphazard process: 'The courts look to the construction of the statute, relying upon a number of "presumptions" for guidance, but in practice there are so many conflicting presumptions, with variable weightings, that it can be extremely difficult to predict how the courts will respond to a particular statute.'[173] This may be contrasted with the broad purposive approach to interpretation adopted by the CJEU and seen in cases such as *Dillenkofer* above, which seeks to identify the context, aims and objectives of the legislation in question. The narrow scope of the domestic tort bears little relation to a form of liability which is prepared to find liability for breach of European Union law, be it breach of primary legislation (Treaty articles), secondary legislation (a failure to implement a Directive correctly) or administrative decisions (a refusal to issue a licence).[174] A distinct form of reasoning is required.

The above analysis suggests that classifying *Francovich* liability as breach of statutory duty is unlikely to be of assistance to courts interpreting this new form of liability and, in fact, fails to highlight to courts the distinctive nature of this area of tort law. This, it is submitted, may be seen in the *Three Rivers* case above, but also

[168] Health and safety at work legislation is distinguished by the Commission on the basis that it regulates the employment relationship and the status of the employer is thereby irrelevant – in other words, there is no 'public' dimension: ibid, para 4.79.

[169] See, eg, recent case law involving regulators such as the Health and Safety Executive: *Thames Trains Ltd v Health and Safety Executive* [2003] EWCA Civ 720 (duty owed by HSE to anyone affected by the railway being unsafe did not give rise to individual rights for passengers and train operators).

[170] Caranta, for example, contrasts the declining scope of governmental liability in English tort law with the introduction of *Francovich* liability: 'Governmental Liability after *Francovich*' (1993) 52 *Cambridge Law Journal* 272.

[171] *X* (n 163).

[172] *X* (n 163) 731 per Lord Browne-Wilkinson.

[173] *Clerk and Lindsell* (n 32) para 9-02.

[174] eg, Case C-5/94 *R v Ministry of Agriculture, Fisheries and Food ex p Hedley Lomas (Ireland) Ltd* [1996] ECR I-2553; [1997] QB 139 (refusal to issue a licence for the export of live sheep to Spain).

in relation to the other conditions. In the competition law case of *Crehan v Inntrepreneur Pub Company*,[175] for example, the tort of breach of statutory duty was relied upon by the defendants to argue that Mr Crehan's claim should be restricted to the kind of loss the law in question was intending to prevent.[176] This, as stated above, is a classic requirement of the tort of breach of statutory duty,[177] and would have served indeed to defeat Mr Crehan's claim. The Court of Appeal struggled with this argument– 'as a matter of English law, [it] is correct'[178] – but ultimately deferred to the EU principle of effectiveness and the fact the ECJ had been willing to entertain a wider claim for damages in the earlier ruling of *Courage Ltd v Crehan.*[179]

Crehan provides a good illustration of the tension which exists between traditional principles of English tort law and the new compensatory regime. There is a clear distinction between domestic and EU forms of reasoning. *Francovich* liability requires the courts to appreciate the hybrid nature of this tort, which is part EU/part national, and avoid resort to purely domestic reasoning, which is particularly dangerous in this area due to the common law's traditionally conservative approach towards public authority liability in tort. In *Crehan*, the point was not pursued. Once again, the court did not find it necessary to initiate an Article 267 reference and the argument was not dealt with on appeal. It is a good example nevertheless of the need to distinguish breach of statutory duty from its '*sui generis*' counterpart.

In view of the above analysis, one might enquire why the English courts have resisted the introduction of a new tort. Is it mere conservatism and the comfort of the familiar or are there more profound reasons for failing to recognise a European form of tort law? One element would seem to be a fear of uncontrolled expansion of liability. It is undoubtedly true that lawyers, schooled in a system of nominate torts, will feel more comfortable with expanding incrementally an existing form of liability rather than introducing a new cause of action with which they are unfamiliar and which, it is claimed, will lead to uncertainty. Lower courts require guidance and, in particular, that the conditions for liability can be identified with sufficient clarity. On this basis, it was easier in *Factortame (No 7)* to identify the correct limitation period by reference to an existing cause of action rather than speculating how to treat a new form of tort law.[180] Further, there remains the concern whether the judiciary, rather than Parliament, should create new causes of

[175] *Crehan v Inntrepreneur Pub Company* [2004] EWCA Civ 637; [2004] 2 CLC 803 (action for breach of Art 101, TFEU).

[176] Here, to confine losses to financial loss caused by distortion at distribution level – a loss Mr Crehan had neither pleaded nor proved (argument not dealt with at HL).

[177] See the classic case of *Gorris v Scott* (1874) LR 9 Exch. 125 (relied upon in *Crehan*). For a more recent application, see *Fytche v Wincanton Logistics plc* [2004] UKHL 31; [2004] 4 All ER 221 (regulations intended to protect employees from risk of injury from impact damage, not frostbite).

[178] *Crehan* (n 175) para 158.

[179] *Courage Ltd v Crehan* (C 453/99) [2002] QB 507.

[180] Although Stanton argues that even this was unnecessary in that s 2 deals with actions 'founded on tort': Stanton, 'New Forms' (n 154) 329–30.

action. Judges, under the doctrine of separation of powers, are less than keen to be seen to create new law.[181] This is noticeable in the judgment of Lord Hoffmann in rejecting the creation of a tort of privacy in *Wainwright v Home Office*.[182] His Lordship argued that such a tort required a detailed approach which could only be achieved by legislation rather than the broad brush of common law principle. His Lordship is not alone in this view. The Court of Appeal in *Patel v Patel*,[183] for example, held that no tort of harassment existed in the common law and that any claim would have to be supported by an existing tort, such as trespass. It was for Parliament to bring in this new form of liability, which, in fact, occurred.[184] Such caution may also be regarded as understandable when facing the politically controversial area of EU law.

Such domestic concerns run into trouble, however, when faced with *Francovich* liability. It is not for the UK Parliament to dictate the character of this form of tortious liability and establish its policy basis. *Francovich* liability was created over 20 years ago by the European Court of Justice. The initial view that EU law would not require States to create new remedies in the national courts to ensure the observance of EU law has now been qualified, notably in the light of *Francovich* itself. On this basis, the content of the tort and its conditions for liability are set by the CJEU, not the UK Supreme Court. Classification is therefore not a question of deference to Parliament, but a question of how best to label a new form of liability which represents a hybrid of English and EU law.

ii. Concluding Remarks

Such analysis leads to the conclusion that the current choice by the English courts to classify *Francovich* liability as a '*sui generis*' form of the traditional tort of breach of statutory duty is misguided. It has been argued that it is also damaging in that it fails to highlight the true nature of liability and leads the courts into false analogies. As Stanton has observed, breach of statutory duty has little to offer to *Francovich* liability in terms of interpretative assistance or authority.[185] Labelling can make a difference. It would therefore be preferable for the common law to accept that there is a distinct tort of State liability for breach of EU law with its own conditions and for which purposive reasoning and reference to EU law is helpful. A realisation is also needed that the Article 267 TFEU procedure is not simply an obstacle to the timely resolution of claims, but may assist in avoiding interpretative divergences at national level.

[181] Note the perceptive comments of Lord Reid on the judicial role: 'The Judge as Law Maker' (1972) 12 *Journal of Public Teachers of Law* 22.

[182] *Wainwright v Home Office* [2003] UKHL 53; [2004] 2 AC 406. This is discussed further in ch 6.

[183] *Patel v Patel* [1988] 2 FLR 179

[184] The Protection from Harassment Act 1997.

[185] Stanton, 'New Forms', (n 154) 329–30.

C. Extending Liability: The Future Impact of *Francovich*

This final section will examine signs that *Francovich* liability may extend beyond its current remit of State liability. At present, liability is confined to claims against the State, emanations of the State and public authorities found to be acting in breach of EU law. It therefore provides a new head of public authority liability in private law in addition to that existing in English contract law, property law and under the traditional torts of negligence, trespass, breach of statutory duty, the Human Rights Act 1998 and the tort of misfeasance in public office.[186] Two important developments by the CJEU will be noted here. First, the Court of Justice has extended *Francovich* liability to claims against the court of last instance in a Member State. Secondly, and perhaps more drastically, it has allowed claims against private parties in relation to directly effective Treaty provisions. The impact of these developments will be examined below.

i. National Courts of Last Instance as Defendants

The key case here is the 2003 decision of the ECJ in *Köbler v Austria*,[187] which establishes that a court of final appeal may be sued for failing to refer a matter to the CJEU or for giving an erroneous ruling where it amounts to a manifest infringement of the applicable law. The case itself involved a claim by an academic criticising the decision to refuse him a salary increment for 15 years service on the basis that he had not worked for the entire period in Austria, but elsewhere in the EU. This, it was argued, contravened Article 45 TFEU on freedom of movement of workers in the EU. His initial action was rejected by the Austrian Supreme Administrative Court (Verwaltungsgerichtshof); the Court making and then withdrawing a preliminary reference to the ECJ in the incorrect belief that the matter had been resolved by an earlier ECJ decision. His second action against the State finally led to a reference of which the central question was whether the Supreme Court of a Member State could be liable under the principle of State liability.

The ECJ found that, in the light of the essential role played by the judiciary in the protection of rights derived by individuals under EU rules, the full effectiveness of those rules would be called into question and the protection of rights weakened if an action could not be brought against the court of a Member State adjudicating at last instance.[188] It was therefore a natural extension of the principle of State liability. Nevertheless, such liability would be exceptional and a breach of EU law would only be regarded as sufficiently serious if, having regard to the

[186] For a summary, see T Endicott, *Administrative Law*, 2nd edn (Oxford, Oxford University Press, 2011) chs 14–15.

[187] *Köbler* (n 135).

[188] Reference was also made to broader notion of State liability in international law which include acts by the legislature, executive and judiciary: *Köbler* (n 135) para 32.

specific nature of the judicial function and the legitimate requirements of legal certainty, the court 'has manifestly infringed the applicable law'.[189] This condition would be applied in the light of all relevant factors which include the degree of clarity and precision for the rule infringed, whether the infringement was intentional, whether the error of law was excusable or inexcusable, the position taken, where applicable, by a EU institution, and non-compliance by the court in question with the obligation to make a reference for a preliminary ruling under Article 267(3) TFEU.[190] The last factor is an addition to the traditional *Brasserie du Pêcheur* list of factors and brings into question the ability of courts to avoid references under the CILFIT doctrine.[191] The later decision of *Traghetti del Mediterraneo SpA (In Liquidation) v Italy*[192] makes it clear that liability is exceptional and applies not only to refusals to apply EU law, but poor interpretations of the relevant legal principles. Intentional fault was not required – intention being only a relevant factor. On this basis, a national rule requiring intentional fault infringed EU law in that it imposed a requirement stricter that the manifest infringement test.[193]

In extending the concept of 'State' to include courts of last instance, the case raises difficult questions of both a constitutional nature (which court will rule on the validity of a judgment of a court of last instance and what happens if this ruling is appealed to the court of last instance?)[194] and policy (diminution in legal certainty and judicial authority).[195] In relation to the last point, the ECJ was dismissive: 'the existence of a right of action . . . could be regarded as enhancing the quality of a legal system and thus in the long run the authority of the judiciary'.[196] The UK government in its representations to the ECJ in *Köbler* argued further that as a matter of principle no action in damages should be brought against the Crown in respect of judicial decisions, noting in particular the difficulties it might cause to a unitary court system with a strict doctrine of stare decisis. Again one

[189] *Köbler* (n 135) para 53. The error of the Austrian court was not judged 'sufficiently serious' as the law had not been clear at the time and so any infringement was not 'manifest in nature'. For a comparison with the application of state unity theory in international law, see A Davies, 'State Liability for Judicial Decisions in European Union and International Law' (2012) 61 *International &Comparative Law Quarterly* 585.

[190] *Köbler* (n 135), para 55.

[191] Namely, that the correct application of EU law is so obvious as to leave no scope for any reasonable doubt as to the manner in which the question raised is to be resolved: 283/81 *CILFIT v Ministry of Health* [1982] ECR 3415, para 16.

[192] C173/03 *Traghetti del Mediterraneo SpA (In Liquidation) v Italy* [2006] ECR I-5177; [2006] 3 CMLR 19.

[193] Ibid, para 46: 'Community law also precludes national legislation which limits such liability solely to cases of intentional fault and serious misconduct on the part of the court, if such a limitation were to lead to exclusion of the liability of the Member State concerned in other cases where a manifest infringement of the applicable law was committed, as set out in paras 53 to 56 of the *Köbler* judgment.' See also C-379/10 *Commission v Italy* 24 November 2011 (nyr).

[194] H Scott and N Barber, 'State Liability under *Francovich* for Decisions of National Courts' (2004) 120 *Law Quarterly Review* 403.

[195] See P Wattel, '*Köbler, CILFIT and Welthgrove*: We Can't Go On Meeting Like This' (2004) 41 *Common Market Law Review* 177, who argues that the *Köbler* judgment is a source of legal uncertainty and procedural entanglements and will lead to even more arrears in the decision of cases, both at national and ECJ level .

[196] *Köbler* (n 135) para. 43.

sees the tensions between domestic common law concerns and EU policy. Such concerns were dismissed.

The question remains how 'exceptional' liability will be. Beutler suggests that only in rare cases will the national court be deemed to fall below the standard of manifest infringement.[197] Biondi and Farley agree: *Köbler* has a very high symbolic value but on a practical level its impact may not be so great.[198] It does, however, expose the English courts to a new form of liability, as discussed by the Court of Appeal in *Cooper v Attorney General*.[199] Here, Cooper argued that the Court of Appeal (the court of last instance in this case) was in breach of Directive 85/337/EEC,[200] having misinterpreted its provisions. The Court of Appeal found that a breach had occurred: the court had failed to order a reference to the ECJ for a preliminary ruling to clarify the question in issue. In considering the factors identified in *Köbler*, the Court recognised that the case concerned a difficult point of law arising in a specialist field and that there was no case law of the ECJ on the point. The Court of Appeal had reached a considered, albeit incorrect, decision not to make a reference, but this was not of itself a manifest breach and the failure to make a reference was excusable. The Court concluded that 'the claimant needs to overcome high hurdles in order to establish a claim based on *Köbler* liability, and that claims based on *Köbler* liability are likely to be rare.'[201] For a breach to be manifest, the Court held it must be evident that there is a breach,[202] for example, where the ECJ has already decided the point or where it may be inferred from ECJ case law. Importantly, it found that a failure to make a reference where a question is not *acte clair* does not automatically lead to *Köbler* liability unless it is obvious from EU law that there is a EU issue and there are no mitigating circumstances.[203] Timing is particularly relevant. The court must consider the state of the law at the time of the ruling and not with the benefit of hindsight.

It is interesting that the English court, in emphasising the exceptional nature of liability where the breach must not only be manifest but 'evident' (query whether this is a higher standard), has adopted a narrow interpretation of this head of liability. This is consistent with the approach seen earlier in this chapter, but again threatens a potential discordance with other Member States. Perhaps the true significance of this head of liability, however, is in the balance of powers between the EU and common law courts. In *Köbler*, the ECJ not only extends the scope of *Francovich* liability, but holds the national court itself accountable. The case also

[197] See B Beutler, 'State Liability for Breaches of Community Law by National Courts: Is the Requirement of a Manifest Infringement of the Applicable Law an Insurmountable Obstacle' (2009) 46 *Common Market Law Review* 773. See also D Nassimpian, 'And We Keep On Meeting: (De)fragmenting State Liability' (2007) 32 *European Law Review* 819.

[198] A Biondi and M Farley, *The Right to Damages in European Law* (The Hague, Kluwer Law International, 2009) 69.

[199] *Cooper v Attorney General* [2010] EWCA Civ 464; [2011] 2 WLR 448.

[200] On the assessment of the effect of certain public and private projects on the environment: [1985] OJ L175, p 40.

[201] *Cooper* (n 199) para 128 per Arden LJ.

[202] Ibid, para 68 per Arden LJ.

[203] Ibid, para 70.

demonstrates that common law concerns, raised expressly by the UK government in *Köbler*, will not necessarily prevent developments at EU level which will in turn create individual rights to sue in the English courts. *Köbler* thus indicates the continued vitality of this area of law.

ii. Private Parties as Defendants

As seen above, *Francovich* liability gives private individuals the right to sue the State for serious breaches of EU law in the national courts. The notion of the 'State' is, as we have seen, taken broadly, but excludes private individuals. Nevertheless, Van Gerven has argued that in respect of infringements of directly effective Treaty provisions, the full effect of EU law would be impaired if an individual or undertaking could not obtain damages from a private individual who had breached EU law.[204] Such 'horizontal' claims have been brought in relation to the directly effective competition law provisions of the TFEU. In *Courage v Crehan*,[205] the ECJ recognised that a private individual could be sued for damages for breach of Article 101 TFEU.[206] The case involved a beer tie agreement, by which Mr Crehan (the landlord of a public house) had agreed to a 20-year tied-brewery lease with the Courage brewery which required the purchase of a fixed minimum quantity of beer. The ECJ found that '[t]he full effectiveness of Article [101 TFEU] and, in particular, that practical effect of the prohibition laid down in Article [101(1)] would be put at risk if it were not open to any individual to claim damages for loss caused to him by a contract or by conduct liable to restrict or distort competition.'[207]

It is noticeable that, although the wording resembles that of the Court in *Francovich*, sharing the goal of ensuring the effectiveness of EU law, the ECJ in *Courage* did not purport to apply *Francovich* liability nor did it establish any substantive conditions for liability. There is no mention, for example, of the need for a 'sufficiently serious' breach. The court merely stated that, in the absence of EU rules governing the matter, it is for the domestic legal system of each Member State to lay down the procedural rules governing such actions, provided that such rules are not less favourable than those governing similar domestic actions (principle of equivalence) and that they do not render practically impossible or excessively difficult the exercise of rights conferred by Community law (principle of effectiveness).[208] This led some commentators to question to what extent this

[204] W van Gerven, 'Bridging the Unbridgeable: Community and National Laws after *Francovich* and *Brasserie*' (1996) 45 *International & Comparative Law Quarterly* 507, 530–32. See also the comments of former Advocate General van Gerven in C-128/92 *Banks v British Coal Corporation* [1994] ECR I-1209: 'The full effect of Community law would be impaired if the former individual or undertaking did not have the possibility of obtaining reparation from the party who can be held responsible for the breach of Community law – all the more so, evidently, if a directly effective provision of Community law is infringed' (para 43).

[205] C-453/99 *Courage v Crehan* [2001] ECR I-6297.

[206] This prohibits cartels and other agreements or concerted practices that restrict competition.

[207] *Courage* (n 205) para 26.

[208] Ibid, para 29.

establishes an autonomous claim under EU law,[209] or, at least, a hybrid claim in which EU law defines the rights and obligations of the parties and national law gives an answer subject to the EU standards of effectiveness and equivalence.[210] In the subsequent case of *Manfredi v Lloyd Adriatico Assicurazioni SpA*,[211] the ECJ simply re-iterated that 'any individual can claim compensation for the harm suffered where there is a causal relationship between that harm and an agreement or practice prohibited under Article [101 TFEU]'[212] Such liability was thus seen as a logical development of the effectiveness doctrine, but with considerable discretion granted to the national courts. Nebbia and Szysczak suggest that it appears to be part of a general trend of widening the scope of obligations under EU law.[213]

The implications of *Courage* outside the competition law context remain unclear. Craig and De Búrca question to what extent it will extend even to other Treaty provisions outside competition law such as those on free movement or discrimination.[214] Van Gerven comments, 'To be sure, thanks to *Crehan* there is now a legal basis in Community law to claim damages, but the conditions for liability to arise remain uncertain.'[215] If extended outside the competition law context, it is submitted that such authority should logically be confined to provisions in Treaties (and regulations) which have horizontal and direct effect. This would exclude directives for which there is clear authority that they do not have horizontal direct effect.[216] Stanton et al agree that claims should be limited to directly effective Treaty provisions, fearing that otherwise there may be a risk of opening the floodgates of liability.[217]

At present, therefore, there is little evidence that *Francovich* liability will be extended to private individuals.[218] Komninos asserts that, in fact, it is a logical

[209] A Komninos, 'New Prospects for Private Enforcement of EC Competition Law: *Courage v Crehan* and the Community Right to Damages' (2002) 39 *Common Market Law Review* 447.

[210] N Reich, 'Horizontal Liability in EC Law: Hybridization of Remedies for Compensation in case of Breaches of EC Rights' (2007) 44 *Common Market Law Review* 705.

[211] Joined cases C-295/04 and 298/04 *Manfredi v Lloyd Adriatico Assicurazioni SpA* [2006] ECR I-6619.

[212] Ibid, para 61.

[213] P Nebbia and E Szysczak, 'White Paper on Damages Actions for Breach of the EC Antitrust Rules' (2009) 20 *European Business Law Review* 635, 637.

[214] Craig and De Búrca, *EU Law* (n 5) 247.

[215] W van Gerven, '*Crehan* and the Way Ahead' (2006) 17 *European Business Law Review* 269, 272. See also K Havu, 'Horizontal Liability for Damages in EU Law: The Changing Relationship of EU and National Law' (2012) 18 *European Law Journal* 407, who also comments at 414 that *Courage* and *Manfredi* have opened up the discussion regarding the details of horizontal liability in EU law rather than in any way closing it.

[216] Case 43/75 *Defrenne v SABENA* [1976] ECR 455; [1976] 2 CMLR 98 and Case 152/84 *Marshall v Southampton and SW Hampshire Health Authority* [1986] ECR 723, [1986] 1 CMLR 688. Art 288 TFEU states that directives are binding on Member States only.

[217] Stanton et al, *Statutory Torts* (n 34) 266–67. For a discussion, see Dougan, *National Remedies* (n 136) and S Drake, 'Scope of *Courage* and the Principle of "individual liability" for Damages: Further Development of the Principle of Effective Judicial Protection by the Court of Justice' [2006] *European Law Review* 41.

[218] See D Leczykiewicz, 'Private Party Liability in EU Law: In Search of a General Regime' (2009) 12 *Cambridge Yearbook of European Legal Studies* 257, who argues that it is clear from ECJ case law that no principle of private party liability analogous to the principle of Member State liability exists.

impossibility: it is a precondition for the civil liability of private individuals that there should be horizontal direct effect of the rule in question and it is impossible to separate the enforceability of the rules from the question of liability for their breach.[219] Bearing in mind that *Francovich* liability remains distinct from the doctrine of direct effect in that the provision breached *need not* be directly effective and indeed it covers the misapplication (or non-application) of directives which do not have horizontal direct effect, this presents a significant obstacle to future expansion. Nevertheless, this is an area of law in which the CJEU has again shown considerable dynamism; a factor any national court would be wise to recognise.

Conclusion

This chapter has examined the impact of *Francovich* liability on the English law of torts and how the English courts have adapted to deal with this new form of liability. A number of observations may be made. English tort lawyers have not welcomed this form of liability with open arms. Pedagogically, it has been left to EU lawyers, who, naturally, pay little attention to its application at national level. This leaves a worrying gap in our discussion of this area of law. Further, by labelling *Francovich* liability '*sui generis* breach of statutory duty', the courts have sought to reconceptualise the Eurotort as a variant of a well-established common law tort, so well established that little discussion is needed. I have attempted in this chapter to show that discussion *is* needed to ensure that English lawyers (academics, practitioners, judges) fully understand how this area of law operates. At the very least, the English courts are paying insufficient notice to its '*sui generis*' status and, it is submitted, the easiest way to resolve this situation is to highlight the special nature of this tort by giving it the title, State liability for breach of EU law. The 'label' of breach of statutory duty, it is argued, is both misleading and obstructive, hiding and obfuscating the true nature of this tort, fundamentally making it appear less European. Recognition of its status as a distinct tort is, in my view, far more likely to give rise to a clearer understanding of its special character and to consistent application across Member States than grafting it onto an existing tort to which it bears little relation in practice.

Concerns may also be raised as to the application of *Francovich* liability by the English courts. It is a hybrid tort, requiring national courts to apply a threefold test established by the Court of Justice. Reich has described how the coexistence of national procedural autonomy and the necessity of properly enforcing EU law has led to remedies which are based on national law, but reshaped under the influence of EU law.[220] Inevitably, this gives rise to tensions in adapting to new forms of reasoning and methods of statutory interpretation. Some blame, admittedly, may

[219] Komninos, 'New Prospects' (n 209) 471.
[220] Reich, 'Horizontal Liability' (n 210) 709.

be placed at the doors of the Court of Justice. It is clear that, at times, the CJEU seems to be walking a tightrope between intervention and respect for national procedural autonomy and that, by deferring unduly to the national courts, fails to provide sufficient guidance to ensure the consistent application of the law across Member States. Particular concerns have been raised in this chapter in relation to conditions 1 and 3 of *Francovich* liability. Without a definition of 'direct causation', for example, what, indeed, is to prevent national courts from continuing to apply the tests with which they are most familiar, even if the net result is to block the claim itself (consider, for example, *Brasserie du Pêcheur* in the Bundesgerichtshof)? Nevertheless, the English courts do need to recognise that they cannot pursue a conventional common law approach to questions of breach, statutory interpretation and causation and that they should refer to CJEU case law for guidance. Equally, reluctance at times to stay litigation and undertake an Article 267 referral does not assist matters. Arnull has remarked that '[t]he issue is no longer whether the *CILFIT* criteria should be relaxed, but how their abuse can be prevented',[221] noting a profound loss of confidence by senior members of the English judiciary in the CJEU. Accepting, as noted above, that some blame must fall on the CJEU itself for failing to do more to respond to the problems confronting the national courts, Arnull nevertheless argues that it is for national courts to learn to accept the role assigned to them rather than continuing to adhere to national legal traditions.[222]

Francovich liability provides, perhaps, the clearest practical example of the changes English tort law faces as a result of UK Membership of the European Union. It shows how the relationship between the European and national courts continues to evolve and raises questions of procedural and substantive autonomy. *Factortame* itself brought the UK government to account, and served to demonstrate the potential impact of this new form of liability. Ultimately, the aim of *Francovich* liability is to ensure the effectiveness of EU law and to protect the rights of citizens. Without a focus on these goals, with the distraction of the label of '*sui generis* breach of statutory duty', one might question to what extent the English courts are currently providing a truly effective remedy for breach by the State of EU law.

[221] A Arnull, 'Keeping Their Heads Above Water? European Law in the House of Lords' in J Lee (ed) *From House of Lords to Supreme Court: Judges, Jurists and the Process of Judging* (Oxford, Hart Publishing, 2011) 129, 147.

[222] Ibid, 148.

5

Tort Law and Human Rights: A European Culture of Rights?

> [T]he question does arise whether the law of tort should evolve, analogically and incrementally, so as to fashion appropriate remedies to contemporary problems or whether it should remain essentially static, making only such changes as are forced upon it, leaving difficult and, in human terms, very important problems to be swept up by the Convention. I prefer evolution.
>
> (Lord Bingham)[1]

Introduction

This chapter will examine the impact of the European Convention on Human Rights and its case law on the development of English tort law. As noted in chapter one, the Convention dates back to 1950 and came into force in 1953. The United Kingdom was influential in its drafting and ratified the Convention in 1951.[2] However, it was only in 1966 that British citizens were permitted to petition the European Court of Human Rights (ECtHR) in Strasbourg.[3] The most significant date for English tort law is 2 October 2000: the date when the Human Rights Act 1998 (HRA 1998) came into force. The introduction of the Act marked a significant step for claimants. The declared aim of the Labour government was to bring (human) rights home.[4] Claimants would no longer have to exhaust national remedies before taking their case to the ECtHR, but could, subject to the terms of the Act, raise human rights challenges in their own national courts.

[1] *D v East Berkshire Community Health NHS Trust and others* [2005] UKHL 23; [2005] 2 AC 373, para 50 per Lord Bingham.

[2] For a study of the significance of the Convention for Britain until 1966, see AWB Simpson, *Human Rights and the End of Empire: Britain and the Genesis of the European Convention*, rev edn (Oxford, Oxford University Press, 2004). The Convention was drafted substantially by Conservative politician and lawyer, Sir David Maxwell-Fyfe (who became Conservative Lord Chancellor as Viscount Kilmuir) and the UK became the first state to ratify the convention, on 8 March 1951.

[3] See, generally, RCA White and C Ovey, *Jacobs, White & Ovey: The European Convention on Human Rights*, 5th edn (Oxford, Oxford University Press, 2010) ch 2; D Harris et al, *Harris, O'Boyle & Warbrick: Law of the European Convention on Human Rights*, 2nd edn (Oxford, Oxford University Press, 2009) ch 1.

[4] Labour Party, *Bringing Rights Home: Labour's Plans to Incorporate the European Convention on Human Rights into UK Law* (London, Labour Party, 1996).

The Act naturally provoked much interest from the legal community with considerable speculation on its potential to affect rights in the private and public law context.[5] The Act contains no indication of its impact of the law of tort, but does establish a cause of action where a public authority[6] is found to act in a way which is incompatible with a Convention right, listed in Schedule 1 to the Act.[7] Remedies are set out in section 8, which provides that:

> In relation to any act (or proposed act) of a public authority which the court finds is (or would be) unlawful, it may grant such relief or remedy, or make such order, within its powers as it considers just and appropriate.

Damages may be awarded in civil proceedings,[8] but are discretionary and no award will be made unless, taking account of all the circumstances of the case, including any other remedy granted and the consequences of any decision in respect of that act, the court is satisfied that the award is necessary to afford just satisfaction to the person in whose favour it is made.[9] It may, therefore, suffice to make a declaration of derogation of rights. The Act also provides for a short limitation period of one year.[10]

At face value, sections 6 to 8 of the Act establish an independent cause of action with a distinct limitation period and remedial discretion which may be relied upon by claimants as an alternative to a tort claim against a public authority. However, this is not the whole story. Tort law is potentially affected in two ways. First, courts under section 3 of the Act must interpret legislation so far as possible in a way which is compatible with the Convention rights. Although tort law is primarily case-based, statutes do play a role, for example the Defamation Acts of 1996 and 2013, the Fatal Accidents Act 1976 and the defence of statutory author-

[5] Notable commentaries included K Starmer, *European Human Rights Law: The Human Rights Act 1998 and the European Convention on Human Rights* (London, Legal Action Group, 1999); J Wadham and H Mountfield, *Blackstone's Guide to the Human Rights Act 1998*, 1st edn (Oxford, Blackstone Press, 1998); S Grosz, J Beatson and P Duffy (eds), *Human Rights: The 1998 Act and the European Convention* (London, Sweet and Maxwell, 1999).

[6] Under HRA 1998, s 6(3), the term 'public authority' includes a court or tribunal, and any person certain of whose functions are functions of a public nature. On the definition of 'public authority', see *Aston Cantlow v Wallbank* [2003] UKHL 37; [2004] 1 AC 546 where Lord Nicholls (para 12) suggested that although there could be no test of universal application, the factors to be taken into account included the extent to which in carrying out the relevant function the body is publicly funded, or is exercising statutory powers, or is taking the place of central government or local authorities, or is providing a public service. The emphasis is thus on the nature of the function, not the person discharging it. See D Oliver, 'Functions of a Public Nature under the Human Rights Act' [2004] *Public Law* 329; J Landau, 'Functional Public Authorities after *YL*' [2007] *Public Law* 630.

[7] HRA 1998, ss 6 and 7. The Act does not include all Convention rights, but does cover the most significant rights under the Convention, namely Art 2 (right to life), Art 3 (prohibition of torture), Art 4 (prohibition of slavery and forced labour), Art 5 (right to liberty and security), Art 6 (right to a fair trial), Art 7 (no punishment without law), Art 8 (right to respect for private and family life), Art 9 (freedom of thought, conscience and religion), Art 10 (freedom of expression), Art 11 (freedom of assembly and association) and Protocol 1, Art 1 (protection of property) which have the potential to impact on tort law principles.

[8] Provided the court has the power to award damages or to order the payment of compensation: HRA 1998, s 8(2).

[9] HRA 1998, s 8(3).

[10] HRA 1998, s 7(5).

ity in nuisance. These must now be interpreted in a convention-compliant manner when possible. Secondly, and more controversially, courts, as 'public authorities' under section 6(3) of the Act, must act in a way which is compatible with Convention rights. If applied to their adjudicative function, this opens up the possibility of a 'horizontal' application of human rights, that is, not simply by the citizen against a public body (vertical application), but between private citizens themselves. The Act makes no express provision for horizontal application, but nevertheless provoked a vociferous debate whether it required courts to develop the common law in a Convention-consistent manner,[11] or should simply be viewed as controlling the power of the State over the individual.[12] A more persuasive line of argument is that of 'indirect horizontality' by which the courts should try to interpret the law in a Convention-compliant manner.[13] The question remained, however, how judges, deciding English tort law cases, would take account of Convention rights in private law litigation. In her 2001 work *Tort Law & Human Rights*,[14] Wright predicted that English judges would struggle to deal with the overarching general legal principles of the ECHR. She also noted that the HRA 1998 would present a far greater challenge to the courts than that of the European Communities Act 1972. In 1973, EU law had still been in its infancy. By contrast, by 2000, the case law under the ECHR was well developed.

More than 10 years later, we are inevitably in a far better position to review the *actual* impact of the Act. This chapter will examine how the Act has influenced the development of English law of tort. It will focus on the torts where it has most commonly been raised and therefore had the most impact, namely the torts of defamation, negligence, trespass to the person, and private nuisance.[15] It will not examine the more radical development of a *new* form of tort law to protect individual privacy rights which, as a distinct cause of action, deserves its own chapter and will be considered in chapter six. As will be seen, in contrast to the last two chapters on EU law, the courts have been more willing to acknowledge openly the influence of the Convention and the case law of the ECtHR. Indeed some have argued that the English courts have been far too willing to follow Strasbourg case law despite its lack of precedential value.[16] The question remains whether, almost

[11] Full horizontality was most famously advocated by HWR Wade, 'Horizons of Horizontality' (2000) 116 *Law Quarterly Review* 217. See also J Morgan, 'Questioning the "true effect" of the Human Rights Act' (2002) 22 *Legal Studies* 259.

[12] R Buxton, 'The Human Rights Act and Private Law' (2000) 116 *Law Quarterly Review* 48.

[13] Commentators differ as to the extent of this interpretation obligation on the courts: compare G Phillipson, 'The Human Rights Act, "horizontal effect" and the Common Law: A Bang or a Whimper?' (1999) 62 *Modern Law Review* 824 and M Hunt, 'The "horizontal effect" of the Human Rights Act' [1998] *Public Law* 423 (who argues for strong indirect horizontal effect).

[14] J Wright, *Tort Law & Human Rights: The Impact of the ECHR on English Law* (Oxford, Hart Publishing, 2001) (2nd edn due in 2015).

[15] These torts are the most significant in this area. Inevitably there is some case law under other torts, but it is limited and piecemeal e.g. does the statutory tort of harassment conflict with the right to freedom of expression under Art 10 (*Howlett v Holding* [2006] EWHC 41 (QB))?

[16] R Masterman, 'Aspiration or Foundation? The Status of the Strasbourg Jurisprudence and the "Convention Rights" in Domestic Law' in H Fenwick, G Phillipson and R Masterman (eds), *Judicial Reasoning under the UK Human Rights Act* (Cambridge, Cambridge University Press, 2007) 75.

15 years after the introduction of the HRA 1998, there has been a change to the character of English tort law. Have we experienced a move towards an approach to human rights consistent with the practice of the Strasbourg court? This discussion is particularly apposite in view of the current policy of the Conservative government to replace the Human Rights Act with a domestic framework of human rights, the British Bill of Rights.[17] If, as Wright suggested in 2001, English lawyers have had to change their mind-set in favour of analysing and developing English law from a human rights perspective,[18] then any reform may be too late to prevent a change in interpretative practice and a willingness to favour a European human rights culture. As will be seen in this chapter, the reality is not so clear. Changes have occurred, but one should not underestimate the resistance of English tort law to external influences.

I. Defamation

Even prior to the 1998 Act, there is evidence that English courts had at times found reference to the Convention helpful, for example where the relevant law was ambiguous or the common law undeveloped or uncertain.[19] This is particularly evident in the context of the tort of defamation. Barendt has noted that freedom of expression has long been influential in the law and that the development of defences such as justification, fair comment and absolute and qualified privilege can only be explained as based on the need to protect freedom of speech.[20] Lord Keith in *Derbyshire CC v Times Newspapers Ltd*[21] declared seven years prior to the entry into force of the HRA 1998 that 'in the field of freedom of speech there was no difference in principle between English law on the subject and article 10 of the Convention'.[22] There were, however, indications prior to October 2000 that some areas of defamation might need reconsideration in the light of the Convention, for example in relation to excessive awards of damages by juries. The Court of Appeal in the pre-Act case of *Rantzen v Mirror Group Newspapers (1986) Ltd*[23] had been prepared to accept that in applying section 8 of the Courts and Legal Services Act 1990, it would have to give proper weight to the guidance given

[17] www.conservatives.com/Policy/Where_we_stand/Justice.aspx

[18] Wright, *Tort Law* (n 14) 1.

[19] A Lester, 'Human Rights and the British Constitution' in J Jowell and D Oliver, *The Changing Constitution*, 7th edn (Oxford, Oxford University Press, 2011) 76–77. See also *R v Secretary of State for the Home Department Ex p Brind* [1991] 1 AC 696, 760, per Lord Ackner.

[20] E Barendt, 'Balancing Freedom of Expression and the Right to Reputation: Reflections on *Reynolds* and Reportage' (2012) 63 *Northern Ireland Legal Quarterly* 59, 60.

[21] *Derbyshire CC v Times Newspapers Ltd* [1993] AC 534, 551.

[22] Ibid, 551, relying on Lord Goff in the breach of confidence case, *Attorney-General v Guardian Newspapers Ltd. (No. 2)* [1990] 1 AC 109, 283–84. See also Buckley J in *Goldsmith v Bhoyrul* [1998] QB 459.

[23] *Rantzen v Mirror Group Newspapers (1986) Ltd* [1994] QB 670, 691.

by the House of Lords and by the European Court of Human Rights. On this basis, the common law 'if properly understood' required the courts to subject large awards of damages to a more searching scrutiny than has been customary in the past. [24] Neill LJ noted that 'Where freedom of expression is at stake . . . recent authorities lend support for the proposition that article 10 has a wider role and can properly be regarded as an articulation of some of the principles underlying the common law.'[25] It is, however, the House of Lords decision in *Reynolds v Times Newspapers Ltd*[26] which serves to bridge the pre- and post-Act case law, decided in October 1999 just one year before the Act came into force.

A. *Reynolds*: A New Legal Landscape

The facts of *Reynolds* are well known. An article in the *Sunday Times* had discussed the resignation of the former Taoiseach of the Irish government, Albert Reynolds, and the collapse of his coalition government. Mr Reynolds alleged that the article had implied that he had deliberately and dishonestly misled the Irish Parliament and his cabinet colleagues. The House of Lords rejected the claim for a wide generic defence of qualified privilege for the publication of political information, but did express a willingness to review the qualified privilege defence. Lord Nicholls found that:

> The elasticity of the common law principle enables interference with freedom of speech to be confined to what is necessary in the circumstances of the case. This elasticity enables the court to give appropriate weight, in today's conditions, to the importance of freedom of expression by the media on all matters of public concern . . . Above all, the court should have particular regard to the importance of freedom of expression. The press discharges vital functions as a bloodhound as well as a watchdog. The court should be slow to conclude that a publication was not in the public interest and, therefore, the public had no right to know, especially when the information is in the field of political discussion. Any lingering doubts should be resolved in favour of publication.[27]

Reynolds privilege thus protects publication of defamatory matter to the world at large where publication was in the public interest and the publisher has acted responsibly in publishing the information.[28] The court's starting point is the non-exhaustive list of ten factors identified by Lord Nicholls in the *Reynolds* case itself.[29] The House of Lords later clarified in *Jameel v Wall Street Journal Europe*

[24] Ibid, 692. This was noted, with approval, by the ECtHR in *Tolstoy Miloslavsky v United Kingdom* (A/323) (1995) 20 EHRR 442: giving a jury an unrestricted discretion to set the amount of defamation damages would contravene Art 10 ECHR.

[25] *Rantzen* (n 23) 691.

[26] *Reynolds v Times Newspapers Ltd* [2001] 2 AC 127.

[27] Ibid, 204–5.

[28] *Jameel v Wall Street Journal Europe SPRL (No.3)* [2006] UKHL 44; [2007] 1 AC 359; *Loutchansky v Times Newspapers Ltd (No.2)* [2001] EWCA Civ 1805; [2002] QB 783. Defamation Act 2013 s 4 replaces the *Reynolds* test with the defence of 'publication on matter of public interest'.

[29] *Reynolds* (n 26) 205.

SPRL (No 3)[30] that these factors were pointers to be considered in the context of each particular case and not a series of hurdles to be negotiated by publishers, as had been interpreted by some of the lower courts, and that weight should be given to the professional judgment of an editor or journalist in the absence of an indication that the decision to publish was made in a casual or careless manner.

What is important in terms of Europeanisation is the weight placed by the court on human rights jurisprudence and recognition of a new 'legal landscape'.[31] By endorsing Strasbourg case law such as *Lingens v Austria*,[32] the House was recognising that international standards under the ECHR were a legitimate concern for the domestic court. Further, in developing the qualified privilege defence with particular reference to the media, no mention was made of the fact that newspapers are not usually 'public authorities', against whom the Act would permit a claim for breach of Convention rights. In reshaping a key defamation defence, their Lordships accepted without question that Convention rights would have horizontal impact on private party claims, and that the tort of defamation in future would develop in the light of not only domestic concerns but with reference to Convention jurisprudence. Lord Phillips in the later case of *Joseph v Spiller*[33] remarked that it was now necessary for the Supreme Court, when considering suggested developments in the common law of defamation, to take account of the Convention and the case law of the ECtHR. This would be particularly relevant to defences such as *Reynolds* privilege and fair/honest comment[34] – the Strasbourg court attaching particular importance to the extent to which the subject of a publication is a matter of public interest.[35]

Sections B–D below will examine the impact in practice of this development. They will consider the extent to which English defamation law has changed to accommodate Article 10 concerns. It should be noted, however, from the start that Article 10 freedom of expression must be balanced against the right of the claimant to protect his or her reputation. Paragraph 2 of Article 10 provides that freedom of expression may be restricted for the protection of the reputation of others if such restrictions are prescribed by law, pursue a legitimate aim and are necessary in a democratic society; the last requirement usually proving the point of contention. Further, the ECtHR now recognises that the Article 8 ECHR right to private life extends to protection of one's reputation.[36] As Lord Nicholls stated

[30] *Jameel v Wall Street Journal Europe SPRL (No 3)* [2006] UKHL 44; [2007] 1 AC 359, para 33.

[31] Lord Steyn in *Reynolds* (n 26) 206.

[32] *Lingens v Austria* (1986) 8 EHRR 407.

[33] *Joseph v Spiller* [2010] UKSC 53; [2011] 1 AC 852, para 73.

[34] See Eady J, eg, in *Sugar v Associated Newspapers Ltd* (unreported) 6 February 2001: 'Fair comment is one of the means adopted in this jurisdiction in our attempts to comply with the public policy objectives nowadays embodied in article 10 of the European Convention on Human Rights.' Note also his comments in *Branson v Bower (No 2)* [2002] QB 737.

[35] *Joseph* (n 33) para 78.

[36] See, eg, *Chauvy & others v France* (64915/01) (2005) 41 EHRR 29; *Cumpana v Romania* (33348/96) (2005) 41 EHRR 200; *Greene v Associated Newspapers Ltd* [2004] EWCA Civ 1462; [2005] QB 972; *Pfeifer v Austria* (12556/03) (2007) 48 EHRR 175, paras 33 and 35, *In re Guardian News and Media Ltd* [2010] UKSC 1; [2010] 2 AC 697, paras 37–42.

in *Reynolds*, 'this appeal concerns the interaction between two fundamental rights: freedom of expression and protection of reputation.'[37]

B. Changes in the Light of the HRA 1998: Qualified Privilege, Damages and *O'Shea*

i. Qualified privilege

The development of *Reynolds* privilege is perhaps the best-known example of the impact of the HRA 1998 on the tort of defamation. Although the case was decided before the commencement of the Act, their Lordships had in mind the fact that Convention rights were about to be introduced into domestic law and effectively determined that the existing law of defamation did not cater adequately for the importance of Article 10 ECHR. The aim was clearly to liberalise the law. As Lord Nicholls stated in *Bonnick v Morris*:

> Stated shortly, the *Reynolds* privilege is concerned to provide a proper degree of protection for responsible journalism when reporting matters of public concern. Responsible journalism is the point at which a fair balance is held between freedom of expression on matters of public concern and the reputations of individuals. Maintenance of this standard is in the public interest and in the interests of those whose reputations are involved. It can be regarded as the price journalists pay in return for the privilege.[38]

Nevertheless the courts' initial reaction, as noted by the House of Lords in *Jameel*,[39] was to apply the *Reynolds* test conservatively. In *Jameel*, the House of Lords regarded such an approach as subverting the liberalising intention of the *Reynolds* decision. Here an article written by an experienced journalist, approved by senior staff and non-sensational in tone and (apparently) factual in content was deemed exactly the sort of journalism which *Reynolds* privilege exists to protect. In the words of Baroness Hale, 'We need more such serious journalism in this country and our defamation law should encourage rather than discourage it.'[40] In this light, the Supreme Court ruling in *Flood v Times Newspapers*[41] in 2012 is important. The Court reiterated the need for a more liberal interpretation of the *Reynolds* test than that adopted by Court of Appeal[42] and that it was for the courts to balance Article 10 against the right to reputation protected by Articles 10.2 and 8: 'The importance of the public interest in receiving the relevant information has to be weighed against the public interest in preventing the dissemination of defamatory allegations, with the injury

[37] *Reynolds* (n 26) 190. See also Laws LJ in *Waterson v Lloyd* [2013] EWCA Civ 136; [2013] EMLR 17, who notes 'the common law's increasing focus in this area on the balance to be struck between public interest and individual right': para 67.

[38] *Bonnick v Morris* [2003] 1 AC 300, 309.

[39] *Jameel* (n 30).

[40] *Jameel* [2006] UKHL 44, para 150.

[41] *Flood v Times Newspapers* [2012] UKSC 11; [2012] 2 AC 273.

[42] *Flood v Times Newspapers* [2010] EWCA Civ 804; [2011] 1 WLR 153. See D Tan, 'The *Reynolds* Privilege Revitalised' (2013) 129 *Law Quarterly Review* 27.

that this causes to the reputation of the person defamed.'[43] The Court held that the denunciation of a public officer (here a senior police officer) for corruption was a matter of obvious public importance and interest, and might justifiably appear to the journalists to be supported by a strong circumstantial case. A responsible journalist would take reasonable steps to satisfy himself that the allegation was true. On the facts, the journalists had taken reasonable steps to verify that there was a serious possibility that DS Flood had been guilty of corruption.

Further, post 2000, the courts have developed the defence of 'reportage', which Lord Phillips clarified in *Flood* to be a special, and relatively rare, form of *Reynolds* privilege. The key issue here is that it is not the content of the reported allegation that is of public interest, but the *fact* it was made. Neutral and disinterested reporting of the fact that certain statements were made, with no attempt to endorse, embellish or adopt the statement,[44] will therefore give parties a defence and, to a certain extent, diminish the harshness of the repetition rule in defamation.[45] In such circumstances, the public interest will justify the publication of facts that carry defamatory inferences without imposing on the journalist any obligation to attempt to verify the truth of those inferences. The position is quite different, however, where the public interest in the allegation lies in its content and in the fact that it might be true: the situation in *Flood*. There is obviously a fine line to be drawn here, and the defence has only been successful in two cases to date.[46] In *Roberts v Gable*, Sedley LJ advised that 'because the reportage defence modifies the repetition rule in the interests of *Reynolds* privilege, it needs to be treated restrictively'.[47]

These examples indicate that the influence of Convention case law has been openly recognised by the courts. In *Jameel*, contrary to the views of the majority, Lord Hoffmann and Baroness Hale maintained that *Reynolds* amounted to a new public interest defence. As they pointed out, in contrast to the traditional form of qualified privilege, it is the material which is privileged, not the occasion on which it is published, and malice is no longer treated as a separate factor.[48] In *Flood*, Lord Phillips had no doubt that this was correct.[49] On this basis, the introduction of the HRA1998 has led to a new defamation defence – *Reynolds* privilege – now acknowledged by section 4, Defamation Act 2013.

[43] *Flood* (n 41) para 44 per Lord Phillips.

[44] See *Galloway v Telegraph Group Ltd* [2006] EWCA Civ 17; [2006] EMLR 11: *Daily Telegraph* found to have gone a long way to adopt and embellish the allegations contained in documents found by its reporter.

[45] That is, that every repetition is a new publication of the defamatory statement.

[46] *Al-Fagih v HH Saudi Research and Marketing (UK)* [2001] EWCA Civ 1634; [2002] EMLR 13 and *Roberts v Gable* [2007] EWCA Civ 721; [2008] QB 502. The defence failed in *Charman v Orion Publishing Group Ltd* [2007] EWCA Civ 972; [2008] 1 All ER 750, *Galloway* (n 44) and *Prince Radu of Hohenzollern v Houston* [2008] EWCA Civ 921; [2009] EMLR 13.

[47] *Roberts v Gable* [2007] EWCA Civ 721, para 74.

[48] *Jameel* (n 40) para 46 per Lord Hoffmann and para 146 per Baroness Hale.

[49] *Flood* [2012] UKSC 11, para 38. See also Lord Mance (para 138): 'British courts have developed the defence of public interest privilege under the influence of principles laid down in the European Court of Human Rights.'

It may nevertheless be questioned how great has been the impact of the ECHR in practice. Freedom of expression is recognised, but was, of course, relevant prior to the 1998 Act. Signs exist also of conservatism by the courts, for example, the reluctance of Lords Bingham, Hope and Scott in *Jameel* to recognise a new defence of public interest. The Court of Appeal in *Galloway* openly queried whether the Strasbourg cases raised by counsel would be of more than limited assistance if used as comparators for the facts of the case, since their facts varied considerably.[50] Question marks also arise as to the defence of reportage more generally. While Ward LJ in *Roberts v Gable* was content to state that the defence was 'in tune and in step with the Convention and the Strasbourg jurisprudence',[51] commentators have queried whether it is in fact compatible with Article 8 and suggested that, at the very least, reportage as a defence is not compelled by Strasbourg jurisprudence.[52] The disagreement between the Supreme Court and Court of Appeal in *Flood* highlights that the balance between freedom of expression and the right to protect one's reputation is far from straightforward and while the Act has encouraged courts to address this issue more openly, it has not necessarily made the task any easier.

ii. Damages

The question of excessive damages in defamation had been addressed by the ECtHR in 1995. In *Tolstoy v United Kingdom*,[53] the Court had indicated that such awards would be likely to amount to a violation of Article 10 ECHR in the absence of steps to control them. These steps were taken and, indeed, continued to be taken after the implementation of the 1998 Act.[54] The 2005 Strasbourg case of *Steel v United Kingdom*[55] is relevant in this context. The Court found that the denial of legal aid to two individuals defending defamation proceedings against a multinational company (McDonalds) had breached their right to a fair trial under Article 6 ECHR. *Steel* also gave guidance on damages and stated that, under the Convention, an award of damages must bear a reasonable relationship of proportionality to the injury to the reputation suffered and that, in this case, the sums awarded against the applicants had been very substantial when compared to their

[50] *Galloway* [2006] EWCA Civ 17, para 83.

[51] Ibid, para 52.

[52] G Busuttil, 'Reportage: A Not Entirely Neutral Report' (2009) 20 *Entertainment Law Review* 44. See also J Bosland, 'Republication of Defamation under the Doctrine of Reportage: The Evolution of common Law Qualified Privilege in England and Wales' (2011) 31 *Oxford Journal of Legal Studies* 89, 109, who argues that the defence is doctrinally distinct from the *Reynolds* test. It was nevertheless retained in the new Defamation Act 2013, s 4(3).

[53] *Tolstoy v United Kingdom* (1995) 20 EHRR 442, para 51. An award of £1.5m by a jury under the pre-*Rantzen* regime was held to be excessive having regard to the absence of any judicial guidance.

[54] *Rantzen v Mirror Group Newspapers* [1994] QB 670 was followed by *John v Mirror Group Newspapers Ltd* [1997] QB 586. Post 2000, cases such as *Kiam v MGN Ltd* [2002] EWCA Civ 43; [2003] QB 281 and *Gur v Avrupa Newspaper Ltd* [2008] EWCA Civ 594; [2009] EMLR 4 indicate that large awards of damages will, in future, be subjected to a more searching scrutiny than had been customary in the past.

[55] *Steel v United Kingdom* (68416/01) (2005) 41 EHRR 22.

modest resources.[56] This last comment might seem to challenge the fact that, as a matter of general principle, English tort law does not regard the defendant's means in assessing damages. *Steel*, however, has had little impact on court practice. The authors of *Gatley on Libel and Slander* comment that the ruling may be explained as applying only to exemplary damages.[57] Dyson LJ in *Gur v Avrupa Newspaper Ltd* also expressed the view that such a fundamental change to a well-established principle could only be made by the House of Lords.[58] In contrast, the Article 6 point on the absence of legal aid for defamation has been dealt with by the introduction of conditional fees and the UK government has sought to address criticisms that provision for success fees for counsel may place a disproportionate restriction on the defendant's freedom of expression.[59]

While, therefore, we can say that the Convention has impacted on defamation damages, it is more difficult to link this to the introduction of the HRA 1998. The question of excessive damages may continue to concern the courts, but this is far from being a fresh concern and intervention to control jury awards has long been viewed as desirable.[60] In fact, it has been left to the UK government to grasp the nettle of fundamental reform. Defamation Act 2013, section 11, provides that in future, trials should be without a jury unless the court orders otherwise. In practice, removing the jury from assessment of damages is likely to prove far more successful in reducing excessive damages awards than intervention under the influence of Convention rights.

iii. O'Shea

A defamatory statement must refer to the claimant. In *Hulton & Co v Jones*,[61] it was established that even if the defendant had no intention of referring to a real individual, the test was one of strict liability which would be satisfied if a reasonable reader might think that the statement referred to the claimant. Intention was therefore irrelevant. In *O'Shea v MGN Ltd*,[62] Morland J considered whether this rule was compatible with Article 10 ECHR when faced with a claim by Ms O'Shea that she had been mistaken for a glamour model in an advertisement for an adult Internet service in the defendants' newspaper. She argued that ordinary sensible

[56] Ibid, para 96.

[57] P Milmo et al, *Gatley on Libel and Slander*, 11th edn (London, Sweet and Maxwell, 2008) para 35.29.

[58] *Gur v Avrupa Newspaper Ltd* [2008] EWCA Civ 594, para 25 (obiter).

[59] This was denied by the House of Lords in *Campbell v Mirror Group Newspapers Ltd (Costs)* [2005] UKHL 61; [2005] 1 WLR 3394, but Strasbourg disagreed: *MGN Ltd v United Kingdom* (39401/04) (2011) 53 EHRR 5. See Legal Aid, Sentencing and Punishment of Offenders Act 2012, s 44.

[60] See, eg, the Faulks Committee Report on Defamation (Cmnd 5909, 1975) which recommended that the right to trial by jury be abolished, though discretion would remain, and Sir Thomas Bingham MR in *John v MGN Ltd* [1997] QB 586, 609: 'Whatever the theoretical attractions of this approach, its practical disadvantages have become ever more manifest. A series of jury awards in sums wildly disproportionate to any damage conceivably suffered by the plaintiff has given rise to serious and justified criticism of the procedures leading to such awards.'

[61] *Hulton & Co v Jones* [1910] AC 20.

[62] *O'Shea v MGN Ltd* [2001] EMLR 40.

readers, who were aware of her close resemblance to the model, would have concluded that she had consented to appear on a highly pornographic website. The judge distinguished *Hulton* on the basis that theoretically the existence of an individual with the same name could have been discovered, whereas it would have been impossible to check if a picture resembled another. Liability would impose an 'impossible burden' on the publisher, which was contrary to Article 10 ECHR.[63] The Court of Appeal proved less enthusiastic, however, in the later case of *Baturina v Times Newspapers Ltd*;[64] Lord Neuberger MR suggesting that the judge's reasoning might well be justified as a small extension of the *Reynolds* defence.[65] On this basis, the decision has been approved, but its reasoning questioned.

These three examples represent the main influence of Article 10 on the development of post-2000 defamation law. The key point here is that these developments are far from revolutionary. An extension of qualified privilege, curbing excessive damages and reducing the harshness of the *Hulton* rule had all been advocated prior to the Act.[66] There have, of course, been other cases in which reference has been made to Article 10 ECHR. In *Thornton v Telegraph Media Group Ltd*,[67] for example, Tugendhat J suggested that defamation should have a threshold of seriousness so as to exclude trivial claims. This was justified on the basis of existing law[68] and as 'required' by Article 10 and the principle of proportionality.[69] Again, despite reference to human rights, his Honour seems to be building on existing law which permits defamation claims to be struck out for abuse of process and indeed his judgment may simply be seen as a plea for courts to be more willing to strike out apparently trivial claims, now heard by the UK government in enacting section 1 of the Defamation Act 2013. The Court of Appeal in *Jameel v Dow Jones & Co Inc*[70] equally relied on both the introduction of the new Civil Procedures Rules and the Article 10 right of freedom of expression to justify halting defamation proceedings for abuse of process when they could not be said to be serving the legitimate purpose of protecting the claimant's reputation.

Further, although HRA 1998 section 3 permits courts to reinterpret statutory provisions in a Convention-compatible way, little use has been made of this section. In *Culnane v Morris*,[71] Eady J was prepared to reinterpret section 10, Defamation Act 1952, to permit qualified privilege as a defence to a charge of defamation by or on behalf of a candidate in an election, notwithstanding the actual statutory wording and previous authority to the contrary. However, much

[63] Ibid, para 43. Morland J was additionally concerned that liability would inhibit investigative journalism into drug dealing, corruption, child abuse and prostitution.

[64] *Baturina v Times Newspapers Ltd* [2011] EWCA Civ 308; [2011] 1 WLR 1526.

[65] Ibid, paras 29–30.

[66] Morland J commented in *O'Shea* (n 62) para 30: 'The harshness of the strict liability principle has long been the subject of concern'.

[67] *Thornton v Telegraph Media Group Ltd* [2010] EWHC 1414 (QB); [2011] 1 WLR 1985.

[68] *Sim v Stretch* [1936] 2 All ER 1237.

[69] *Thornton* (n 67) para 90.

[70] *Jameel v Dow Jones & Co Inc* [2005] EWCA Civ 75; [2005] QB 946, para 55.

[71] *Culnane v Morris* [2005] EWHC 2438 (QB); [2006] 1 WLR 2880 (relying on Arts 6 and 10 ECHR).

will depend on the wording of the statute in question. In *Maccaba v Lichtenstein*,[72] for example, the court held that the clear wording of section 2, Defamation Act 1952, rendered any different construction impermissible. Equally, in *Warren v Random House Group Ltd*,[73] in finding that the offer of amends procedure under Defamation Act 1996 was compatible with Articles 6 and 10 ECHR, the Court of Appeal found that there was no question of a court reading down provisions of the Act which were already consistent with the HRA 1998.

The Act has encouraged the courts to be more interventionist. Nevertheless, the developments seen above are perhaps less extensive than might have been anticipated. The next two sections will examine why, despite the introduction of the HRA 1998, there has been limited change to the tort of defamation, indicating that the English courts have preferred to retain the basic structure of the tort despite criticism from academics and lawyers alike.

C. Unsuccessful Challenges under the HRA 1998: The Presumption of Falsity, the Presumption of Damage and Publication on the Internet

Tony Weir, one of the strongest critics of the English tort of defamation, described it as the most difficult and oddest of all torts:

> [D]efamation is odd at the very core ... [The claimant] can get damages (swingeing damages!) for a statement made to others without showing that the statement was untrue, without showing that the statement did him the slightest harm, and without showing that the defendant was in any way wrong to make it ... Are we still in the law of tort?[74]

Weir in this quotation criticises three elements of the modern defamation action: the presumption of falsity (the law presumes the statement injuring the claimant's reputation to be false), the presumption of damage (libel is actionable per se) and its strict liability character. While *O'Shea* above considered this final point, Weir's first and second criticisms were considered in the course of the *Jameel* litigation. More recently, concerns have also arisen that defamation rules are too stringent in relation to Internet publications and serve to 'chill' freedom of expression. The response of the courts to these criticisms will be examined below.

i. *Presumption of Falsity*

Unusually the burden of proof lies on the defendant in defamation to rebut the presumption that the statement is false. This has been justified on the basis of the difficulty for the claimant in proving a negative, that is, that the defamatory statement was untrue,[75] and that it is the defendant who made the charge in the first

[72] *Maccaba v Lichtenstein* (Summary Judgment) [2004] EWHC 1580 (QB).

[73] *Warren v Random House Group Ltd* [2008] EWCA Civ 834; [2009] QB 600.

[74] T Weir, *A Casebook on Tort*, 10th edn (London, Sweet and Maxwell, 2004) 519.

[75] See WVH Rogers, *Winfield and Jolowicz on Tort*, 18th edn (London, Sweet and Maxwell, 2010) para 12-26.

place.[76] However, it has equally been argued that the presumption has a chilling effect on free speech in that it deters criticism because of fears that it may be difficult to prove the statement true in court.[77] To date, this controversial rule has withstood challenge in Strasbourg in *McVicar v United Kingdom*[78] and more recently in *Wall Street Journal Europe SPRL v United Kingdom.*[79] In the latter case, the ECtHR maintained its position that the presumption of falsity which requires the defendant to raise the defence of justification is generally compatible with Article 10. The English courts have also maintained that it is not a disproportionate interference with the right to freedom of expression for a defendant to be required to justify the 'essence or substance or sting' of any attack on an individual's reputation: 'It meets the legitimate purpose, recognised by Article 10(2), of protecting people from the publication of damaging and unjustified falsehoods.'[80] It was therefore neither disproportionate nor unacceptable in a democratic society to limit justification to the fundamental damage caused by a publication and to test exaggeration and error separately by allowing defences of fair comment and qualified privilege, provided that these gave adequate weight and liberty to press freedom. On this basis, Weir's criticism, despite Article 10, still stands. Defamation Act 2013, section 2 reaffirms the defence of justification or truth; the Government seeking broadly to reflect the current law while simplifying and clarifying certain elements of the defence.[81]

ii. Presumption of Damage and Corporate Claimants

It is also long-standing principle that libel is actionable per se, that is damage is presumed. Neither the Faulks' Report of 1975[82] nor Sir Brian Neill's review on the

[76] Milmo et al, *Gatley* (n 57) para 11.3: the claimant may thus argue that he should be regarded as innocent until proven guilty.

[77] See D Milo, *Defamation and Freedom of Speech* (Oxford, Oxford University Press, 2008) 283, who argues that it places a disproportionate restriction of freedom of expression in public matters.

[78] *McVicar v United Kingdom* (46311/99) (2002) 35 EHRR 22, para 87: The requirement that the applicant prove the substantial truth was justified in the circumstances, including the very grave nature of the allegations.

[79] *Wall Street Journal Europe SPRL v United Kingdom* (Admissibility) (28577/05) (2009) 48 EHRR SE19: application by the WSJE which had been sued by Jameel for libel. In *Jameel (Mohammed) and Another v Wall Street Journal Europe Sprl* [2005] EWCA Civ 74; [2005] QB 904, the Court of Appeal had refused to permit the applicants to raise this point as the parties had conducted the case on the premise that any defamatory meaning that the article bore was presumed to be untrue unless the publishers pleaded and proved justification, but noted that it would require a major reform to the law of defamation. See also *Europapress Holding v Croatia* (25333/06) (2011) 53 EHRR 27: requiring a publisher to prove to a reasonable civil standard that defamatory statements were substantially true did not violate Art 10 ECHR.

[80] *Berezovsky v Forbes Inc (No.2)* [2001] EWCA Civ 1251; [2001] EMLR 45, para 12 per Sedley LJ. The Court also confirmed that the current interpretation of Defamation Act 1952 s 5 was convention-compliant.

[81] Explanation Notes to Defamation Act 2013, para 13. Note that s 2(4) abolishes the common law defence of justification and, accordingly, repeals s 5 of the Defamation Act 1952.

[82] The Faulks Committee on Defamation, in its Report (Cmnd 5909) (1975) para 336 did, however, recommend that libel actions by trading corporations should be limited to cases where the trading corporation could establish either that it had suffered special damage or that the defamation was likely to cause it financial damage, but this was never implemented.

Practice and Procedure in Defamation in 1991[83] recommended change. The Court of Appeal in *Jameel v Dow Jones* re-iterated the view that this general principle should be retained in the absence of a convincing case that it was in conflict with Article 10 of the Convention.[84] The presumption is, however, more contestable in relation to corporate claimants. Tony Weir had argued in 1972 that 'There is still some justification, however, for the rule that the human plaintiff need not prove any harm. If the statement is defamatory, he will feel bad and others will think badly of him'. In contrast, a company has no feelings, nor social relations, and in the absence of proof of harm, it would be a 'grim perversion of values' to prefer the interest in maintaining a corporate image to the protection of free speech.[85] Lord Hoffmann in 2004 agreed:

> In the case of an individual, his reputation is a part of his personality, the "immortal part" of himself and it is right that he should be entitled to vindicate his reputation and receive compensation for a slur upon it without proof of financial loss. But a commercial company has no soul and its reputation is no more than a commercial asset, something attached to its trading name which brings in customers. I see no reason why the rule which requires proof of damage to commercial assets in other torts, such as malicious falsehood, should not also apply to defamation.[86]

The majority of the House of Lords in *Jameel*, however, disagreed. It confirmed pre-existing authority[87] that a company with a trading reputation in England and Wales would be entitled to pursue a remedy in defamation without being required to allege or prove that the publication complained of had caused it actual damage. There was nothing in the Human Rights Act 1998 or Article 10 that required a different conclusion. Libel claimants, whether real or legal persons, should be treated in the same manner. It was also noted that the ECtHR in *Steel and Morris v United Kingdom*[88] had determined this to be a matter on which the Contracting State enjoyed a margin of appreciation and it was therefore for the domestic court to determine how the balance was to be struck between the competing rights of freedom of expression and the right of the company to limit the damage of allegations harming its reputation. It did recognise, however, that in the absence of proof of loss, only modest damages should be awarded.

The key issue again is that despite the arguments of the minority based on the right to freedom of expression, the Convention did not lead to a change in the

[83] Report of the Working Group of the Supreme Court Procedure Committee, chaired by Lord Justice Neill, *Report on Practice and Procedure in Defamation* (1991).

[84] *Jameel (Yousef) v Dow Jones & Co Inc* [2005] EWCA Civ 75; [2005] QB 946, para 37.

[85] JA Weir, 'Local Authority v Critical Ratepayer: A Suit in Defamation' (1972) 30(2) *Cambridge Law Journal* 238, 239.

[86] *Jameel v Wall Street Journal Europe SPRL (No.3)* [2006] UKHL 44, [91]. See also Baroness Hale at para 158.

[87] *South Hetton Coal Co Ltd v North Eastern News Association Ltd* [1894] 1 QB 133: law of libel to be one and the same for all claimants.

[88] *Steel and Morris v United Kingdom* (68416/01) (2005) 41 EHRR 403, para 94.

domestic position.[89] Indeed, the decision in *Steel* was cited by the majority in support of their reasoning. Change again has been introduced by a UK, not European, source. Section 1(1) of the Defamation Act 2013 now provides that a statement will not be considered defamatory unless publication has caused or is likely to cause serious harm to a claimant's reputation, establishing, as noted above, a threshold of seriousness for all claims. More importantly, in this context, section 1(2) adds that in relation to bodies that trade for profit (which will, of course, include companies), an action cannot be brought unless it can show that publication has caused or is likely to cause serious financial loss. This latter requirement – the subject of considerable debate in the House of Commons[90] – serves to demonstrate the ongoing role of domestic, rather than European, policy in shaping both defamation law and the right to free expression.

iii. Defamation and the Internet

A final point of contention in recent times has been that of the Internet. It has revolutionised communication across the world. One person may comment on a blog and that comment may be accessed by millions of people. While such a development may be praised in terms of freedom of expression, naturally it has also given rise to concerns that defamatory statements may be published far more easily and widely than previously. The tort of defamation has found it particularly difficult to adapt organically to such developments. In chapter three, we discussed the problem of the liability of Internet service providers (ISPs) whose sites permit others to make defamatory statements and the attempt of the Electronic Commerce Directive 2000/31/EC[91] to provide a European response capable of preventing the disproportionate imposition of liability on ISPs.

The Court of Appeal in *Loutchansky v Times Newspapers (No 2)*[92] examined whether the repetition rule[93] should apply to archive material on the Internet. This gives rise to problems for newspapers placing articles in an online archive in that every click on the article will amount to a new publication which will trigger its own one year time limit, potentially extending (depending on the interest of the public in the article) the limitation period indefinitely. The Court rejected replacing the much criticised multiple publication rule with a single publication

[89] Beattie argues that the majority deference to corporate reputation would appear to be another example of the bias of the English courts towards the protection of reputation: K Beattie, 'New Life for the *Reynolds* "public interest defence"? *Jameel v Wall Street Journal European*' [2007] *European Human Rights Law Review* 81, 89.

[90] Which defeated the additional proposal of the House of Lords that corporations performing a public function should not have an action in defamation in relation to a statement concerning that function.

[91] Directive 2000/31/EC of the European Parliament and of the Council of 8 June 2000 on certain legal aspects of information society services, in particular electronic commerce, in the Internal Market (Directive on electronic commerce): [2000] OJ L178/1, implemented by the Electronic Commerce (EC Directive) Regulations 2002 SI 2002/2013.

[92] *Loutchansky v Times Newspapers (No 2)* [2001] EWCA Civ 1805; [2002] QB 783.

[93] Deriving from *Duke of Brunswick v Harmer* (1849) 14 QB 185.

rule which had been adopted in the United States, despite the argument that to do otherwise would chill freedom of expression. The current rule was justified as necessary and proportionate in a democratic society for the protection of reputation. The maintenance of an archive was seen as a comparatively insignificant aspect of freedom of expression in that it dealt with stale news and any damages award would be likely to be modest. Strasbourg again failed to intervene. The Court in *Times Newspapers (Nos 1 and 2) v United Kingdom*[94] accepted that where the defendants' attention had been drawn to the fact that a libel action had been initiated in relation to an article and it could, as suggested by the Court of Appeal, simply have placed a qualifying notice on the article indicating that the veracity of the article was disputed, there had not been a disproportionate interference with the right to freedom of expression. Again it has been left to the UK government to introduce a change of policy. Section 8 of the Defamation Act 2013 provides that where a person publishes a statement to the public and subsequently publishes (whether or not to the public) substantially the same statement, the time limit for defamation will be treated as having accrued on the date of the first publication: in other words, the single publication rule. This marks a significant step in favour of freedom of expression, but one introduced by the UK government, not the ECtHR.

D. Why So Little Change?

Following the HRA 1998, it is clear that the courts have been far more willing to address openly the tension which exists in defamation between protection of reputation and the restrictions it thereby places on the defendant's freedom of expression. Reference to Article 10 ECHR appears in judgments, together with citation of Strasbourg jurisprudence. Commentators have noted that English libel law may be said to be broadly consonant with the approach of the ECtHR to freedom of expression.[95] Nevertheless, as noted above, the tort of defamation has withstood challenges based on Article 10 to some of its most contestable rules and it has been left to the UK legislator to intervene. In proposing reform in 2011, the UK government argued that legislation was needed to strengthen the right to speak and debate freely in the light of a number of cases where it was felt that the law did not give sufficient protection.[96]

[94] *Times Newspapers (Nos 1 and 2) v United Kingdom* (3002/03 and 23676/03) [2009] EMLR 14. The Court did, however, express concern that, on different facts, libel proceedings against a newspaper after a significant lapse of time might, in the absence of exceptional circumstances, give rise to a disproportionate interference with press freedom under Art 10 ECHR.

[95] G Phillipson, 'The "global pariah", the Defamation Bill and the Human Rights Act' (2012) 63 *Northern Ireland Legal Quarterly* 149, 156.

[96] See, eg, the Simon Singh litigation, although finally resolved in his favour: *British Chiropractic Association v Singh* [2010] EWCA Civ 350; [2011] 1 WLR 133; S Boseley, 'Simon Singh and the Silencing of the Scientists', *Guardian*, 25 February 2010. See now Defamation Act 2013, s 6, which provides that the publication of a statement in a scientific or academic journal (whether published in electronic form or otherwise) will be privileged if certain conditions are met.

The reasons why we have not seen fundamental change to the tort of defamation following the Act appear to be two-fold. First, since 2004, the Strasbourg and the domestic courts have accepted that reputation falls to be protected under Article 8 ECHR. This means that neither Article 8 nor Article 10 should take precedence, despite the wording of section 12(4) HRA 1998 which states that the court must have particular regard to the importance of the Convention right to freedom of expression.[97] By requiring that Article 10 rights are balanced against those of Article 8, it is inevitable that arguments based on freedom of expression will not always succeed and this has diminished the impact of Article 10. Secondly, the difficulties experienced by the courts in identifying guiding principles from Strasbourg jurisprudence have led them to fall back onto their own resources. The nature of Strasbourg case law – for example, its focus on the particular facts of each case and frequent resort to the margin of appreciation doctrine – limits its ability to provide clear interpretative guidance.[98] In reality, the development of the law has been left to the national court, which will determine when it is desirable to tip the balance in favour of free speech. What we have seen is a gradual evolution towards more open recognition of the value of freedom of expression. Nevertheless, the basic framework of the defamation tort remains in place.

Such analysis serves to cast doubt on the suggestion that the HRA 1998 has introduced a new 'European' legal landscape into English law. The key changes – *Reynolds* privilege and the reportage extension – build on existing case law. Although the courts appear more confident in developing a public interest defence based on the right to freedom of expression, this right has a long common law history, as highlighted in the case of *Greene v Associated Newspapers Ltd*.[99] Here, it was questioned whether, following the HRA 1998, the courts would continue to be reluctant to grant interim relief to restrain a libel except where it was clear that that defence would fail.[100] Brooke LJ traced the right of the press to free speech back to Blackstone in 1769 and found the proposition that the HRA 1998 had actually weakened the inhibitions which judges felt before imposing prior restraint on the press 'surprising'.[101] In affirming the current approach as consistent with Article 10 ECHR,[102] the Court found that the English courts had long been required to strike a balance between freedom of expression and the protection of reputation.[103]

[97] See *Re S (a child)* [2004] UKHL 47; [2005] 1 AC 593, para 17 per Lord Steyn. The significance of this development was noted in A Mullis and A Scott, 'The Swing of the Pendulum: Reputation, Expression and the Re-centring of English Libel Law' (2012) 63 *Northern Ireland Legal Quarterly* 27.

[98] Consider, eg, *Steel v United Kingdom* (68416/01) (2005) 41 EHRR 22, discussed above.

[99] *Greene v Associated Newspapers Ltd* [2004] EWCA Civ 1462; [2005] QB 972.

[100] As stated in *Bonnard v Perryman* [1891] 2 Ch 269.

[101] *Greene* [2004] EWCA Civ 1462, para 1.

[102] Thereby following the rule in *Bonnard v Perryman* [1891] 2 Ch 269 and distinguishing the test from the less stringent test applicable for breach of confidence: *Cream Holdings Ltd v Banerjee* [2005] 1 AC 253.

[103] Lord Kilbrandon in *Cassell v Broome* went so far as to refer to a 'constitutional right to free speech': [1972] AC 1027, noted by Lord Steyn in *Reynolds* (n 26) 207, who commented that by categorising this basic and fundamental right as a constitutional right, its higher normative force was emphasised.

On this basis, *Reynolds* privilege did not involve a legal transplant (as discussed in chapter two), but an evolution of pre-existing law and common law values. The HRA 1998 gave the English courts the basis on which to justify such a development and perhaps accelerated the speed of change, but it did not involve the introduction of alien 'European' concepts into English law. Rather it permitted the courts to extend existing tort defences in a manner consistent with domestic policy grounds. On this basis, it is perhaps *O'Shea* rather than *Reynolds* which represents a challenge to common law orthodoxy and the best example of reform based on the ECHR. It is interesting, therefore, to note that its impact has been less than impressive and the Court of Appeal has recently sidelined it as a minor extension of the *Reynolds* defence.

II. Public Authority Liability in Tort

While defamation is perhaps the most obvious area in which we would expect human rights reasoning to be influential, the HRA 1998 has also had impact on other areas of law such as negligence and private nuisance. In these areas, the focus has been primarily on claims against public authorities. Here, the common law has traditionally adopted a restrictive approach to liability. The HRA 1998 has as a result presented the common law with a dilemma. The claimant may now have an action against the public authority under sections 6 and 7 of the Act for breach of Convention rights, which may result in an award of damages under section 8. In this light, is it legitimate for the common law to continue to reject claims in tort even where the public body has acted in breach of Convention rights? The Act gives no guidance, but it has been argued that the courts, as public authorities, should at least attempt to develop the common law in a Convention-compliant manner. As Steele has remarked, '[o]ne of the real tests for the law of tort is the need to consider whether protected interests, and circumstances of protection, should be realigned to reflect Convention rights'.[104]

This section will start with the tort of negligence where, following the ECtHR's ruling in *Osman v United Kingdom*,[105] the English courts found themselves faced with a major challenge to the iconic common law concept of the 'duty of care'.

A. The Tort of Negligence

Traditionally, the common law has adopted a restrictive approach to public authority liability in negligence. English courts have declined to deal with questions of pure policy on the basis that they are non-justiciable, and therefore a matter for

[104] J Steele, *Tort Law: Text, Cases and Materials*, 2nd edn (Oxford, Oxford University Press, 2010) 24.
[105] *Osman v United Kingdom* (23452/94) (2000) 29 EHRR 245.

Parliament, not the courts. Even where the matter is justiciable, the courts have found reasons why the imposition of liability would not, in the language of *Caparo v Dickman*,[106] be 'fair, just and reasonable'. For example, in the classic case of *X v Bedfordshire CC*,[107] the House of Lords argued that public authorities operating in sensitive areas such as social services within a statutory framework which involved an interdisciplinary system of care should not owe a duty of care. Victims had access to a statutory complaints procedure, such delicate areas were a 'fertile ground in which to breed ill feeling and litigation' and the imposition of such a duty might well lead the authorities to adopt a more cautious and defensive approach to their duties in addition to resulting in a diversion of money and human resources.[108] Further, in many claims, the allegation is not one of positive misconduct, but that the local authority had negligently *failed* to intervene to prevent a third party from causing harm to the victim, for example by not arresting a potential murderer in the course of a police investigation or not rehousing a potential threat to the local community. The courts will only rarely impose liability for omissions and thus will be reluctant to impose liability on a public body for its failure to exercise its statutory powers.[109]

Post 2000, however, public authorities will face claims under the Act that their conduct led to a violation of a Convention right, notably, in the context of personal injury claims, the Article 2 right to life and Article 3 prohibition of torture. For social services, negligent acts or omissions may also amount to a violation of the Article 8 right to private and family life.[110] What is distinctive about these obligations is that they may also impose positive duties on the public authority to act. Article 2, for example, imposes a primary duty on the State to refrain from taking life save in the exceptional circumstances described in Article 2.2. It also imposes positive duties to conduct a proper and open investigation into deaths for which the State may be responsible and to protect life in certain circumstances.[111] The latter duty has two elements: the 'systems or framework' duty which is a general duty on the State to put in place a legislative and administrative framework designed to provide effective deterrence against threats to life and the so-called 'operational duty' to take, in certain circumstances, preventive measures to protect the life of an individual from the danger posed by another individual. In *Osman v United Kingdom*,[112] the ECtHR rejected the argument that this positive obligation would only arise in relation to failures amounting to gross dereliction

[106] *Caparo v Dickman* [1990] 2 AC 605.
[107] *X v Bedfordshire CC* [1995] 2 AC 633 (conjoined with *M (a minor) v Newham LBC*).
[108] Ibid, 749–51 per Lord Browne-Wilkinson.
[109] *Stovin v Wise* [1996] AC 923.
[110] Property rights are further protected by Art 1, Protocol 1 (right to property), but are qualified by public interest considerations: 'Every natural or legal person is entitled to the peaceful enjoyment of his possessions. No one shall be deprived of his possessions except in the public interest and subject to the conditions provided for by law and by the general principles of international law.'
[111] Summarised most recently by Lord Dyson JSC in *Rabone v Pennine Care NHS Foundation Trust* [2012] UKSC 2; [2012] 2 AC 72, para 12.
[112] *Osman* (n 105).

or wilful disregard of the duty to protect life. Although it was important not to impose an impossible or disproportionate burden on the authorities, the Court held that a breach would occur where the authorities knew or ought to have known at the time of the existence of a real and immediate risk to the life of an identified individual or individuals from the criminal acts of a third party and that they failed to take measures within the scope of their powers which, judged reasonably, might have been expected to avoid that risk.[113] Article 3 equally implies a positive duty on the State to provide protection against torture or to inhuman or degrading treatment or punishment,[114] and, in common with *Osman*, this includes reasonable steps to prevent ill-treatment of which the authorities had or ought to have had knowledge.[115]

It is also without doubt that public authorities are obvious targets for such claims. They are solvent and in a position by virtue of their statutory powers to intervene when ordinary citizens are unable to assist. The question remains as to the extent to which it is desirable to society to render them liable for injuries caused by third parties on the basis that they had the *power* to intervene.[116]

i. Osman, Z *and* D *: Finding a Proper Balance between ECHR and Domestic Law*

In view of the importance of the rights outlined above, it is perhaps surprising that it was the Article 6 ECHR right to a fair trial which first raised the question of how negligence law should respond to the introduction of the HRA 1998.[117] In *Osman v United Kingdom*,[118] the Strasbourg court found that a decision of the English Court of Appeal that the police owed no duty of care for policy reasons to victims injured in the course of an investigation amounted to breach of Article 6. In following the earlier House of Lords decision in *Hill v Chief Constable of West Yorkshire*[119] that liability would not be 'fair, just and reasonable', the Court of Appeal was found to have conferred a blanket immunity on the police for their acts and omissions during the investigation and suppression of crime, amounting

[113] Ibid, para 116. The duty goes beyond the protection of individuals from attack by third parties and in certain circumstances extends to the protection of individuals from harming themselves: *Keenan v United Kingdom* (27229/95) (2001) 33 EHRR 913 (prisoner committing suicide).

[114] *Z v United Kingdom* (29392/95) (2002) 34 EHRR 97.

[115] Ibid, para 73. See also *E v Chief Constable of the Royal Ulster Constabulary* [2008] UKHL 66; [2009] 1 AC 536.

[116] On the hostility of the English courts to this subset of liability, see J Stapleton, 'Duty of Care: Peripheral Parties and Alternative Means of Deterrence' (1995) 111 *Law Quarterly Review* 301; C McIvor, 'Getting defensive about police negligence: the Hill principle, the Human Rights Act 1998 and the House of Lords' (2010) 69 *Cambridge Law Journal* 133, 141.

[117] Art 6.1: In the determination of his civil rights and obligations or of any criminal charge against him, everyone is entitled to a fair and public hearing within a reasonable time by an independent and impartial tribunal established by law.

[118] *Osman v United Kingdom* (23452/94) (2000) 29 EHRR 245, appeal from *Osman v Ferguson* [1993] 4 All ER 344 (CA).

[119] *Hill v Chief Constable of West Yorkshire* [1989] AC 53.

to an unjustifiable restriction on an applicant's right to have a determination on the merits of his or her claim against the police in deserving cases.[120]

Osman represents a fascinating example of the tensions and potential for misunderstanding which can occur between courts with different legal traditions. The judgment of the ECtHR, delivered on 28 October 1998, suggested that previous common law practice might now be under threat. In adopting a broad reading of the right to access to the court, the Strasbourg put under the spotlight any perceived immunities,[121] but also the court's case management powers, for example the ability to strike out a statement of case under CPR rule 3.4. The decision did, however, receive mixed reviews from common law commentators. Some were positive, praising, in particular, a more generous approach to claims against the police.[122] Others were more hostile. Gearty, for example, found the reasoning of the Strasbourg court to be deeply flawed, accusing it of seeking to develop the concept of the right of access to a court as a means of critically assessing the content of the domestic law before it.[123] English judges were also willing to express their discontent and concern at what they regarded as a misguided interpretation of the common law. Lord Hoffmann commented extra-judicially that the decision filled him with apprehension in that 'it is challenging the autonomy of the courts and indeed the Parliament of the United Kingdom to deal with what are essentially social welfare questions involving budgetary limits and efficient public administration.'[124] Lord Browne-Wilkinson's view in *Barrett v Enfield LBC* is equally pertinent:[125]

> I confess that I find the decision of the Strasbourg court extremely difficult to understand. . . . The problems in applying this reasoning to the English law of negligence are many and various . . . [A] holding that it is not fair, just and reasonable to hold liable a particular class of defendants whether generally or in relation to a particular type of activity is not to give immunity from a liability to which the rest of the world is subject. It is a prerequisite to there being any liability in negligence at all that as a matter of policy it is fair, just and reasonable in those circumstances to impose liability in negligence.

In other words, the Strasbourg court had failed to understand completely the common law duty of care concept. Under *Caparo*, the decision whether it is fair, just and reasonable to impose a liability in negligence on a particular class of

[120] *Osman* (n 118) paras 150–51.

[121] eg, the traditional immunity from negligence of barristers in court: *Arthur JS Hall & Co v Simons* [2002] 1 AC 615.

[122] eg, LCH Hoyano, 'Policing Flawed Police Investigations: Unravelling The Blanket' (1999) 62 *Modern Law Review* 912.

[123] CA Gearty, 'Unravelling *Osman*' (2001) 64 *Modern Law Review* 159. See also M Lunney, 'A Tort Lawyer's View of *Osman* v *United Kingdom*' (1999) 10 *King's College Law Journal* 238 and P Craig and D Fairgrieve, '*Barrett*, Negligence and Discretionary Powers' [1999] *Public Law* 626, 630.

[124] 'Human rights and the House of Lords' (1999) 62 *Modern Law Review* 159, 164.

[125] *Barrett v Enfield LBC* [2001] 2 AC 550, 558–59. His Lordship had notably given the leading judgment in *X v Bedfordshire*. Note also criticism of Lord Woolf MR in *Kent v Griffiths* [2001] QB 36, 51: 'it would be wrong for the *Osman* decision to be taken as a signal that, even when the legal position is clear and an investigation of the facts would provide no assistance, the courts should be reluctant to dismiss cases which have no real prospect of success.'

would-be defendants depends on weighing in the balance the total detriment to the public interest from holding such a class liable in negligence as against the total loss to all would-be claimants if they do not have a cause of action in respect of the loss they have individually suffered. The doctrine of precedent would render any such decision binding. This is conceptually distinct from an absolute immunity from liability.

The opposition was thus twofold: that the ECtHR had failed to appreciate how the duty of care concept operated in English law and further failed to recognise the utility of the striking out procedure as part of the court's case management powers to expedite litigation and save expense. It also encouraged some commentators to give vent to anti-European and anti-human rights opinions, warning that 'it is unwise to endorse a dubious arrogation of power . . . Nations should decide for themselves whether public funds should be directed to victims of past malfunction in public services or used to reduce the number of such malfunctions in the future . . . [T]o answer this question in terms of "human rights" is frankly absurd.'[126]

Nevertheless, in a number of decisions, the English courts did seek to comply with *Osman v UK* by refusing to strike out claims against public authorities.[127] In *Phelps v Hillingdon LBC*,[128] the House of Lords was further prepared to find a local education authority vicariously liable for the acts of its education officers performing the authority's functions with regard to children with special educational needs, such as dyslexia. Such decisions are remarkable in that the litigation was commenced prior to the Act, but the English judges were prepared to remodel the common law to avoid any perceived inconsistency with the *Osman* judgment.

In the 2002 decision of *Z v United Kingdom*,[129] the ECtHR sought to respond to common law criticism[130] and accepted that a finding of no duty of care should not be characterised as either an exclusionary rule or an immunity which deprived the applicant of access to a court.[131] The inability of the applicants to sue the local authority was acknowledged to flow from the principles governing the substantive right of action in domestic law. The Court also acknowledged that there was no reason to consider the striking-out procedure as per se offending the principle of access to a court.[132] The UK government has praised this decision for highlighting that the 'dialogue' between English judges and the ECtHR is reciprocal and the respect shown by the Strasbourg court for the close analytical attention paid

[126] T Weir, 'Down Hill: All the Way?'(1999) 58 *Cambridge Law Journal* 4, 7.

[127] See, eg, *Barrett v Enfield LBC* [2001] 2 AC 550 (refusal to strike out negligence actions by children in care); *L (A Child) and another v Reading Borough Council* [2001] EWCA Civ 346; [2001] 1 WLR 1575 (refusal to strike out negligence claim against police); *W v Essex County Council* [2001] 2 AC 592 (refusal to strike out parents' claim for psychiatric injury).

[128] *Phelps v Hillingdon LBC* [2001] 2 AC 619.

[129] *Z v United Kingdom* (29392/95) (2002) 34 EHRR 3.

[130] Ibid, para 100: 'The Court considers that its reasoning in *Osman* was based on an understanding of the law of negligence . . . which has to be reviewed in the light of the clarifications subsequently made by the domestic courts and notably by the House of Lords.'

[131] *Z* (n 129) para 96.

[132] *Z* (n 129) para 97. See also *TP v United Kingdom* (2002) 34 EHRR 2, para 56.

by the English courts to the Convention.[133] In *Z* and *TP v United Kingdom*,[134] which involved appeals from the conjoined cases of *X v Bedfordshire CC* and *M v Newham LBC*, the Court rejected claims for breach of Article 6, but found breaches of Articles 3 (*Z*) and 8 (*TP*). Claims were therefore permissible against public authorities, but in future would focus on other Convention rights, notably Articles 2, 3 and 8.

For judges nervous of the impact of the ECHR on English tort law, this represented something of a victory. Whereas *Osman* threatened the operation of the duty of care 'gateway' to negligence claims, Articles 2 and 3 would be confined to cases of extreme harm (loss of life; inhuman treatment)[135] and Article 8 is a right qualified by matters of public interest. Nevertheless the Court of Appeal in *D v East Berkshire Community NHS Trust*[136] demonstrated that even Article 8 could lead the common law court to review its previous practices. Despite the fact that the HRA 1998 did not apply to the facts (which predated the Act), the Court found it necessary to consider whether the introduction of the Act had affected the common law principles of negligence. In a judgment, which may be regarded as questionable in terms of the doctrine of precedent,[137] it was held that having regard to Convention case law,[138] notably *Z*, and cases such as *Barrett* and *Phelps* which had significantly restricted the effect of the *X v Bedfordshire*, the House of Lords decision in *X* – that victims of child abuse could not sue the public authority for negligently failing to remove them from abusive households – could not survive:

> In the context of suspected child abuse, breach of a duty of care in negligence will frequently amount to a violation of Article 3 or Article 8. The difference, of course, is that those asserting that wrongful acts or omissions occurred before October 2000 will have no claim under the Human Rights Act 1998. This cannot, however, constitute a valid reason of policy for preserving a limitation of the common law duty of care which is not otherwise justified. On the contrary, the absence of an alternative remedy for children who were victims of abuse before October 2000 militates in favour of the recognition of a common law duty of care once the public policy reasons against this have lost their force.[139]

This did not, however, assist the parents wrongly accused of child abuse by the public authorities. In view of the potential conflict of interest between the welfare

[133] DCA, *Review of the Implementation of the Human Rights Act* (July 2006)11

[134] *Z* and *TP v United Kingdom* (28945/95) (2002) 34 EHRR 2.

[135] Breach of Art 2 had been raised in *Osman*, but the Court had not been persuaded that the police at any decisive stage had known or ought to have known that the lives of applicants' family were at real and immediate risk.

[136] *D v East Berkshire Community NHS Trust* [2003] EWCA Civ 1151; [2004] QB 558 (also known as *JD*). Joined with *MAK v Dewsbury Healthcare NHS Trust* and *RK v Oldham NHS Trust*. The claim for breach of Art 6 was rejected, consistent with *Z v United Kingdom*.

[137] See J Wright, '"Immunity" No More: Child Abuse Cases and Public Authority Liability in Negligence After *D v East Berkshire Community Health NHS Trust*' (2004) 20 *Journal of Professional Negligence* 58, 61.

[138] As required by s 2(1) of the 1998 Act.

[139] *D* (n 136) para 83.

of the child and the interest of the parent to keep the child, the court ruled that there were cogent reasons of public policy for concluding that there should not be a duty of care to parents where child care decisions were being taken. A majority of the House of Lords supported this position.[140] Steele remarks that the House of Lords' refusal in *D* to extend the duty of care to the parents, largely on ground that it would inhibit the effective performance of the defendants' statutory duties, shows that traditional common law reasoning has not yet been wholly expunged from English law.[141] Nevertheless, the decision, by indicating that even House of Lords authority could be reviewed in the light of the 1998 Act and its subsequent case law, demonstrates the potential impact of the Act on the common law duty of care.

ii. A Parting of the Ways: Van Colle, Jain and Rabone

D left unresolved, however, how the courts would react when the claimant was able to bring an alternative claim under the 1998 Act. By the time of *Lawrence v Pembrokeshire CC*[142] in 2007, public authority decisions were being challenged under the Act, although in this case Mrs Lawrence had arguably missed the one year deadline. The Court rejected in no uncertain terms the argument that the existence of a HRA claim would actually strengthen the case for a common law duty of care to parents accused of abuse. It maintained that social services owed no duty of care: 'The development proposed would fundamentally distort the law of negligence in this area, putting at risk the protection for children which it provides in its present form.'[143] A potential claim under sections 6 and 7 of the Act for breach of Article 8 was considered to 'complement' the common law and the decision of the House of Lords in *D* therefore remained good law.

In drawing a line between claims under the Act and those at common law, the courts have relied on the distinctive nature of HRA claims which have their own limitation period (section 7(5)) and remedial framework (section 8). Unlike tort, no award of damages is to be made unless, taking account of all the circumstances of the case, the court is satisfied that the award is necessary to afford just satisfaction to the person in whose favour it is made.[144] In determining whether to award damages, or the amount of an award, the court must take into account the prin-

[140] *D v East Berkshire Community Health NHS Trust* [2005] UKHL 23; [2005] 2 AC 373 (Lord Bingham dissenting). For criticism of this argument, see MA Jones, 'Child Abuse: When the Professionals Get It Wrong' (2006) 14 *Medical Law Review* 264. On appeal to the ECtHR (*MAK v United Kingdom* (45901/05) (2010) 51 EHRR 14), the Court found in the parent's favour in terms of breach of Art 8, although some of the interferences were found to have pursued the legitimate aim of protecting the rights of the child. The claim under Art 3 was rejected. On this basis a sum of €2,000 was awarded in respect of non-pecuniary damage (plus costs). For criticism, see K Greasley, 'A Negligent Blow to Children at Risk: *MAK and RK v United Kingdom*' (2010) 73 *Modern Law Review* 1026

[141] I Steele, 'Public Law Liability: A Common Law Solution?' (2005) 64 *Cambridge Law Journal* 543.

[142] *Lawrence v Pembrokeshire CC* [2007] EWCA Civ 446; [2007] 1 WLR 2991.

[143] Ibid, para 55 per Auld LJ.

[144] HRA 1998, s 8(3). These circumstances include any other relief or remedy granted and the consequences of any court decision in respect of that act.

ciples applied by the ECtHR under Article 41 of the Convention.[145] There is therefore no right to damages, merely a power for the court to make an award.[146] As Clayton and Tomlinson note, this signifies that we are not looking at a constitutional tort, but a public law remedy distinct from tort law.[147] Lord Bingham in *R (on the application of Greenfield) v Secretary of State for the Home Department*[148] expressly stated that the 1998 Act was not a tort statute:

> Its objects are different and broader. Even in a case where a finding of violation is not judged to afford the applicant just satisfaction, such a finding will be an important part of his remedy and an important vindication of the right he has asserted . . . [T]he purpose of incorporating the Convention in domestic law through the 1998 Act was not to give victims better remedies at home than they could recover in Strasbourg but to give them the same remedies without the delay and expense of resort to Strasbourg.

In directing English courts to consider the decisions of the Strasbourg court instead of domestic precedents,[149] his Lordship emphasised that damages should not be assessed on the basis of tort law, but that the court should award an 'equitable' sum which the court judges to be fair in the individual case. This is likely to be less generous than its tort counterpart.[150] Lord Reed, more recently, suggested that over time such awards could be 'naturalised', using case law under section 8 for guidance.[151]

The treatment of HRA 1998 and tort claims as complementary actions, existing 'side by side', received support from the House of Lords in the important conjoined decisions of *Van Colle v Chief Constable of Hertfordshire; Smith v Chief Constable of Sussex Police*.[152] In the first case, *Van Colle*, the parents of a murder victim had brought a claim under the HRA 1998, alleging that the failure of the police to

[145] HRA 1998, s 8(4).

[146] D Fairgrieve, 'The Human Rights Act 1998, Damages and Tort Law' [2001] *Public Law* 695. 'It is to be noted that, in terms of judicial remedies, section 8 of the Human Rights Act 1998 makes it clear that the award of damages is a discretionary one': *R. (on the application of Faulkner) v Secretary of State for Justice* [2009] EWHC 1507 (Admin), para 37 per Blair J. On the policy choices facing the courts, see G McLay, 'Tort and Constitutional Damages: Towards a Framework' [2012] *Public Law* 45.

[147] R Clayton and H Tomlinson, 'The Human Rights Act and Its Impact on the Law of Tort' in TT Arvind and J Steele, *Tort Law and the Legislature: Common Law, Statute and the Dynamics of Legal Change* (Oxford, Hart Publishing, 2012). Bagshaw further argues that in view of such provision, it would be pointless for tort law to duplicate such protection: R Bagshaw, 'Tort Design and Human Rights Thinking' in D Hoffman (ed), *The Impact of the UK Human Rights Act on Private Law* (Cambridge, Cambridge University Press, 2011).

[148] *R (on the application of Greenfield) v Secretary of State for the Home Department* [2005] UKHL 14; [2005] 1 WLR 673, para 19.

[149] His Lordship did, however, note that English judges are not inflexibly bound by Strasbourg awards, but that they should not aim to be significantly more or less generous than the court might be expected to be in a case where it was willing to make an award at all. Clayton disputes whether taking account of 'principles' applied by the ECtHR (under s 8(4)) entails an obligation to 'mirror' decisions as to quantum, but this has generally been the practice of the English courts: R Clayton, 'Damage Limitation: The Courts and Human Rights Act Damages' [2005] *Public Law* 429.

[150] Contra: J Varuhas, 'A Tort-based Approach to Damages under the Human Rights Act 1998' (2009) 72 *Modern Law Review* 750 who argues for a tort-based approach to damages under the HRA (rejected in *R (on the application of Pennington) v Parole Board* [2010] EWHC 78 (Admin), para 6).

[151] *R (on the application of Sturnham) v Parole Board* [2013] UKSC 23; [2013] 2 WLR 1157, para 29.

[152] *Van Colle v Chief Constable of Hertfordshire; Smith v Chief Constable of Sussex Police* [2008] UKHL 50; [2009] 1 AC 225.

prevent their son being murdered by the very person he was due to give evidence against in a criminal trial (Brougham) violated Articles 2 and 8 of the Convention. In contrast, Smith (having missed the deadline for the HRA 1998) had brought his claim at common law, alleging that the failure of the police to take seriously death threats against him by a former partner had led to his attempted murder during which he had nearly lost his life. While such a claim would fail in the light of the earlier authority of *Hill v Chief Constable of West Yorkshire*,[153] which the House of Lords had approved (with some reservations) in 2005,[154] it was argued that the common law should now be developed in the light of Convention rights, here the Article 2 right to life. Lord Bingham indeed remarked that 'one would ordinarily be surprised if conduct which violated a fundamental right or freedom of the individual did not find a reflection in a body of law ordinarily as sensitive to human needs as the common law.'[155] The case thus represented an attack on core tort law principle, namely the policy grounds in *Hill* that liability for police misconduct in the investigation and suppression of crime would lead to defensive and over-cautious conduct and a significant diversion of resources.[156] The claimants sought to bypass *Hill* by relying on the Act (*Van Colle*) or, more drastically, by asserting that the doctrine of indirect horizontal effect would require the common law tort of negligence to be developed in a Convention-compliant way (*Smith*).[157]

The court rejected the claim in *Van Colle* unanimously. Applying the test stated in *Osman v UK*,[158] breach of Article 2 would arise where 'the authorities knew or ought to have known at the time of the existence of a real and imminent risk to the life of an identified individual or individuals from the criminal acts of a third party and that they failed to take measures within the scope of their powers which, judged reasonably, might have been expected to avoid that risk.'[159] On the facts, Brougham had been charged with a minor offence, had no record of violence and no explicit death threats had been reported to the police. Their Lordships found that, in the circumstances, the police could not have reasonably anticipated that there was a real and immediate risk to Van Colle's life. Being a witness for the prosecution at trial did not suffice. Further, there was no breach of Article 8 in that the police could not be said to have interfered with Van Colle's right to respect for his family life and his personal autonomy. This ruling was subsequently supported by the Strasbourg court itself.[160] This relatively narrow interpretation

[153] *Hill v Chief Constable of West Yorkshire*, [1988] QB 60.

[154] *Brooks v Comr of Police of the Metropolis* [2005] UKHL 24; [2005] 1 WLR 1495.

[155] *Van Colle* (n 152) para 58.

[156] *Hill* (n 153) 63 per Lord Keith.

[157] Noticeably even Lord Bingham, who supported Smith's claim, did not advocate the application of direct horizontal effect in this case, i.e. that the existence of a Convention right would call for the instant manufacture of a corresponding common law right where none exists: (n 155).

[158] *Osman* (n 105).

[159] Ibid, para 116.

[160] *Van Colle v United Kingdom* (7678/09) (2013) 56 EHRR 23. Judge Garlicki nevertheless warned the English courts that, in applying the *Osman* Art 2 test, they should bear in mind that it is not set in stone. The Convention is a living instrument and the threshold of what is required from authorities may need to rise in the light of contemporary conditions.

of Article 2 demonstrates the limits of the HRA 1998 to respond to claims of police misconduct.[161] In *Savage v South Essex Partnership NHS Foundation Trust*,[162] the House of Lords noted that the *Osman* test would, in practice, be more difficult to establish than negligence which might be satisfied by casual acts of negligence by staff. In view of the high threshold to be satisfied, Baroness Hale observed that liability should not persuade the professionals to behave any more cautiously or defensively than they are already persuaded to do by the ordinary law of negligence.[163]

While liability under the Act was interpreted narrowly, the majority in *Smith* rejected the negligence claim completely. In the absence of 'special circumstances',[164] the *Hill* policy grounds would prevail and any change in the law was best left to Parliament rather than the courts.[165] In the words of Lord Hope, 'the interests of the wider community must prevail over those of the individual.'[166] Lord Bingham, in the minority, had argued for a 'liability principle': if a member of the public (A) furnishes a police officer (B) with apparently credible evidence that a third party whose identity and whereabouts are known presents a specific and imminent threat to his life or physical safety, B owes A a duty to take reasonable steps to assess such threat and, if appropriate, take reasonable steps to prevent it being executed.[167] Such a test was dismissed by the majority as creating uncertainty in that it would be difficult to determine whether evidence was 'apparently credible' or a threat 'imminent' in each case.[168]

Van Colle and *Smith* are important for two reasons. First, they confirm the view of the House of Lords that, following the introduction of the 1998 Act, there is little incentive to modify rules of tort law when a claim is available under the Act. Secondly, they show the unwillingness of the common law courts to make policy changes. In choosing to defer to Parliament rather than develop the common law in a more Convention-friendly manner, the courts adopted an approach at odds with the early stance of the Court of Appeal in *D* above.

This position was confirmed in the subsequent decision of *Jain v Trent SHA*.[169] The Jains' nursing home business had been ruined when a health authority, on facts later found to be largely unsubstantiated, obtained *ex parte* order without

[161] The threshold (real and immediate risk to life) is acknowledged to be high: *In re Officer L* [2007] 1 WLR 2135, para 20, per Lord Carswell. The claimant also failed in *Mitchell v Glasgow City Council* [2009] UKHL 11; [2009] 1 AC 874, although Lord Rodger (para 69) questioned whether the relationship of landlord and secure tenant would (unlike the police) in fact give rise to a positive Art 2 obligation to protect the tenant's life.

[162] *Savage v South Essex Partnership NHS Foundation Trust* [2008] UKHL 74; [2009] 1 AC 681. Comment: N Allen, 'Saving Life and Respecting Death: A Savage Dilemma' (2009) 17 *Medical Law Review* 262.

[163] *Savage* (n 162) para 100.

[164] See Lord Nicholls of Birkenhead in *Brooks v Commissioner of Police of the Metropolis* [2005] 1 WLR 1495, para 6.

[165] *Van Colle* (n 152) para 102 per Lord Phillips CJ.

[166] *Van Colle* (n 152) para 75.

[167] *Van Colle* (n 152) para 44.

[168] See, eg, Lord Hope in *Van Colle* (n 152) para 77.

[169] *Jain v Trent SHA* [2009] UKHL 4; [2009] 1 AC 853.

notice from a magistrate to close down the home. Despite their successful appeal, four months had passed during which their business had collapsed. Their Lordships, although very sympathetic, were not prepared to allow a claim in tort for pure economic loss. As a matter of policy, a duty of care might inhibit those exercising the power to protect vulnerable patients in nursing homes.[170] Further, parties involved in judicial (or quasi-judicial) proceedings were traditionally not owed a duty of care by the opposing side.[171] Although the force of these reasons might be questioned,[172] the leading judgment of Lord Scott is important here. His Lordship, in reaching his decision, considered what would have been the position of the Jains if the Human Rights Act 1998 had been in force at the relevant time.[173] The fact that, in his view, the Jains would have had a sound case under the Act for breach of Article 1 Protocol 1 (peaceful enjoyment of possessions) and Article 6 (right to a fair trial) ECHR led him to reject a claim in tort on the basis that 'Parliament had already legislated and had provided a domestic law remedy.'[174]

The 2012 decision of the Supreme Court in *Rabone v Pennine Care NHS Foundation Trust*[175] takes this division a step further. Here, an adult voluntary patient, who had been assessed as a high risk of suicide, had, against her parents' wishes, been allowed two days' home leave during which she committed suicide. The claim of the estate for negligence had been settled in the estate's favour,[176] but in this action, her parents claimed that that the hospital had breached its operational obligation under Article 2 ECHR to protect mentally ill patients where there was a real and immediate risk of suicide. It was recognised by the court that the parents' loss (essentially distress at the events which occurred) would not be recoverable under the common law of negligence. Section 1A of the Fatal Accidents Act 1976 restricts bereavement damages for parents to cases where the deceased is a minor. This did not, however, prevent the court developing the parallel claim for distress damages under the HRA 1998. The hospital had assumed responsibility for an extremely vulnerable young person and in view of the real risk she would take her own life if allowed home, had made a decision which no reasonable psychiatric practitioner would have made. Moreover, by adopting a broad interpretation of 'victim' under Article 34 of the Convention to include the

[170] *Cf D v East Berkshire Community NHS Trust* [2003] EWCA Civ 1151, para 86.

[171] See *Elguzouli-Daf v Commissioner of Police of the Metropolis* [1995] QB 335.

[172] eg, L Blom-Cooper, 'When the Private Lawyer Should Go Public' [2009] *Public Law* 195.

[173] The authority's application and the magistrate's order had been made some two years before the Act came into force. Baroness Hale also addressed the human rights point. Lord Rodger, in contrast, refused to speculate on this point since counsel had not made submissions on this point: at para 41. This point, therefore, was one raised by the court, not the litigants. The Jains did indeed take their case to Strasbourg and the case was ultimately settled for £733,500: *Jain v United Kingdom* (39598/09) [2010] ECHR 411.

[174] *Jain* (n 169) para 11. See also *Watkins v Secretary of State for the Home Department* [2006] UKHL 17; [2006] 2 AC 395, where the House of Lords unanimously refused to reform the tort of misfeasance in public office in the light of the HRA 1998; Lord Bingham arguing that 'it may reasonably be inferred that Parliament intended infringements of the core human (and constitutional) rights protected by the Act to be remedied under it and not by development of parallel remedies' (para 26).

[175] *Rabone v Pennine Care NHS Foundation Trust* [2012] UKSC 2; [2012] 2 AC 72.

[176] For £7,500 representing funeral expenses and pre-death pain and suffering.

parents of the deceased,[177] the Court was able to award Ms Rabone's parents £5,000 each with an indication that this was on the low side. Lord Dyson commented that 'the family ties between Mr and Mrs Rabone and Melanie were very strong . . . [T]he fact that the very risk which they feared and warned the authorities against eventuated must have made the death all the more distressing for them. This was a bad case of breach of the article 2 operational duty.'[178]

Rabone, since supported by *Reynolds v UK*,[179] demonstrates a more proactive approach to Convention rights in which the denial of a negligence claim encourages a more generous interpretation of Convention rights. A similarly robust approach was taken by the Supreme Court in *Smith v Ministry of Defence*.[180] Here, despite the controversial nature of the subject-matter, namely military procurement and the equipment used by soldiers in combat zones, the majority of the Supreme Court[181] refused to strike out claims based on Article 2 ECHR. It held that the *Osman* test could apply in relation to decisions taken on the ground concerning the provision of military vehicles and equipment as well as their deployment, provided it was interpreted in a way which did not impose an unrealistic or disproportionate burden on the authorities.[182] As in *Rabone*, the Supreme Court asserted that a domestic court may go further than the current jurisprudence of the ECtHR when its conclusions flow naturally from existing Strasbourg case law.[183]

Both decisions are not, however, without problems. The minority in *Smith* expressed concern that the majority was anticipating, in the absence of clear guidance, how the ECtHR would decide the issue and the English courts should not 'advance way ahead of anything that it has yet decided'.[184] This raises the essential question of who makes European human rights law. The accepted view is that the correct interpretation of the Convention can only be authoritatively expounded by the Strasbourg court,[185] but the Supreme Court in *Smith* was divided whether its decision could be said to be based on guidance from Strasbourg (the majority view) or amounted to an extension of the law in the absence of directly relevant guidance from Strasbourg (the minority view). In *Rabone*, in contrast, the court expressed frustration with the lack of guidance from Strasbourg and resorted to

177 HRA 1998, s 7(1), provides that the person bringing a claim for breach of a Convention right must be a 'victim'. The Supreme Court argued that it was abundantly clear from the jurisprudence of the ECtHR that parents can be 'victims' under Art 34, and hence also under HRA 1998, s 7: see, eg, *Yasa v Turkey* (22495/93) (1999) 28 EHRR 408 (nephew of deceased).

178 *Rabone* [2012] UKSC 2, para 87.

179 *Reynolds v UK* (2694/08) (2012) 55 EHRR 35.

180 *Smith v Ministry of Defence* [2013] UKSC 41; [2013] 3 WLR 69 (although, in this case, the negligence case was allowed to proceed to trial).

181 Lords Mance, Wilson and Carnwath JJSC dissenting in part.

182 *Smith* (n 180) para 78.

183 See Lord Browne in *Rabone* (n 178) para 112.

184 Lord Mance (n 180) para 143. See also Lord Carnwath at para 156: 'We cannot determine the limits of Article 2'. Lord Mance suggested that this case presented a good example of where a preliminary reference procedure similar to Art 267 TFEU would be beneficial for human rights law: para 151.

185 *R (Ullah) v Special Adjudicator* [2004] UKHL 26; [2004] 2 AC 323, para 20 per Lord Bingham.

the more familiar common law notions of incremental development[186] and the concept of 'assumption of responsibility'. Lord Mance in both cases expressed concern that the ECtHR in *Osman* was creating a new substantive form of tort law, which would overlap with domestic tort law in cases involving death or the risk of death.[187] This raises again the spectre of loss of autonomy in the domestic court and, arguably, one explanation of the robust approach of the Supreme Court in *Rabone* and the majority in *Smith* is that the English court was asserting some measure of interpretative control over the *Osman* test.

One might nevertheless question whether the Supreme Court in *Rabone* paid sufficient attention to the consequences of developing the *Osman* operational duty distinct from the tort of negligence. Baroness Hale commented that 'We are here because the ordinary law of tort does not recognise or compensate the anguish suffered by parents who are deprived of the life of their adult child.'[188] The law remains that stated in section 1A of the Fatal Accidents Act (FAA) 1976. The UK government[189] in 2011 refused to adopt the recommendations of the Law Commission in its 1999 Report, *Claims for Wrongful Death*,[190] which had advocated an extension to the scope of bereavement damages in tort. If the claimants had sought to challenge section 1A under the HRA 1998, they would, by virtue of sections 3 and 4 of the Act, have been confined to arguing for a re-interpretation of the section (difficult in the light of its clear wording) or, more likely, for a declaration of incompatibility under section 4. Yet, by allowing parents an award of £5,000 each under the HRA 1998, the parents did in fact receive bereavement damages, contrary to the provisions of the FAA 1976. This is justified on the basis that a separate cause of action was relied upon, but clearly it will impact on how tort actions are pleaded in future. Tettenborn has accused the court of bypassing democracy; according a benefit to claimants 'at the behest of a judge notwithstanding the decision of an elected government not to grant it'.[191]

The fact remains that *Rabone* and *Smith* throw into question how the division between the HRA 1998 and tort law will operate in practice. *Smith* raises the issue of the relationship between the UK and Strasbourg courts and the extent to which operational liability under *Osman* is becoming a distinct form of 'tort-like' liability. *Rabone* also highlights the tensions between the HRA 1998 and tort claims when tort law policy indicates a more restrictive approach to liability. By focusing

[186] Advocated, of course, by Brennan J in *Sutherland Shire Council v Heyman* (1985) 157 CLR 424, 481, and approved by Lord Bridge in *Caparo v Dickman* [1990] 2 AC 605, 618.

[187] *Smith* (n 180) para 142. Note also his comments in *Rabone* (n178) para 121.

[188] *Rabone* (n 178) para 92.

[189] See Ministry of Justice, 'Civil Law Reform Bill: Response to Consultation' (2011) 3.

[190] Law Commission, *Claims for Wrongful Death*, Report No 263 6.12–6.18: a parent should be able to recover for the death of his or her child, irrespective of whether that child was under eighteen years or not, married or not, and whether legitimate or illegitimate.

[191] A Tettenborn, 'Wrongful Death, Human Rights, and the Fatal Accident Act' (2012) 128 *Law Quarterly Review* 327, 330. Contrast the view of Andenas that *Rabone* is a welcome clarification of the relationship between national courts and the ECtHR which will stand as authority for a long time: M Andenas, 'Leading from the Front: Human Rights and Tort Law in *Rabone* and *Reynolds*' (2012) 128 *Law Quarterly Review* 323.

on the question of liability under Article 2 ECHR, the Supreme Court paid little attention to one issue which arises in relation to concurrent remedies, namely that of consistency.[192] While the Supreme Court in these cases was clearly not as interventionist as the Court of Appeal has been on a number of occasions,[193] these recent decisions do indicate a greater willingness to address and develop incrementally Strasbourg jurisprudence rather than waiting for the ECtHR to provide directly relevant guidance. Nevertheless, while it may be encouraging to see the domestic courts taking a more proactive approach to the application of human rights law in English law, the 4:3 split in *Smith* does indicate that, as yet, the Supreme Court is far from being of one mind how to resolve the 'difficult line' between national law and substantive Convention rights.

There exists, therefore, an active (and ongoing) debate as to the impact of the HRA 1998 on the development of public authority liability in the tort of negligence. Yet, public authority liability arises in relation to a number of other torts. Since 2000, the English courts have considered the extent to which Convention rights should influence how the courts treat claims involving intentional harm (trespass to the person), neighbourhood pollution (private nuisance) and defamatory statements made by public bodies or their employees. Such liability is not necessarily devoid of policy concerns. A decision by the police to contain protesters to avoid a risk of violence and disorder (commonly known as 'kettling') may lead to claims of false imprisonment and a deprivation of liberty within Article 5 of the Convention.[194] A failure by a statutory undertaker to prevent sewage and surface water flooding the claimant's property after heavy rain due to stretched resources may give rise to claims for an actionable nuisance and that the flooding constituted an unjustified interference with the claimant's rights under Article 8 and Article 1 of Protocol 1 ECHR.[195] Equally a warning to alert council staff that the claimant was potentially violent may lead to claims of defamation and breach of Article 8 ECHR.[196] In all these claims, the question for the court is the extent to which Convention rights under the HRA 1998 should influence the development of tort liability.

B. Trespass to the Person

The key tort here is false imprisonment. While claims for battery and assault will generally be dealt with by criminal law, false imprisonment remains an important means by which the lawfulness of detention by the police and prison authorities

[192] See, eg, *Henderson v Merrett Syndicates Ltd* [1995] 2 AC 145, 184.

[193] See, eg, in addition to *D v East Berkshire*, *Smith v Chief Constable of Sussex Police* [2008] EWCA Civ 39; [2008] HRLR 23 and *Watkins v Secretary of State for the Home Department* [2004] EWCA Civ 966; [2005] QB 883 (both overturned on appeal).

[194] *Austin v Commissioner of Police of the Metropolis* [2009] UKHL 5; [2009] 1 AC 564.

[195] *Marcic v Thames Water Utilities Ltd* [2003] UKHL 66; [2004] 2 AC 42.

[196] *Clift v Slough BC* [2010] EWCA Civ 1484; [2011] 1 WLR 1774.

may be challenged.[197] It is thus a tort with a strong 'constitutional' element.[198] Post 2000, such cases are likely to raise the dual question whether the detention in question amounts to false imprisonment and/or it amounts to a deprivation of liberty under Article 5 ECHR. Article 5 may be described as a limited right, that is, a right which can be restricted in explicit and finite circumstances as set out in the article itself or subject to restrictions implied by the ECtHR.[199] It involves a two-stage test – (1) Has there been an interference constituting a 'deprivation of liberty'? (2) If so, was the deprivation justified under one of the six categories in subparagraphs (a)–(f), and 'in accordance with a procedure prescribed by law'? The framework of Article 5 is thus distinct from that of the tort of false imprisonment. It seeks to ensure that liberty is not interfered with arbitrarily and that any deprivation of liberty complies with procedural and substantive principles of fairness and justice.[200]

The leading case is that of *Austin v Commissioner of Police of the Metropolis*.[201] This controversial case involved claims following a demonstration which had involved a large group of protesters converging on Oxford Circus in central London. The police, fearing violence and disorder, had responded by imposing a cordon around the area, enclosing thousands of people for over seven hours (a practice known as 'kettling'). The claimants had been caught in the mêlée and sought damages for false imprisonment and under the Human Rights Act 1998 for breach of their rights to liberty guaranteed by Article 5 ECHR. It was accepted that the claimants had not been violent, threatened violence nor breached the peace nor threatened to do so. The case raised directly, therefore, the question how these two causes of action would interact. At first instance Tugendhat J had expressed concern that there might be some difficulty in aligning these two causes of action.[202] False imprisonment would not be found where the defendant could rely on the defence of necessity or more generally lawful authority. In contrast, deprivation of liberty could only be permitted if the defendants could establish one of the specific exceptions stated in Article 5(1)(a)–(f).[203] Further the very

[197] It may of course be raised against a private party, but such claims are rare e.g. *Robinson v Balmain New Ferry* [1910] AC 295.

[198] Steele, *Tort Law* (n 104) 68.

[199] J Wadham et al, *Blackstone's Guide to the Human Rights Act 1998*, 6th edn (Oxford, Oxford University Press, 2011) para 2.28.

[200] S Foster, *Human Rights and Civil Liberties*, 3rd edn (Harlow, Pearson Education, 2011) 274.

[201] *Austin v Commissioner of Police of the Metropolis* [2007] EWCA Civ 989; [2008] QB 660 (appealed to House of Lords on Art 5 only: [2009] UKHL 5; [2009] 1 AC 564).

[202] *Austin v Commissioner of Police of the Metropolis* [2005] EWHC 480 (QB); [2005] HRLR 20, para 46.

[203] 'No one shall be deprived of his liberty save in the following cases and in accordance with a procedure prescribed by law: (a) the lawful detention of a person after conviction by a competent court; (b) the lawful arrest or detention of a person for non-compliance with the lawful order of a court or in order to secure the fulfilment of any obligation prescribed by law; (c) the lawful arrest or detention of a person effected for the purpose of bringing him before the competent legal authority on reasonable suspicion of having committed an offence or when it is reasonably considered necessary to prevent his committing an offence or fleeing after having done so; (d) the detention of a minor by lawful order for the purpose of educational supervision or his lawful detention for the purpose of bringing him before

concept of 'imprisonment' under the tort has been found to differ from that of 'deprivation of liberty' under Article 5; a distinction accepted by the ECtHR in *HL v United Kingdom*.[204] On this basis, while false imprisonment requires actual restraint of a individual who wishes to leave – the essence of the tort being that there must *in fact* be a complete deprivation of, or restraint upon, the claimant's liberty[205] – the 'deprivation of liberty' test requires that liberty is not interfered with arbitrarily and will be satisfied where the patient is merely under continuous supervision and control and not free to leave.[206]

In *Austin*, the Court of Appeal dealt with the two claims consecutively, finding it 'convenient' to consider the position at common law first. It found that there had been sufficient restraint on the claimants to amount to the tort of false imprisonment, but that in this very exceptional case, where there had been a reasonable belief that there were no other means whatsoever whereby a breach or imminent breach of the peace could be obviated, the lawful exercise by third parties of their rights might be curtailed by the police.[207] On this basis, the defence of necessity could provide a valid defence for the police's actions. This finding was not appealed.

In contrast, the Article 5 claim was treated differently. The exceptions under Article 5(1)(a)–(f) do not include a defence of necessity as such. Nor is any reference made to the interests of public safety or the protection of public order as one of the cases in which a person may be deprived of his liberty. Nevertheless the Court of Appeal held that, in the circumstances, the original imposition of the cordon could not properly be regarded as the kind of arbitrary detention that would amount to deprivation of liberty within Article 5. This led to the rather odd conclusion that the claimants were falsely imprisoned (but this could be justified in the exceptional circumstances), but were not deprived of their liberty under Article 5. This controversial finding was approved by the House of Lords on appeal. Lord Hope argued that 'there is room, even in the case of fundamental rights as to whose application no restriction or limitation is permitted by the Convention, for a pragmatic approach to be taken which takes full account of all the circumstances . . . The ambit that is given to article 5 as to measures of crowd control must, of course, take account of the rights of the individual as well as the interests of the community.'[208] On this basis, provided any steps taken were in good faith and proportionate to the situation, the confinement and restriction of

the competent legal authority; (e) the lawful detention of persons for the prevention of the spreading of infectious diseases, of persons of unsound mind, alcoholics or drug addicts or vagrants; (f) the lawful arrest or detention of a person to prevent his effecting an unauthorised entry into the country or of a person against whom action is being taken with a view to deportation or extradition.'

[204] *HL v United Kingdom* (45508/99) (2005) 40 EHRR 32, para 90.

[205] *R v Bournewood Community and Mental Health NHS Trust Ex p. L* [1999] 1 AC 458, 486 per Lord Goff.

[206] *HL* (n 204). Comment: A Pedain, 'Requiem for a Fairytale' (2005) 64 *Cambridge Law Journal* 11.

[207] Relying on the power to act to prevent an imminent breach of the peace stated in *R (Laporte) v Chief Constable of Gloucestershire Constabulary* [2006] UKHL 55; [2007] 2 AC 105.

[208] *Austin v Commissioner of Police of the Metropolis* [2009] UKHL 5, para 34.

movement imposed would not be deemed arbitrary and would not amount to an infringement of Article 5.

These rulings are clearly questionable. Civil liberties lawyers, in particular, have expressed concern at a 'pragmatic' approach to human rights. Feldman argues that the real issue is that Article 5(1) is not sufficiently well drafted to deal with containment short of arrest for preventative purposes.[209] This argument receives support from the later ruling of the Strasbourg court in *Austin v United Kingdom*.[210] Here, the Court acknowledged the difficulties involved in policing modern societies, perhaps unforeseen when the Convention was drafted. On this basis, Article 5 should not be interpreted in a way to make it impracticable for the police to fulfil their duties of maintaining order and protecting the public provided they comply with the underlying principle of Article 5, which is to protect the individual from arbitrariness.[211]

In terms of Europeanisation, what we see here is a clear line being drawn between the development of the common law and the interpretation of Article 5. This mirrors the approach taken by the courts in negligence, discussed above. *Austin* reveals also the frustration of the English courts with the failure of the Convention right in question to provide the necessary flexibility to respond 'pragmatically' to what it deemed to be the exceptional circumstances of the Oxford Circus incident. The HRA 1998 may present claimants with the possibility to sue public authorities for breach of Convention rights, but, in this case at least, it is the common law which appears to be influencing the interpretation of Article 5. This is far from the concept of indirect horizontal effect which academics had predicted prior to the coming into force of the Act.

C. Private Nuisance

The tort of private nuisance, which protects against undue interference with the claimant's use and enjoyment of land, has equally faced a number of challenges based on the introduction of the HRA 1998, notably that the current law is inconsistent with Article 8 (right to respect for private and family life, home and correspondence) and/or Article 1 of Protocol 1 (right to peaceful possession of land). As Nolan has noted, it is Article 8 which is the most important right in this con-

[209] D Feldman, 'Containment, Deprivation of Liberty and Breach of the Peace' (2009) 68 *Cambridge Law Journal* 243. See also H Fenwick, 'Marginalising Human Rights: Breach of the Peace, "Kettling", the Human Rights Act and Public Protest' [2009] *Public Law* 737 and D Mead, 'Of Kettles, Cordons and Crowd Control: *Austin v Commissioner of Police for the Metropolis* and the Meaning of "deprivation of liberty"' [2009] *European Human Rights Law Review* 376.

[210] *Austin v United Kingdom* (39692/09) (2012) 55 EHRR 14 (no breach of Art 5).

[211] Ibid, para 56. See also *R (on the application of Sturnham) v Parole Board* [2013] UKSC 23; [2013] 2 WLR 1157. For criticism, see D Mead, 'Kettling Comes to the Boil before the Strasbourg Court: Is It a Deprivation of Liberty to Contain Protesters en masse?' (2012) 71 *Cambridge Law Journal* 472; A Ashworth, 'Human Rights: Article 5: Application to Measures of Crowd Control by Police' [2012] *Criminal Law Review* 544.

text.[212] Article 8.1 sets out a substantive right, placing a positive obligation on the State to protect the right to respect for private and family life, while Article 8.2 qualifies the right where the interference is 'in accordance with the law' and pursuing an aim or aims that are legitimate and can be regarded as 'necessary in a democratic society'.[213] Significantly, Article 8 does not require claimants to have a 'right to land' and has been successfully relied upon in cases where the State has been found to have breached its positive duty to protect its citizens against environmental nuisances.[214] The focus of English case-law to-date has been on public authority liability – it should be noted that the privatised utility companies do satisfy the definition of 'public authority' under section 6 of the 1998 Act[215] – and there has been limited case law involving private parties.[216] While this may change in the future, in view of the case law discussed below, such claims would be most likely to arise in relation to the impact of section 3 HRA 1998 on the defence of statutory authority.[217]

There is, however, an immediate tension between the tort of private nuisance, described in the 1997 House of Lords decision in *Hunter v Canary Wharf Ltd*[218] as a tort to land,[219] and the protection of individual *human* rights. In *Hunter*, the majority of the House of Lords asserted that only claimants with a right to land could bring a claim, thereby rejecting the attempt by the Court of Appeal to broaden the scope of the tort to protect individuals occupying the property as a home. Only Lord Cooke (dissenting) sought guidance from international standards such as Article 8 ECHR[220] which focus on the needs of individuals resident on land. The stage was thus set for a clash between the narrow rules of standing stated in *Hunter* and the broader rules of Article 8. The majority's decision came under fire as early as January 2002. In *McKenna v British Aluminium Ltd*,[221] the claimants were children who were residents, but possessed no interest in land. They argued

[212] D Nolan, 'Nuisance' in D Hoffman (ed), *The Impact of the UK Human Rights Act on Private Law* (Cambridge, Cambridge University Press, 2011) 166.

[213] Art 8.2 ECHR: There shall be no interference by a public authority with the exercise of this right except such as is in accordance with the law and is necessary in a democratic society in the interests of national security, public safety or the economic well-being of the country, for the prevention of disorder or crime, for the protection of health or morals, or for the protection of the rights and freedoms of others.

[214] See, eg, *López -Ostra v Spain* (16798/90) (1995) 20 EHRR 277 and *Guerra v Italy* (14967/89) (1998) 26 EHRR 357.

[215] eg, Thames Water Utilities in the *Marcic* litigation discussed below. As a statutory sewage undertaker responsible for the sewers, it was deemed a public authority for the purposes of HRA 1998, s 6.

[216] But see *McKenna v British Aluminium Ltd* [2002] Env LR 30 below.

[217] See Nolan, 'Nuisance' (n 212) 188.

[218] *Hunter v Canary Wharf Ltd* [1997] AC 655.

[219] Ibid, 687 per Lord Goff. See also Professor Newark's classic article: 'The Boundaries of Nuisance' (1949) 65 *Law Quarterly Review* 480.

[220] *Hunter* (n 218) 714. His Lordship also cited Art 16, United Nations Convention on the Rights of the Child. In related proceedings concerning dust nuisance, the European Commission on Human Rights in *Khatun v United Kingdom* (38387/97) (1998) 26 EHRR CD212 considered that Art 8.1 applied to all the applicants whether they were the owners of the property or merely occupiers living on the property, but that any interference was justified in the public interest under Art 8.2.

[221] *McKenna v British Aluminium Ltd* [2002] Env LR 30 (striking out decision of Chancery Division (Birmingham District Registry)).

that, following the 1998 Act, they had a right to sue in nuisance or under 'a common law tort analogous to nuisance'. Neuberger J found that

> there is a real possibility of the court concluding that in light of the different landscape, namely Article 8.1 now being effectively part of our law, it is necessary to extend or change the law, even though, in circumstances where the Convention was no part of English law, the majority of the House of Lords thought otherwise. There is obviously a powerful case for saying that effect has not been properly given to Article 8.1 if a person with no interest in the home, but who has lived in the home for some time and had his enjoyment of the home interfered with, is at the mercy of the person who owns the home, as the only person who can bring proceedings.[222]

At this early stage, therefore, it seemed that the 1998 Act might challenge the long-standing perception of private nuisance as a tort protecting land rights rather than the personal interests of residents, despite clear approval of this basis by the House of Lords in 1997. Two further decisions confirmed that the lower courts at least were prepared to interpret private nuisance to reflect Convention values. In *Dennis v Ministry of Defence*,[223] Buckley J accepted that the common law should develop consistently with European decisions involving human rights and rejected the option that the human rights claim should be treated separately from the nuisance claim. This would, in his Honour's view, reflect adversely on the flexibility of the common law.[224] Equally, the Court of Appeal in *Marcic v Thames Water Utilities Ltd*[225] was unwilling to follow the court below in rejecting a claim of private nuisance but permitting a claim under the HRA 1998, and held that the common law should be reinterpreted in the light of the fair balance to be struck between the protection of human rights and the general interest of the community found in Article 8 and Article 1 of Protocol 1 ECHR. Parker, commenting at the time, remarked that '*Marcic* is a salutary reminder that the impact of the ECHR on the tort of nuisance must not be underestimated'.[226]

However, on appeal, the judgment of the House of Lords in *Marcic* in December 2003 manifested a very different vision of the interaction of the HRA 1998 and private nuisance.[227] Utility undertakers such as Thames Water operate within a statutory framework and a claim under the common law action in nuisance was found to be inconsistent with the comprehensive statutory scheme laid down in the Water Industry Act 1991. This did not prevent a claim under the HRA 1998, but the scheme in question was found to be convention-compliant. The law required a fair balance to be struck between the interests of persons whose homes

[222] Ibid, paras 52–53.

[223] *Dennis v Ministry of Defence* [2003] EWHC 793 (QB); [2003] Env LR 34 (noise nuisance created by RAF Harrier Jump Jets at a nearby training base).

[224] Ibid, para 46.

[225] *Marcic v Thames Water Utilities Ltd* [2002] EWCA Civ 64; [2002] QB 929. See also *Pemberton v Southwark LBC* [2000] 1 WLR 1672, 1684 per Clarke LJ (Art 8 a relevant factor in extending standing in private nuisance to tolerated trespassers).

[226] B Parker, 'A Continued Nuisance' (2002) 61 *Cambridge Law Journal* 260, 263. See also D Rook, 'Property Law and the Human Rights Act 1998: A Review of the First Year' [2002] *Conveyancer* 316.

[227] *Marcic v Thames Water Utilities Ltd* [2003] UKHL 66; [2004] 2 AC 42.

and property were affected and the interests of other people, such as customers and the general public. The House found that the scheme struck a reasonable balance; Parliament acting well within its bounds as policy maker.[228]

In rejecting the claim, their Lordships placed considerable emphasis on the decision of the Grand Chamber of the ECtHR in *Hatton v United Kingdom*.[229] This had accepted that, in the light of the fundamentally subsidiary nature of the Convention, national courts were in principle better placed than an international court to evaluate local needs and conditions and that the role of the domestic policy maker should be given special weight.[230] In their Lordships' view, future litigants would be better advised to pursue their claims under the statutory scheme, with the long stop availability of judicial review. The approach of the House of Lords is revealing. A Strasbourg case is relied upon, but as a means to justify the primacy of domestic policy making. In bringing policy home, the court is defending a national statutory scheme against challenge from both the law of tort and rights recognised by the HRA 1998.

The more recent decision of the Court of Appeal in *Dobson v Thames Water Utilities Ltd*[231] indicates that private nuisance has also moved towards the division of tort and HRA claims which we saw earlier in relation to claims for public authority liability in negligence and false imprisonment. In *Dobson*, local residents had raised test cases for nuisance and negligence arising from odour and mosquitoes allegedly caused by the negligent operation of the defendants' sewage treatment works. Breach of Article 8 ECHR was also pleaded. The Court of Appeal placed the claimants in two categories: those with proprietary rights able to claim under private nuisance and the Act, and those without, who could only claim under the Act, thereby implicitly rejecting the suggestion in *McKenna* that the standing rule in *Hunter* should be challenged. Lord Bingham's judgment in *Greenfield* was relied upon to illustrate the distinct remedial regimes. In the words of Waller LJ:

> The Convention serves principally public law aims; the principal objective is to declare any infringement and to put a stop to it. Compensation is ancillary and discretionary. The interests of the individual are part of the equation, but so are those of the wider public.[232]

For those able to bring an action for damages in private nuisance, the Court held that it was 'highly improbable, if not inconceivable'[233] that it would be appropriate to award a further sum for breach of Article 8. Controversially, even parties without standing to sue in private nuisance might be confined to a declaration under the Act where the owner in whose home they were resident had obtained damages

[228] Ibid, para 43 per Lord Nicholls.
[229] *Hatton v United Kingdom* (36022/97) (2003) 37 EHRR 28 (the Heathrow night flights case).
[230] Ibid, para 97, thereby acknowledging the margin of appreciation granted to national courts.
[231] *Dobson v Thames Water Utilities Ltd* [2009] EWCA Civ 28; [2009] 3 All ER 319.
[232] Ibid, para 42 .
[233] Ibid, para 50.

in private nuisance. Any award would be a 'highly significant consideration'[234] when determining whether damages were appropriate under section 8(3). This section provides that no award of damages should be made unless, taking account of all the circumstances of the case, including other relief granted, it is necessary to accord just satisfaction to the victim. The Court found that in assessing damages for loss of amenity in nuisance, the court would take account of the actual experience of all persons in occupation of the property (not simply the claimant). On this basis, any damages awarded in nuisance should be regarded as 'other relief' under section 8(3). Such a view is difficult to understand from the perspective of individual human rights. Tofaris asks how an occupant can meaningfully be said to derive a benefit from damages awarded to another party.[235] One might also enquire why, in awarding damages for a 'tort to land', the number of people on the property is a relevant concern and how this may be reconciled with the view of Lord Hoffmann in *Hunter* that damages should not be increased merely because more people are in occupation and therefore suffer greater discomfort.[236] As a result of *Dobson*, residents without a right to land will be less likely to be awarded damages for breach of Article 8 under the HRA 1998.[237]

This does not signify, however, that the HRA 1998 has had no impact on litigation involving nuisance claims, but simply that it has done little to 'reshape' the existing tort cause of action. It should be recalled that in *Marcic* the House of Lords did find it necessary to assess whether the statutory scheme could be justified as in the public interest and found that it provided a proportionate mechanism for striking a fair balance between the interests of customers whose properties were prone to sewer flooding and the interests of other customers who would have had to finance the cost of constructing more sewers. Equally in *Hatton*, the ECtHR found Article 8.1 to be engaged and proceeded to assess the substantive merits of the UK Government's decision (subject to a wide margin of appreciation) and to scrutinise the decision-making process to ensure compatibility with Article 8 and that due weight had been accorded to the interests of the individual.[238] Decision-making processes under statutory schemes must therefore be Convention-compliant or risk challenge. It is unsurprising, therefore, that challenges have also arisen in the contested area of planning law. The HRA 1998 will therefore operate to ensure both due process in relation to such schemes and that public authorities engage in a balancing exercise between competing rights. As Pill LJ stated in *Lough*, 'Recognition must be given to the fact that article 8 and

[234] Ibid, para 45.

[235] S Tofaris, 'Damages for Sewage Smells in Nuisance and under the Human Rights Act 1998' (2009) 68 *Cambridge Law Journal* 273.

[236] *Hunter* (n 218) 706.

[237] Ramsey J confirmed in *Dobson v Thames Water Utilities Ltd* [2011] EWHC 3253 (TCC); 140 Con LR 135 that for those claimants without a proprietary interest, no damages were necessary to provide just satisfaction under the Act, given that (a) the damages awarded to the property owners had reflected the loss of amenity of the whole family; (b) a declaration of rights had been made; and (c) other remedies were available under the Environmental Protection Act 1990 s 80 and s 82 and under s 94 of the Water Industry Act 1991.

[238] (2003) 37 EHRR 28, para 99.

article 1 of the First Protocol are part of the law of England and Wales.'[239] Nevertheless, cases such as *Dobson*[240] also indicate the unwillingness of the courts to modify established common law rules of private nuisance. This suggests that even if a challenge were to be brought against a private party on the basis of Article 8, alleging horizontal effect, a court would be reluctant to advocate change.

In terms of Europeanisation, therefore, the above analysis suggests that, despite early promise, the tort of private nuisance has not absorbed Convention rights. Claims under the Act will stand side by side with those for private nuisance. More significantly, in terms of compensation, *Dobson* indicates that a restrictive approach will be adopted towards the award of damages under the Act. One may only speculate to what extent recognition of the potentially crippling financial implications of liability for public authority undertakers, as noted in *Marcic*,[241] has influenced this approach, thereby enabling the courts to avoid what are essentially disputes about public resource allocation.[242] While there have been some suggestions that Strasbourg case law may encourage the courts to find a breach of Convention rights where no compensation has been awarded for the rights violated,[243] there is little evidence that this is influencing current practice and Nolan has suggested that the English courts should be careful not to read too much into the slim authority of the admissibility decision of *S v France* without considering fully its ramifications for domestic law.[244]

It is clear that there are still a number of unresolved matters in relation to the interaction of the tort of private nuisance and the HRA 1998. Nevertheless, this section has identified a similar pattern to that observed in other public authority cases: a move to parallel claims, treatment of the HRA as providing a distinctive remedial framework, some reference to Strasbourg case law but with evidence that the English courts find it difficult to translate its often fact-specific conclusions into a useful form of precedent. One thing is clear. Private nuisance, despite the HRA, has continued to operate as a tort focusing on the needs of those with *proprietary*, rather than human, rights.

[239] *Lough v First Secretary of State* [2004] EWCA Civ 905; [2004] 1 WLR 2557, para 48.

[240] See also *Arscott v Coal Authority* [2004] EWCA Civ 892; [2005] Env LR 6 where the 'common enemy rule', which entitles an occupier to take steps to protect her property against an external threat such as flooding, was held to be Convention-compatible.

[241] See, eg, KL Morrow, 'The Rights Question: The Initial Impact of the Human Rights Act on Domestic Law relating to the Environment' [2005] *Journal of Planning Law* 1010, 1015. The House of Lords would also have been aware of the award of £950,000 damages, payable by the Ministry of Defence, in *Dennis* above.

[242] H Wilberg, 'Public Resource Allocation, Nuisance and the Human Rights Act 1998' (2004) 120 *Law Quarterly Review* 574; M Lee, 'Private Nuisance in the House of Lords: Back to Basics' (2004) 15 *King's College Law Journal* 417, 422.

[243] On the basis of *S v France* (1990) 65 DR 250. See also Lord Nicholls in *Marcic* (para 45) who indicated that those administering the statutory scheme might wish to reconsider whether the minority who suffered damage as a result of the inadequacy of the sewerage system should receive some compensation borne by those who enjoy the benefit of effective drainage.

[244] Nolan, 'Nuisance' (n 212) 177. See also C Miller, 'Environmental Rights in a Welfare State? A Comment on DeMerieux' (2003) 23 *Oxford Journal of Legal Studies* 111.

D. Defamation

Defamation, in contrast to the other torts examined above, has accepted that Convention rights may influence the treatment of common law claims against public authorities. In *Clift v Slough BC*,[245] Ms Clift brought an action against the council for defamation. The council raised the defence of qualified privilege: that it had a duty to warn employees and certain partner institutions of the threat it believed had been posed by the claimant, they had a corresponding interest in receiving the information, and that the statement had been made without malice. Noting that the council was a public authority under section 6 HRA 1998 and therefore bound to act in a way compatible with Convention rights, the Court held that the council was obliged to respect Ms Clift's Article 8 right to reputation, unless the interference could be justified under Article 8.2. Here, although the protection of the safety of all council employees and even the employees of the partner organisations was a legitimate aim sufficiently important to justify an interference with Ms Clift's Article 8 rights, publication of the words to supernumerary employees, who were not likely to be directly approached by Ms Clift, was a disproportionate interference with her rights. The qualified privilege defence failed – the council could not argue that they were under a duty to publish material which amounted to a breach of Article 8 ECHR.

It is interesting to note that in limiting the ability of the public authority to rely on the qualified privilege defence, the Court expressly rejected the argument that it should adopt the approach of the House of Lords in *Smith v Chief Constable of Sussex Police*.[246] Ward LJ remarked that:

> Since section 6 of the Human Rights Act 1998 requires the court to act compatibly with a Convention right, the court is bound to give effect to article 8 if the point arises as it squarely does in this case. We simply cannot duck it, rule it irrelevant or ignore its implications for qualified privilege, leaving Ms Clift with her human rights claim only.[247]

This different approach is closer to the Court of Appeal decision in *Smith* which was, of course, rejected by the House of Lords. The Court was also prepared to ignore the cost implications of rendering a public authority liable for defamation damages – the 'diversion of resources' argument used in the negligence cases – in this context. *Clift* may be justified as being largely consistent with the approach adopted for defamation generally, as seen in section I of this chapter, namely that

[245] *Clift v Slough BC* [2010] EWCA Civ 1484; [2011] 1 WLR 1774. Comment K Hughes, 'Defamation and the Human Rights Act 1998' (2011) 70 *Cambridge Law Journal* 296.

[246] Ibid, para 39. Contrast with the earlier decision of *W v Westminster City Council* [2005] EWHC 102 (QB); [2005] 4 All ER 96 (Note): publication by social workers, at a child protection case conference, of a report containing defamatory words was protected by qualified privilege, but nevertheless breached the claimant's Art 8 rights.

[247] *Clift* (n 245) para 46. See also *Thompson v James* [2013] EWHC 515 (QB) where the local authority was successful in its defence of qualified privilege.

domestic law is being shaped to respond to rights under the HRA 1998 and in the light of Strasbourg jurisprudence (although Ward LJ cites only English case law in his judgment). As such it is treated as a distinctive area of tort law in which public law duties under the HRA are capable of reframing substantive rules of private law.[248] It does, however, create inconsistency in terms of public authority liability in tort. While the victim of public authority incompetence may be entitled to tort-based damages if the injury is to her reputation (*Clift*), damages will be refused if the result is near death (*Smith*). This result seems somewhat arbitrary to say the least.

Conclusion

The Human Rights Act 1998 sought to bring (human) rights home. For tort lawyers, the question was the degree to which the Act would impact on domestic law and lead to changes in core tort law principle. If the courts, as public authorities, were expected to act in a Convention-compliant manner, it was inevitable that claimants would argue that tort law should be developed in the light of Convention rights. As this chapter has illustrated, arguments for reform of English tort law have been raised primarily in relation to the torts of defamation, negligence, nuisance and false imprisonment. Yet, while defamation might have seemed the most obvious target for reform, particularly in view of rules which had been criticised for 'chilling' freedom of expression, this tort remains remarkably unchanged. This is despite the objections of counsel and the existence of established Strasbourg jurisprudence on freedom of expression. The most obvious development – the *Reynolds* defence – does not conflict with existing common law policy and is perhaps better characterised as an incremental development from existing law, which had already recognised the importance of freedom of expression prior to the Act, rather than a radical change. Convention rights may have hastened this development, but can scarcely take sole credit. In reality, the force of the Article 10 right has been weakened by Strasbourg itself in recognising that Article 8 is capable of protecting an individual's reputation, giving rise to competing rights which must be balanced on the facts of each case. It has been left to the UK government (hardly an enthusiastic advocate of the Convention) to propose new legislation to protect the freedom of expression.

Beyond defamation, the impact of the Convention, after a somewhat tumultuous start provoked by the decision in *Osman v UK*, has been limited. The seriousness of

[248] There is also the added complication in this context that since 'public authorities' are not regarded as victims under Art 34 and possess no human rights under the Convention (see *Aston Cantlow v Wallbank* [2003] UKHL 37; [2004] 1 AC 546, para 8), the public authority is arguably unable to assert any countervailing arguments under Art 10: see A Mullis and A Scott, 'The Swing of the Pendulum: Reputation, Expression and the Re-Centring of English Libel Law' (2012) 63 *Northern Ireland Legal Quarterly* 27, 51.

the rights invoked (primarily Articles 2, 3 and 5) has led to a focus on claims against public authorities. By virtue of their statutory powers, local authorities are capable of intervening to protect against threats to life or of torture. The police and prison service are also the most obvious targets for claims of deprivation of liberty. Equally in nuisance Article 8 claims have generally involved issues of serious environmental pollution caused by companies regarded as public authorities under the Act. The prevalence of claims against public authorities has inevitably led to the question of how tort law and claims under HRA 1998 interact. The decision to treat the claims in the alternative is significant. The HRA 1998 is treated as possessing its own distinct cause of action. In the words of Lord Hope in *Van Colle*:

> [T]he common law, with its own system of limitation periods and remedies, should be allowed to stand on its own feet side by side with the alternative remedy. Indeed the case for preserving it may be thought to be supported by the fact that any perceived shortfall in the way that it deals with cases that fall within the threshold for the application of the *Osman* principle can now be dealt with in domestic law under the 1998 Act.[249]

This division serves a number of goals. It leaves domestic tort law policy intact. The HRA 1998 is thus left to develop its own precedents. In cases such as *Jain*,[250] the HRA action was indeed used to justify *not* changing tort law in the claimants' favour. It also serves to maintain the existence of policy bars to liability, seen in cases such as *Hill*[251] and *D v East Berkshire Community Health NHS Trust* (re parental liability).[252] Domestic tort policy survives, subject to limited intervention under the HRA 1998.

Nevertheless, a number of concerns may be identified at what is essentially a defensive approach to Convention rights. In *Rabone v Pennine Care NHS Foundation Trust*,[253] as seen above, drawing a line between a claim in tort and under the HRA 1998 led the Supreme Court to underestimate the possibility of a conflict between the section 7 action and section 1A of the Fatal Accidents Act 1976. Concurrent actions must operate consistently. More broadly, Steele has suggested that the reluctance to embrace Convention rights might be explained as a fear of loss of control to Strasbourg.[254] Consider, for example, the extra-judicial view of Lord Hoffmann in a public lecture:

> Whatever one may say about the wisdom or even correctness of decisions of the Court of Justice in Luxembourg, no one can criticise their legitimacy in laying down uniform rules for the European Union in those areas which fall within the scope of the Treaty.

[249] *Van Colle* [2008] UKHL 50, para 82.

[250] *Jain v Trent SHA* [2009] UKHL 4.

[251] *Hill v Chief Constable of West Yorkshire* [1989] AC 53.

[252] *D v East Berkshire Community Health NHS Trust* [2005] UKHL 23; [2003] EWCA Civ 1151. Nolan further argues that the Court of Appeal ruling in *D* might not survive the decision of the House of Lords in *Gorringe v Calderdale MBC* [2004] UKHL 15; [2004] 1 WLR 1057: D Nolan, 'The Liability of Public Authorities for Failing to Confer Benefits' (2011) 127 *Law Quarterly Review* 260.

[253] *Rabone* (n175).

[254] J Steele, '(Dis)owning the Convention in the Law of Tort' in J Lee (ed), *From House of Lords to Supreme Court: Judges, Jurists and the Process of Judging* (Oxford, Hart Publishing, 2011).

> But the Convention does not give the Strasbourg Court equivalent legitimacy. As the case law shows, there is virtually no aspect of our legal system, from land law to social security to torts to consumer contracts, which is not arguably touched at some point by human rights . . . I do not suggest belief that the United Kingdom's legal system is perfect but I do argue that detailed decisions about how it could be improved should be made in London, either by our democratic institutions or by judicial bodies which, like the Supreme Court of the United States, are integral with our own society and respected as such.[255]

The courts' mixed reaction to Strasbourg case law may be seen in two recent cases. In *Marcic*, the House of Lords welcomed a decision which gave the domestic courts a margin of appreciation. In *Smith v Ministry of Defence*, the Supreme Court sought to 'interpret' the jurisprudence of the ECtHR to determine the scope of the *Osman* operational duty. In both cases, the English court is attempting to assert some form of control over the interpretation of Convention law and its interface with national tort law provisions.

Stepping back and reviewing the relationship between tort law and the HRA 1998 over the last 15 years, a distinction may be drawn between different causes of action. When English lawyers think of the torts of negligence and private nuisance, for example, they think in terms of duties of care and undue interference with the claimant's use and enjoyment of land. The emphasis is on the wrongful conduct of the defendant, not the violation of the claimant's right.[256] An English lawyer would therefore assert that the defendant owes the claimant a duty of care, not that the claimant has a general right not to be injured.[257] Conceptually, therefore, tort lawyers do not think in terms of human rights in these contexts.[258] On this basis, by divorcing tort claims from those arising under the HRA 1998, the courts are simply adhering to this traditional interpretation of tort law. This may be unadventurous, but should not surprise.

The distinct remedial structure found under the HRA 1998 has also served to preserve this conceptual division between these forms of tort law and the award of just satisfaction under the HRA. By focusing on the violation of rights, section 8 adopts a framework more familiar to public lawyers, namely, a short limitation period for claims where damages are not the primary remedy. In the public law context, for example, it is not unusual for a declaration that a right has been violated to be deemed the more appropriate and proportionate remedy in the

[255] Lord Hoffmann, 'The Universality of Human Rights' (2009) 125 *Law Quarterly Review* 416, 429–30.

[256] See A Mason, 'Human Rights and the Law of Torts' in P Cane and J Stapleton (eds), *The Law of Obligations* (Oxford, Clarendon Press, 1998) 14, who argues that the law of torts remains in essence the offspring of its history, a body of principles developed around particular causes of action.

[257] See PH Winfield, 'Duty in Tortious Negligence' (1934) 34 *Columbia Law Review* 41; *Stubbings v Webb* [1993] AC 498, 508. Stevens, however, dismisses this distinction as mere semantics: a duty is merely the obverse of a right: R Stevens, *Torts and Rights* (Oxford, Oxford University Press, 2007) 291. Whatever the theoretical merits of this argument, the question here is how the courts reason in practice which is, in this context, duty-based.

[258] See G Samuel, '"Le droit subjectif" and English Law' (1987) 46 *Cambridge Law Journal* 264.

circumstances.[259] By stressing the public law dimension, the courts have sought to justify a division between claims, giving rise to Lord Bingham's statement in *Watkins*[260] that 'the primary role of the law of tort is to provide monetary compensation for those who have suffered material damage rather than to vindicate the rights of those who have not'. [261] If we focus on the nature of the torts in question, the fact remains that negligence and private nuisance do not, at present, set out to protect human rights. They focus on private law duties and obligations and seek to compensate for proven losses. They are not actionable per se. On this basis, one can justify the division between tort claims from those under the HRA 1998. This does not address, of course, the normative question whether the nature of these torts *should* change. Many have argued, for example, that private nuisance should focus more on human beings than rights over land.[262] However, at present, there is no obvious consensus in favour of such a development. Lawyers, such as Nolan, have continued to argue that tort law has its own distinctive rationales, concepts and principles and that alignment with the HRA 1998 would lead to incoherence.[263] In the absence of general agreement that the fundamental nature of the torts of nuisance and negligence need to change, the English courts have essentially played it safe. Developing the torts of negligence and private nuisance in a Convention-compliant manner would have required a fundamental change to the character of the tort and the English courts have simply refused to take this step.

In contrast, looking at the tort of defamation, this tort has long made reference to the right to protect one's reputation and the public interest in promoting freedom of expression in a democracy.[264] The public dimension, therefore, is self-evident. Lord Coleridge CJ in *Bonnard v Perryman*[265] in 1891 remarked that 'The right of free speech is one which it is for the public interest that individuals should possess, and, indeed, that they should exercise without impediment, so long as no wrongful act is done.' The dialogue of rights therefore already existed prior to the HRA 1998, which merely provided a clearer framework – Article 10 v Article 8 – within which to continue the debate. It is unsurprising, therefore, that the HRA 1998 has been directly applied to defamation law and the *Van Colle* division rejected. The very nature of the tort renders it inevitable.

[259] McLay, 'Tort and Constitutional Damages' (n 146) 50.

[260] *Watkins v Secretary of State for the Home Department* [2006] UKHL 17, para 9.

[261] Steele has criticised this functional distinction and she is correct to state that tort law does at time vindicate rights: J Steele, 'Damages in Tort and under the Human Rights Act: Remedial or Functional Separation?' (2008) 67 *Cambridge Law Journal* 606. Nevertheless, it may be argued that as a generalisation, his Lordship is correct. For an alternative justification of this division, see F du Bois, 'Human Rights and the Tort Liability of Public Authorities' (2011) 127 *Law Quarterly Review* 589.

[262] J Wightman, 'Nuisance: The Environmental Tort? *Hunter v Canary Wharf* in the House of Lords' (1998) 61 *Modern Law Review* 870; P Cane, 'What a nuisance!' (1997) 113 *Law Quarterly Review* 515.

[263] D Nolan, 'Negligence and Human Rights Law: The Case for Separate Development' (2013) 76 *Modern Law Review* 286.

[264] See, eg, J Laws, 'Law and Democracy' [1995] *Public Law* 72. For its history, see P Mitchell, *The Making of the Modern Law of Defamation* (Oxford, Hart Publishing, 2005).

[265] *Bonnard v Perryman* [1891] 2 Ch 269, 284.

The situation in relation to false imprisonment is more contentious. Many would argue that false imprisonment is a tort dealing with a right to self-determination and that a right not to be deprived of one's liberty would fit neatly within this tort. Hickman has argued that while the common law has an affinity for duty-based reasoning, a distinction exists in tort law between actions that focus on breach of duty by the tortfeasor, such as negligence and nuisance, and those actions that focus on the rights of the claimant, such as trespass and false imprisonment.[266] As seen above, this is not how the House of Lords has interpreted the relationship between Article 5 ECHR and false imprisonment. In the *Austin* case,[267] by distinguishing the tort from Article 5, the court rendered a distinct treatment of claims inevitable. Only by questioning the legitimacy of the *Bournewood*[268] and *Austin* ruling, which many have done, would it be permissible to interpret false imprisonment with reference to Article 5 jurisprudence. In finding a pragmatic resolution in *Austin* due to the failure of Article 5 to make specific allowances for matters of necessity, the House of Lords created an artificial division between the tort and the Convention right. Domestic policy has served to trump arguments that false imprisonment should be developed in a Convention-compliant manner. This is unfortunate to say the least.

The conclusion must be that, in terms of Europeanisation, English tort law is far from supporting a European culture of rights. We have seen greater citation of Strasbourg jurisprudence and that the domestic courts are looking to the ECtHR for guidance and turning away from Commonwealth comparisons.[269] There is also some dialogue – a form of cross-reference between domestic and European court which we do not see in the ordinary tort law.[270] Nevertheless, as observed by Dame Mary Arden, the courts have only developed tort law by reference to Convention rights and values when it was found to be appropriate for *domestic* law reasons.[271] On this basis, the torts of negligence, private nuisance and, more questionably, false imprisonment remain intact. In contrast, in defamation, the development of the *Reynolds* defence has continued a pre-Act move towards greater recognition of freedom of expression. Tort law policy thus remains centred around domestic policy concerns, much, one suspects, to the relief of Lord Hoffmann. While such a conclusion may seem an anti-climax after the dizzy heights of *Osman v UK*, the key point is that the courts are refusing to interpret

[266] TR Hickman, 'Tort Law, Public Authorities and the HRA 1998' in D Fairgrieve, M Andenas and J Bell (eds), *Tort Liability of Public Authorities in Comparative Perspective* (BIICL, 2002) 21.

[267] *Austin v Commissioner of Police of the Metropolis* [2009] UKHL 5; [2007] EWCA Civ 989.

[268] *R v Bournewood Community and Mental Health NHS Trust Ex p. L* [1999] 1 AC 458.

[269] See Lord Bingham in *Sheldrake v DPP* [2004] UKHL 43; [2005] 1 AC 264, para 33: 'Some caution is . . . called for in considering different enactments decided under different constitutional arrangements. But, even more important, the United Kingdom courts must take their lead from Strasbourg. In the United Kingdom cases I have discussed our domestic courts have been trying, loyally and (as I think) successfully, to give full and fair effect to the Strasbourg jurisprudence.'

[270] See M Amos, 'The Dialogue between United Kingdom Courts and the European Court of Human Rights' (2012) 61 *International & Comparative Law Quarterly* 557.

[271] 'Human Rights and Civil Wrongs: Tort Law under the Spotlight' [2010] *Public Law* 140, 153.

certain torts on the basis of a rights-based framework and until they do so, no fundamental change is likely. It remains to be seen whether the optimistic view of Steele that tort law may become more receptive to rights-based reasoning once the *Osman* saga fades into ancient history turns out to be correct.[272]

This somewhat negative conclusion contrasts with the topic of chapter six. This chapter will examine how the HRA 1998 has led the English courts to develop a means of protecting privacy rights based on Article 8 of the Convention. This is despite the express refusal by Lord Hoffmann in *Wainwright v Home Office*[273] to recognise a tort of invasion of privacy. The development of this new cause of action and its impact on the relationship between tort law and human rights law will be the focus of the next chapter.

[272] J Steele in MA Jones (ed), *Clerk and Lindsell on Torts*, 20th edn (London, Sweet and Maxwell, 2010) para 14-93. Contrast Nolan, 'Negligence' (n 263) 302: 'the process of convergence would serve to distort the law of negligence both by undermining established principles and by introducing alien concepts.'

[273] *Wainwright v Home Office* [2003] UKHL 53; [2004] 2 AC 406.

6

A Right to Personal Privacy in the English Law of Torts?

Introduction

In examining the influence of European human rights law on English tort law, undoubtedly the most dynamic area is that of privacy law. Parliament, when debating the Human Rights Bill, questioned whether this would introduce through the back door a new law of privacy.[1] Although this was denied by the UK government, a general expectation existed that when the Human Rights Act 1998 came into force, the English courts would be able to fashion some protection for Article 8 privacy rights. This indeed has occurred and, despite the assertion by Lord Hoffmann as late as 2003 that it was for the legislator, not the courts, to establish a detailed law of privacy,[2] the House of Lords in *Campbell v Mirror Group Newspapers Ltd* in 2004[3] recognised that the law would protect to a certain extent the right to privacy, even where a celebrity had been photographed in a public street.

The interface between European human rights law and English law in this area has been, however, less than straightforward. The HRA 1998 does not permit a claim based on breach of Article 8 ECHR, but rather, under sections 6 and 7, an action against a public authority for failing to act in a Convention-compliant manner. This offers little assistance in a field where most claims will be against privately owned media defendants. Some form of horizontal effect is therefore required by which private parties may be sued for breach of Article 8.[4] The English courts have favoured indirect horizontal effect and have adapted the equitable doctrine of breach of confidence to provide protection for informational privacy. This new form of breach of confidence, however, is distinct from the traditional doctrine. It is based on balancing the right to privacy against the right to free expression. It has, as its focus, the protection of the claimant's reasonable expectation of privacy and

[1] A point raised by Lord Wakeham, chair of the Press Complaints Council, in the House of Lords: see HL Deb 24 November 1997, vol 583 col 771.

[2] *Wainwright v Home, Office* [2003] UKHL 53, [2004] 2 AC 406, para 33.

[3] *Campbell v Mirror Group Newspapers Ltd* [2004] UKHL 22; [2004] 2 AC 457.

[4] See AL Young, 'Mapping Horizontal Effect' in D Hoffman (ed), *The Impact of the UK Human Rights Act on Private Law* (Cambridge, Cambridge University Press, 2011).

the need to protect his or her autonomy and dignity against unfair intrusion. It is also an area of law where Strasbourg case law has proven particularly influential, assisted by the ongoing battle between Princess Caroline of Monaco and the German press.

This chapter will examine how the English courts have developed privacy protection under the HRA 1998 and the extent to which this new form of action represents the most overt example of the Europeanisation of modern tort law. If, and this remains controversial, the English courts have created a new tort which seeks to protect Article 8 ECHR rights, then this marks a significant step in the relationship between the English and Strasbourg courts. Yet, while it is without doubt that protection now exists in English law for breach of informational privacy and that this is due to the implementation of the HRA 1998, the courts have been reticent as to its classification. It is still tied to the equitable action for breach of confidence, albeit with explicit recognition that it is distinct from the traditional action which continues to focus on misuse of confidential information, usually in a commercial or employment context. Further, protection will be confined to the obtaining and distributing information without consent. *Wainwright v Home Office* stands as authority that there is no tort of privacy per se. On this basis, breaches of privacy which do not amount to misuse of private information, such as the illegal personal search in *Wainwright*,[5] fall outside this cause of action.

In examining how the courts have responded to the challenge of developing privacy rights, this chapter will consider two questions. First, to what extent has the ECHR influenced the development of a new form of breach of confidence protecting informational privacy and, secondly, almost 15 years after the introduction of the HRA 1998, can we now say that the English courts have developed a genuinely 'European' form of tort law shaped by the jurisprudence of the European Court of Human Rights?

[5] Although a future Wainwright could bring an action under the HRA 1998 provided the defendant was a public authority. Lord Hoffmann noted in *Wainwright* that had the Human Rights Act 1998 been applicable on the facts, the Wainwrights could have brought an action under HRA 1998, ss 6 and 7 for breach of their Art 8 rights, but doubted whether they would have been successful: [2003] UKHL 53, para 51. A subsequent ruling of the ECtHR found, however, in the claimants' favour: *Wainwright v United Kingdom* (12350/04) (2007) 44 EHRR 40 (illegal strip search in breach of Art 8 ECHR). On the limitations of a breach of confidence action in protecting broader privacy rights, see E Reid, '*Wainwright v United Kingdom*: Bringing Human Rights Home?' (2007) 11 *Edinburgh Law Review* 83.

I. From Breach of Confidence to a 'Tort' of Misuse of Private Information

A. Ad hoc Protection at Common Law and Statute

The right to privacy, which Warren and Brandeis famously described as 'the right to be let alone' in 1890,[6] has long provoked public debate. Warren and Brandeis' article highlights that concerns of press intrusion into private lives are not new.[7] Yet, thanks to new technology, the modern media is particularly capable of intrusion and can distribute information to vast numbers of people at the press of a button. UK newspapers are also noted for their apparently insatiable appetite for information relating to the private lives of celebrities. Recently the Leveson Report into the Culture, Practices and Ethics of the Press[8] highlighted the need for greater regulation of press conduct and the ability (and willingness) of the media to intrude into very personal aspects of the private lives not simply of celebrities, but of newsworthy individuals.[9] The question of the balance to be reached between a free press and personal privacy therefore goes beyond private litigation to become a matter for public concern and debate.

Nevertheless, in contrast to the United States and despite widespread recognition that the common law contains gaps rendering it unable to protect deserving claimants from unwarranted invasions of privacy,[10] English law continues to resist the introduction of a general privacy tort. The general view until the 1990s was that protection could be obtained from existing common law and statutory remedies. For example, home-owners are protected from intrusion by the torts of trespass[11] and private nuisance. Perhaps less obviously, the tort of defamation was

[6] S Warren and L Brandeis, 'The Right to Privacy' (1890) 4 *Harvard Law Review* 19, adopting the language of TM Cooley, *A Treatise on the Law of Torts*, 2nd edn (Chicago, Callaghan, 1888) 29. The US has long recognised the need for privacy protection: see United States Restatement (Second) of Torts paras 652A-652I) (1977) which recognises four types of invasion of privacy: intrusion, appropriation of name or likeness, unreasonable publicity and placing a person in a false light. Note, also the influential article of WL Prosser, 'Privacy' (1960) 48 *California Law Review* 383.

[7] They complained in 1890 that 'Instantaneous photographs and newspaper enterprise have invaded the sacred precincts of private and domestic life; and numerous mechanical devices threaten to make good the prediction that "what is whispered in the closet shall be proclaimed from the house-tops".' It is also commonly believed that the article followed Warren's own experiences of press intrusion: DJ Solove et al, *Privacy, Information and Technology* (New York, Aspen, 2006) 11.

[8] Leveson LJ, *An Inquiry into the Culture, Practices and Ethics of the Press*, HC 780 (London, TSO, 2012): www.official-documents.gov.uk/document/hc1213/hc07/0780/0780.asp (hereafter Leveson Report)

[9] The Leveson Report (n 8) noted that 'For the seventh time in less than 70 years, a report has been commissioned by the Government which has dealt with concerns about the press. It was sparked by public revulsion about a single action – the hacking of the mobile phone of a murdered teenager': Executive Summary, para 1.

[10] Acknowledged by Lord Hoffmann in *Wainwright* (n 2) para 18. See BS Markesinis, 'Our Patchy Law of Privacy: Time to Do Something About It' (1990) 53 *Modern Law Review* 802.

[11] See *Entick v Carrington* (1765) 2 Wils KB 275; 95 ER 807.

invoked in *Tolley v Fry*,[12] where the claimant's image had been used as a caricature in an advertisement for the defendants' chocolate bars. Equally, statutes such as the Copyright, Designs and Patents Act 1988,[13] the Protection from Harassment Act 1997 and the Data Protection Act 1998[14] provide some protection against unwanted intrusion, together with extra-legal mechanisms such as the Codes of Practice applicable to the media. However, such an ad hoc approach has its limitations. Aerial photographs of a country house were found not to be actionable in trespass in that the rights of a landowner do not extend to airspace exceeding that necessary for the ordinary use and enjoyment of land.[15] Equally members of the family living in the home, but without rights to land, cannot sue in private nuisance.[16]

The limitations of such piecemeal protection were identified by the Court of Appeal in *Kaye v Robertson* in 1991.[17] In this case, Kaye, a well-known television actor, had been seriously injured in an accident and placed in a private hospital room with a notice on the door barring visitors. Nevertheless, reporters from a tabloid newspaper managed to enter his room and obtain an 'interview' with photographs,[18] which it sought to publish as a 'great old-fashioned scoop'. The Court of Appeal was clearly troubled by the fact that such reprehensible conduct failed to find an obvious remedy in tort.[19] Eventually, resort was made to the tort of malicious falsehood on the basis that the newspaper's allegation that the story and photograph had been taken with Kaye's consent was clearly false, and that Kaye had lost the right to sell his first interview after the accident for profit. The result was less than satisfactory. The injunctive relief granted did not prevent the newspaper publishing photographs of Kaye in his hospital bed, but simply prevented it from claiming that he had voluntarily consented to the so-called interview. More fundamentally, the gross invasion of the privacy had, of necessity,

[12] *Tolley v Fry* [1931] AC 333: Tolley (a famous amateur golfer) successfully sued the defendants on the basis of the innuendo that he had violated his amateur status by permitting his image to be used in the advert. Section 8 (as amended) of the Rehabilitation of Offenders Act 1974 further offers some limited protection of privacy in that truth is not a defence where the defendant has maliciously published details of a person's distant criminal past. Defamation is subject, of course, to a defence of truth which confines its protection to statements which are untrue.

[13] Copyright law offers some protection of privacy rights where the claimant owns the copyright of the work or photograph disclosed: section 85, Copyright, Designs and Patents Act 1988. See also *Williams v Settle* [1960] 1 WLR 1072.

[14] Which extends the rights of individuals to control the use of personal data stored on computers or manually.

[15] *Bernstein v Skyviews Ltd* [1978] 1 QB 479.

[16] *Hunter v Canary Wharf Ltd* [1997] AC 655, overturning the Court of Appeal's decision in *Khorasandjian v Bush* [1993] QB 727 that the daughter of the house (who was a licensee) could obtain an injunction for private nuisance to stop harassment by a former boyfriend.

[17] *Kaye v Robertson* [1991] FSR 62.

[18] The newspaper claimed that Kaye had consented to an interview, even though he was unable to recollect the incident 15 minutes after the event.

[19] Trespass to the person failed as the use of flash photography by itself did not amount to battery. Nor did Kaye have sufficient possessory rights to bring an action for trespass to land. Defamation (that is, the newspaper had falsely stated that Kaye had consented to give an exclusive interview to the *Sunday Sport*) equally failed as the court was not prepared to impose an interim injunction except in the clearest of cases.

been re-characterised as a complaint that Kaye had been denied the ability to profit from his ill-health, which not only diminished the gravity of the intrusion but also arguably portrayed the victim in a less favourable light. Bingham LJ spoke for many when he commented that 'this case nonetheless highlights, yet again, the failure of both the common law of England and statute to protect in an effective way the personal privacy of individual citizens.'[20] Glidewell LJ agreed that the facts of the case gave a graphic illustration of the desirability for legislative intervention to protect the privacy of individuals.[21]

Writing extra-judicially in 1996, Lord Bingham noted the particular mental pain and distress that such intrusions were capable of causing which might have far greater impact than mere bodily injury.[22] His Lordship re-iterated that while the current law did, to a very large extent, already protect personal privacy, it did not go far enough and recommended legislative intervention or, failing this, intervention by the courts.[23] The view was therefore that it was for the UK legislator to intervene. This did not signify that English litigants had neglected the possibility of bringing an action before the ECtHR. In *Peck v United Kingdom*,[24] Mr Peck had been filmed in a public street without his consent by a CCTV camera moments after he had attempted to commit suicide. The ECtHR held that disclosure of the CCTV footage constituted a serious interference with his right to respect for private life, breaching Article 8 ECHR. It concluded that 'Article [8] protects a right to identity and personal development, and the right to establish and develop relationships with other human beings and the outside world and it may include activities of a professional or business nature. There is, therefore, a zone of interaction of a person with others, even in a public context, which may fall within the scope of "private life".'[25] Nevertheless, the UK's limited response to the ECtHR's decision in *Malone v UK*[26] is revealing. Faced with a decision that lack of any legal regulation of state interceptions of private communications (in other words, phone-tapping) was contrary to Article 8, the UK government chose to address the issue narrowly, introducing a specific Act, the Interception of Communications Act 1985, to deal with this. Further, Lord Hoffmann in *Wainwright* dismissed the *Peck* case as showing no more than the need, in English law, for a system of control of the use of film from CCTV cameras.[27] The European Commission of Human Rights in *Earl Spencer v United Kingdom*[28] was also persuaded by the UK government that English law did not breach Article 8 on the basis that the

[20] *Kaye* (n 17) 70.
[21] *Kaye* (n 17) 66.
[22] Lord Bingham, 'Should There Be a Law to Protect Rights of Personal Privacy?' [1996] *European Human Rights Law Review* 450, 451.
[23] Ibid, 461–62.
[24] *Peck v United Kingdom* (44647/98) (2003) 36 EHRR 41.
[25] Ibid, para 57.
[26] *Malone v UK* (8691/79) (1985) 7 EHRR 14.
[27] *Wainwright* [2003] UKHL 53, para 33.
[28] *Earl Spencer v United Kingdom* (1998) 25 EHRR CD 105 (photograph of Lady Spencer in private clinic).

applicant could have pursued an action for breach of confidence and therefore had not exhausted their domestic remedies.

The legislature continued to resist any general protection of privacy per se.[29] Then Home Secretary Jack Straw, on the introduction of the HRA, stated that 'we have no plans to introduce legislation creating a general law of privacy'.[30] Lord Chancellor, Lord Irvine nevertheless added that:

> I believe that the true view is that the courts will be able to adapt and develop the common law by relying on existing domestic principles in the laws of trespass, nuisance, copyright, confidence and the like, to fashion a common law right to privacy . . . They may have regard to the convention in developing the common law, as they do today.[31]

B. Incremental Development: Extending Breach of Confidence

By the time the HRA was implemented, therefore, there were signs of a growing judicial dissatisfaction with the piecemeal approach to protection of privacy and a clear indication by the government that it would not introduce privacy legislation, but would leave it to the courts to 'fashion' a suitable legal framework. The HRA indicated the decisions of the ECtHR would be helpful in this task; section 2(1) providing that, in determining a question in connection with Convention rights, the courts should take into account decisions of the ECtHR. It remained an open question how such developments would take place.

The vehicle chosen was the equitable action for breach of confidence. At first glance, this may appear an odd choice. As Lord Browne-Wilkinson VC commented in *Stephens v Avery*, 'The basis of equitable intervention to protect confidentiality is that it is unconscionable for a person who has received information on the basis that it is confidential subsequently to reveal that information'.[32] The classic doctrine thus has three requirements:

(i) The information in question has the necessary quality of confidence about it;
(ii) The information was imparted in circumstances importing an obligation of confidence;[33] *and*

[29] See, eg, the Calcutt Review of Press Self-Regulation, which had recommended that the government should give further consideration to the introduction of a new tort of infringement of privacy (Cmnd 2135, London, HMSO, 1993), para 17. The National Heritage Committee, *Fourth Report on Privacy and Media Intrusion* (HC 294-II, March 1993) had also recommended that a Protection of Privacy Bill should be introduced, although this was rejected by the government in 1995: *Privacy and Media Intrusion: The Government's Response*, Cmnd 2918 (London, HMSO, 1995), para 4.13. For a review of the national debate on privacy law 1961–95, see R Errera, 'The Twisted Road from *Prince Albert* to *Campbell*, and Beyond: Towards a Right of Privacy?' in M Andenas and D Fairgrieve (eds), *Tom Bingham and the Transformation of the Law: A Liber Amicorum* (Oxford, Oxford University Press, 2011) 377–83.

[30] *Official Report*, Commons, 2 July1998, col. 541.

[31] HL Deb 24 November 1997, col 785.

[32] *Stephens v Avery* [1988] Ch 449, 455. He added at 456: 'The [equitable] jurisdiction is based . . . on the duty to be of good faith.'

[33] This extends beyond legal relationships: see *Stephens* (n 32) (duty of confidence owed by former friend in relation to the details of a sexual relationship between two women).

(iii) There must be an unauthorised use or disclosure of that information.[34]

On this basis, trade secrets and commercially sensitive information can be protected; the defendant acting unconscionably in ignoring the obligation of confidence imposed upon him or her. However, if the quality of confidentiality is lost, for example by information entering the public domain, or never acquired, for example in relation to useless information or trivia, no liability will arise. Such confidential information might, of course, relate to private matters,[35] and the action has long been recognised to provide some protection for privacy,[36] but it offers little to protect claimants from media intrusion. As Morgan has commented,[37] it is difficult to consider photographs taken covertly with a long range lens by the paparazzi as information imparted in confidence. More fundamentally, breach of confidence is an equitable response to the defendant's *unconscionable* disclosure of information imparted in confidence and does not seek to protect the claimant from intrusion into his or her private life.

Nevertheless, prior to the Act, the courts had significantly widened the application of the action to the extent that it could be applied to disclosure of private information.[38] Lord Goff in *AG v Guardian Newspapers Ltd (No 2)*[39] suggested that the requirement of a pre-existing confidential relationship between the parties (requirement [ii]) was not always essential. His Lordship suggested that claimants should be able to claim where an obviously confidential document had been wafted by an electric fan out of a window into a crowded street or where a private diary had been dropped in a public place and picked up by a passer-by. Lord Keith in the same case commented that 'the right to personal privacy is clearly one which the law should in this field seek to protect'.[40] Laws J later supported Lord Goff's extension, remarking that, in such a case, 'the law would protect what might reasonably be called a right of privacy, although the name accorded to it would be breach of confidence'.[41] Although the statements of Lord Goff and Laws J were obiter, they were later described as 'persuasive dicta' by the courts.[42] As recognised by Strasbourg itself in

[34] MA Jones (ed), *Clerk and Lindsell on Torts*, 20th edn (London, Sweet and Maxwell, 2010) para 27-06; *Coco v AN Clark (Engineers) Ltd* [1969] RPC 41, 47 per Megarry J. It is unclear whether detriment to the claimant is an essential ingredient, but *Clerk and Lindsell* (n 34) finds that the claimant must at least show apprehended damage in future if an injunction is to be granted.

[35] Consider, eg, *Argyll v Argyll* [1967] Ch 302 (revelation of marital confidences).

[36] Consider, eg, the famous case of *Prince Albert v Strange* (1849) 2 De G & Sm 652; 1 Mac & G 25 (unauthorised publication of private etchings of Royal family).

[37] J Morgan, 'Privacy in the House of Lords, Again' (2004) 120 *Law Quarterly Review* 563.

[38] See H Fenwick and G Phillipson, 'Confidence and Privacy: A Re-Examination' (1996) 55 *Cambridge Law Journal* 447.

[39] *AG v Guardian Newspapers Ltd (No 2)* [1990] AC 109, 281–82. Lord Walker in *OBG Ltd v Allan* commented that 'The most important single step in the course of the law's recent development has been the speech of Lord Goff of Chieveley in *Attorney-General v Guardian Newspapers Ltd (No 2)*': [2007] UKHL 21, para 272.

[40] *AG v Guardian Newspapers Ltd (No 2)* [1990] AC 109, 255.

[41] *Hellewell v Chief Constable of Derbyshire* [1995] 1 WLR 804 at 807, opining that publishing a photo taken with a telephoto lens of a private act would amount to as much of a breach of confidence as finding a letter or diary in which the private act was recounted.

[42] *Douglas and Others v Hello! Ltd (No 1)* [2001] QB 967, 1012 per Keene LJ.

Earl Spencer v United Kingdom,[43] the action for breach of confidence provided the most flexible basis for protecting privacy rights even before the HRA 1998 came into force and was able to accommodate a Convention-style balancing process between private information and freedom of expression. On this basis, an action which sought to protect both commercial secrets and personally confidential information could be extended to the wrongful disclosure of private information.

i. From Douglas to Campbell: Absorbing Articles 8 and 10 into Breach of Confidence

In *Douglas v Hello! Ltd*,[44] this opportunity was grasped by the Court of Appeal. While their Lordships differed in approach, all agreed that the action for breach of confidence could apply even if the information had been gathered by an intruder with whom no relationship of confidence had been established. Sedley LJ perhaps went furthest in holding that English law has reached a point 'at which it can be said with confidence that the law recognises and will appropriately protect a right of personal privacy'.[45] This was attributed to the flexibility of the common law and the impact of the HRA 1998 which, in his view, required the courts to take into account Article 8 ECHR by virtue of the court being a 'public authority' under section 6 of the Act. Such open acceptance of strong indirect horizontal effect has rarely been followed.[46] Nevertheless, it is clear that the courts have sought to develop a form of breach of confidence which protects the fundamental value of personal autonomy inherent in the right to privacy. Keene LJ recognised that whatever label is attached to the cause of action, this new form of breach of confidence was distinct from the traditional action which sought to protect confidential information arising from commercial and employment relationships.[47]

The significance of Convention rights in this process was highlighted by Lord Woolf CJ in *A v B plc*:[48]

> [A]rticles [8 and 10 ECHR] have provided new parameters within which the court will decide, in an action for breach of confidence, whether a person is entitled to have his privacy protected by the court or whether the restriction of freedom of expression which such protection involves cannot be justified . . . The court is able to achieve this by absorbing the rights which articles 8 and 10 protect into the long-established action for breach of confidence. This involves giving a new strength and breadth to the action so that it accommodates the requirements of those articles.

[43] *Earl Spencer v United Kingdom* (1998) 25 EHRR CD 105 (photograph of Lady Spencer in private clinic). Contrast, however, *Peck v United Kingdom (44647/98)* (2003) 36 EHRR 41.

[44] *Douglas (No 1)* (n 42). See N Moreham, '*Douglas and Others v Hello! Ltd*: The Protection of Privacy in English Private Law' (2001) 65 *Modern Law Review* 767.

[45] *Douglas (No 1)* (n 42) 997.

[46] See, however, Baroness Hale in *Campbell* (n 3) para 132 who openly supported strong indirect horizontal effect, but contrast Lord Nicholls in the same case, para 18 who found it unnecessary to address this 'controversial question'.

[47] *Douglas (No 1)* (n 42) 1012.

[48] *A v B plc* [2002] EWCA Civ 337; [2003] QB 195, para 4.

A new form of the action for breach of confidence was thus developed in which a relationship of confidence (required under the traditional form) was replaced by recognition of the Article 8 right that 'Everyone has the right to respect for his private and family life, his home and his correspondence'. This is, however, a qualified right and restrictions would thus be permitted where they pursue a legitimate aim, are justified by a pressing social need and are proportionate.[49] Further, while the House of Lords in *Wainwright v Home Office*[50] continued to reject any broad privacy action, the new breach of confidence action would protect one particular aspect of privacy: wrongful disclosure of private information.

The House of Lords in *Campbell v Mirror Group Newspapers Ltd*[51] confirmed that there had been 'a shift in the centre of gravity of the action for breach of confidence when it is used as a remedy for the unjustified publication of personal information'. In this case, supermodel Naomi Campbell had sought damages against a newspaper for publishing articles disclosing her treatment for drug addiction with photographs taken covertly of her in a street leaving a group therapy meeting. The House of Lords found that having previously denied publicly taking drugs, the newspaper had been entitled to publish the fact of her drug addiction, but that (by a majority)[52] it had gone too far in publishing details of her therapy and publishing photographs which, although taken in a public place, added to the overall intrusion into Campbell's private life. In determining whether confidence has been breached, Lord Nicholls confirmed that the values enshrined in Articles 8 and 10 were now part of the action for breach of confidence; which had shaken off the limiting constraint of the need for an initial confidential relationship; a development 'spurred' by the enactment of the 1998 Act.[53] His Lordship also acknowledged the significant influence of the Convention and Strasbourg jurisprudence in this area over a number of years, now rendered explicit in framing the cause of action which he preferred to call 'the tort of misuse of private information'.[54] The question, therefore, was whether in respect of the disclosed facts the claimant had a reasonable expectation of privacy.[55] A distinction would be drawn between

[49] Art 8.2:

> There shall be no interference by a public authority with the exercise of this right except such as is in accordance with the law and is necessary in a democratic society in the interests of national security, public safety or the economic well-being of the country, for the prevention of disorder or crime, for the protection of health or morals, or for the protection of the rights and freedoms of others.

[50] *Wainwright v Home Office* [2003] UKHL 53, para 35.

[51] *Campbell* (n 3), para 51 per Lord Hoffmann. Appeal to the ECtHR for violation of Art 10 was rejected by a majority of 6:1: *MGN Ltd v United Kingdom* (39401/04) (2011) 53 EHRR 5.

[52] Lord Nicholls and Lord Hoffmann dissenting.

[53] *Campbell* (n 3) paras 11–17.

[54] *Campbell* (n 3) para 16. See, eg, *Cornelius v De Taranto* [2000] EWHC 561 (QB); [2001] EMLR 12. His Lordship also recognised the particular intrusive effect of photographs: 'In general photographs of people contain more information than textual description. That is why they are more vivid. That is why they are worth a thousand words' (para 31); a factor supported in *Von Hannover* (below). See also *Douglas v Hello! Ltd (No 3)* [2005] EWCA Civ 595, paras 84–90.

[55] A test which can be traced back to the Strasbourg cases of *PG and JH v United Kingdom* (44787/98) [2001] ECHR 550, para 57 and *Peck v United Kingdom (44647/98)* (2003) 36 EHRR 719, para 62: see Lord Hope in *Campbell* (n 3) para 122.

identifying whether the information is private and whether it is proportionate to prevent disclosure of such information, having regard to the competing Convention right of freedom of expression.

Campbell thus identified that an existing common law cause of action had been transformed to reflect the framework of Article 8 and 10 rights.[56] Yet while the House of Lords was prepared to recognise the influence of Convention rights both before and after the 1998 Act, it also acknowledged the incremental nature of this development which could be traced back to Lord Goff in *AG v Guardian Newspapers*. To the more cautious Lord Hoffmann, the decision to develop the law to protect an individual's autonomy and dignity reflected both common law and Convention values and illustrated the capacity of the common law to adapt itself to the needs of contemporary life.[57] Nevertheless, the language of debate had changed: from this point analysis would focus on the right to respect for private life and the countervailing right to freedom of expression.[58] Further, despite the specific wording of section 12(4) HRA 1998 which seemed to give particular emphasis to freedom of expression,[59] the House of Lords chose to follow the approach of the ECtHR and confirmed that neither Article 8 nor Article 10 would have pre-eminence over the other.[60] In *Re S (a child)*,[61] Lord Steyn was able to conclude that, in the light of *Campbell*, four propositions could be clearly stated:

> First, neither article has *as such* precedence over the other. Secondly, where the values under the two articles are in conflict, an intense focus on the comparative importance of the specific rights being claimed in the individual case is necessary. Thirdly, the justifications for interfering with or restricting each right must be taken into account. Finally, the proportionality test must be applied to each. For convenience I will call this the ultimate balancing test.

This 'ultimate balancing test' has provided useful guidance to the courts.[62]

A number of points may be noted. Absorption of Articles 8 and 10 ECHR into breach of confidence has produced a new form of the action distinct from traditional breach of confidence and one which betrays the obvious influence of European human rights law. Lord Nicholls in *Douglas v Hello!* in the House of

[56] See also G Phillipson, 'Transforming Breach of Confidence? Towards a Common Law Right of Privacy under the Human Rights Act' (2003) 66 *Modern Law Review* 726.

[57] *Campbell* (n 3) para 50.

[58] See Lord Hope in *Campbell* (n 3) para 86.

[59] 'The court must have particular regard to the importance of the Convention right to freedom of expression'.

[60] See Resolution 1165 (1998) of the Parliamentary Assembly of the Council of Europe, para 11: 'The Assembly reaffirms the importance of everyone's right to privacy, and of the right to freedom of expression, as fundamental to a democratic society. These rights are neither absolute nor in any hierarchical order, since they are of equal value.'

[61] *Re S (a child)* [2004] UKHL 47; [2005] 1 AC 593, para 17 (emphasis in text).

[62] Cited in *McKennitt v Ash* [2006] EWCA Civ 1714, para 46; *Browne v Associated Newspapers Ltd* [2007] EWCA Civ 295, para 39; *Associated Newspapers Ltd v HRH Prince of Wales* [2006] EWCA Civ 1776, para 52.

Lords[63] noted that 'As the law has developed breach of confidence, or misuse of confidential information, now covers two distinct causes of action, protecting *two* different interests: privacy, and secret ("confidential") information. It is important to keep these two distinct.'[64] Secondly, the terminology of 'breach of confidence' continues to be used, despite recognition that it is distinct from the traditional equitable remedy. Finally, while section 2(1) of the Act indicated that the English courts should take into account of Strasbourg case law, the relevant case law at that time was somewhat meagre and gave little guidance, leaving much to the State's margin of appreciation.[65] In particular, the balance between protection of privacy rights and freedom of the press appeared difficult to pin down. Baroness Hale in *Campbell* remarked that:

> It is much less straightforward when two Convention rights are in play, and the proportionality of interfering with one has to be balanced against the proportionality of restricting the other. As each is a fundamental right, there is evidently a 'pressing social need' to protect it. The Convention jurisprudence offers us little help with this. The ECtHR has been concerned with whether the state's interference with privacy (as, for example, in *Z v Finland* (1997) 25 EHRR 371) or a restriction on freedom of expression (as, for example, in *Jersild v Denmark* (1994) 19 EHRR 1, *Fressoz and Roire v France* (2001) 31 EHRR 2, and *Tammer v Estonia* (2001) 37 EHRR 857) could be justified in the particular case. In the national court, the problem of balancing two rights of equal importance arises most acutely in the context of disputes between private persons.[66]

This was, however, about to change.

ii. From Von Hannover (No 1) *to* Von Hannover (No 2)*: Strasbourg Case Law and the 'Tort' of Breach of Confidence*

In June 2004, one month after *Campbell*, the ECtHR gave judgment in *Von Hannover v Germany*[67] in relation to a series of complaints by Princess Caroline of Monaco concerning press photographs taken of her and her husband in public places without her consent. Princess Caroline is a well-known member of the royal family of Monaco, but holds no official role. Many of the photos represented mundane scenes, showing the applicant shopping or alone on a bicycle or on horseback or even tripping over an obstacle at the Monte Carlo Beach Club. The Court held that publication of the photographs infringed her Article 8 right despite the fact that they were taken in public places. There is 'a zone of interaction of a person with

[63] *Douglas v Hello!* [2007] UKHL 21; [2008] 1 AC 1 (more commonly known by the first action in this case: *OBG Ltd v Allan*). The claim by the Douglases against *Hello*! magazine was not in issue in the appeal, to which the Douglases were not parties.

[64] *Douglas* (n 63) para 255 (emphasis added). See also Lord Hoffmann, 'Whatever may have been the position of the Douglases, who, as I mentioned, recovered damages for an invasion of their privacy, *OK!*'s claim is to protect commercially confidential information and nothing more' (para 118).

[65] G Phillipson, 'The Human Rights Act, "Horizontal Effect" and the Common Law: A Bang or a Whimper?' (1999) 62 *Modern Law Review* 824, 841.

[66] As noted by Baroness Hale in *Campbell* (n 3), para 140.

[67] *Von Hannover v Germany* (Application no 59320/00) (2005) 40 EHRR 1.

others, even in a public context, which may fall within the scope of "private life"'.[68] In a passage of particular relevance to the 'ultimate balancing test' outlined above, the Strasbourg court found:

> [T]hat a fundamental distinction needs to be made between reporting facts – even controversial ones – capable of contributing to a debate in a democratic society relating to politicians in the exercise of their functions, for example, and reporting details of the private life of an individual who, moreover, as in this case, does not exercise official functions. While in the former case the press exercises its vital role of 'watchdog' in a democracy by contributing to 'impart[ing] information and ideas on matters of public interest', it does not do so in the latter case.[69]

Here published photos and accompanying commentaries which related exclusively to details of the applicant's private life, of which the sole purpose was to satisfy the curiosity of readers, were not deemed to contribute to any debate of general interest to society despite the applicant being known to the public. On this basis, publication of photographs of celebrities, even when taken in public, could be restricted where publication did not contribute to a debate of general interest. Even the famous should be able to enjoy a 'legitimate expectation' of protection of and respect for their private life.[70] Further, the ECtHR acknowledged that although the wording of Article 8 indicates that it protects individuals against arbitrary interference by public authorities, it also imposes positive obligations on the State to secure respect for private life even in the sphere of private litigation.[71]

Von Hannover appears to go further than *Campbell*. While affirming the role of the courts in protecting privacy rights, the balance is tipped in favour of privacy unless the publication in question relates to a debate of general interest. This may be contrasted with the approach of the House of Lords in *Campbell*, where Baroness Hale questioned whether there was anything essentially private about a supermodel being photographed out shopping for a bottle of milk; a judgment with which Strasbourg would seem to differ.[72] While the court in *Campbell* therefore appeared to accept that some intrusion was the price of celebrity even if it was not a 'high order of freedom of speech',[73] *Von Hannover* indicated a more censorious approach to celebrity photos even when taken in public places. The decision also came soon after Lord Bingham in *R (on the application of Ullah) v Special Adjudicator*[74] stated the so-called 'mirror principle', that is, that in the absence of

[68] *Von Hannover* (n 67), para 50, echoing *Peck v United Kingdom* (44647/98) (2003) 36 EHRR 719, para 57.

[69] *Von Hannover* (n 67) para 63.

[70] *Von Hannover* (n 67) para 69.

[71] *Von Hannover* (n 67) para 57. Nicol J commented in *Ferdinand v MGN Ltd* [2011] EWHC 2454 (QB) that 'it is now beyond argument that it also encompasses a positive obligation to put in place a system to protect an individual's private life from interference by non-state entities such as the media': para 39.

[72] *Campbell* (n 3) para 154. See NA Moreham, 'Privacy in Public Places' (2006) 65 *Cambridge Law Journal* 606.

[73] *Campbell* (n 3) para 154.

[74] *R (on the application of Ullah) v Special Adjudicator* [2004] UKHL 26; [2004] 2 AC 323, para 20.

some special circumstances, the court should follow any clear and constant jurisprudence of the ECtHR.[75] Following *Ullah*, it was inevitable that English courts would look to Strasbourg for authority as to the interpretation of Convention rights. In the words of Lord Bingham, '[t]he duty of national courts is to keep pace with the Strasbourg jurisprudence as it evolves over time: no more, but certainly no less'.[76]

The Court of Appeal in *McKennitt v Ash*[77] thus gave 'respectful attention' to *Von Hannover*, acknowledging that it extended the reach of Article 8 beyond that which had previously been understood, and refused to confine the case to issues of media harassment.[78] Buxton LJ affirmed that while the English courts have to proceed through the tort [sic][79] of breach of confidence, the rules will be found in the jurisprudence of Articles 8 and 10: 'Those articles are now not merely of persuasive or parallel effect but . . . the very content of the domestic tort that the English court has to enforce.'[80] In this light, the view in the earlier case of *A v B*[81] that public figures must expect and accept greater media scrutiny, particularly if acting as a role model whose conduct is emulated by others, was deemed suspect. In a questionable application of the doctrine of precedent, Buxton LJ ruled that, in not citing Convention authority in applying the balancing exercise, *A v B* could no longer be regarded as binding authority on the contents of Articles 8 and 10 and therefore it was appropriate to look to *Von Hannover* instead.[82] Such comments have led commentators to suggest that judicial support can be identified for granting the HRA 1998 direct horizontal effect in privacy claims.[83] It is important, however, not to get carried away. McKennitt had a clear claim for breach of confidence, indeed she could argue that the disclosures by her former friend in her book, *Travels with Loreena McKennitt: My Life as a Friend*, were covered by traditional breach of confidence rules. The Court conceded that McKennitt did not need to go anywhere near *Von Hannover* to establish her case.[84] Further the judgment of Buxton LJ in *McKennitt v Ash* is most useful in providing a clear articulation of the two stage test for liability, namely:

[75] *Campbell* was decided on 6 May 2004, *Ullah* on 17 June 2004 and *Von Hannover* on 24 June 2004.
[76] *Ullah* (n 74) at para 20.
[77] *McKennitt v Ash* [2006] EWCA Civ 1714; [2008] QB 73.
[78] *McKennitt* (n 77) para 41, relying on *Sciacca v Italy* (Application 50774/99) (2006) 43 EHRR 20, paras 27 and 29.
[79] Buxton LJ here misquoted the Court of Appeal in *Douglas v Hello (No 3)* [2005] EWCA Civ 595; [2006] QB 125, para 53 which had, in fact, referred to the 'action for breach of confidence'. The Court in that case went further at para 96 concluding that 'the cause of action of breach of confidence means that it does not fall to be treated as a tort under English law'.
[80] *McKennitt* (n 77) para 11. Contrast this view with his Lordship's pre-HRA view, expressed extrajudicially in R Buxton, 'The Human Rights Act and Private Law' (2000) 116 *Law Quarterly Review* 48.
[81] *A v B plc* (n 48).
[82] *McKennitt* (n 77) para 64.
[83] N Moreham, 'Privacy and Horizontality: Relegating the Common Law' (2007) 123 *Law Quarterly Review* 373. See also TDC Bennett, 'Horizontality's New Horizons: Re-Examining Horizontal Effect: Privacy, Defamation and the Human Rights Act: Part 1' (2010) 21 *Entertainment Law Review* 96 and J Morgan, '*Hello*! Again: Privacy and Breach of Confidence' (2005) 64 *Cambridge Law Journal* 549.
[84] *McKennitt* (n 77) para 37.

(i) Is the information private in the sense that it is in principle protected by Article 8? (the reasonable expectation of privacy test).

If no, that is the end of the case. If yes, then,

(ii) In all the circumstances, must the interest of the owner of the private information yield to the right of freedom of expression conferred on the publisher by Article 10? (the 'balancing exercise').[85]

While such a test lacks detail, the courts have found it to provide a valuable framework on which to build. Subsequent case law has thus established that some information, such as that contained in Prince Charles' private diaries, will obviously be private.[86] In less obvious cases, the Court of Appeal advised in *Murray v Express Newspapers plc*[87] that a broad approach should be taken which takes account of all the circumstances of the case. These include the attributes of the claimant, the nature of the activity in which the claimant was engaged, the place at which the invasion of privacy occurred, the nature and purpose of the intrusion, the absence of consent and whether it was known or could be inferred, the effect on the claimant, and the circumstances in which and the purposes for which the information came into the hands of the publisher.[88] In *Murray*, the fact that the claimant was a child of 19 months, who had been photographed in the street without his parents' consent, was deemed a relevant concern. Equally the courts will take account of any pre-existing relationship of confidence.[89]

In determining the 'balancing exercise' at stage (ii), the courts have recognised the need for proportionality in qualifying one right against another. This will require an intense focus on the facts. Lord Phillips MR in the *Prince of Wales* case noted that the views of the Strasbourg court were helpful here; *Von Hannover* drawing a distinction between reporting private information capable of contributing to a public debate and that which does not.[90] The content of the article, therefore, whether it is a matter of political debate or mere 'tittle-tattle', will be important in determining whether the publication contributes to a general debate of legitimate public interest.[91] His Lordship also noted an important public interest in the observance of duties of confidence.[92] There is also a 'public interest' in exposing the truth and putting the record straight, as seen in *Campbell*.[93]

[85] *McKennitt v Ash* [2008] QB 73, para 11.

[86] *HRH Prince of Wales v Associated Newspapers Ltd* [2006] EWCA Civ 1776, para 25. Sexual activity between consenting adults on private property is also generally deemed private: *Mosley v News Group Newspapers Ltd* [2008] EWHC 1777 (QB), para 98; *Ntuli v Donald* [2010] EWCA Civ 1276, [2011] EMLR 10.

[87] *Murray v Express Newspapers plc* [2008] EWCA Civ 446; [2009] Ch 481.

[88] *Murray* (n 87) para 36.

[89] See *McKennitt* (n 62) para 15; *Browne v Associated Newspapers Ltd* [2007] EWCA Civ 295; [2008] QB 103 (mere fact of a pre-existing relationship is not enough and will depend on the particular item of information in question which may extend to business activities).

[90] *HRH Prince of Wales v Associated Newspapers Ltd* [2006] EWCA Civ 1776, paras 50–51.

[91] *Campbell* (n 3) para 148 per Baroness Hale.

[92] *Prince of Wales* (n 90) para 67: 'a significant element to be weighed in the balance is the importance in a democratic society of upholding duties of confidence that are created between individuals.' See also *McKennitt* (n 62) para 15.

[93] *Campbell* (n 3) paras 24, 58 and 151.

Murray did, however, bring to the fore the question of the relationship between *Von Hannover* and *Campbell* in applying this two-fold test. JK Rowling's son had been photographed in a public street on a family outing to a café; an everyday occurrence in family life. The Court focused on the right of the child (as distinct from his famous mother) to respect for privacy which would be judged in the particular circumstances of this case. Notably, however, the Court held itself under the doctrine of precedent to be bound by *Campbell*, not *Von Hannover*.[94] Both cases were, in any event, distinguished; the court finding it arguable that a child had a reasonable expectation of privacy, particularly in the light of increasing recognition of the rights of children in many different contexts.[95] The Court nevertheless concluded that it had little doubt that the Strasbourg court would have reached the same decision on the assumed facts. Subsequent case law has affirmed that in balancing Article 8 and 10 rights, particular weight will be given to the rights of any children likely to be affected by the publication, even when the publication relates to private information relating to their parent[96] or step-parent.[97]

Post *Campbell*, therefore, the English courts have adopted a more explicit focus on Articles 8 and 10 ECHR in framing the action for breach of confidence/misuse of private information. By deeming these Articles to give the 'content' to the action, it becomes a logical necessity to consider rulings of the ECtHR. *Von Hannover* has received particular attention, appearing at a time when the English courts were seeking to establish a test for determining when the right to informational privacy has been breached. As such, this seems, therefore, a clear example of Europeanisation where the English courts are actively turning to Strasbourg for guidance how to develop English law. Yet, as Moreham suggests in her commentary on *McKennitt*, the reality is less clear-cut. Strasbourg case law rarely gives the detailed guidance needed to formulate common law 'rules'.[98] In particular, the Strasbourg court has been reluctant to identify specific categories into which private life can be divided or principles on which its decisions are based.[99] Lord Mance has equally commented that *Von Hannover* gives little assistance in determining how to deal with the middle ground between serious political debate and

[94] *Murray* [2008] EWCA Civ 446, para 20, following *Kay v Lambeth LBC* [2006] UKHL 10; [2006] 2 AC 465 that, in the event of a conflict between a decision of the Supreme Court and the ECtHR, lower courts must follow the former.

[95] *Murray* (n 94) para 57: 'the law should indeed protect children from intrusive media attention, at any rate to the extent of holding that a child has a reasonable expectation that he or she will not be targeted in order to obtain photographs'.

[96] *K v News Group Newspapers Ltd* [2011] EWCA Civ 439; [2011] 1 WLR 1827. Comment: TDC Bennett, 'The Relevance and Importance of Third Party Interests in Privacy Cases' (2011) 127 *Law Quarterly Review* 531, who notes the reference to the protection of children's rights in international law.

[97] *Rocknroll v News Group Newspapers Ltd* [2013] EWHC 24 (Ch): grave risk of children being subjected to teasing or ridicule at school about behaviour of their new step-father, which might damage the relationship he was trying to establish with them.

[98] Moreham, 'Privacy and Horizontality' (n 83) 376.

[99] NA Moreham, 'The Right to Respect for Private Life in the European Convention on Human Rights: A Re-Examination' [2008] *European Human Rights Law Review* 44, 45: 'The right is ill-defined and amorphous'.

invasive photography of mundane personal activities.[100] This gives the courts maximum flexibility but, from a common law perspective, at the price of uncertainty. The risk of over-reliance on the Strasbourg Court has also been emphasised recently in the Court's 2012 decision in *Von Hannover v Germany (No 2)*[101] where Princess Caroline of Monaco brought a further complaint of media intrusion and the publication of photographs without her consent. While the Grand Chamber maintained that an initial essential criterion was that the photos or articles in the press contributed to a debate of general interest, it found that a photograph of the applicants on a skiing holiday accompanied by an article regarding the health of Princess Caroline's father, Prince Rainier of Monaco, did not violate Article 8. It was not 'unreasonable' of the national court to find that the photos in question contributed to some degree to a debate of general interest: how the prince's children reconciled their obligations of family solidarity with the legitimate needs of their private life. The Court side-stepped the argument that this would encourage the media to circumvent privacy rules by linking intrusive photographs to some event of contemporary interest, arguing that any such practice could be met by bringing a case in the appropriate national court. The Court further emphasised the margin of appreciation awarded to the Contracting State in determining whether and to what extent an interference with freedom of expression is necessary. It emphasised that while the Strasbourg court has a supervisory function, its task is not to act as an appeal court but to review, in the light of the case as a whole, whether national decisions are compatible with the relevant provisions of the Convention.[102] As Pillans has remarked, any English lawyer hoping that the Grand Chamber would 'lay down the law' on privacy and intrusion and give clear guidance will have been very disappointed by this decision.[103]

Combined with the *Axel Springer AG v Germany* decision,[104] these decisions seem to suggest a far more generous approach to freedom of expression than that previously stated in *Von Hannover (No 1)* and greater deference to the national court.[105] This does raise difficulties, however, for common lawyers seeking to apply *Von Hannover (No 1)* as part of the test in English law. If the Strasbourg court is now prepared to take a broader view of the question of matters of 'public debate', how is an English court supposed to apply this test on a day-to-day basis? Again, English lawyers find themselves struggling with the very nature of Convention case law

[100] J Mance, 'Human Rights, Privacy and the Public Interest: Who Draws the Line and Where?' (2009) 30 *Liverpool Law Review* 263, 278.

[101] *Von Hannover v Germany (No 2)* (40660/08) (2012) 55 EHRR 15.

[102] *Von Hannover (No 2)* (n 101) para 105.

[103] B Pillans, 'Private Lives in St Moritz: *Von Hannover v Germany (No 2)*' [2012] *Communications Law* 63, 66.

[104] *Axel Springer AG v Germany* (39954/08) (2012) 55 EHRR 6 (decision released the same day as *Von Hannover (No 2)*). The Grand Chamber noted that 'Where the balancing exercise between those two rights [Arts 8 and 10] has been undertaken by the national authorities in conformity with the criteria laid down in the Court's case law, the Court would require strong reasons to substitute its view for that of the domestic courts': para 88.

[105] See E Reid, 'Rebalancing Privacy and Freedom of Expression' (2012) 16 *Edinburgh Law Review* 253.

which treats the Convention as a 'living instrument' to be developed in the light of contemporary conditions. More positively, Pillans suggests that the margin of appreciation recognised in *Von Hannover (No 2)* strongly supports the position that current English privacy law is compatible with Convention rights.

The *McKennitt* twofold test has thus been given content by the courts in establishing factors relevant to both parts of the test. This is consistent with guidance from Strasbourg,[106] but in building a test based on factors identified incrementally by case law this is also very much a common law approach. The case law of the European Court will be relevant and *Von Hannover (No 1)* has had a particular impact on the English courts, but, it will be recalled, will not be binding if in conflict with English authority. The result is a hybrid action: a new action, developed incrementally from the equitable action for breach of confidence, but now with its own framework and 'European' character in that its content is based on Articles 8 and 10, ECHR. The question remains: how does this European/common law hybrid action fit into the English common law? In examining the Europeanisation of English *tort* law, are we looking at a tort, a principle of equity or some other form of action?

II. A 'Euro' Tort of Misuse of Private Information?

As noted above, despite the description of liability as the tort of misuse of private information in *Campbell*,[107] the courts have been reluctant to relinquish the label of 'breach of confidence', albeit with an implicit understanding that this label is not to be taken too seriously and that we are really dealing with a new distinct form of 'breach of confidence' which protects informational privacy. Indeed, 'original' breach of confidence will still be relevant where the claimant is not in a position to invoke Article 8.[108] Lord Phillips MR in *Douglas v Hello! Ltd* concluded that:

> [I]n so far as private information is concerned, we are required to adopt, as the vehicle for performing such duty as falls on the courts in relation to Convention rights, the cause of action formerly described as breach of confidence . . . We cannot pretend that we find it satisfactory to be required to shoe-horn within the cause of action of breach of confidence claims for publication of unauthorised photographs of a private occasion.[109]

Such a comment is revealing in that it indicates both that the courts are uncomfortable with the 'breach of confidence' label, but also that they believe that they

[106] See, eg, the criteria for the balancing exercise set out in *Von Hannover (No 2)* paras 108–13. *Axel Springer* (n 104) added two further criteria: the method of obtaining information and its veracity; severity of sanction imposed on the publisher: paras 93 and 95.

[107] *Campbell* (n 3) para 14 per Lord Nicholls.

[108] For instance in relation to commercial information. See *Ferdinand v MGN Ltd* [2011] EWHC 2454 (QB) para 106 per Nicol J.

[109] *Douglas v Hello! Ltd* (n 54), para 53.

are committed to this vehicle to protect privacy rights. This section of the chapter will argue that this compromise solution – the so-called 'tort' of breach of confidence[110] – does the law no justice at all. To continue to utilise such a misleading label almost 15 years after the implementation of the HRA 1998 portrays the English judiciary as conservative and still tied to the old causes of action.[111] Articles 8 and 10 ECHR do not focus on betrayals of confidences, but on protecting the claimant's right to informational privacy as an aspect of his or her own individual wellbeing. The action seeks to protect personal dignity and integrity.[112] Logically, therefore, the time has come to recognise the true nature of this action by simply changing the label from 'tort of breach of confidence' to 'tort of misuse of private information'.

Such analysis should not be dismissed as a mere academic desire for conceptual neatness. As seen in chapter four, classification may affect the very nature of the cause of action. By confusing the equitable action for breach of confidence with a tort of breach of confidence, the law fails to give guidance on basic questions such as to which remedies are available (those in equity or those in tort?) and other procedural rules. While the question of limitation is unlikely to be a problem in this context (claimants generally acting immediately to protect their privacy),[113] in *Douglas*, classification of the cause of action did make a difference. In ruling that the action was part of breach of confidence, the Court held with some reluctance that the choice of law provisions for determining issues relating to tort would not apply to this cause of action.[114] Further, while the courts have, by necessity, been required to determine the nature of injunctive relief in this context – holding in *Cream Holdings Ltd v Banerjee*[115] that the test for interim injunctive relief was distinct from that of defamation – the question of assessment of damages remains under-analysed. This is partly due to the nature of the claims themselves and the fact that, as Eady J has commented, 'an infringement of privacy

[110] This term can be traced back to Sedley LJ in *Douglas (No 1)* (n 42) 998.

[111] Contrast the approach of the majority of the New Zealand Court of Appeal in *Hosking v Runting* [2004] NZCA 34; [2005] 1 NZLR 1 where Tipping J commented that

> it is more jurisprudentially straightforward and easier of logical analysis to recognise that the confidence and privacy, while capable of overlapping, are essentially different concepts . . . While it may be possible to achieve the same substantive result by developing the equitable cause of action, I consider it legally preferable and better for society's understanding of what the Courts are doing to achieve the appropriate substantive outcome under a self-contained and stand-alone common law cause of action to be known as invasion of privacy (para 246).

Note, however, that the majority came to a more restrictive view of privacy rights than that adopted by the Court of Appeal in the JK Rowling case.

[112] *Browne v Associated Newspapers Ltd* [2007] EWCA Civ 295; [2008] QB 103, para 34; *Von Hannover v Germany* (2005) 40 EHRR 1, para 50. As Lord Hoffmann stated in *Campbell* (n 3), 'What human rights law has done is to identify private information as something worth protecting as an aspect of human autonomy and dignity': para 50.

[113] In any event, the limitation period would be six years on either the basis of tort or breach of confidence. Nevertheless, it might be argued that a more focused analysis would raise the question whether it should be confined to one year in common with defamation and indeed the HRA 1998 itself.

[114] *Douglas v Hello! Ltd* [2005] EWCA Civ 595, para 96.

[115] *Cream Holdings Ltd v Banerjee* [2004] UKHL 44; [2005] 1 AC 253.

cannot ever be effectively compensated by a monetary award'.[116] Yet, while the primary remedy in these cases is almost always an injunction, the courts do have jurisdiction to award damages in addition or in lieu. The courts have in any event awarded damages in a number of cases after publication of the information in question.[117] In *Mosley v News Group Newspapers Ltd*,[118] the court was prepared to award £60,000 in view of the injury to feelings, embarrassment and distress caused by publication, which included the placing of video extracts on the newspaper's website of private sexual activities in which the claimant was involved. This included aggravated damages,[119] but not exemplary (or punitive) damages. Again, this raises the question of the relationship between equitable breach of confidence (where exemplary damages may not be awarded) and tort (where they may).[120] In rejecting the claim for exemplary damages in this context, Eady J acknowledged that it remained a matter for speculation whether a future Supreme Court would follow Lord Nicholls' classification of invasion of privacy as a tort and concluded that, on the authorities as they stood, it would be something of a 'departure' for a first instance judge to award such damages. This ignores the obvious analogy with tort law where exemplary damages are awarded, notably in defamation actions where the publisher has deliberately published untrue statements calculated to make a profit in excess of any compensatory damages payable.[121] In view of the fact that the Leveson Inquiry has recommended that exemplary damages should be available for actions for breach of privacy in addition to defamation,[122] it remains to be seen whether a future court would continue to reject the possibility of exemplary damages in this context.

Further remedial uncertainty may be identified in the context of an award of account of profits. In *Douglas*, the court readily accepted that if Hello! Ltd had made a profit on the publication, the Douglases would have been entitled to seek

[116] *Mosley* (n 86) para 231.

[117] In *Campbell* (n 46) 22, the House of Lords restored the order for £3,500 damages to compensate Ms Campbell for the invasion of her informational privacy and injury to her feelings (£2,500 compensatory/£1,000 aggravated damages), but, as Clarke notes, no effort was made to discuss the jurisdictional basis of a compensatory monetary remedy: L Clarke, 'Remedial Responses to Breach of confidence: The Question of Damages' (2005) 24 *Civil Justice Quarterly* 316, 330.

[118] *Mosley v News Group Newspapers Ltd* [2008] EWHC 1777 (QB); [2008] EMLR 20. See also *McKennitt* (n 62) (£5,000). In *Mosley v United Kingdom* (48009/08) (2011) 53 EHRR 30, the ECtHR rejected Mosley's argument that Art 8 ECHR required a prior notification rule by which newspapers, intending to publish details of an individual's private life, must notify the individual in advance and thereby give him or her the opportunity to apply for an interlocutory injunction to block publication. See C Hunt, 'Strasbourg on Privacy Injunctions' (2011) 70 *Cambridge Law Journal* 489 who argues that the need for such a rule is clear.

[119] The court noted that the video footage of the claimant had been freely accessible on the *News of the World*'s website and that it had persisted in its reference to the unproven Nazi allegations.

[120] *Rookes v Barnard* [1964] AC 1129.

[121] In *Cassell v Broome* [1972] AC 1027, for example, the House of Lords held that the court should investigate whether the defendant was aware of the fact that what he was planning to do was against the law (or had shown reckless disregard as to whether the proposed conduct was legal or illegal) and had nevertheless decided to carry on because the prospects of material advantage outweighed the prospects of material loss. See also *John v MGN Ltd* [1997] QB 586 at 618 *per* Bingham MR.

[122] *An Inquiry into the Culture, Practices and Ethics of the Press: Executive Summary* (November 2012) para 72: www.official-documents.gov.uk/document/hc1213/hc07/0779/0779.pdf

an account of that profit.[123] Account of profits is, however, as an equitable remedy more readily associated with the traditional action of breach of confidence than tort law. It is widely acknowledged to be available for equitable wrongs such as passing off, infringement of trademarks, and copyrights and patents.[124] Its role in the law of tort is far more controversial. Current authority indicates that account of profits (or restitutionary damages) will only be awarded for torts protecting intellectual property rights such as passing off,[125] with some indication that it may extend to torts which involve the misappropriation of property rights more generally, such as trespass to land or conversion. There is, in contrast, clear authority excluding this remedy for torts such as nuisance and breach of statutory duty.[126] On this basis, unless the misuse of private information could be classified as interference with a proprietary right – which at present seems unlikely[127] – account of profits should not be awarded for this tort.[128] Again this point has not been directly addressed by the courts. Clarke has convincingly argued that the claim for monetary remedies based on gain to the defendant, rather than loss to the claimant, should be restricted to claims where there is a relationship of confidence between the parties:

> '[B]reach of confidence', as developed by the House of Lords in *Campbell*, has become another civil law wrong, where the remedy must compensate for loss to the claimant, not strip profit from the defendant. Instead of trying to find some jurisdictional basis for awarding compensation for an equitable wrong, instead we should drop the categorisation of breach of confidence as an equitable cause of action, recognise it as a civil wrong, and award compensatory remedies. Only where there is a further interest in preserving relationships of trust and confidence, so that we wish to prevent the wrong occurring at all, is there a justification for a strict deterrent action, based on profit-stripping.[129]

The issue here is that it is difficult to respond to questions relating to the assessment of damages and other procedural matters without a clear understanding of whether we are dealing with an equitable cause of action or a form of tort law. The current obfuscation as to the classification of the cause of action renders answering such basic questions more problematic than it needs to be. The courts are

[123] *Douglas* (n 114) para 249.

[124] See *Attorney General v Blake* [2000] UKHL 45; [2001] 1 AC 268, 279 per Lord Nicholls.

[125] A Burrows, *The Law of Restitution*, 3rd edn (Oxford, Oxford University Press, 2011) 646.

[126] See *Stoke-on-Trent City Council v W & J Wass Ltd* (No 1) [1988] 1 WLR 1406; *Forsyth-Grant v Allen* [2008] EWCA Civ 505; [2008] Env LR 41 [rejected for tort of nuisance]; *Devenish Nutrition Ltd v Sanofi-Aventis SA* [2008] EWCA Civ 1086; [2009] Ch 390 [rejected for tort of breach of statutory duty].

[127] *Douglas No 3* (n 114) paras 118–19.

[128] See Arden LJ in *Devenish Nutrition* (n 126) para 2. The Court of Appeal in *Walsh v Shanahan* [2013] EWCA Civ 411 nevertheless asserted that account of profits could be awarded for the tort of misuse of information, applying it, however, in the context of a traditional breach of confidence action.

[129] Clarke, 'Remedial Responses' (n 117) 335. See also D Friedmann, 'The Protection of Entitlements via the Law of Restitution: Expectancies and Privacy '(2005) 121 *Law Quarterly Review* 400, 417: under the 'restitution for wrongs' approach the prospects of recovering in restitution for the invasion of privacy, even if the invasion is regarded as a tort, do not seem particularly bright. Contra: N Witzleb, 'Justifying Gain-based Remedies for Invasion of Privacy' (2009) 29 *Oxford Journal of Legal Studies* 325.

unlikely to reach a clearly reasoned answer to the question whether exemplary damages or account of profits are suitable remedies to this action without understanding the nature of the action itself.

A. Why Obfuscate?

The obvious question to ask is: why have the courts been so reluctant to acknowledge openly this new cause of action? As seen above, the current position is confusing (in that the courts refer intermittently to the action as based in equity, tort or a mixture of both) and threatens its coherent legal development. It would seem logical, therefore, to recognise a new tort of misuse of private information which focuses upon the protection of human autonomy and dignity.

One primary reason for the courts' reluctance is that they do not wish to be seen to make new law. This was evident before the Act when the Court of Appeal in *Kaye* expressed its dissatisfaction with the failure of the common law to protect privacy rights and asked the legislator to intervene. The HRA 1998 did mark some limited intervention by the legislature, but the Act makes no explicit reference to any form of horizontal effect,[130] and Lord Irvine indicated that it would be for the courts to develop incrementally existing protection for privacy rights. This, as we have seen, has occurred. The courts have, however, been careful to proceed cautiously and avoid becoming embroiled in the academic debate relating to the horizontal effect of the HRA. Phillipson has argued that such evasion is at least semi-deliberate and reflects the inevitable ambivalence of the judiciary when faced with a statute which seeks to allow an international treaty to penetrate into the common law, thereby threatening traditional common law reasoning and the judiciary's autonomy in developing it.[131] The unwillingness of the House of Lords to grant leave to appeal in a number of decisions on the question of privacy also indicates a degree of caution, which favours the gradual incremental development of the law.[132] This ensures that the judges are not seen to 'make' law. As Eady J stated in *Mosley*, 'it is not simply a matter of "unaccountable" judges running amok.'[133] The courts have no intention of creating a new and untested tort and a number of judges have openly rejected direct horizontal effect in favour of developing the breach of confidence action.[134] Somewhat ironically, advocates of direct horizontal effect, such as Bennett, have served only to underline the need for such caution by arguing that there should be a wide-ranging, overarching action for

[130] Phillipson, 'The Human Rights Act' (n 65) 825, has commented that 'the Act's impact on the common law governing relations between private persons is prima facie its area of greater obscurity'.

[131] G Phillipson, 'Clarity Postponed: Horizontal Effect after *Campbell*' in H Fenwick, G Phillipson and R Masterman (eds), *Judicial Reasoning under the UK Human Rights Act* (Cambridge, Cambridge University Press, 2007).

[132] See, eg, *McKennitt* (n 62).

[133] *Mosley* (n 86) para 7.

[134] See, eg, Baroness Hale (with whom Lord Carswell agreed) in *Campbell* (n 46) para 132: 'The 1998 Act does not create any new cause of action between private persons.'

'unlawful interference with Article 8 rights'.[135] The prospect of such a dramatic change to the existing structure of the law is unlikely to find favour with the common law judiciary, characterised by Sedley LJ as having a 'perennial need (for the best of reasons, that of legal certainty) to appear not to be doing anything for the first time'.[136] Fear of opening the floodgates of liability, uncontrolled privacy rights, confronting an angry press (or, more positively, being seen to undermine the right to a free press) and exceeding the delicate balance between judge and legislator all contribute to discouraging the English courts from such bold intervention. There is little indication that the English courts are ready or willing to embrace a general tort of breach of privacy at present.

In this light, it is easy to see why the current position might seem attractive to the judiciary. The courts are able to respond to claimants' needs and protect Article 8 rights (in relation to informational privacy at least) without causing a major change to the existing legal framework. Breach of confidence had been developed by the common law courts to provide broader protection for private information prior to the HRA 1998 and the courts have simply accelerated this process, with the deemed approval of Parliament which enacted the HRA. This poses no threat to the separation of powers or the current remedial framework. Yet post *Von Hannover*, the English courts have become increasingly frank as to how the law has changed. In *McKennitt v Ash* and subsequent case law, the courts have formulated a test based on the balancing of Articles 8 and 10 ECHR. Reference is made to Strasbourg case law and Strasbourg doctrines such as proportionality. Equally, the term 'tort' is appearing regularly in judgments, admittedly often as the 'tort' of breach of confidence, suggesting a move towards recognition of a basis in the law of tort. The genie is escaping the bottle, despite the initial caution of the courts. There is now a cause of action which seeks to protect the personal autonomy and dignity of an individual from unwarranted intrusions into his or her right to informational privacy.

It is submitted, therefore, that consistently with the incremental approach adopted by the courts, the next step is to recognise that this new action, previously called 'breach of confidence', is part of English tort law. It has evolved, with the assistance of the HRA 1998 and in the light of the ECHR, from traditional breach of confidence into the tort of breach of confidence[137] and the final stage in its development is to recognise it as a tort of misuse of private information. A limited tort of informational privacy or misuse of private information will provide the law with a clearer framework, permitting it to develop in a controlled environment with the added certainty of an existing tort law framework. This is not radi-

[135] TDC Bennett, 'Horizontality's New Horizons – Re-Examining Horizontal Effect: Privacy, Defamation and the Human Rights Act: Part 1' (2010) 21 *Entertainment Law Review* 96 and TDC Bennett, 'Horizontality's New Horizons – Re-Examining Horizontal Effect: Privacy, Defamation and the Human Rights Act: Part 2' (2010) 21 *Entertainment Law Review* 145.

[136] *Douglas (No 1)* (n 42) 997.

[137] See, eg, R Clayton and H Tomlinson, 'The Human Rights Act and Its Impact on the Law of Tort' in TT Arvind and J Steele, *Tort Law and the Legislature: Common Law, Statute and the Dynamics of Legal Change* (Oxford, Hart Publishing, 2012) 446.

cal law-making, but simply the next logical step in a process that can be traced back to *AG v Guardian Newspapers*. One of the strengths of the common law is its adaptability to social change and this seems a good opportunity to demonstrate this strength.

B. A Euro-Tort?

One last question remains. Bearing in mind the influence of Convention rights noted in this chapter, to what extent would this new tort be shaped by European human rights law? The very content of the tort, we are told, is provided by Articles 8 and 10 ECHR and concepts such as 'proportionality' and 'reasonable expectation of privacy' owe much to the Strasbourg court. This question is implicit in the *Mosley* case where one of the reasons given by Eady J for rejecting an award of exemplary damages was that such damages were likely to be incompatible with Article 10.2 in that they are neither prescribed by law nor necessary in a democratic society where compensatory damages are available. He added that since a claim for invasion of privacy involved the direct application of Convention values, it would be 'somewhat eccentric' to introduce an 'alien anomaly from the common law' in the shape of exemplary damages, bearing in mind they are not granted in Strasbourg.[138] Recognition of the role of the jurisprudence of the ECtHR in shaping English law may also be seen in the judgment of Buxton LJ in *McKennitt v Ash*, discussed above, who expressed his willingness to develop English law with reference to Strasbourg (*Von Hannover*), rather than English (*A v B*), authority.[139]

Yet it is submitted that these judgments overstate the 'Europeanisation' element of the new tort. The comments of Buxton LJ are obiter and Eady J was dealing with the point at first instance. Bearing in mind the difficulties which the courts have experienced in finding definitive answers within Strasbourg jurisprudence, and, in particular, the tendency (discussed in chapter five above) to limit the impact of the Convention in other areas of English tort law, it is unlikely that English courts will suddenly enthusiastically embrace Europeanisation in this context. As previously explained, the generality and fact-specific analysis of the Strasbourg court continue to frustrate common law judges, despite the patient warning of Lord Mance that 'it is perhaps worth remembering expressly that individual section decisions of the court are not, and may not respond well to the same close linguistic analysis that a common lawyer would give to, binding precedents'.[140] The English judiciary may be actively referring to Strasbourg case law and citing it in its judgments, but by its

[138] *Mosley v News Group Newspapers Ltd* [2008] EWHC 1777 (QB), para 196. See *BB v United Kingdom* (2004) 39 EHRR 635, para 36; *Anufrijeva v Southwark London Borough Council* [2003] EWCA Civ 1406; [2004] QB 1124, para 55. This reflects the general position in Continental civil law: see H Koziol and V Wilcox (eds), *Punitive damages: Common Law and Civil Law Perspectives*,Tort and Insurance Law (Vienna, Springer, 2009).

[139] *McKennitt* (n 62) para 64.

[140] *Rabone v Pennine Care NHS Foundation Trust* [2012] UKSC 2; [2012] 2 AC 72, para 123.

very nature, it often fails to give the specific guidance expected of a common law precedent and will require development at national level, which we have seen in cases such as *McKennitt* and *Murray*. The House of Lords in *Kay v Lambeth LBC*[141] has further determined that, in the event of a conflict between a decision of the Supreme Court and the ECtHR, lower courts must follow the Supreme Court. It will therefore be for the English courts to develop this area of law, with reference to the Convention and its jurisprudence, but also buoyed by the margin of appreciation granted to Contracting States by the Strasbourg court itself. In the light of the willingness of the Leveson Inquiry to contemplate exemplary damages, the question perhaps should be characterised not as a matter of European civil law versus the common law, but rather one of legal evolution: will English law continue to follow the path of equitable causes of action or the law of tort? In Australia, for example, which, in contrast to New Zealand[142] continues to adhere to the breach of confidence framework, the Victorian Court of Appeal in *Giller v Procopets*[143] ruled that exemplary damages would not be awarded in equity.[144] It is submitted that acceptance of a tort of misuse of private information would provide a clearer means of resolving this issue, based on principle rather than a technical point of classification.

Conclusion

Commenting extra-judicially in 2009, Lord Mance noted that a narrow view which confined Article 8 privacy rights to claims against public authorities under the HRA 1998 was never a realistic possibility. In his Lordship's view, it was inevitable that, following the HRA, the Convention would have some horizontal effect in the field of privacy.[145] Such a development is consistent with the view of the ECtHR that States have a positive obligation to ensure Article 8 rights of individuals are protected.[146] The result has been the development by the English courts of a private law action protecting privacy rights, at least in the context of misuse of private information. What is interesting from the perspective of Europeanisation is the centrality of Convention rights in this area of English law. Academic analysis as late as 2006 which attempted to draw closer analogies between English and other Commonwealth

[141] *Kay* (n 94).

[142] In *Hosking v Runting* [2004] NZCA 34; [2005] 1 NZLR 1 New Zealand accepted the existence of a free-standing tort of breach of privacy by giving publicity to private and personal information.

[143] *Giller v Procopets* [2008] VSCA 236, para 437, following the decision of the NSW Court of Appeal in *Harris v Digital Pulse Pty Ltd* (2003) 56 NSWLR 298 and citing *Mosley* (n 86).

[144] *Gurry on Breach of Confidence* argues that the claims in both *Mosley* and *Giller* failed due to the lack of authority and that in reality they leave the door open for a higher court to rule in favour of exemplary damages: T Aplin et al, *Gurry on Breach of Confidence*, 2nd edn (Oxford, Oxford University Press 2012) paras 19.38–19.40.

[145] J Mance, 'Human Rights, Privacy and the Public Interest: Who Draws the Line and Where?' (2009) 30 *Liverpool Law Review* 263, 266.

[146] See, eg, *Von Hannover (No 1)* (n 67) para 57.

jurisdictions[147] now seems dated in an environment where the very content of liability is determined with reference to Articles 8 and 10 ECHR and Strasbourg case law. Yet such bold statements contrast with the unwillingness of the English courts to recognise openly the novelty of this legal development. In seeking to retain the label of breach of confidence, the English courts have avoided giving a clear ruling on the question of horizontal effect, much debated by academic commentators.[148] The courts have simply applied Convention rights to private party litigation. Those judges who touch on this point have not done so with one voice. David Hoffman has commented that

> there is no overall theory of how the HRA works horizontally which has received judicial approval, or even been adopted generally – indeed, sometimes the Convention rights are simply applied without any consideration of whether there is an obligation to do so, and whether or not they apply as between individuals. It is not surprising that different courts in different areas have taken different views about what the HRA requires of them, depending on factors such as the level of regulation, the interaction between common law and statute, or the interests at stake.[149]

This leaves the courts with a dilemma. Recognition of a new tort of misuse of private information effectively threatens to bring the issue of horizontal effect into the open. Retaining the label 'breach of confidence' and developing the law incrementally avoids dealing with such issues, but, as seen above, leads to conceptual confusion – a 'tort' of breach of confidence? – and a lack of clarity as to the relationship between traditional and new breach of confidence. Nevertheless, this chapter has shown that the law has evolved following the introduction of the HRA 1998 in October 2000. It is submitted that the English courts are on the brink of recognising a tort of misuse of private information and that this should be the next incremental step. It will, however, be confined to informational privacy. Lord Hoffmann's fears of a 'blockbuster' tort of privacy[150] remain unfounded. As Morgan has observed, by developing the action incrementally from breach of confidence, there is no scope for a wider action protecting non-informational privacy.[151] Recognition of a limited tort would not involve the introduction of any high level generalisation of principle causing uncertainty, but a cause of action which would force the courts to focus more sharply on the relevant purpose and scope of the protection given and remove the 'shadow' of traditional breach of

[147] eg, R Mulheron 'A New Framework for Privacy? A Reply to *Hello!*' (2006) 69 *Modern Law Review* 679, who commented that the impact of the HRA was beyond the scope of the article.

[148] To, it must be said, the frustration of leading academics in this field: See, eg, G Phillipson, 'Privacy: The Development of Breach of Confidence: The Clearest Case of Horizontal Effect?' in D Hoffman (ed), *The impact of the UK Human Rights Act on Private Law* (Cambridge, Cambridge University Press, 2011); G Phillipson and A Williams, 'Horizontal Effect and the Constitutional Constraint' (2011) 74 *Modern Law Review* 878.

[149] D Hoffman, 'Conclusions' in D Hoffman (ed), *The impact of the UK Human Rights Act on Private Law* (Cambridge, Cambridge University Press, 2011) 381.

[150] *Wainwright v Home Office* (n 27) para 18.

[151] J Morgan, 'Privacy, Confidence and Horizontal Effect: "*Hello*" Trouble' (2003) 62 *Cambridge Law Journal* 444, 469.

confidence.[152] Such a tort would, of course, be supplemented by actions against public authorities under the HRA for breaches of Article 8 ECHR (dealing with the scenario in *Wainwright* itself) together with existing statutory and case law provision for other breaches of privacy. It remains an open question whether the courts will continue to push to extend privacy rights beyond this point. Commentators continue to argue for broader protection of privacy rights,[153] but the courts at present seem unwilling to venture further, regarding a broader privacy tort as beyond their constitutional and institutional capacities.[154]

The result is a form of privacy law which is framed in terms of Convention rights, but applied by the common law courts using a methodology which mixes reference to the Strasbourg jurisprudence with the traditional common law incremental development of principle via case law. Such a process may be contrasted with the development of privacy law in other European states which have introduced privacy rights expressly into their Civil Codes[155] or recognised privacy as a right which their Civil Code should protect.[156] Despite the comments of Markesinis, little reference has been made by the English courts to the development of privacy law in other European jurisdictions.[157] While privacy thus remains the most 'European' of the areas of law examined in this book so far, it cannot be denied that the English courts continue to express concerns as to the quality of Strasbourg judgments,[158] and even the merits of a Strasbourg-framed human rights discourse; Lord Hoffmann notably emphasising the need to recognise domestic policy imperatives and expressing concern at the ability of the Strasbourg court to provide useful guidance on issues arising at domestic level.[159]

[152] T Aplin, 'The Future of Breach of Confidence and the Protection of Privacy' (2007) 7 *Oxford University Commonwealth Law Journal* 137, 164. See also CDL Hunt, 'Rethinking surreptitious takings in the law of confidence' [2011] *Intellectual Property Quarterly* 66.

[153] Moreham, for example, argues that 'physical' privacy intrusions which do not involve the publication of private information should be included within the common law action: N Moreham, 'Privacy in the Common Law: A Doctrinal and Theoretical Analysis' (2005) 121 *Law Quarterly Review* 628. See also R Mulheron 'A New Framework for Privacy? A Reply to *Hello!*' (2006) 69 *Modern Law Review* 679.

[154] G Phillipson, 'Privacy: The Development of Breach of Confidence: The Clearest Case of Horizontal Effect?' in D Hoffman (ed), *The Impact of the UK Human Rights Act on Private Law* (Cambridge, Cambridge University Press, 2011) 163.

[155] eg, Art 9 of the French Civil Code, introduced under a statute of 1970 (Act No 70-643 of 17 July 1970). See Errera, 'The Twisted Road' (n 29) 393–99.

[156] See, eg, Germany which, influenced by Arts 2(1) and 1(1) of its Basic Law (*Grundgesetz*), recognised privacy as a right (*Persönlichkeitsrecht*) protected by para 823(1) of its Civil Code in the 1950s: see H-J Cremer, *Human Rights and the Protection of Privacy in Tort Law: A Comparison between English and German Law* (Abingdon, Routledge-Cavendish, 2010).

[157] BS Markesinis, C O'Cinneide, J Fedtke and M Hunter-Henin, 'Concerns and Ideas about the Development of English Law of Privacy (and How Knowledge of Foreign Law Might be of Help)' (2004) 52 *American Journal of Comparative Law* 133.

[158] Recently the former President of the ECtHR conceded that the Strasbourg Court needed to strive for greater clarity and consistency in expressing its judgments to avoid exasperating national judges and that an increased dialogue between judges at national and the European level would be desirable: N Bratza, 'The Relationship between the UK Courts and Strasbourg' (2011) 5 *European Human Rights Law Review* 505, 511.

[159] Lord Hoffmann, 'The Universality of Human Rights' (2009) 125 *Law Quarterly Review* 416.

To conclude, the current legal position rests on an acknowledgement that Parliament, by means of the HRA 1998, gave the courts a green light to construct a new framework to support privacy rights with reference to the ECHR.[160] The equitable action of breach of confidence presented the courts with a cause of action which was flexible enough to bring in the test of balancing Article 8 and 10 ECHR rights with the added benefit of avoiding the need to create a new form of liability. This led to the current legal position: a 'tort' of breach of confidence, shaped by Convention rights, but developed by the common law courts. It may be seen as representing the best and worst of common law legal development – an unwillingness to embrace open change, but at the same time supporting the incremental development of a remedy providing some protection of privacy rights. Perhaps the words of Sedley LJ in *Douglas v Hello! Ltd*, five weeks after the implementation of the HRA 1998, were prophetic of how the common law in this field would develop:

> The common law, and equity with it, grows by slow and uneven degrees. It develops reactively, both in the immediate sense that it is only ever expounded in response to events and in the longer-term sense that it may be consciously shaped by the perceived needs of legal policy . . . Nevertheless, we have reached a point at which it can be said with confidence that the law recognises and will appropriately protect a right of personal privacy.[161]

The fact remains that the best example of the Europeanisation of English tort law identified in this book lacks conceptual coherency and remains tied to traditional causes of action. Further, we might even question whether the courts have indeed accepted this as an area of tort law at all. It seems clear that the role of European human rights law has yet to be embraced by the English tort law community. One case (*Von Hannover (No 1)*) does not a revolution make. It remains to be seen whether recognition of a tort of informational privacy will make a difference and finally make English tort lawyers take human rights more seriously.[162]

[160] See also Hoffman, 'Conclusions' (n 149) 380.
[161] *Douglas (No 1)* (n 42), 997.
[162] Paraphrasing the title of the famous book of the late Professor Dworkin: R Dworkin, *Taking Rights Seriously* (London, Duckworth, 1977).

7

Europeanisation and English Tort Law: The Way Forward

> Relish the opportunity or resent the intrusion, we cannot ignore the fact that European law is here to stay. The real question . . . is how the legal scientist should respond to it.
>
> (David Ibbetson)[1]

The 'Europeanisation' of English tort law has taken place in two ways. Membership of the European Union has led to the introduction of EU law into the domestic legal system and the development of State liability for breaches of EU law. *Francovich* liability has required the courts to integrate a new form of tort liability into the existing tort law framework and represents a cause of action formulated not by the domestic courts, but by the Court of Justice of the European Union (CJEU) itself. The Human Rights Act 1998 has confirmed the importance of rights under the European Convention on Human Rights (ECHR) and has acted as a stimulus for the development of protection of privacy rights (or, at least, of a right to informational privacy). It has further encouraged English judges to consider how tort law should develop alongside public authority liability under sections 6–8 of the Act.

This chapter will seek to draw together the themes of this book. So far this book has examined the challenges of Europeanisation and identified signs of judicial resistance to these new sources of law, considered to threaten the autonomy of English tort law and the common law 'way of doing things'. This final chapter will propose solutions, in particular how the English tort law community, be it lawyers, judges, academics or students, can better understand European influences and respond more positively to the changes they bring. It is indicative of national attitudes that these new sources of law are still labelled 'alien', despite the fact that EU law has been applicable in the UK from 1973 and the UK signed the ECHR in 1951 and brought Convention rights 'home' in 2000. I will argue that a genuine understanding of how Europeanisation has actually influenced English tort law – which I have sought to provide in this book - should lead to an approach which looks forwards rather than backwards to the halcyon days of the 'common law

[1] DJ Ibbetson, 'A Reply to Professor Zimmermann' in TG Watkin, *The Europeanisation of Law* (London, UKNCCL, 1998) 224.

family'. Many English tort lawyers still view themselves as having a closer relationship with other Commonwealth jurisdictions than Continental Europe. Australian Professor, Jane Stapleton, an internationally renowned tort lawyer, wrote in 2007 that 'The common law world seems, at least to me, to be rich enough for most needs of tort practitioners and judges in English-speaking jurisdictions'.[2] However, for tort lawyers based in the UK, the combination of the European Communities Act 1972 and Human Rights Act 1998 signifies that they cannot remain bunkered in the common law world. As shown in chapter two above, this is not an option and adaptation is required to new ways of reasoning and interpreting legislative material. Nevertheless, chapters three to six have raised concerns that there has been a tendency to 'anglicise' these new sources and use common law modes of reasoning to render them more acceptable to the community at large. This has led to the unsatisfactory results, notably new causes of action being labelled 'breach of statutory duty' and 'breach of confidence' despite being conceptually distinct from these traditional causes of action. Chapters three and five have further highlighted a willingness to isolate these new sources of law to avoid cross-infection with existing common law principles of tort law.

Ultimately the question is one of adaptability. If tort law can respond to social change at a domestic level, can it do so in relation to European sources of law? Is the English legal system ready to become part of Europe or will the perception remain of the 'common law' as a bastion against all things European?

I. Finding Solutions

I have argued in this book that English private lawyers need to do more to understand these new sources and should recognise that Europeanisation is not simply a matter for politicians and public lawyers, but private lawyers as well. English private law is not immune from EU or European human rights discourse and lawyers need to engage with these new areas of law. This section will examine ways in which this may be better achieved, ranging from the construction of a new European framework of tort law principles to the adoption of a fresh approach to Europeanisation which will provide a genuine insight into its content and context.

A. A New Framework for European Tort Law

This study has shown that English lawyers find it difficult to use sources of law which differ from those of the traditional common law. It is particularly problematic in an area of law which is largely judge-made and to which legislative

[2] J Stapleton, 'Benefits of Comparative Tort Reasoning: Lost in Translation' (2007) *Journal of Tort Law* 1, 33.

intervention is minimal. English judges must thus master not only new rules of law, but seemingly vaguely drafted Treaty or Convention provisions phrased often in a 'Euro' language with which they are unfamiliar. One proposed solution in the context of EU law has been to draft afresh new principles of European tort law. Here, UK lawyers would join with other EU lawyers to develop a new language of tort law which would be country-neutral and seek to rationalise and improve existing national law. Stimulated by proposals from the 1980s to develop a unified European form of contract law to boost inter-state trade[3] and support from the European Parliament for a European Civil Code,[4] a number of organisations have proposed common principles of tort law derived from the legal traditions of Europe. They have received funding from the European Commission and some national governmental bodies such as Austrian Federal Ministry of Justice and their work has been widely disseminated and translated into a number of European languages. Their aim is to overcome misunderstandings based on national legal traditions and move towards a European understanding of how tort law should operate.

i. The Principles of European Tort Law/Book VI of the Draft Common Frame of Reference

In recent years, the work of the European Group on Tort Law (EGTL), the Study Group on a European Civil Code (SGECC) and the Joint Network on European Private Law has proven to be particularly influential.[5] The EGTL published in 2005 its *Principles of European Tort Law* (PETL).[6] In 2009, the SGECC published the final version of its own set of principles relating to 'non-contractual liability arising out of damage caused to another'.[7] The SGECC was also one of the key

[3] See, eg, the work of the Lando Commission, published as O Lando and HG Beale (eds), *Principles of European Contract Law Parts 1 and 2* (The Hague, Kluwer Law International, 1999), O Lando, E Clive, A Prum and R Zimmermann (eds), *Principles of European Contract Law: Part 3* (The Hague, Kluwer Law International, 2003). The European Commission's Communications of 2001, 2003 and 2004 led to the proposal for a Common European Sales Law ('Proposal for a Regulation of the European Parliament and of the Council on a Common European Sales Law' COM (2011) 635 final). See European Commission, 'Communication from the Commission on European Contract Law' COM (2001) 398 final, 'A More Coherent European Contract Law: An Action Plan' COM (2003) 68 final and 'European Contract Law and the Revision of the *acquis*: The Way Forward' COM (2004) 651 final.

[4] The support of the European Parliament for some form of harmonised instrument may be traced back to its resolution of 26 May 1989 recommending action to bring into line the private law of the Member States: [1989] OJ C158\400.

[5] Christian von Bar's ambitious *The Common European Law of Torts: Volumes One and Two* (Oxford, Oxford University Press, 1998 and 2000) also merits an honourable mention, covering 16 systems of tort law and drawing out their key characteristics, thereby providing a valuable source for future researchers.

[6] The European Group on Tort Law, *Principles of European Tort Law. Text and Commentary* (Wien, Springer, 2005) (PETL). This work is supplemented by a series of volumes which discuss the most relevant factors in establishing liability such as wrongfulness, causation, damage, fault and the area of strict liability: see, for example, J Spier and H Koziol (eds), *Unification of Tort Law: Causation*, Principles of European Tort Law (The Hague, Kluwer Law International, 2000).

[7] www.sgecc.net/pages/en/texts/index.draft_articles.htm. See now C von Bar (ed), *Principles of European Law: Non-Contractual Liability Arising out of Damage Caused to Another* (Oxford, Oxford University Press, 2009)

participants of the Joint Network on European Private Law which, in 2009, published the full version of the Draft Common Frame of Reference (DCFR).[8] The DCFR represented the culmination of an ambitious research project, funded by the European Commission,[9] to find a framework for both improving existing EU law and developing a common European law of contract. The Joint Network went further and the DCFR provides definitions, principles and importantly model rules covering most of European private law. Book VI of the DCFR contains draft principles of tort law (or to use the neutral language of the DCFR, Non-contractual liability).[10]

These projects have a number of factors in common. All seek to provide a model form of tort law which goes beyond national traditions and provides the best solutions for Europe.[11] They seek, therefore, not to summarise the status quo, but look forward. All involve lawyers from both common and civil law jurisdictions,[12] with considerable expertise in the tort law of their own jurisdiction. Further, while conceding that these are academic projects and it is for the law-makers to determine how they will be used, the drafters clearly hope to inspire future law-makers to take account of their provisions which deal with fundamental policy questions varying from victim compensation to the role of strict liability in deterring harmful behaviour. The introduction to the DCFR states that it is an independent piece of research which it hopes will contribute to a harmonious and informal harmonisation of private law.[13] PETL similarly seeks to show 'the potential for harmonising tort law in Europe in the future and how this could be achieved'[14] and possibly act as a signpost for the drafting of future directives and/or regulations.[15]

These statements indicate that these academic projects deal with future law-making. One might question, therefore, how they will assist current practitioners

[8] C von Bar and E Clive (eds), *Principles, Definitions and Model Rules of European Private Law: Draft Common Frame of Reference.* Full Edition (Munich, Sellier, 2009 and Oxford, Oxford University Press, 2010) (DFCR).

[9] Funded as a 'Network of Excellence' under the European Commission's sixth Framework Programme for Research and Technological Development, Priority 7 – FP6-2002-Citizens-3, Contract No 513351.

[10] The drafters sought to increase accessibility and intelligibility by avoiding technical language drawn from any one legal system: DFCR (n 8) Introduction para 48.

[11] PETL (n 6) Introduction, para 20. See G Wagner, 'The Project of Harmonising European Tort Law' (2005) 42 *Common Market Law Review* 1269; K Oliphant, 'Rival Perspectives on European Tort Law: A Comparative Analysis' in H Koziol and BC Steininger (eds.), *European Tort Law 2009* (Berlin, de Gruyter, 2010) 666.

[12] But note complaints that the Nordic countries have been neglected: M Schultz, 'Disharmonization: A Swedish Critique of Principles of European Tort Law' (2007) 18 *European Business Law Review* 1305. Inevitably also the common law, as a minority jurisdiction in Europe, has provided fewer representatives than civil law jurisdictions.

[13] DFCR (n 8) Introduction, para 8.

[14] BA Koch, 'Principles of European Tort Law' (2009) 20 *King's Law Journal* 203, 205. See also BA Koch, 'The "European Group on Tort Law" and its "Principles of European Tort Law"' (2005) 53 *American Journal of Comparative Law* 189.

[15] H Koziol, 'Comparative Law : A Must in the European Union: Demonstrated by Tort Law as an Example' (2007) 1(3) *Journal of Tort Law*, Art 5, 2.

and judges attempting to gain a better understanding of European influences. The essential problem is that their utility is diminished by their ambition. In seeking to provide future European principles of tort law, they seek to replace and improve the existing law. In proposing reform, therefore, they go beyond the more limited focus of this work which addresses how English tort law is being changed by European influences and seek to create a new pan-European law of torts. This may be seen below by examining the core provision of PETL and the DCFR. Both commence with a 'basic' rule:

> Article 1:101 PETL
>
> (1) A person to whom damage to another is legally attributed is liable to compensate that damage.
> (2) Damage may be attributed in particular to the person (a) whose conduct constituting fault has caused it; or (b) whose abnormally dangerous activity has caused it; or (c) whose auxiliary has caused it within the scope of his functions.
>
> Book VI.-1:101 DCFR[16]
>
> (1) A person who suffers legally relevant damage has a right to reparation from a person who caused the damage intentionally or negligently or is otherwise accountable for the causation of the damage.
> (2) Where a person has not caused legally relevant damage intentionally or negligently that person is accountable for the causation of legally relevant damage only if Chapter 3 so provide.

These provisions illustrate the policy choice of the drafters to adopt the style of a traditional civil code – codified model rules to be supplemented by academic commentary – and to identify 'neutral' legal terminology which is not indicative of a particular European legal system.[17] While the decision to follow the format of a code is unsurprising bearing in mind the majority of representatives from these groups come from civil law jurisdictions, it does render it more difficult to map onto a common law legal landscape.[18] An English lawyer is equally unlikely to find references to 'legally attributed damage'[19] or 'legally relevant damage'[20] helpful in trying to understand differences between common and civil law legal reasoning. More fundamentally, by constructing a new system of tort law which is not tied to traditional national approaches, PETL and the DCFR provide a critique on current law but offer little in terms of guidance for lawyers who wish to understand and apply the law currently in place. They offer also little insight into the interface

[16] This provision is identical to the equivalent provision in the principles drafted by the SGECC, which, for this reason, will not be examined in this section.

[17] Van Dam comments that these provisions provide a good illustration of the difficulties and pitfalls of harmonisation in that they are so basic that it is hard to disagree with the provisions, but they provide little real guidance: C van Dam, *European Tort Law*, 2nd edn (Oxford, Oxford University Press, 2013) para 607.

[18] Stapleton, 'Benefits of Comparative Tort Reasoning' (n 2) 43.

[19] Defined in Ch 2 of PETL, Arts 2:101 to 2:105

[20] Defined in Ch 2 of DCFR, Arts 2:101 to 2:211.

of human rights and European tort law and the tension between transposed Directives and existing forms of domestic law.[21]

While, therefore, interesting in terms of the future development of European private law and in outlining the key policy debates which affect every system of tort law – fault v strict liability? corrective v distributive justice? judicial discretion v legislative certainty? – the projects do not assist us greatly in understanding existing European legal influences. It is submitted, nevertheless, that they do have some positive impact in terms of Europeanisation. English tort lawyers who may previously never have considered looking at civil law have found themselves invited to participate in drafting committees and attend conferences outlining the differences between different European legal systems. As a result, they have become increasingly aware of the value of understanding other legal systems and the utility of cross-jurisdictional dialogue. The involvement of UK tort law professors such as Rogers and Oliphant, for example, has led to the inclusion of European tort law material in standard student tort textbooks.[22] New journals, such as the *Journal of European Tort Law*, which is available in English and online, have encouraged the dissemination of knowledge about different legal systems.[23] The harmonisation of European tort law may not be on the political agenda,[24] but the very existence of PETL and the DCFR has served to highlight, in the words of the late Lord Bingham, that there is a world elsewhere, beyond the common law.[25]

ii. Identifying the Common Core of European Tort Law Principle?

If proposals for new principles of European tort law offer little assistance, may less ambitious projects which seek to identify the extent to which there are, in fact, similar principles underlying European tort law systems prove more useful? The Common Core of European Private Law Project,[26] launched in 1995, does exactly that. It seeks to unearth the 'common core' of European private law, i.e. what is different and what is already common among the different legal systems of Europe, subdividing the research area into general categories of contracts, torts

[21] DCFR Book VI.-2:203 does recognise (unlike PETL) the infringement of dignity, liberty and privacy as legally relevant damage, but the drafters were unable to gain consensus on the treatment of protection of reputation which is left to national law (VI.-2: 203(2)). Some recognition is made of existing EU tort law, for example the Product Liability Directive is dealt with in the DCFR (VI.-3: 204) but not in PETL.

[22] WVH Rogers, *Winfield and Jolowicz on Tort*, 18th edn (London, Sweet and Maxwell, 2010); M Lunney and K Oliphant, *Tort Law: Text and Materials*, 5th edn (Oxford, Oxford University Press, 2013).

[23] Interestingly the most downloaded article in 2013 was K Oliphant, 'Cultures of Tort Law in Europe' (2013) 3 *Journal of European Tort Law* 147–57.

[24] C van Dam, 'European Tort Law: Features of a Diverse Landscape' in C Twigg-Flesner, *The Cambridge Companion to European Union Private Law* (Cambridge, Cambridge University Press, 2010) 171, who argues strongly against the advisability of such a measure. See also van Dam, *European Tort Law* (n 17) para 612.

[25] TH Bingham, '"There is a World Elsewhere": The Changing Perspectives of English Law' (1992) 41 *International and Comparative Law Quarterly* 513.

[26] www.common-core.org/ (also known as the Trento group).

and property. Bussani,[27] Infantino and Werro comment that such a common core is worth revealing 'in order to obtain at least the main outline of a reliable geographical map of Europe's multi-legal framework' and distinguish their project from the 'integrative' harmonisation project of the European Group on Tort Law and Study Group on a European Civil Code.[28] On this basis, in its publications, it has identified common features of tort law across jurisdictions.

Again this is useful in highlighting the relationship between the different systems of Europe. Although the resulting publications have been somewhat ad hoc in terms of their coverage of tort law topics[29] and cover a limited number of jurisdictions,[30] the research does examine to what extent convergence (or otherwise) between European Member States may be found. This serves to increase our knowledge of the operation of tort law across European Member States. The focus is once again, however, on core private law and the contributions remain primarily of academic interest. As such, they offer limited assistance to lawyers trying to gain a better understanding of current European influences on domestic law.

It is submitted, therefore, that grand projects such as the publication of PETL or the DCFR are of academic interest in proposing a new framework for European tort law and may, indeed, prove influential in the drafting of future EU legislation, but do little to help bridge the existing gap between the English common law and European sources of law which differ in terms of style and language. On this basis, what is proposed is a more practical approach; one which seeks to assist the English tort law community to better understand and apply these new sources of law.

B. A New Approach to Europeanisation: OED (Openness, Education, Dialogue)

This book has identified a number of difficulties experienced by the courts and legal community generally in correctly applying and understanding European

[27] Mauro Bussani, in fact, launched the project with Ugo Mattei, with Franz Werro acting as Chairperson of the Torts Groups.

[28] M Bussani, M Infantino and F Werro, 'The Common Core Sound: Short Notes on Themes, Harmonies and Disharmonies in European Tort Law' (2009) 20 *King's Law Journal* 239, 240.

[29] The volumes cover, for example, pure economic loss, strict liability and personality rights, but one might question whether these are the most significant areas of tort law in Europe where similarities need to be found: M Bussani and VV Palmer, *Pure Economic Loss in Europe*, The Common Core of European Private Law (Cambridge, Cambridge University Press, 2003), F Werro and VV Palmer, *The Boundaries of Strict Liability in European Tort Law*, The Common Core of European Private Law (Bern, Stämpfli; Durham, NC, Carolina Academic Press, 2004) and G Brüggemeier, A Colombi Ciacchi and O Callaghan (eds), *Personality Rights in European Tort Law* (Cambridge, Cambridge University Press, 2010).

[30] The volume on pure economic loss, for example, covered 13 jurisdictions (Austria, Belgium, England, France, Germany, Greece, Italy, Portugal, Scotland, Spain, Sweden and Finland, the Netherlands), while the volume on strict liability a slightly different 12 (Austria, Denmark, England, Finland, France, Germany, Greece, Italy, Portugal, Scotland, Spain, the Netherlands). The limited discussion of Scandinavian and Eastern European countries may be noted.

influences affecting the common law of tort. It has sought to highlight that reference to EU and human rights law is not optional, but the result of UK legislation. The law of tort must, therefore, respond to these new forms of law which require changes to how we interpret law and read case law. Nevertheless, chapters three and five have highlighted attempts by the courts to confine these new sources to a limited category of claims. The decision, for example, in *Van Colle v Chief Constable of Hertfordshire*[31] (discussed above in chapter five) that claims under the HRA 1998 would exist side-by-side with claims against public authorities in negligence indicates both the reluctance of the courts to alter the traditional character of many nominate torts and a desire by the judiciary to retain autonomy in terms of legal development. Further, chapters four and six indicate that, even where the courts have no choice but to apply EU law due to the *Francovich* ruling[32] or are given the green light by Parliament to develop existing law in the light of Convention jurisprudence to fill the gap in privacy protection, the courts will seek to avoid creating new forms of tort law and will diminish the European character of the resulting European/common law hybrid cause of action by giving it a more familiar label such as 'breach of statutory duty' or 'breach of confidence'.

The way forward, it is submitted, may be characterised by three words: openness, education, dialogue. Openness signifies receptivity of the legal community to these new sources of law and a willingness to look beyond national policy frameworks and to consider new ways of approaching the law. To achieve this requires education, ie, ensuring that the legal community is aware of these new influences and of their differences and similarities with the common law. To apply this law successfully, however, a third element is needed: dialogue. Without ensuring an exchange of views between all members of the legal community within Europe, a consistent application and understanding of European law will be impossible to achieve. These three factors will be examined below.

i. Openness

Chapters three to six have given numerous examples where the English judiciary has proven resistant to the 'alien' reasoning of the European courts. From the ongoing influence of fault-based reasoning in product liability cases in chapter three to the separation of HRA-based and tort-based actions against public authorities in chapter five, English judges have been seen to adopt an approach which reduces the influence of these legal transplants to a bare minimum. Caruso has noted that such an entrenched attitude may be found in other European legal systems where the judiciary has sought to avoid institutional disempowerment by clinging to national legal doctrines and passively resisting European integration.[33] This is more than path dependency – the instinctive adoption of familiar rules –

[31] (Conjoined with *Smith v Chief Constable of Sussex Police*) [2008] UKHL 50; [2009] 1 AC 225, see, in particular, Lord Hope at para 82.

[32] C6/90 *Francovich v Italian Republic* [1991] ECR I-5357; [1993] 2 CMLR 66.

[33] D Caruso, 'The Missing View of the Cathedral: The Private Law Paradigm of European Legal Integration' (1997) 3 *European Law Journal* 3.

but expressive of national discomfort at a perceived attack to the internal coherence of the common law. Whenever possible, therefore, we have seen that the courts have sought to retain control of tort policy.[34]

One might question whether such resistance represents an over-reaction to the perceived threat of Europeanisation. Chapters three and four indicate (i) the limited impact of EU legislation and case law on English tort law, and (ii) that directives, by their very nature, give Member States considerable discretion in terms of implementation.[35] Increasingly the doctrine of subsidiarity is paving the way for greater co-operation between the EU and Member States. Equally chapters five and six indicate incremental development of tort law and human rights can occur in a controlled manner, even if the current approach towards torts such as false imprisonment appears far too restrictive. Yet it is not solely the courts who have displayed nervousness towards Europeanisation. Chapters three and five have highlighted the dissatisfaction of the UK government with some forms of European intervention, indeed taking for itself the policy initiative in relation to health and safety legislation and defamation claims against Internet service providers. It remains to be seen whether recent statutory limitations on the ability of employees to claim for breach of statutory duty in relation to transposed EU health and safety directives will be found to be in compliance with EU law.

Narrow construction of European legislation and case law, combined with an unwillingness to recognise new areas of tort law, has led to some questionable legal decisions. Such a reaction seems out of proportion to the risks Europeanisation actually presents to the common law system. It further gives rise to the possibility that the courts may find themselves in conflict with the obligations imposed by the European Communities Act 1972 and the Human Rights Act 1998. Sections 2 and 3 HRA 1998 impose interpretative obligations on the courts and while the Act does not expressly deal with the question of its horizontal effect, chapter six has highlighted evidence that the UK government expected some form of horizontal application. In relation to EU law, there is an obligation to apply correctly EU legislation and indeed, in the light of *Köbler v Austria*,[36] the possibility of legal action against a court of final appeal for failing to refer a matter to the CJEU or for giving an erroneous ruling where it amounts to a manifest infringement of the applicable law. While chapters three and four concede that the CJEU and European Commission could do more to give guidance to national courts, the resistance of the national courts to change does not render this process any easier.

The fact remains that by choosing to enact the 1972 and 1998 statutes, the UK Parliament introduced new legal sources into English law. This has led to changes to English tort law, affecting, to a certain extent, the autonomy of the English courts to make tort law policy. A refusal to recognise this fact will not change its

[34] For the relationship of the English courts and tort policy, see J Bell, *Policy Arguments in Judicial Decisions* (Oxford, Clarendon Press, 1983) ch III.

[35] Van Dam, for example, has described State liability for breach of EU law as a dog which 'barks but hardly bites': C van Dam, 'European Tort Law' (n 24) 164.

[36] Case 224/01 *Köbler v Austria* [2003] ECR I-239; [2004] QB 848.

validity. It is submitted that the way forward must be to take a more positive view of such developments. Europeanisation is capable of improving the quality of English tort law and this book has highlighted benefits in terms of consumer protection, workplace safety and the enhanced protection of human rights. Tort law has never been static and there is no reason why it should not embrace these goals. There remains a need, however, to understand fully how to apply and interpret these new legal sources, without which misunderstandings will continue to arise.

ii. Education

It is argued, therefore, that the English legal community needs to be open to change and to make more effort to understand these new legal sources. In terms of legal education, steps have been taken. EU law and human rights law are now a compulsory element of the law degree in England and Wales. This measure was, however, only introduced in the 1990s[37] and in a country where most judges are over 50 and therefore studied law 30 years earlier, there will clearly be a time lag until this new generation of lawyers joins the judiciary. Naturally, lawyers participating in the legal process will have studied these subjects, but the fact remains that the increased importance of EU law and the implementation of the HRA 1998 have occurred more recently and there is likely to be an 'education' gap in ensuring that the legal community is aware of these changes to English tort law. It has been interesting in examining judgments in this book to note that judges with EU or human rights experience such as Lord Slynn, Lord Mance, Lord Bingham and Lord Justice Sedley have proven particularly adept at applying these new sources.

More significantly, a key obstacle remains the characterisation of EU and human rights law as 'public' law. Private lawyers can be insular. Despite the tradition of Dicey, lawyers tend to think of themselves as public or private lawyers. Labelling EU and human rights law 'public law' essentially lets private lawyers off the hook. There is little incentive to engage in the time and effort of mastering these areas of law. Leading practitioners' text *Clerk and Lindsell*, for example, contains only three paragraphs on *Francovich* liability and other references to EU and human rights law are integrated within individual tort chapters.[38] Student textbooks may be more receptive to new influences, but the fact remains that the traditional law degree syllabus places little emphasis on non-common law sources and certainly does not provide the incentive for more detailed treatment. Part 1 of the Consumer Protection Act 1987[39] is thus taught as part of UK consumer law or

[37] Taking my degree in 1989, for example, few of my fellow students chose to opt for the obscure EEC law option, preferring more conventional options such as family and labour law.

[38] MA Jones (ed), *Clerk and Lindsell on Torts*, 20th edn (London, Sweet and Maxwell, 2010) paras 9-46–9-48.

[39] Transposing Council Directive 85/374/EEC of 25 July 1985 on the approximation of the laws, regulations and administrative provisions of the Member States concerning liability for defective products: [1985] OJ L210, 29.

as a response to the limitations of *Donoghue v Stevenson*[40] manufacturers' liability. This presents a distorted picture of what is in reality part of a European harmonisation process, seeking to provide uniform protection to consumers injured by defective products across all Member States. One might question how many students (or even their lecturers) are aware that this is a specific area of maximum harmonisation,[41] and may indeed be characterised as 'Brussels' first serious attempt to wrest from the Member States a measure of their previously undivided control over their respective tort law'.[42]

Understanding Europeanisation therefore requires us to think how we educate the private law community. This applies from individual law students to our Supreme Court justices. Educators need to consider how to integrate these new sources of law into the tort law syllabus. Greater emphasis on the evolving nature of English tort law will serve to break down barriers and ensure a clearer understanding of the relevant law. The hope of this author is further that knowledge will diminish the fear of the unknown and that a legal community which understands how Europeanisation operates and its limited impact on English tort law will be less wary of embracing these new sources.

iii. Dialogue

Successful understanding of Europeanisation also requires dialogue. EU law and the 1998 Act grant the English courts a considerable discretion to interact with European institutions. The Article 267 TFEU preliminary reference procedure, in particular, gives courts at all levels the opportunity to refer questions of interpretation of EU law to the Luxembourg court and thus introduces a dialogue between national and European courts.[43] Commentators have noted the power this gives national courts in relation to the executive and legislative branches of government, as seen in the *Factortame* litigation.[44] Equally, section 2(1) of the Human Rights Act 1998 expressly requires the English courts to 'take into account' the case law of the Strasbourg court when determining questions relating to Convention rights, leaving it to the English courts to decide how onerous this duty should be. Amos has noted the attempts by the Strasbourg court to promote dialogue by developing the principle of subsidiarity, in its application of the mar-

[40] *Donoghue v Stevenson* [1932] AC 562

[41] As mentioned in ch 3, the fact that two of the leading statute books for contract, tort and restitution contain no reference to the relevant EU Directive is unfortunate to say the least.

[42] Caruso, 'The Missing View' (n 33) 15.

[43] Helfer and Slaughter describe it as a 'form of power-sharing': L Helfer and AM Slaughter, 'Toward a Theory of Effective Supranational Adjudication' (1997) 107 *Yale Law Journal* 273, 310. Lord Mance has commented, however, that dialogue by preliminary reference, with its unclear division between interpretation and application and the often overly condensed and limited reasoning of the CJEU, is not always the easiest way to resolve difficult issues: Lord Mance, 'The Interface between National and European Law' Second Lecture in honour of Sir Jeremy Lever QC 1 February 2013, (see now (2013) 38 *European Law Review* 437 at 443). His Lordship argued that the CJEU should improve its dialogue with national courts by engaging with national jurisprudence and thereby appearing less hierarchical: at 445.

[44] See, eg, JHH Weiler, *The Constitution of Europe* (Cambridge, Cambridge University Press, 1999) 197.

gin of appreciation and by a new vigorous approach to interpretation of Article 13 (the right to an effective remedy), supported by extra-judicial statements by members of the court.[45] Indeed, the *Osman* saga, detailed in chapter five,[46] demonstrates the willingness of the Strasbourg Court to change its position when faced with national opposition indicating a misunderstanding of the domestic law. The case law in chapter five indicates a far from interventionist stance by this Court. The Department for Constitutional Affairs, reviewing the implementation of the 1998 Act in 2006, concluded that:

> There is no doubt that the Human Rights Act has also established a 'dialogue'; between English judges and the European Court of Human Rights. The close analytical attention paid by the English courts to the European Convention on Human Rights case law is respected in Strasbourg, and has become influential on the way it approaches English cases. This in part accounts for the significant reduction in a number of adverse decisions against the UK Government by the European Court of Human Rights since the Human Rights Act came into effect.[47]

The response of the English courts has, however, been mixed. As noted in chapter four, the English courts have demonstrated reluctance to utilise the Article 267 TFEU preliminary reference procedure, preferring to resolve questions of law in the domestic courts whenever possible. Views were also noted that the procedure simply slowed down the judicial process and added to costs. Equally, in relation to human rights, Lord Hoffmann in the 2009 Annual Judicial Studies Board Lecture (published in the *Law Quarterly Review*)[48] openly questioned the legitimacy of the Strasbourg court, as opposed to the national court, to interpret the content of human rights in domestic law. One might also question whether the 'mirror' principle advocated by Lord Bingham in *Ullah*,[49] that the English courts should, in the absence of special circumstances, follow any clear and constant jurisprudence of the European Court of Human Rights, has placed an undue restriction on this dialogue. While a useful rule of thumb – as Lord Slynn observed, there seems little point in contradicting a clear ruling by the Strasbourg Court if the case is likely to be successfully appealed to it at a later date[50] – it should not be interpreted as a rule of stare decisis, encouraging the English courts to view Strasbourg decisions as binding authority. As discussed in chapters two, five and six, the judgments of the European Court of Human Rights are ill-suited to such

[45] M Amos, 'The Dialogue between United Kingdom Courts and the European Court of Human Rights' (2012) 61 *International and Comparative Law Quarterly* 557, 560. See, eg, former President of the Court (and British lawyer), Sir Nicholas Bratza, 'The Relationship between the UK Courts and Strasbourg' [2011] *European Human Rights Law Reports* 505.

[46] *Osman v United Kingdom* (23452/94) (2000) 29 EHRR 245 and Z *v United Kingdom* (29392/95) (2002) 34 EHRR 3.

[47] Department for Constitutional Affairs, *Review of the Implementation of the Human Rights Act* 38/06 (2006) 4.

[48] Lord Hoffmann, 'The Universality of Human Rights' (2009) 125 *Law Quarterly Review* 416.

[49] *R (on the application of Ullah) v Special Adjudicator* [2004] UKHL 26; [2004] 2 AC 323, para 20.

[50] *R (Alconbury Developments Ltd and Others) v Secretary of State for the Environment, Transport and the Regions* [2001] UKHL 23; [2003] 2 AC 295, para 26 per Lord Slynn.

an interpretation and the Strasbourg court does not regard itself as a final court of appeal. Commentators have expressed concern that the mirror principle should not prevent the domestic courts from developing human rights law proactively:[51] a view shared also by Lord Irvine and Baroness Hale.[52]

Dame Mary Arden has observed that there is a tendency to accept Europeanisation when it matches domestic law policy but not where it goes against the grain of some established principle of domestic law. [53] Caruso attributes this to a fear of loss of control over civil adjudication, encouraging the national courts to 'cling to the dogmas of national private law'.[54] Such tensions are arguably not assisted by opposition by sections of the UK media to any form of European intervention into English law[55] and scepticism by a number of Members of Parliament to the continued role of the UK within the EU and the Council of Europe. Nevertheless a more positive approach to dialogue has obvious benefits. Conversation is, after all, a two-way form of communication. By not engaging in discussion, one's voice will never be heard. If English lawyers wish to have input into the development of EU law and the interpretation of the ECHR, then it is necessary to engage in dialogue and utilise the opportunities available to get their views across. Engagement will encourage involvement in the Europeanisation process, which will assist in diminishing the 'European threat' and lead to an increased understanding and awareness of the nature of EU and European human rights law. As Arden notes, a 'lively' dialogue may actually increase the ability of the national courts to develop law, permitting more development at a local level.[56] At the very least, refusing to engage in such a dialogue and then questioning the legitimacy of the Luxembourg and Strasbourg courts to affect English law seems to amount to a step backwards, ignoring the impact of the 1972 and 1998 Acts on English law and the ability of Europeanisation to improve both the quality of English tort law and its ability to protect the vulnerable in society.

[51] For recent criticism, see R Clayton 'Smoke and Mirrors: The Human Rights Act and the Impact of Strasbourg Case Law' [2012] *Public Law* 639, who argues that it would be preferable if domestic courts regarded the ECtHR case law as a floor, not a ceiling.

[52] Lord Irvine of Lairg, 'A British Interpretation of Convention Rights' [2012] *Public Law* 237; Baroness Hale, '*Argentoratum locutum*: Is Strasbourg or the Supreme Court Supreme?' (2012) 12 *Human Rights Law Review* 65. See also Lord Bingham, 'Constitutional Change: Unfinished business', lecture 4 December 2013.

[53] 'Human Rights and Civil Wrongs: Tort Law under the Spotlight' [2010] *Public Law* 140, 153.

[54] (n 33) 26. See also J Steele, '(Dis)owning the Convention in the Law of Tort' in J Lee (ed), *From House of Lords to Supreme Court: Judges, Jurists and the Process of Judging* (Oxford, Hart Publishing, 2011) 127.

[55] UK tabloids remain openly sceptical of the impact of Europe (in which it generally conflates EU and ECHR law) and, in particular, the negative impact of free movement of workers within the EU (consider, for example, *Daily Mail* headline of 7 June 2013 'Cashpoint Card Snatches Treble: Romanian Crime Gangs Responsible for 92% of Thefts from Cash Machines, Police Believe') and the rulings of the Strasbourg court ('We Must Put an End to the Europe Madness. Calls to Boycott ECHR for Life Sentences Ruling', *Daily Express*, 10 July 2013).

[56] See (n 53). See also C Harlow, 'Voices of Difference in a Plural Community' (2002) 50 *American Journal of Comparative Law* 339, 367.

II. Conclusions

This book has identified the sometimes tense relationship between English tort law and EU and European human rights law. It has noted the limited impact of EU law on the English legal system. EU Directives have targeted very specific areas of law and the focus has been on individual policy initiatives rather than establishing general principles of tort law.[57] Such a fragmented approach may be explained in terms of the EU's functional approach to private law, seeking to promote the effective functioning of the internal market and respect for EU law rather than establish new principles of European tort law.[58] The choice of minimum harmonisation directives (the Product Liability Directive being the exception) has also served to diminish their impact. Directives give States a considerable amount of discretion in terms of transposition, which inevitably allows Member States to 'adjust' the provisions to suit local conditions. The CJEU has also played a very limited role in policing the correct transposition of EU Directives into national law. Even where the CJEU has proven more assertive and set out a new principle of European tort law – State liability for breach of EU law – it has left questions of procedure to the national courts together with the application of the *Brasserie du Pêcheur* liability conditions (subject to the principles of equality and effectiveness). The English courts' relatively narrow interpretation of the law has gone largely unchallenged.[59]

Equally, in the human rights sphere, the courts have sought to confine human rights within the framework of the 1998 Act whenever possible. With the exception of defamation, the courts have sought to divide claims against public authorities into two categories with different remedial frameworks: claims under the HRA 1998 and claims in the law of tort. The aim is to avoid cross-infection and on this basis, the existence of the alternative HRA claim has been used as a justification for *not* changing the law of tort.[60] Privacy law does appear to be the exception. Here the courts have embraced horizontal claims based on breach of Article 8 ECHR and this has led to a number of high profile claims involving footballers, supermodels and even the former head of the governing body of Formula One asserting their right to privacy in the English courts. However, this apparently

[57] The impact of EU law has been described as 'pointillist', consisting of a series of isolated steps without amounting to a system: A Harmathy, 'The Impact of the Practice of the European Court of Justice on the Civil and Commercial law of the Member States of the European Union' (2010) 18 *European Review of Private Law* 429, 431. See also T Wilhelmsson, 'Private Law in the EU: Harmonised or Fragmented Europeanisation' (2002) 10 *European Review of Private Law* 81.

[58] See Van Dam, *European Tort Law* (n 17) paras 610-5 and 611.

[59] For criticism of the application of *Francovich* liability in England and Germany, see T Lock, 'Is Private Enforcement of EU Law through State Liability a Myth? An Assessment 20 Years after *Francovich*' (2012) 49 *Common Market Law Review* 1675. Niglia also notes evidence that the German and Italian courts have defied or avoided EU directives to preserve their interpretative autonomy: L Niglia, 'The Non-Europeanisation of Private Law' (2001) 4 *European Review of Private Law* 575.

[60] See *Jain v Trent SHA* [2009] UKHL 4; [2009] 1 AC 853.

progressive attitude has been marred by the unwillingness of the court to create a new form of action or address the considerable academic writing in this field, leaving English law with a 'tort' of breach of confidence: a cause of action which simply does not exist.

In this chapter, I have sought to explain how this situation might be improved. Attempts by groups of academics to 'rationalise' European tort law and propose a new tort framework as a point of reference for European legislators may be interesting, but look to the future and offer little assistance in resolving current difficulties in understanding the integration of EU and European human rights sources within our common law legal system. My conclusion is, therefore, more practical. The solution must lie in addressing the negative attitudes of the legal community, together with the often misguided 'common law' interpretation of European sources. By improving our knowledge base – which indeed is the *raison d'être* of this book – we can remove our fear of the unknown and engage on a more equal basis with these new forms of law. This chapter has also sought to address another form of prejudice – that of the division between private and public law. EU and human rights law are not simply the remit of public lawyers. Ultimately, however, negative attitudes can only be overcome by being open to new influences and engaging with them positively through dialogue. As an Erasmus co-ordinator of long-standing, I have seen the positive effect that studying in another European legal system for a term or a year can have on students. The Erasmus student exchange programme demonstrates the interaction of the factors of openness, education and dialogue. For those students who remain tied to the English legal system and unwilling to adapt to new modes of teaching, the Erasmus year can be unpleasant and frustrating. The students who prosper most are those who talk to the other students and their professors, attend classes and are ready to experience new ways of engaging in university life and study. While I do not propose to send our Supreme Court on a year long exchange programme, the point is obvious: Europeanisation is an ongoing process in which EU law and European human rights law have become part of English law and this will inevitably affect tort law. Despite the current political debate over Europe, it remains very unlikely that the UK will withdraw from the European Union. Even if it were possible for the UK to withdraw from the European Convention on Human Rights,[61] no mainstream political party is suggesting that there will be no Bill of Human Rights within English law and any such Bill will inevitably be influenced by the interpretation of Convention rights. Equally, it seems very unlikely that the privacy genie can be returned to the bottle.

[61] Query whether membership of the EU would permit this, particularly if the EU becomes, as it currently intends, a signatory to the Convention. Nevertheless the UK government established in 2011 a Commission on a Bill of Rights, whose report, *A UK Bill of Rights?: The Choice Before Us*, published in December 2012, recommended (by a majority) that there is a strong argument in favour of a UK Bill of Rights. The government accepts, however, that any change is unlikely to occur before the 2015 general election.

Europeanisation, whether we like it or not, has changed English law. Where we have a choice is in determining how we approach this process and whether we look away or react positively and ensure that we fully understand the nature of tort law in the twenty-first century. The strength of the common law is its versatility and ability to respond to change. The judiciary has a key role in its development. It is to be hoped that English law will play to these strengths in recognising the role of tort law in protecting the rights of citizens both in terms of EU law and in terms of human rights.

Index

abuse of process 133
Academy of European Law (ERA) 3–4
access to court, right of 143–5
account of profits 187–9
***acte clair* doctrine** 38, 108, 119
aggravated damages 106–7, 187
airspace, trespass to 172
Amos, M 27, 28, 206–7
analogy, reasoning by 18
Andenas, M 97
applicable law 108, 116–17, 204
Arden, M, Dame 167, 208
Arnull, A 18, 52, 122
Arvind, TT 33
Association of European Administrative Judges (AEAJ) 39
Australia 192
autonomy *see* **national autonomy; personal autonomy**

bad faith 97–8 *see also* **good faith**
Baker, JH 7
balancing exercises
  freedom of expression 128–9, 131, 136, 139
  negligence 142–6
  nuisance 160–1
  privacy 176, 178–9, 181–2, 190
Banking Directive 95–8, 108
Barendt, E 126
Bell, J 35–7
Bennett, TDC 189–90
bereavement damages 150–2
Beutler, B 118
bias 33–4, 39
Bingham, T (Lord Bingham) 20, 22–3, 36, 38, 41, 123, 131–2, 147–9, 159, 166, 173, 180–1, 201, 205, 207
Biondi and Farley. The Right to Damages in European Law 94, 98, 118
Blackstone, W 139
blood products infected with Hepatitis C 51, 55
Brandeis, L 171
***Brasserie du Pêcheur* case** 92–5, 99, 102–7, 117, 209
breach of confidence 169, 174–95, 197, 203, 210
breach of statutory duty
  account of profits 188
  damages 110–14
  directives 43, 86
  European Communities Act 1972 111–12
  Francovich liability 93–4, 109–15, 121–2, 197, 203
  Health and Safety Framework Directive 63–72, 204
  interpretation 111–13, 115
  nominate tort, as 110–11
  public authorities, liability of 112–14, 116
  reform 70–2
  sui generis breach 110, 114, 121–2
British Bill of Rights, proposal for 28, 126
British Institute of International and Comparative Law (BIICL) 38–9
Bussani, M 202
but for test 58, 105–6

caching 78–9
Callaghan, B 66
canon law 6
Caruso, D 9–10, 15, 208
causation 45, 58, 60, 62, 86, 92–4, 103–7, 113, 122
causes of action *see also* **breach of statutory duty; *Francovich* liability; privacy, recognition**
of tort of invasion of
  causation 107
  classification 188–9
  common law 90, 203
  Francovich liability 196
  Human Rights Act 1998 124, 160, 164–6
  new causes 90, 114–15, 168, 189, 197
  public authority liability 124
  transplants 34
Chalmers, D 100
Charter of Fundamental Rights of the EU 14
child abuse 145–6
civil law systems
  codes and codification 5, 6, 9, 14, 20, 172, 198, 200–1
  common law 6–8, 14, 16–17, 29–30, 200–1
  Draft Common Frame of Reference 200–1
  European Convention on Human Rights 14, 200–1
  European Court of Human Rights 17
  exemplary damages 192
  integration 28–9
  model forms of tort law 199
  policy 200
  principles 5, 7, 200–1
  privacy 192, 194
  transplants 14, 16, 29–30

civil wrongs, tort as law of 5–8
Clarke, L 188
Clayton, R 147
Clerk and Lindsell on Torts 93–4, 110, 205
***CILFIT* criteria** 117, 122
codes and codification 5, 6, 9, 14, 20, 172, 198, 200–1
Collins, H 28
Common Core of European Private Law Project 201–2
common core of European Tort Law Principle, identification of 201–2
common law 196–7, 200–3, 211
- causation 62
- causes of action 90, 203
- civil law systems 6–8, 14, 16–17, 29–30, 200–1
- culture 1, 3, 15
- damages 62, 192
- defamation 126, 139–40
- directives 85, 87–8
- Draft Common Frame of Reference 200–2
- Englishness 1–2, 5
- EU law as public law 8–9
- European Communities Act 1972 1–2, 17, 27, 34, 204, 197
- European Convention on Human Rights 14, 17, 29, 140, 176, 185
- false imprisonment 155–6, 167
- *Francovich* liability 98, 102–3, 108, 119, 121–2, 197
- freedom of expression 126, 139–40
- Health and Safety Framework Directive 68, 72
- Human Rights Act 1998 1–2, 27, 34–6, 140, 143, 146–9, 156–8, 195, 197
- integration 14, 16, 28–9, 85, 87–8, 203–4
- interpretation 14, 204, 210
- legal culture 1, 6, 35
- legal reasoning 8, 14, 18, 32, 49, 87, 102, 108, 146, 167, 189, 200
- model forms of tort law 199
- national autonomy 8, 189, 196
- negligence 140–1, 143–4, 149, 152
- new sources of law 197–8
- openness 203
- precedent 117–18
- Product Liability Directive 16, 49, 51–2, 61–3
- remoteness 62
- sufficiently serious breach 99–100
- traditional approach 3
- transplants 27, 29–30, 40
- values 4–8, 28, 30, 35, 140

common principles of tort law 198
Commonwealth comparisons 167, 192, 197
comparative law 3, 33–5, 38–9, 103
compensation *see* **damages**
competition law 43, 44, 109, 114
conditional fees 132
confidentiality 169, 174–95, 197, 203, 210
constitutional elements, torts with 147, 154
Consultative Council of European Judges (CCJE) (CoE) 36, 39
Consumer Protection Act 1987, Part I 11, 16, 47, 48–62, 86, 205–6
continuing education 3–4
contraceptive pill litigation 60
contract law 2, 84, 198–9
contributory negligence 45, 74–7
convergence 30, 202
copyright 188
Copyright, Designs and Patents Act 1988 172
corporate claimants in defamation actions 136–7
Corradetti, C 37
Council of Bars and Law Societies of Europe (CCBE) 3, 39
Council of Europe's Consultative Council of European Judges 36, 39
Council of the Notariats of the EU (CNUE) 3
Court of Justice (CJEU) *see also* **preliminary references**
- application of law 17–19
- caseload 88
- common law 18
- concurring or dissenting opinions 18, 22
- deference 58, 87–8, 93, 106, 115, 184
- delay 88
- European Court of Human Rights 9, 22
- *Francovich* liability 89–95, 102–8, 115–22, 209
- guidance 204
- interpretation 17–22
- judicial dialogue 38, 49
- judicial notice 18
- language of judgments 35
- legitimacy 208
- rise in cases 10
- suitability of judges and advocates-general, panel on 36
- supervision 62, 86, 89
- transplants 16, 40

Craig, P 42–3, 55, 120
cross-jurisdictional European dialogue 1–4, 31, 34–40, 144–5, 167, 201, 206–8
culture 1, 3, 6, 15, 28–37, 167
cryptotypes 33

damages
- aggravated damages 106–7, 187
- bereavement damages 150–2
- breach of statutory duty 110–14
- common law 62
- compensation culture 81
- contributory negligence 75–7
- defamation 126–7, 131–2, 136, 138, 163
- Environmental Liability Directive 43
- EU law as public law 13

European Convention on Human Rights 25, 140
excessive awards 126–7, 131–2
exemplary or punitive damages 106–7, 132, 187, 189, 191–2
Francovich liability 89, 91–2, 95, 100–1, 106–7, 110–14, 117–20
freedom of expression 126–7, 131–2, 136, 138
Health and Safety Framework Directive 71
Human Rights Act 1998 13, 124, 165
injury to feelings 187
just satisfaction 124, 146–7, 160, 165
loss of amenity 160
loss of profits 106
mitigation 104
Motor Insurance Directives 75–6
negligence 75–7, 146–7, 150–2, 166
nuisance 159–60, 166
privacy 186–9
Product Liability Directive 60, 62, 86
public authority liability 112, 140
restitutionary damages 107
sufficiently serious breach 100–1
data protection 172
Davies, G 100
de Búrca, G 42–3, 55, 120
declarations of incompatibility 25
defamation *see also* **defamation and freedom of expression; defamation claims against ISPs**
damages 163, 187
Defamation Act 1996 124–5
Defamation Act 2013 124–5
Human Rights Act 1998 124–5, 162–3
negligence 162–3
privacy 169–70
private and family life, right to respect for 162
proportionality 162
public authority liability 162–4
qualified privilege 162
resources, diversion of 162–3
defamation and freedom of expression 126–40
absolute privilege 126
abuse of process 133
balancing rights 128–9, 131, 136, 139
burden of proof 134–5
chilling effect 134–5, 163
common law 126, 139–40
conditional fees 132
conservatism 131
corporate claimants and presumption of damage 136–7
damage, presumption of 134
damages 126–7, 131–2, 136, 138
Defamation Act 1952 134
Defamation Act 1996 134
Defamation Act 2013 132–3, 137
defences 126, 128, 134–5
European Convention on Human Rights 126–40
European Court of Human Rights 128, 130–1, 135–9, 163
excessive awards 126–7, 131–2
exemplary damages 132
fair/honest comment/honest opinion 126, 128, 135
falsity, presumption of 134–5
Human Rights Act 1998 11, 126–40
Internet 132–3, 134, 137–8
interpretation 129, 133–4, 139
juries 126–7, 132
justification or truth defence 126, 135
legal aid 131–2
malice 130
margin of appreciation 136, 139
multiple publication rule 137–8
offers of amends 134
O'Shea case 132–3, 134, 140
policy 137
political expression 127
prior restraint 139
private and family life, right to respect for 128–9, 131, 139, 166
proportionality 131–2, 133, 135, 138
public authority liability 128, 153, 162–4, 166, 167
public interest defence 127–31, 139, 166
qualified privilege 126–31, 133–5, 139–40
repetition rule 130, 137–8
reportage, defence of 130–1, 139
reputation 42, 78, 82, 84, 128–32, 136, 138–9, 166
restrictions 128–9
Reynolds privilege 127–9, 132, 139–40
single publication rule 137–8
strict liability 132, 134
time limits 137–8
defamation claims against ISPs 11, 44, 77–84
authors, editors or publishers 79–80, 82
caching 78–9
consistency 83–4
Defamation Act 1996 77, 79–80, 84, 86
Defamation Act 2013 82–3
defences 45, 77–84
Electronic Commerce Directive 45, 77–84, 85–6, 137
Electronic Commerce (EC Directive) Regulations 2002 78–81
freedom of expression 78, 81, 84
hosts 78–9, 82
identity of authors 82–3
innocent dimension 77
Law Commission 85–6
mere conduits 78
notice and take-down procedure 82
policy 84, 87, 204

defamation claims against ISPs (*cont*):
private and family life, right to respect for 81
reform 82, 85–62
removal or disablement 78–80, 82–3
defective goods *see* **Product Liability Directive**
deference 58, 87–8, 93, 106, 115, 184
Denning, A, (Lord Denning) 5, 20, 75–6, 109
Deposit Guarantee Schemes Directive 98
development risks defence 49, 54–9, 62, 86
Dicey, AV 205
different, whether European law is 34–40
Diplock, K (Lord Diplock) 39, 109
direct applicability 9
direct causal link 92–4, 103–7, 113, 122
direct effect
Francovich liability 90–2, 95, 97, 112, 119–21
Health and Safety Framework Directive 71
horizontal direct effect 52
interpretation 19, 21
legal education 35
private law 9–11
Product Liability Directive 52
remedial autonomy of national courts 10–11
vertical direct effect 5
directives *see* **EU directives**
discrimination 120
Donoghue v Stevenson 4–5, 11, 45, 47, 60, 206
Draft Common Frame of Reference (DCFR) 198–201
Durant, IC 106
duty of care
Health and Safety Framework Directive 68, 72–3, 84
negligence 13, 140, 142–4, 146, 165, 167

ecclesiastical courts 7
economic loss 58, 106, 108, 150
education *see* **legal education**
effective remedy, right to an 207
effectiveness, principle of
causation 103, 105, 106
Francovich liability 89–92, 94, 103, 105, 106, 112, 114, 116, 119–20
individuals, intention to confer rights on 119–20
Product Liability Directive 57–8, 86
remedial autonomy of national courts 10–11
Electronic Commerce Directive 16, 45, 77–84, 85–6, 137
employers' liability *see* **Health and Safety Framework Directive**
employment relationships and privacy 176
Environmental Liability Directive 43
equivalence, principle of
causation 103, 106–7
Francovich liability 90, 94, 103, 106–7, 119–20
individuals, intention to confer rights on 119–20
Product Liability Directive 57–8, 86
remedial autonomy of national courts 10–11
Erasmus student exchange programme 35–6, 210
EU directives 42–88 *see also* **Motor Insurance Directives and road accidents; Product Liability Directive; transposition and implementation of directives**
autonomy of national courts 84
Banking Directive 95–8, 108
breach of statutory duty 43, 86
common law, assimilation of EU law into 85, 87–8
competition law 43–4
consistency 85–6
Deposit Guarantee Schemes Directive 98
divergence from tort policy 44, 77–84
Electronic Commerce Directive 16, 45, 77–84, 85–6, 137
enforcement procedure 86–7
evidence of Europeanisation 44–5
Francovich liability 91–3
harmonisation 43, 45, 85, 88
Health and Safety Framework Directive 11, 44, 63–73, 85
integration 27
interpretation 45, 86–8
maximum harmonisation 84, 86
nature and scope of directives 84–5
negligence 86
new European tort law principles and their impact, existence of 84
Package Holiday Directive 97–8, 103–4
policy 44–5, 77–84, 87–8, 209
preliminary references 86–7
Principles of European Tort Law 201
private law 45
public and private law 43
strict liability 45, 86
EU law *see also* **Court of Justice (CJEU); direct effect; EU directives; *Francovich* liability; integration; legal transplants**
Charter of Fundamental Rights of the EU 14
civil law systems 14
comparative law 33
cross-jurisdictional European dialogue 3–4, 206–8
decisions 42
different, whether EU law is 34–40
direct applicability 9
economic role of EU 9–10
'Euro' language, development of 198
European Commission 4, 86, 198, 204
European Convention on Human Rights, accession to 14
Europeanisation, meaning of 3
general principles of EU law 14, 19, 38, 92
indirect effect 10–11, 21, 51–2, 55, 91

institutional liability of EU 19–20
interpretation 14, 197, 204
lack of awareness of European influences 8–14
legal education 34–6, 37, 61–3, 205–6
precedent 14, 18
private law 3, 8–13, 43
public law 8–9, 13
recommendations and opinions 42
regulations 42
supremacy of EU law 21–2, 27–8, 37
treaties 10, 14, 17–18
values 30
withdrawal from EU 210
'Euro' language, development of 198
European Centre of Tort and Insurance Law (ECTIL) 4
European Civil Code, proposal for 198
European Commission 4, 86, 198, 204
European Communities Act 1972 1, 17–18
breach of statutory duty 111–12
common law 1–2, 17, 27, 34, 204, 197
damages 107
Francovich liability 109–10
integration 27
interpretation 17–18, 197, 204
legal reasoning 34, 197
new sources of law 17–18, 204–5
private law 9
European Convention on Human Rights 123–68 *see also* **European Court of Human Rights (ECtHR); integration; legal transplants; particular rights; public authority liability in tort for breach of Convention rights**
accession of EU 14
Charter of Fundamental Rights of the EU 14
civil law systems 14
common law 14, 17, 29, 140, 176, 185
defamation 126–40
different, whether human rights law is 34–40
Human Rights Act 1998 2, 12, 16, 22–6, 123–4, 196
interpretation 14, 204
judicial dialogue 37–8, 40, 144–5
lack of awareness of European influences 8–14
living instrument principle 24, 185
negligence 142–53, 207
Principles of European Tort Law 200–1
public authorities 16
public law 8
supervision 184
Treaty on European Union 14
values 35
victims, definition of 150–1
withdrawal 210
European Court of Human Rights (ECtHR) *see also* **integration; legal transplants**
civil law systems 17
comparative law 33
concurring or dissenting opinions 22
Court of Justice 9, 22
cross-jurisdictional European dialogue 37–8, 40, 206–8
damages 25
defamation 128, 130–1, 135–9, 163–4
different, whether human rights law is 34
freedom of expression 128, 130–1, 135–9
language of judgments 35
legal culture 167
legitimacy 207–8
margin of appreciation 24
mirror principle 23, 37, 207–8
negligence 37–8
nuisance 165
persuasive, decisions as being 22
precedent 14, 23
privacy 173–85, 190–4
proportionality 24
public authority liability 162–5
seminars 39
subsidiarity 24
transplants 16, 33
understanding 33
European Court of Justice *see* **Court of Justice (CJEU)**
European Group on Tort Law (EGTL) 198–200, 202
European Judges and Prosecutors Association (EJPA) 39
European Law Institute (ELI) 4, 39
European Network of Councils for the Judiciary (ENCJ) 39
Europeanisation, meaning of 2–4
Euro-scepticism of MPs and media 208
Eurotort *see* ***Francovich*** **liability**
Eveleigh, E, Sir 39
Ewald, W 31, 32
exclusion or limitation of liability 45, 74–6
exemplary or punitive damages 106–7, 132, 187, 189, 191–2
exhaustion of local remedies 12, 94, 123, 174
expression, freedom of *see* **freedom of expression**
extension of liability 114, 116–21

Facebook 78
Factortame **litigation** 19–20, 100–1, 109, 111–12, 114, 206
failure to act *see* ***Francovich*** **liability**
fair hearing, right to a 13, 132, 150
fair, just and reasonable test 141–4
Fairgrieve, D 97
false imprisonment 153–6, 204
common law 155–6, 167
constitutional elements, torts with 154
deprivation of liberty test 154–5, 167
duty of care 167

false imprisonment (*cont*):
good faith 155–6
Human Rights Act 1998 154–6
imprisonment, definition of 154–5
indirect horizontal effect 156
interpretation 167
justification for deprivation of liberty 154
kettling by police 153–6
liberty and security, right to 153–6, 167
necessity 154–5, 167
police 153–6, 164
prison 153–4, 164
procedural fairness 154
proportionality 155–6
public authority liability 116, 153–5, 163, 167
third parties 155
fatal accidents 124–5, 150–2, 164
Faulks Report 135–6
fault
Francovich liability 102–3, 109, 117
policy 201
Product Liability Directive 45, 46–7, 49, 51, 53, 60–2, 203
strict liability 11, 201
sufficiently serious breach 102–3
Feldman, D 156
Fenwick, H 13
final appeal courts as defendants 116–19
financial services 43, 95–8, 108
First Non-Life Insurance Directive 96–8
Fleming on Torts 6
floodgates argument 120, 190
Flume, W 6
France 104, 106
***Francovich* liability** 11–12, 42, 89–122, 205
abuse of a dominant position 109
autonomy of national courts 12
Brasserie du Pêcheur case 92–5, 99, 103–7, 117, 209
breach of statutory duty 93–4, 109–16, 121–2, 197, 203
causation 92–4, 103–7, 113, 122
classification 109–15, 121
common law 98, 102–3, 108, 119, 121–2, 197
conditions for liability 92–110, 113–14, 119–22, 209
Court of Justice and UK courts, relationship between 89–95, 99–108, 115–22, 209
damages 89, 91–2, 95, 100–1, 106–7, 110–14, 117–20
development of state liability 90–3, 196
direct effect 90–2, 95, 97, 112, 119–21
directives, implementation of 91–3
effectiveness, principle of 89–92, 94, 103, 105–6, 112, 114, 116, 119–20
equivalence, principle of 90, 94, 103, 106–7, 119–20
European Communities Act 1972 109–12
extension of liability 114, 116–21
Factortame litigation 100–1, 109, 111–12, 114
fault 102–3, 109, 117
harmonisation 96
Health and Safety Framework Directive 71
indirect effect 91
individuals, intention to confer rights on 92–8, 108–10, 113, 119–21
interpretation 95, 98–100, 103–5, 108–9, 111–13, 115, 117–18, 121–2, 209
last instance courts as defendants 116–19
legal reasoning 113–14, 121
misfeasance in public office 111
national autonomy 12, 93–109, 121–2
policy 115, 117
preliminary references 89, 94–6, 99–101, 108, 115–18, 122
proportionality 90
public authorities, liability of 112–14, 116
selective deference to CJ 93
State, definition of 112, 119
sufficiently serious breach 92–4, 99–103, 105, 113, 116–19
taxonomy of torts 109–15
time limits 94, 101–2, 114
free movement 48, 74, 105, 120
freedom of expression *see also* **defamation and freedom of expression**
Internet service providers 78, 81, 84
privacy 169–70, 177–8, 180, 183–5, 190–5
function of tort law 5–7

Gatley on Libel and Slander 80, 132
Gearty, CA 23, 143
General Council of the Bar 'Foundations of Legal Knowledge' 8
general principles of EU law 14, 19, 38, 92
Germany 14, 105
globalisation 30–1, 32
Goff, R, (Lord Goff) 18, 38, 175, 178
good faith 28, 155–6 *see also* **bad faith**
Granger, M-P 103
Graziadei M 27
Grotius, H 7, 38
Grotius Society 38

Hale, B (Lady Hale) 24–5, 63–4, 68–70, 129–30, 149–50, 152, 179–80, 208
Hancock, M 70–1
harassment 115, 172
harmonisation
directives 43, 45, 85, 88
Francovich liability 96–7
Health and Safety Framework Directive 69–70
maximum harmonisation 48–9, 58, 62, 84, 86, 206
minimum harmonisation 48, 69–70, 85, 209
Motor Insurance Directives 74

Principles of European Tort Law 199
Product Liability Directive 48–9, 57–8, 62–3, 84, 86, 206
private law 3, 199
Hartley, TC 19
Health and Safety Framework Directive 11, 44, 63–73, 85
breach of statutory duty 63–72, 204
civil liability exclusion 71
common law 68, 72
consistency 66
criminal offences 64
daughter directives 65
direct effect 71
duty of care 68, 72–3, 84
foreseeability 69
Francovich liability 71
Health and Safety at Work Act 1974 65–7, 72
Health and Safety Executive 65, 71
interpretation 67–9
minimum harmonisation 69–70
minimum standards 64, 68–9
negligence 64, 66–73
policy 70–1, 87, 204
precautions/preventive measures 64–6, 70–1
proportionality 66
reform 70–2
risk-based approach 66, 71
safe system of work 72
six pack regulations 65–6
'so far as reasonably practicable' 66
standards 45, 64, 67–9
strict liability 67, 70
training 65
transposition 65–7, 73
Heinze, C 87
Hepatitis C, infection of blood products with 51, 55
Hickman, TR 167
Hoffman, D 193
Hoffmann, L (Lord Hoffmann) 30, 39, 115, 130, 136, 143, 160, 165–8, 169, 173, 178, 193–4, 207
horizontal effect
false imprisonment 156
Human Rights Act 1998 125, 181, 189, 192, 204
indirect horizontal effect 125, 148, 156, 169, 176
negligence 148
privacy 169, 176, 181, 189, 192–3, 209–10
private and family life, right to respect for 161
hosts 78–8, 82
Howells, G 58
Human Rights Act 1998
British Bill of Rights, replacement with 28, 126
causes of action 124, 160, 164–6
common law 1–2, 27, 34–6, 140, 143, 146–9, 156–8, 195, 197
cross-jurisdictional European dialogue 207–8
damages 13, 124, 165
declarations 25, 124, 165–6
declarations of incompatibility 25
defamation 11, 124–40, 162–3
different, whether human rights law is 34, 36–7
drafting 123
entry into force 123
European Convention on Human Rights 2, 12, 16, 22–6, 123–6, 196
exhaustion of local remedies 123
false imprisonment 154–6
Fatal Accidents Act 1976 124–5
freedom of expression 11, 126–40
horizontal application 125, 181, 189, 192, 204
individual petitions 123
interpretation 12, 22–6, 124–6, 197, 204
judges 36–7
lack of awareness of European influences 12–13
legal education 205
legal reasoning 34, 197
Lisbon Treaty 14
negligence 125, 142, 146–53, 203
new sources of law 204–5
nuisance 124–5, 157–61, 164
Osman effect 13
parliamentary sovereignty 25–6
planning 160–1
privacy 168, 169, 174, 176–9, 181, 186, 189–95, 209–10
private nuisance 124–5
public authorities 12–13, 116, 124–5, 140–54, 157–65, 196, 203, 209
ratification 123
time limits 124, 165
training of judges 34
trespass to the person 125
human rights law *see also* **European Convention on Human Rights; Human Rights Act 1998**
Charter of Fundamental Rights of the EU 14
legal education 34–5
public law 205–6
transplants 30

Ibbetson, DJ 7
illegality 77–8, 81, 103, 170
impartiality 33–4, 39
implementation of directives *see* **transposition and implementation of directives**
impossibility of legal transplants 29–32
indirect effect 10–11, 21, 51–2, 55, 91
indirect horizontal effect 125, 148, 156, 169, 176

individual rights
Francovich liability 92–8, 108–10, 113, 119–21
Human Rights Act 1998 123
policy 15
private law 10
Infantino, M 202
inhuman or degrading treatment 141–2, 164
injunctions 172, 186–7
injury to feelings, damages for 107, 187
institutions for cross-jurisdictional European dialogue, establishment of 3–4
insurance 96–8, 101–2 *see also* **Motor Insurance Directives and road accidents**
integration 14–17, 27–41, 210
anglicisation 28
civil law principles 28–9
common law 14, 16, 28–9, 85, 87–8, 203–4
cultural identity 28
directives 27
'donor involvement' 27
Europeanisation, meaning of 3
Francovich liability 90
interpretation 28–9
inter-systemic approach 27
resistance 203–4
supremacy of EU law 27–8
intermediaries *see* **defamation claims against ISPs**
International Association of Judges (IAJ) 3, 39
International Law Association (ILA) 36
Internet
cross-jurisdictional European dialogue 4
defamation 11, 44, 77–84, 132–3, 134, 137–8
freedom of expression 132–3, 134, 137–8
Internet service providers, defamation claims against 11, 44, 77–84
interpretation *see also* **preliminary references**
application of law 18–19
breach of statutory duty 111–13, 115
common law 14, 204, 210
Court of Justice 17–22
defamation 129, 133–4, 139
different, whether human rights law is 36
direct effect 19, 21
EU law 14, 17–18, 45, 86–8 , 197, 204
European Convention on Human Rights 14, 204
false imprisonment 167
Francovich liability 95, 98–100, 108–9, 117–18, 121–2, 209
freedom of expression 129, 133–4, 139
Health and Safety Framework Directive 67–9
Human Rights Act 1998 12, 22–6, 124–6, 197, 204
indirect effect 11
integration 28–9
legal culture 34–5
literal interpretation 49, 67–9
localised interpretation 86
Motor Insurance Directives 76–7
negligence 143, 148–52, 165, 167–8
nuisance 158
Parliamentary intention 111
presumptions 113
privacy 181
Product Liability Directive 47, 49–58, 86
purposive approach 18–19, 26, 49, 95, 113, 115
sufficiently serious breach 99–100
transplants 32–4
Irvine, D (Lord Irvine) 23, 174, 189, 208
ius commune 6

Jansen, N 3
Joint Network on European Private Law 198–200
Jolowicz, JA 60–1, 93
Journal of European Tort Law 201
Judge, Igor (Lord Judge) 37
judges *see* **judiciary**
judicial conservatism 114, 131
Judicial Integrity Group (JIG) 36
judicial notice 18
judicial review 112, 159
judiciary
cross-jurisdictional European dialogue 31, 34–40, 144–5, 167, 207
Human Rights Act 1998 36
independence and impartiality 39
law-making 114–15, 189
legal education 205–6
limitations on role 15
professional associations 36, 39
pro-European background 36, 62, 205
public law background 87
training 28–9, 31, 36
'tuners' of law, as 40
Justinian's *Digest* 7

Kahn-Freund, O 28
Kerr, M, Sir 39
kettling 153–6
***Köbler* liability** 118–19, 204
Komninos, A 120–1
Koopmans, T 19

lack of awareness of European influences 8–14
Lando, O 30
languages 20, 35, 198
last instance courts as defendants 116–19
Law Commission 46, 85–6, 102, 112–13, 152
Law Society 'Foundations of Legal Knowledge' 8
Laws, J, Sir 37
Lee, M 73
legal aid 131–2
legal culture 1, 3, 6, 15, 28–37, 167

legal education 8–9, 205–6
common law 8, 14, 18, 32, 49, 87, 102, 108, 146, 167, 189, 200
continuing education 3–4
direct effect 35
Erasmus student exchange programme 35–6, 210
EU law 34–6, 37, 61–3, 205–6
human rights law 34–6, 205
judiciary 205–6
law degrees 8–9, 35, 205–6
legal culture 34
new sources of law 206
openness 203
private law 205–6
Product Liability Directive 61–3
public law, EU and human rights law as 205–6
supremacy of EU law 37
'tuning' of law 40
legal formants 32–3
legal reasoning
analogy, reasoning by 18
common law 62
European Communities Act 1972 34, 197
Francovich liability 113–14, 121
Human Rights Act 1998 197
judicial dialogue 37
legal culture 32
localised legal reasoning 87
transplants 32–3, 41
legal transplants 3, 16–41
application of law 32–3
civil law systems 29–30, 14, 16
common law 27, 29–30, 40
comparative law 33
context 32–3
convergence 30
cross-jurisdictional European dialogue 37–40
different, whether European law is 34–40
epistemological baggage 29–30
globalisation 30–2
harmonisation 29–30
historical baggage 29
ideology 33
impossibility of transplants 29–32
inherent bias 33–4
integration into English legal system 16–17, 27–41
interpretation 32–4
judiciary 31, 37–40
legal culture 29–32, 34–7
legal style and reasoning 32–3, 41
national courts 17–26
new sources of law 17–26
possibility of transplants 32–4
private law 16, 31
public law 31
socio-cultural dimension 29–31
tacit assumptions, role of 33
understanding law 33
values 30
legislative interpretation *see* **interpretation**
legitimate expectations 11, 34–5, 180
Legrand, P 30–1
Leveson Report 171, 187, 192
liberty and security, right to 153–6, 164, 167
life, right to 141–2, 148–53, 164
Lisbon Treaty 14
living instrument principle 24, 185
Lord Chancellor's Advisory Committee on Private International Law 36
loss of a chance, damages for 105–6
loss of amenity, damages for 160
loss of profits, damages for 106
Lunney, M 75–6

MacCormick, N 4–5
Mak, E 20
malicious falsehood 172
Mance, J (Lord Mance) 1, 36, 68, 152, 183–4, 191–2, 205
manifest infringement test 117–18
manufacturers, liability of 47, 49–51, 54, 60–1, 84
margin of appreciation 24, 37, 99, 136, 139, 164, 179, 184–5, 192, 206–7
maritime law 7
Markesinis and Deakin's Tort Law 93
Markesinis, BS 16, 30, 32, 93, 194
Marleasing **principle** 21, 26, 77
Masterman, R 13
McDonald's hot drinks, burns from 52–3
Medicus, D 6
mentally ill persons, risk of suicide by 150–1
mere conduits 78
Merkin, R 76
Michaels, R 3
Miller, L 2–3
mirror principle 23, 37, 180–1, 207–8
misfeasance in public office 95, 97–8, 111, 116
misuse of confidential information, tort of 170, 177–9, 183, 185–93
model forms of tort law 199–200
mitigation 104
Montesquieu, C de 29–30
Monti, G 100
Moreham, NA 183
Morgan, J 175, 193–4
Motor Insurers' Bureau, time limits for claims from 101–2
Motor Insurance Directives and road accidents 43, 74–7, 84
causation 45
civil liability rules 74–6
compulsory insurance 45, 74–5
contributory negligence 45, 74–7

Motor Insurance Directives and road accidents (*cont*):
damages 75–6
exclusion or limitation of liability 45, 74–6
free movement 74
harmonisation 74
interpretation 76–7
novus actus interveniens 74
passengers 45, 74–5
policy 75, 76–7
proportionality 75–7
third parties 74

national autonomy 84, 93–109, 203–4
causation 106
common law 8, 189, 196
diminishing autonomy 15, 41, 152
directives 84
Francovich liability 12, 93–109, 121–2
negligence 143
new sources of law 196, 204–5
peaceful enjoyment of possessions 158
policy 204–5
private and family life, right to respect for 158
procedural autonomy 90, 94, 121–2
nationality discrimination 100–1
natural law 7
Nebbia, P 120
necessity 96–7, 154–5, 167
negligence 140–53
assumption of responsibility 152
balancing exercise 142–6
categories of liability 5
child abuse 145–6
common law 140–1, 143–4, 149, 152
consistency 153
contributory negligence 45, 74–7
damages 146–7, 150–2, 166
defamation 162–3
development of law 5
directives 86
duty of care 13, 140, 142–4, 146, 165, 167
economic loss 150
European Convention on Human Rights 146–53
European Court of Human Rights 142–52, 207
fair hearing, right to a 13, 150
fair, just and reasonable test 141–4
Health and Safety Framework Directive 64, 66–73
horizontal effect 148
Human Rights Act 1998 13, 125, 142, 146–53, 203
interpretation 143, 148–52, 165, 167–8
investigative duty 141
Jain case 149–50
life, right to 141–2, 148–53, 164
misfeasance in public office 97–8
omissions 141
Osman case 13, 37–8, 140, 141–6, 152–3, 163–5, 167–8, 207
peaceful enjoyment of possessions 150
personal injury claims 141
police, immunity of 142–4, 147–9
policy 140–1, 145–6, 148–50, 152–3, 164
positive duties 141–2
precedent 5, 145, 147
preventive measures 141–2
private and family life, right to respect for 141, 148–9
Product Liability Directive 49–54, 59, 61–2
proportionality 142
public authority liability 116, 140–53, 159, 162–8, 203
public interest 144–5
Rabone case 150–3
standard of care 67, 72
striking out 144–5, 151
third parties, injuries caused by 141–2
torture or inhuman or degrading treatment 141–2, 164
Van Colle case 147–9, 203
victims, definition of 150–1
neighbour principle 4–5, 11
Neill Review 135–6
Network of the Presidents of the Supreme Judicial Courts of the EU 39
new causes of action 90, 114–15, 168, 189, 197
new sources of law 11, 17–26, 203–6
New Zealand 192
noise, code of practice on 73
Nolan, D 61, 156–7, 161, 166
nominate torts 110–11, 114
Nourse, M (Lord Nourse) 1, 9
novus actus interveniens 74
nuisance *see* **private nuisance**

Oliphant, K 75–6, 93, 201
omissions 141
openness 203–5, 210
oral contraceptive pill litigation 60
Örücü, E 25, 37–8, 40
***Osman* case** 13, 37–8, 140, 141–6, 152–3, 163–5, 167–8, 207

Package Holiday Directive 97–8, 103–4
Palmer, V 33
parliamentary sovereignty 25–6
passing off 188
patents 188
path dependency 203–4
peaceful enjoyment of possessions 150, 153, 156–8, 160–1
Pearson Commission 46

personal autonomy 121, 148, 170, 176, 178, 189–90
personal injury 42, 47–8, 56, 60, 141
personal protective equipment 67–8
Phillipson, G 13, 189
Pillans, B 184–5
planning 160–1
police 142–4, 147–9, 153–6, 164
policy
consumer protection 15
control of policy 87–8
defamation 84, 87, 204, 137
directives 44–5, 77–84, 87–8, 209
fault 201
Francovich liability 115, 117
freedom of expression 137
Health and Safety Framework Directive 70–1, 87, 204
individual rights 15
model forms of tort law 199
Motor Insurance Directives 75, 76–7
negligence 140–1, 145–6, 148–50, 152–3, 164
nuisance 159
openness 203
precedent 117–18
Principles of European Tort Law 200
public authority liability 154, 167
strict liability 201
values 8
political and social context 32
possibility of legal transplants 32–4
precedent
EU law 14, 18, 117–18
European Court of Human Rights 14, 23
Francovich liability 117–18
nuisance 161
privacy 181, 191–2
preliminary references
acte clair doctrine 38, 108, 119
consistency 38
cross-jurisdictional European dialogue 38, 206–7
directives 86–7
Factortame litigation 206
Francovich liability 89, 94–6, 99–101, 108, 115–18, 122
general principles of EU law 39
localised legal reasoning 87
new sources of law 21
open or evasive answers 87
Product Liability Directive 53–4, 56–8
public law background of judges 87
sufficiently serious breach 99–101
wording and scope of questions 87
Principles of European Tort Law (PETL) 198–202
privacy, recognition of tort of invasion of 169–95
account of profits 187–9
ad hoc protection 171–85
balancing exercise 176, 178–9, 181–2, 190
breach of confidence 169, 174–95, 197, 203, 210
civil law systems 192, 194
codes of practice 172
commercial relationships 176
commercially sensitive information 175
common law 171–4, 183–5, 189–95, 197
damages 186–9, 191–2
data protection 172
defamation 169–70
development of tort 168
employment relationships 176
equity 185–6, 195
European Court of Human Rights 173–85, 190–4
exhaustion of local remedies 174
Francovich liability 115
freedom of expression 169–70, 177–8, 180, 183–5, 190–5
harassment 115, 172
horizontal effect 169, 176, 181, 189, 192–3, 209–10
Human Rights Act 1998 168, 169, 174, 176–9, 181, 186, 189–95, 209–10
incremental development 174–85, 189, 193, 195
informational privacy 169, 185, 190, 193, 195, 196
injunctions 172, 186–7
judicial law-making 115
malicious falsehood 172
margin of appreciation 179, 184–5, 192
mirror principle 180–1
misuse of confidential information, tort of 170, 177–9, 183, 185–93
nuisance 169, 172
personal autonomy 176, 178
positive obligations 180, 192
precedent 181, 191–2
private and family life, right to respect for 169, 172, 176–85, 189–95, 209–10
proportionality 177–9, 182, 191
public authorities 169, 176, 180, 194
public interest 182
reasonable expectation 169–70, 177–8, 180–2
statute, ad hoc protection by 171–4
trespass to land 115, 169, 172
unconscionability 174–5
Von Hannover litigation 170, 179–85, 190, 195
wrongful disclosure of private information 176–7
private and family life, right to respect for
balancing exercise 158
defamation 81, 128–9, 131, 139, 162, 166
horizontal effect 161

private and family life, right to respect for (*cont*):
negligence 141, 148–9
nuisance 153, 156–61, 164
positive obligations 157, 180, 192
privacy 169, 172, 176–85, 189–95, 209–10
proportionality 177
private law
development of European private law 201
EU law 3, 8–13, 43
fragmentation 27
Francovich liability 92
functional approach 209
harmonisation 3, 199
integration 27
legal education 205–6
public law/private law division 210
transplants 16, 31
private nuisance 156–61
account of profits 188
balancing exercise 160–1
common law 158
damages 159–60, 166
declarations 159–60
Human Rights Act 1998 124–5, 157–61, 164
interpretation 158
judicial review 159
loss of amenity, damages for 160
margin of appreciation 165
peaceful enjoyment of possessions 153, 156–8, 160–1
planning 160–1
policy 159
precedent 161
privacy 169, 172
private and family life, right to respect for 153, 156–61, 164
public authority liability 140, 153, 156–61, 163, 164–7
public interest 160
right to land 157–8
statutory authority, defence of 124–5, 157
utility companies 157–8, 164
private parties *see* **individual rights**
procedural fairness 154
Product Liability Directive 44–5, 46–63
ambiguity and imprecision 85
burden of proof 54, 59
but for test 58
causation 58, 60, 62, 86
common law 16, 49, 51–2, 61–3
Consumer Protection Act 1987 11, 16, 47, 48–62, 86, 205–6
consumer law, as part of 61, 205–6
contract law 84
core tort principle, how Directive has changed 58–63
cost/benefit analysis 51, 61, 87
damages, assessment of 60, 62, 86
debates 47, 54, 61–2, 85
defect, concept of 49–53
design defects 53, 60–1
development risks defence 49, 54–9, 62, 86
divergence 49, 86
Donoghue v Stevenson 45, 47, 60, 206
economic loss 58
effectiveness, principle of 57–8, 86
equivalence, principle of 57–8, 86
fault-based regime 45, 46–7, 49, 51, 53, 60–2, 203
guidance 53–8
harmonisation 48–9, 57–8, 62–3, 84, 86, 206
impact 84
indirect effect 51–2, 55
informal dispute resolution 45
interpretation 47, 49–58, 86
limited practical impact 60–1
manufacturers, liability of 47, 49–51, 54, 60–1, 84
marketing defects 53
maximum harmonisation 49, 62–3, 84, 86, 206
nature and scope 48–9
negligence 49–54, 59, 61–2
optional provisions 49, 54, 85
penalty mechanism 86
personal injury and death 47–8, 56, 60
precautions 51–3
preliminary references 53–4, 56–8
Product Liability Convention (Council of Europe) 46–7
property damage 47–8, 56, 60
recitals 51, 53
reform 46, 61–3
remoteness 62, 86
restrictive interpretation 86
reviews of Directive 58–9
Scottish Law Commission 46
standards 48–58
strict liability 11, 45, 46–7, 49–53, 60–2, 87
substitution of parties 56–7
textbooks and teaching 61–3
time limits 56–7, 60
transposition 47, 48, 53–6, 62, 85–6
United States 46–7, 53
vagueness 50
warranties, breach of 59
watering down 49, 85
professional associations 2–4, 36, 38–9
property damage 43, 47–8, 56, 60
proportionality 11, 131–2
damages 131–2
defamation 131–2, 133, 135, 138, 162
European Court of Human Rights 24
Francovich liability 90
freedom of expression 131–2, 133, 135, 138
Health and Safety Framework Directive 66

legal culture 34–5
Motor Insurance Directives 75–7
negligence 142
privacy 177–9, 182, 191
private and family life, right to respect for 177
public authority liability for breach of Convention rights 140–63
breach of statutory duty 112–14, 116
courts as public authorities 125
damages 113, 140
defamation 128, 153, 162–4, 166, 167
European Court of Human Rights 162–5
false imprisonment 116, 153–5, 163–4, 167
Francovich liability 116
freedom of expression 128
Human Rights Act 1998 12–13, 116, 124–5, 140–54, 157–65, 196, 203, 209
judicial dialogue 167
judicial review 112
negligence 116, 140–53, 159, 162–8, 203
nuisance 140, 153, 156–61, 163, 164–7
policy 154, 167
privacy 169, 176, 180, 194
private law 116
State, definition of 112
transplants 16
trespass to the person 116, 153–5, 167
public interest
contributory negligence 75
defamation 127–31, 139, 166
freedom of expression 127–31, 139
negligence 144–5
nuisance 160
privacy 182
public law 8–9, 13, 31, 87, 205–6, 210
Pufendorf, S 7
punitive damages 106–7, 132, 187, 189, 191–2

qualified privilege 126–31, 133–5, 139–40, 162

reform 46, 61–3, 70–2, 82, 85–6, 102, 112–13, 152
Regulation 1/2003 44
Reich, N 121
Reimann, M 59
remedies rather than principle, focus on 4–5
Renaissance humanism 7
remoteness 62, 86
reputation 42, 78, 82, 84, 128–32, 136, 138–9, 166
***Reynolds* privilege** 127–9, 132, 139–40, 163, 167
right to a fair hearing 13, 132, 150
right to an effective remedy 207
right to liberty and security 153–6, 164, 167
right to life 141–2, 148–53, 164
right to respect for private and family life *see* **private and family life, right to respect for**
road accidents 11 *see also* **Motor Insurance Directives and road accidents**
Rogers, WVH 201
Roman law 6–7, 31
Rozakis, C 24

Sacco, R 32–3
Sales, P 23
Schmid, CU 27
Scottish Law Commission 46
Second Motor Insurance Directive 102
Second Restatement of Torts (United States) 46
Sedley, S, Sir 130, 176, 190, 195, 205
separation of powers 34, 115, 190
sewage and surface water, flooding by 153, 159–60
Slynn, G (Lord Slynn) 36, 101, 205, 207
Smith, F 107–8
Smits, JM 30–1
social and political context 32
Society of Comparative Legislation 38
sources of law, dealing with new 11, 17–26, 203–6
Stanton, K 44, 93–4, 97, 100, 115, 120
Stanton, Skidmore, Harris and Wright. Statutory Torts 93
Stapleton, J 35, 63, 86, 197
***stare decisis see* precedent**
State liability for breach of EU law *see* ***Francovich* liability**
static, legal culture as not being 31–2, 34–7
statutory interpretation *see* **interpretation**
Steele, J 140
Steiner, E 104
Straw, J 174
Street on Torts 5
strict liability
compared to fault 11, 201
defamation 132, 134
deterrence 199
directives 45, 86
freedom of expression 132, 134
Health and Safety Framework Directive 67, 70
policy 201
Product Liability Directive 11, 45, 46–7, 49–53, 60–2, 87
striking out 144–5, 151
Study Group on a European Civil Code (SGECC) 198–200, 202
subsidiarity 24, 37, 204, 206–7
substitution of parties 56–7
success fees 132
sufficiently serious breach 92–4, 99–103, 105, 113, 119
suicide by mentally ill persons, risk of 150–1
supremacy of EU law 21–2, 27–8, 37
Szysczak, E 120

tacit assumptions, role of 33
taxonomy of torts 109–15

Tettenborn, A 152
Teubner, G 27–8, 33
textbooks 6, 35, 61–3, 94–5, 201
thalidomide tragedy 46
third parties 74, 141–2, 155
Third Restatement of Torts (United States) 53
Tofaris, S 160
Tomlinson, H 147
torture or inhuman or degrading treatment 141–2, 164
trade secrets 175
trademarks 188
training 28–9, 31, 36, 65 *see also* legal education
transplants *see* legal transplants
transposition and implementation of directives 42–88
 copy-out approach 85
 discretion 85
 Francovich liability 91–3
 guidance 85
 Health and Safety Framework Directive 65–7, 73
 infringement proceedings 54
 Product Liability Directive 47, 48, 53–6, 85–6
 supervision 53–4, 62
treaties and conventions
 EU law 10, 14, 17–18
 national cultures 30–1
Treitel on Contract 6
Trento Common Core project 4
trespass to land 115, 169, 172, 188
trespass to the person 116, 125, 153–5, 167 *see also* false imprisonment
Tridimas, T 93, 104
Tugendhat, M, Sir 39
'tuners' of law, judges as 40
Twitter 78
understanding law 33
Unfair Terms Directive 28, 85
United States 46–7, 169
Usenet newsgroups 78

van Eecke, P 81
Van Erp, S 33
Van Gend en Loos case 19, 90
Van Gerven, W 119–20
Van Hoecke, M 27
vicarious liability 144
victims, definition of 150–1
Volksgeist 30
von Savigny, FC 30

warranties, breach of 59
Warren, E 171
Warrington, M 27
Watson, A 31
Weir, T 134–6
Werro, F 202
Whittaker, S 21–2, 25, 61
Winfield and Jolowicz on Tort 93
Winfield, PH 60–1, 93
Woods, L 107–8
workplace accidents *see* Health and Safety Framework Directive
Wright, J *Tort Law & Human Rights* 125–6
writ system 4, 7
Wurmnest, W 87

Zimmermann, R 6–7, 39